¡Dime más!

Spanish word profiles

PHIL TURK

Hodder & Stoughton

A MEMBER OF THE HODDER HEADLINE GROUP

Acknowledgements

I would like to thank Marisol Díez Cantero, José-Luis García Daza, Jennifer Pulham, Esther Rosillo, Gloria Shumperli Soria and Jenny Wake for their help and advice in the preparation of this book. Also Jane Horwood for her meticulous proof-reading and further helpful suggestions.

I am indebted to the Collins Spanish Dictionary, 3rd and 4th Editions, and the Concise Oxford Spanish Dictionary for their guidance. I have always tried to use my own examples, and apologise if these occasionally coincide with those given in the dictionaries, as the obvious and sometimes the only viable ones!

Finally my thanks to Nat MacBride and Alexia Chan at Hodder & Stoughton Educational for their handling of the manuscript and my queries, and not least to my wife, Brenda, for her usual patience and forbearance during the writing of this book.

Phil Turk
Summer, 1999

Orders: please contact Bookpoint Ltd, 78 Milton Park, Abingdon, Oxon OX14 4TD.
Telephone: (44) 01235 827720, Fax: (44) 01235 400454. Lines are open from 9.00–6.00,
Monday to Saturday, with a 24 hour message answering service.
Email address: orders@bookpoint.co.uk

British Library Cataloguing in Publication Data
A catalogue record for this title is available from The British Library

ISBN 0 340 63151 1

First published 1999
Impression number   10   9   8   7   6   5   4   3   2   1
Year   2005   2004   2003   2002   2001   2000   1999

Copyright © 1999 Phil Turk

Typeset by Transet Limited, Coventry, England.
Printed in Great Britain for Hodder & Stoughton Educational, a division of
Hodder Headline plc, 338 Euston Road, London NW1 3BH by Redwood Books, Trowbridge, Wilts.

Introduction

Why word profiles?

You are probably very aware that for a language dictionary to be of any real use, it has to be very bulky: not something you would wish to carry around with you. Grammar books tend to look at grammar points from a generalised point of view, neatly slotting words into grammatical models and categories.

This book is not a dictionary; nor is it a grammar book. In fact, it sets out to fill the gap between the two. It takes Spanish words or groups of related words, and gives an individualised profile of each. In building up this profile, it deals with any specific grammatical irregularity the word may have, lists the main meanings, with any unexpected ones that you should be alerted to, including 'false friends' (words which don't mean what they look or sound like). Related words are grouped together, so that you can instantly see their relationship; synonyms (words that mean the same) are given, together with a warning where their meanings or uses do not correspond completely.

In order to keep the book to a manageable size, and so that (unlike a large and heavy dictionary) it will fit into your school or college bag, some selection has had to take place. So, words whose meaning or behaviour causes no problem, and about which there is therefore nothing to say, are not included (eg *cortina*: ends in *-a*, predictably feminine, means 'curtain' in the same senses as in English: no comment, not included!) For the same reason, it has not been possible to include every stem or spelling-change verb or noun endings in *-ión/iones* where there is nothing else to say about them!

The main criteria for including words are as follows:

a. mechanical, for example:

- a verb with irregular formation of any of its parts.
- an unexpected noun gender or a reminder about feminine words beginning with a stressed *a/ha*.
- adjectival endings not following the normal pattern.
- any other unexpected grammatical behaviour.
- any special point about spelling or stress.

b. meaning, for example:

- any unexpected or unpredictable meaning.
- 'false friends': words which have a different meaning from a similar English one (and, where there is sometimes confusion, the occasional French one).

c. usage

- the need to avoid confusion between similar-looking or sounding words.
- the need to point out the relative closeness or otherwise of synonyms, and the type of situation or 'register' in which one or the other might be used.
- any interesting observation about the word and the way it is used.

Note also that:

- if the word has a wide range of meanings or functions which are normally dealt with in detail in most grammar books or dictionaries, you will find a summary of the main points and advice as to where to seek more detailed information.

- if the word is used in a large number of idiomatic expressions, you will find a sample and pointers to the most likely source of further information.

- the emphasis is on the way that Spanish words are used in Spain. Common Spanish-Americanisms have been noted (eg *carro* for 'car'), but it has not been possible to note every difference of use, especially as they may apply to only one region of Spanish America.

What you have in this book is therefore a portable bank of valuable information concerning the way 4,000 or so common Spanish words behave, and pointers to the best source of further information as and when you have access to other reference books in, for example, your school or college library.

How to use this book

You can do this in several ways:

- if you have doubts about a particular word or simply want to find out more about it, look it up: words are arranged alphabetically. However, you will find occasionally that within a group of closely related words which have slightly differing endings, strict alphabetical order may not be observed (eg *lamentable* occurs as a derivative from *lamentar* and therefore after it, but in the same paragraph).

- you can learn synonyms of words, and also the slight differences of meaning and nuance between words with similar but not quite identical meanings and uses by following up the numerous cross-references. NB: Some suggested synonyms are not listed in this book if there is nothing else to say about them: these are denoted *syn* (for 'synonym'). Words which are cross-referenced and appear in this book are denoted cf (for 'compare').

- you can simply use it as a 'browser': take a couple of pages a day to read (don't always start at letter A!), and you will take in a great deal of useful and relevant information.

Abbreviations used in the text

Note: *italics* are used in the text in listing and naming words and their parts, also where the text is in Spanish. Otherwise roman (ie normal) type is used. Some abbreviations will occur therefore in italic or roman, depending on where they appear.

abb	abbreviation/abbreviated to
adj	adjective
adv	adverb
cf	compare with
cond/condit	conditional
conj	conjunction
def art	definite article
demons	demonstrative
dim	diminutive

dir obj	direct object
Eng	English
esp	especially
f, fem	feminine
fig	figurative
Fr	French
fut	future
ger	gerund
impf	imperfect
imp subj	imperfect subjunctive
indef art	indefinite article
indic	indicative
indir obj	indirect object
inf	infinitive
interj	interjection
interrog	interrogative
inv	invariable: ie does not change, eg by adding an ending
irreg	irregular
lit	literal(ly)
m, masc	masculine
N	North(ern)
n	noun
NB	note, take note
neg	negative
nf	noun, feminine
nfpl	noun, feminine plural
nfsing	noun, feminine singular
nm	noun, masculine
nmpl	noun, masculine plural
nmsing	noun, masculine singular
num	numeral/number
obj	object
opp	opposite
past part	past participle
pers	personal
pi	present indicative
pl	plural
pos	positive
poss	possessive
prep	preposition

pret	preterite
pron	pronoun
ps	present subjunctive
reg	regular
S	south(ern)
sb	somebody
sing	singular
Sp	Spain/Spanish/Spaniard
Sp Am	Spanish America(n)
sth	something
subjunc	subjunctive
syn/s	synonym/s (ie has the same or similar meaning)
v	verb
vi	intransitive verb: ie one which is used without a direct object
vr	verb, reflexive
vt	transitive verb: ie one which can have a direct object
vti	verb which can be used transitively or intransitively.

Codes for stem and spelling changes

Verbs which have 'radical' or 'stem' changes or spelling changes or both, have these changes noted in *italics* immediately after the indication of type of verb (*vt vi vti vr*) and before their meaning and further commentary. NB: this is a simplified scheme to illustrate these changes simply as a guide when you look up a word.

- *-ue-* Stem change type 1
  pi v*ue*lvo v*ue*lves v*ue*lve ... v*ue*lven
  ps v*ue*lva v*ue*lvas v*ue*lva ... v*ue*lvan
- *-ie-* Stem change type 1
  pi p*ie*nso p*ie*nsas p*ie*nsa ... p*ie*nsan
  ps p*ie*nse p*ie*nses p*ie*nse ... p*ie*nsen
- *-ue-, -u-* Stem change type 2
  pi m*ue*ro m*ue*res m*ue*re ... m*ue*ren
  ps m*ue*ra m*ue*ras m*ue*ra muramos muráis m*ue*ran
  ger m*u*riendo
  pret m*u*rió ... m*u*rieron
  imp subj m*u*riera/m*u*riese and throughout tense

- *-ie-, -i-* Stem change type 2
  pi m*ie*nto m*ie*ntes m*ie*nte … m*ie*nten
  ps m*ie*nta m*ie*ntas m*ie*nta m*i*ntamos m*i*ntáis m*ie*ntan
  ger m*i*ntiendo
  pret m*i*ntió … m*i*ntieron
  imp subj m*i*ntiera/m*i*ntiese and throughout tense
- *-i-* Stem change type 3
  pi p*i*do p*i*des p*i*de … p*i*den
  ps p*i*da p*i*das p*i*da p*i*damos p*i*dáis p*i*dan
  ger p*i*diendo
  pret p*i*dió … p*i*dieron
  imp subj p*i*diera/p*i*diese and throughout tense
- *-zc-* verbs ending in *-ecer, -ocer, -ucir*
  pi pare*zc*o, pareces then as normal
  ps pare*zc*a, pare*zc*as and throughout tense
  NB: verbs ending in *-du*cir have pret cond*u*je, cond*u*jiste, cond*u*jo, cond*u*jimos, cond*u*jisteis, cond*u*jeron

Spelling changes

- *-ce-, -cé* verbs ending in -zar
  ps alcan*ce* and throughout tense
  pret alcan*cé* alcanzaste and as normal
- *-gue-, -gué* verbs ending in -gar
  ps lle*gue* and throughout tense
  pret lle*gué* llegaste and as normal
- *-que-, -qué* verbs ending in -car
  ps sa*que* and throughout tense
  pret sa*qué*, sacaste and as normal
- *-zo, -za-*
  pi ven*zo*, vences and as normal
  ps ven*za* and throughout tense
- *-jo, -ja-* verbs ending in -ger
  pi co*jo* coges then as normal
  ps co*ja* and throughout tense
- *-go, -ga-* verbs ending in -guir
  pi si*go* sigues then as normal
  ps si*ga* and throughout tense
- verbs with *-y-* between vowels
  pi constru*yo* contru*ye*s constru*ye* … constru*ye*n
  ps constru*ya*
  ger constru*ye*ndo

pret construy*ó* … construy*eron*

imp subj construy*era*/construy*ese* and throughout tense

NB: verbs like *leer* which are partially affected in this way have their parts fully explained in the text.

- or -*ú*- verbs ending in –iar or –uar where the -*í*- or -*u*- needs a stress accent

pi fí*o* fí*as* fí*a* … fí*an*   actú*o* actú*as* actú*a* … actú*an*

ps fí*e* fí*es* fí*e* … fí*en*   actú*e* actú*es* actú*e* … actú*en*

A

> **A** is one of the five Spanish vowels.
> - It always has the same full sound value wherever it occurs, even on the end of many words: *agua, azafata, hablar, almacén, alcázar.*
> - It forms diphthongs both ways round with *-i-* (*-y* on the end of a word) and *-u-*: *traiga, hay; farmacia; cuatro; agua, zaguán.*
> - It does not form diphthongs with *-e-* and *-o-*, which are pronounced separately: *lea, cae; leo, roer.*

a *prep*
- to (a place or direction): *vamos a Madrid* we're going to Madrid; *tuerza a la izquierda* turn (to the) left
- occasionally 'at': *a la mesa*, at (the table), although *en* is more frequently the equivalent of 'at': *en la estación*, at the station; in fact be very careful to distinguish use of *a* with motion and *en* with situation: *va a casa* s/he's going home, *está en casa* s/he's at home; *al/en el extranjero* abroad, *a/en alguna parte* somewhere
- to indicate a distance or time taken from somewhere: *a medio kilómetro/ cinco minutos del centro* half a kilometre/five minutes from the centre
- at (a time): *a las dos* at two o'clock; at (a speed): *a cien kilómetros por hora* at 100 kph; at (a price): *los huevos están a un euro veinte* eggs are (at) one euro twenty
- to indicate manner or means: *a pie* on foot; *a mano* by hand
- 'personal' *a* has no translatable meaning and must precede the direct object when this is a definite person: *¿Has visto a Miguel?* Have you seen Miguel?

- occurs between a large number of verbs and a following infinitive, especially verbs of motion, beginning and inviting: *vamos a volver* we're going to go back; *empezó a llover* it started to rain; *nos invitaron a cenar* they invited us to supper
- NB This is merely a selection to indicate some of the main uses. You will find them explained in greater detail in most grammars, and a further selection of uses and phrases in a good dictionary.

abajo *adj* indicates position: below, down below (ie on a lower level); downstairs
- useful phrases: *hacia abajo* downwards; *cuesta abajo* downhill; *río abajo* downstream; *¡Abajo la monarquía!* Down with the monarchy!
- *de abajo* can be used as *adj* meaning 'lower': *el piso de abajo* the lower flat, the downstairs flat
- see also *debajo (de)*

abandonar *vt* to leave, leave behind, abandon
- usually implies deliberate departure but perhaps not as forceful as its Eng equivalent; nonetheless rather stronger in meaning than cf *dejar*
- to give up: *abandoné el tabaco* I gave up smoking
- **abandonarse** *vr* to give in, give up (cf *rendirse*): *abandonarse al alcohol* to give in/give oneself up to drink
- **abandono** *nm* abandonment, ie the act of abandoning; state of moral abandon, degradation

abanico *nm* fan (of traditional Sp type)
- for electric fan use *ventilador*
- **abanicar(se)** *vtr* -que-, -qué to fan (oneself)

abarcar *vt* -que-, -qué to include, comprise, take in, span

□ used in quite a range of expressions, often for a variety of Eng equivalents: *este libro abarca las dos guerras mundiales* this book takes in/covers the two world wars; *su vida abarcó el fin del siglo 19 y el principio del 20* his life spanned the end of the 19th century and the beginning of the 20th

□ a somewhat idiomatic word: take note when you come across it and try to build up a 'library' of its applications!

abastecer *vt* -zc- to supply, provide (*de* with)

□ **abasto** and **abastecimiento** *nm* supply, provision

□ used mainly in commercial context, especially of food

□ cf *suminstrar, proveer*

abatir *vt* conveys the idea of 'bringing down': to demolish, knock down, cut down (tree), shoot down (bird), lay low (eg person with illness); to depress, discourage (person)

□ **abatirse** *vr* conveys both the above meanings intransitively: to drop, fall, dive (eg bird); to get depressed, discouraged

□ **abatimiento** *nm* also conveys both meanings: demolition (of building); depression, dejection (of person)

ablandar *vt* to soften, become less severe (weather)

□ **ablandarse** *vr* to soften, become soft; become less severe (cold or wind)

□ verb from *blando*

abogado/a *nmf* lawyer, barrister

□ but, take care, as Sp and Eng legal terms do not correspond exactly; see also *notario*

abortar *vi* to have a miscarriage; to have an abortion; to lose a baby — either by accident or by intent: the meaning is usually clear from the context!

□ **abortar** *vt* to abort (sth) in all senses

□ **aborto** *nm* abortion; miscarriage

abrasar *vt* to burn up

□ can be used literally, in the sense of *quemar*, but often used of plants etc: 'to parch', 'dry up'

□ **abrasarse** *vr* burn, catch fire, but esp to parch, dry up, (eg land)

□ often has more to do with heat of sun than actual combustion

abrazar *vt* -ce-, -cé to embrace, hug

□ **abrazo** *nm* hug, embrace: *un abrazo de* (at end of letter) love from

□ for 'kiss' see *besar*

abrigar *vt* -gue-, -gué to shelter, protect

□ *abrigar dudas, esperanza, sospechas* to harbour doubts, hope, suspicion, etc

□ **abrigo** *nm* shelter, protection; overcoat, topcoat

abrir *vt* *past part:* *abierto* to open

□ *abrir con llave* to unlock; *abrir un grifo* to turn on a tap

□ **abrirse** *vr* to open

□ you must use the reflexive form when something opens (itself): *la puerta se abrió* the door opened

□ **abierto** *adj/past part* open

□ use with *estar* when applied to shops, doors, windows etc.

□ use with *ser* to describe character: *esta chica es muy abierta y amigable* this girl is very open and friendly

□ **abrebotellas; abrelatas** *nm inv* bottle-opener; tin-opener

□ invariable — no plural form

abrochar *vt* to do up (buttons, clothes, belts, etc); to fasten (eg safety belt *cinturón de seguridad*)

absoluto *adj* absolute, complete, utter

□ **absolutamente** *adv* absolutely, as in Eng: *absolutamente perfecto* absolutely perfect

□ **BUT** beware! Both
absolutamente and **en absoluto**
can also have a negative meaning,
completely the opposite of the usual
Eng meaning: *¿Te molesto?
¡Absolutamente/En absoluto!* Am I
disturbing you? Not at all! If you said
'Am I disturbing you?' 'Absolutely' in
Eng, it would mean you were indeed
disturbing the speaker!

absolver *vt -ue-, past part: absuelto*
to absolve

aburrir *vt* to bore
□ **aburrirse** *vt* to get/become bored,
the action or process of becoming
bored, ie getting into that state;
to express a state of boredom: use
estar aburrido; los niños se aburrieron
the children got bored (ie something
bored them); *los niños estaban
aburridos* the children were bored
(ie they were in that state all the
time)
□ **NB also *ser* aburrido** to be bor**ing**:
la película fue larga y aburrida the
film was long and boring

abusar *vi* to go too far, take advantage
□ *abusar de algo/alguien* to abuse sth/sb
□ **abuso** *nm* abuse; but also unfair
demand, betrayal, excess
□ **abusivo** *adj* improper, corrupt
□ for verbal abuse use *improperios* or
injurias

acá *adv* here, over here
□ more emphatic than cf *aquí*, and
tends to imply motion towards
the speaker, rather like 'hither': *¡ven
acá!* come here! Common in
Sp Am for *aquí; acá y allá* here
and there
□ can sometimes be used in a time
sense, meaning 'now': *hasta acá* up
to now

acabar *vti* to finish, complete, conclude, end
□ in this basic sense, much the same as

terminar, concluir, and can be used
with or without an object: *¿A qué
hora acaba la fiesta?* What time
does the party end? *Acabamos el
proyecto ayer.* We finished the
project yesterday.
□ *acabar con* to put an end to: *acabé
con todo eso* I put a stop to all that
□ *acabar de + inf* to have just: (*pres*)
acabo de volver I've just returned;
(*imp*) *acababa de volver* I had just
returned
□ **acabarse** *vr* to finish (intransitively),
come to an end: *se acabó* it's all over,
it's finished
□ can be used in this sense with indirect
object: *se me acabó la paciencia* my
patience ran out

acaecer *vi -zc-* to happen
□ one of several verbs 'to happen',
perhaps less used than cf *ocurrir, pasar,
suceder, acontecer*
□ **acaecimiento** *nm* event, happening

acaso *adv* perhaps, maybe
□ tends to take subjunctive, especially if
there is some emphasis on doubt
□ *por si acaso* just in case; *por si
acaso lo sabe* if by chance he
knows
□ cf *quizás, tal vez, puede ser*

acceder *vi* to accede, gain access (*a* to)
to: *acceder a la Unión Europea* to gain
entry to the EU
□ also: to agree to + *noun* or *inf*

acción *nf* action (in most senses as Eng)
□ *pl acciones*: also means: (stockmarket)
shares

aceite *nm* oil
□ of most types, including car oil, not
just olive oil, but use *petróleo* for
crude oil

aceituna *nf* olive
□ usual word: *oliva* generally only used
in *aceite de oliva* olive oil

ℹ *All words in this frame have only one c* **❗**

acelerar *vti* to accelerate, quicken
- **acelerador** *nm* accelerator;
  aceleración *nf* acceleration

acento *nm* accent (in most senses); *acento tónico* stress (ie on a syllable)

acentuar *vt -u-: acentúo, acentúas; acentúe* to accentuate, emphasise, stress

aceptar *vt* to accept
- *aceptar a* + inf to agree

---

acercar *vt -que-, -qué* to bring nearer: *acerca una silla* bring up a chair
- **acercarse (a)** *vr* to get nearer (to), to approach
- also: to drop in, call round: *si tienes tiempo, acércate a casa* if you have time, pop in to see us

acertar *vti -ie-* to hit the mark, get right: *(lo) hemos acertado* we've got it right, we've hit the mark
- *acertar a* + inf: to happen to; to manage to, succeed in (cf *conseguir, lograr) acertar con algo* to happen/ stumble upon sth (ie by chance)
- **acertado** *adj* correct, right: *una respuesta acertada* a correct/spot on answer; apt, fitting: *una observación acertada* a fitting remark: means the successful outcome for the particular circumstance: Eng equivalents may be variable
- **acierto** *nm* success (in same sense as cf *éxito*); also: good shot, good hit, guess right (the successful action for the circumstance, as above)
- can also mean 'skill', 'ability', 'discretion': *con todo acierto* with great skill/ability

aclarar *vt* to clarify, make clear (from *claro*)
- to rinse (clothes)
- *vi* to clear (up), get brighter (weather)
- **aclararse** *vr* to catch on, to 'get it'

acoger *vt -jo, -ja-* to welcome, receive (in that sense)
- **acogerse a** *vr* to have recourse to, resort to
- **acogida** *nf* welcome, reception: *tuvimos una buena acogida* we had a good reception
- **acogedor** *adj* acogedora, *acogedores, acogedoras* welcoming, hospitable

acometer *vt* to attack (violently), set upon, charge (in that sense); to tackle (problem, etc); to assail, overcome: *me acometió el sueño* I was overcome by sleep

acomodar *vt* to accommodate (usually only in the sense of 'to come to an arrangement', ie adjust, adapt); to arrange, tidy: *acomodar los estantes* to arrange/tidy the shelves
- for a place to stay or live, use *alojar*
- **acomodarse** *vr (con)* to comply, conform (with); *a* to adapt oneself (to)
- **acomodación** *nf* and **acomodo** *nm* arrangement
- for accommodation where you stay or live, use *alojamiento*
- these words merit further dictionary research

acompañar *vt* to accompany, go with
- *estar/ir acompañado de* to be accompanied by

aconsejar *vt* to advise
- + *inf* or *que* + *subjunctive: te aconsejo hacerlo* or *aconsejo que lo hagas* I advise you to do it
- **aconsejarse** *con alguien de algo vr* to consult sb about sth

acontecer *vi -zc-* to happen, occur
- cf *suceder, pasar, ocurrir, acaecer*
- **acontecimiento** *nm* event, happening; cf *suceso, acaecimiento*

acordar *vt -ue-* to decide, resolve
- + *que* + *subj* to resolve that ...; + *inf* to resolve to

    □ to tune, harmonise (instrument, voices, etc)

    □ **acordarse de** *vr* to remember (+ noun) or + *inf* to remember to; cf *recordar*

    □ to agree (to), although *ponerse de acuerdo* is more common

    □ **acuerdo** *nm* agreement: *¡de acuerdo!* agreed! OK!; *de acuerdo con* in accordance with; *estar de acuerdo* to be agreed/in agreement; *ponerse/quedar de acuerdo* to agree (ie reach an agreement)

acosar *vt* to harass, pester

    □ **acoso** *nm* harassment: *acoso sexual* sexual harassment

acostar *vt* -ue- to lay (sb/sth) down, put to bed

    □ **acostarse** *vr* to lie down (in bed), go to bed

    □ for 'lie down' without the implication of bed use *echarse* or *tumbarse*

    □ *estar acostado* (ie *past part*) to be lying down, be in bed

acostumbrar *vt* to accustom; *acostumbrar a alguien a algo* to accustom sb/get sb accustomed to sth

    □ **acostumbrarse** (*a* + *n* or *inf*) *vr* to get/become accustomed (to), get used (to)

    □ *estar acostumbrado* (*a* + *n* or *inf*) to be accustomed (to)

actitud *nf* attitude (in most senses)

    □ NB spelling: *act-*

    □ *hacia* or *para con,* towards

acto *nm* act (most senses); action, deed

    □ *acto seguido* next, straight after; *en el acto* on the spot, instantaneously

    □ **actual** *adj* present, present-day, current: *la situación actual* the current situation

    □ for 'actual' use *verdadero* or *efectivo*

    □ **actualmente** *adv* at the present time, at present; for 'actually' use *en efecto, efectivamente, en realidad*

    □ **actualidad** *nf* the present (time): *en la actualidad* at the present time, at the moment; *actualidades* current events

    □ **actualización** *nf* modernisation, bringing up to date

    □ **actualizar** *vt* -ce-, -cé to modernise, bring up to date

    □ **actuar** *vi* ú: actúo, actúas; actúe to act

    □ to work, operate, function cf *obrar, operar, funcionar*

    □ to act (in theatre, cinema etc)

    □ *vt* to actuate, ie set in motion

acudir *vi* to come along, turn up (*a* to)

    □ common alternative to *ir/venir*; often implies a purposeful arrival: *todos acudieron a ver lo que pasaba* everyone went along to see what was happening; *acudieron en auxilio* they went/came to the rescue

    □ to turn to, have recourse to: *tuvo que acudir al psicólogo* he had to have recourse to a psychologist

acuerdo see **acordar**

acusar *vt* to accuse (*de* of)

    □ *acusar sorpresa* to show/register surprise

    □ *acusar recibo de* to acknowledge receipt of (letter, package, etc) in formal business language

    □ NB *past part*, besides 'accused' can mean 'pronounced', 'marked': *con un acusado acento inglés* with a marked English accent

    □ **acusarse** *vr* to confess (*de* to): *acusarse de un crimen* to confess to a crime

    □ **acusación** *pl acusaciones nf* accusation

    □ NB spelling: one *c*!

adecuado *adj* adequate

    □ but also, commonly, 'suitable', 'appropriate', 'apt' (*para* for): *rellena los espacios en blanco con la palabra*

adecuada fill the gaps with a suitable word
- **adecuar** *vt* to adapt, make suitable

adelante *adv* forward, ahead (in both time and place)
- *hacia adelante* forwards; *más adelante* further on, later on; *de aquí en adelante* from now on, henceforth; *¡adelante!* come in!, go ahead!
- **adelantar** *vt* to advance, bring forward: to overtake (car etc) *hemos adelantado la fecha de la fiesta* we've brought forward the date of the party; *adelantar el paso de algo* to speed sth up
- *vi* to get ahead, make progress
- **adelantarse** *vr* to move forward, get ahead
- **adelantado** *adj* advanced; *pagar por adelantado* to pay in advance
- **adelanto** *nm* advance(ment), progress, improvement: *adelantos tecnológicos* technological advances/improvements
- cf *avanzar, avance*

adelgazar *vti -ce-, -cé* to make or grow thin, to slim (ie become *delgado*)

ademán *nm pl ademanes* gesture (with hand or body)
- *hacer ademán de + inf* to make as if to; *hacer ademanes* to make signs
- cf *gesto*

además *adv* besides, moreover, furthermore
- **además de** *prep* besides, in addition to

adentro *adv* inside
- same as cf *dentro*
- used after noun in phrases such as *selva adentro* into the forest, within the forest; *decir para sus adentros* to say to oneself
- **adentrarse** *vr en algo* to get (deeper) inside sth

aderezar *vt -ce-, -cé* to prepare, get ready; to dress, embellish (things that need to look good, often food)

adherir *vt -ie-, -i-* to stick, adhere; to join (a party, organisation): *en 1986 España se adhirió a la UE* in 1986 Spain joined the EU
- **adhesión** *nf* adhesion, sticking; (act of) joining (see above), membership

adicto/a *nmf* addict; also *adj* addicted (*a* to)
- **adicción** *nf pl adicciones* addiction

admirar *vt* to admire
- but also NB: to astonish, surprise: *es de admirar su descaro* his cheek is astonishing
- **admirarse** *vr* to be astonished, surprised (*de* at)
- **admiración** *pl admiraciones nf* admiration; but also astonishment, surprise: *punto de admiración* exclamation mark

admitir *vt* to admit
- other meanings much as in Eng, ie to allow (in), to confess
- **admisión** *nf pl admisiones* admission (ie acceptance or confession)
- **admisible** *adj* admissible (ie allowable, acceptable)

adonde or **a donde** *conj* to where
- **¿adónde?** or **¿a dónde?** *interrog* where to?
- both used when there is motion: *¿Adónde vas? Voy adonde no me encontrarás* Where are you going? I'm going (to) where you won't find me
- NB: accent on question form

adversario/a *nmf* adversary; usual word for opponent

advertir *vt -ie-, -i-* to notice, observe; to point out, warn, advise (in that sense); stronger than cf *aconsejar*

☐ **advertencia** *nf* warning; reminder

aéreo *adj* (to do with) air: *los transportes aéreos* air transport; *vía aérea* airmail

afán *pl afanes nm* desire, urge
☐ quite a common word, implying strong desire or hard work or exertion: *hacer algo con afán* to do sth keenly, with zeal
☐ *el afán de + noun* or *inf* the urge, desire for/to: *el afán de tener éxito* the desire to succeed
☐ **afanarse** *vr* to strive hard to (+ *por + inf*): perhaps emphasises personal effort more than cf *luchar por*

afición *pl aficiones nf* fondness, liking (*a* for): *tener afición al helado* to have a liking for ice cream
☐ hobby, pastime: *¿Cuáles son tus aficiones?* What are your hobbies?
☐ NB does not mean 'affection': don't confuse with *afecto, afección*
☐ **aficionado/a** *nmf* enthusiast, amateur (as opposed to professional), fan, supporter (ie anyone who is keen on a hobby, a team, etc)
☐ also used as *adj* with *ser*: *es muy aficionado a la jardinería* he's very keen on gardening
☐ **aficionarse** *vr* to be/become keen (*a* on): *empiezo a aficionarme a la cocina* I'm beginning to get a liking for cooking

afligir *vt -jo, -ja-* to afflict
☐ **afligirse** *vr* to grieve, get upset (in that sense): *se afligió mucho por la muerte de su hermano* she was very upset by the death of her brother
☐ **afligido** *adj* grieving, bereaved (use with *estar*)
☐ **aflicción** *nf pl aflicciones* afflictions; grief, sorrow

afortunado *adj* **afortunadamente** *adv* lucky/luckily, fortunate/ly
☐ NB *a* at the beginning!

afrentar *vt* to affront, insult

afrenta *nf* affront, insult
☐ don't confuse with *afrontar* below

afrontar *vt* to confront, face up to: *los problemas que hay que afrontar* the problems one has to face up to/confront
☐ don't confuse with *afrentar* above!

afuera *adv* outside: *están afuera* they're outside
☐ you don't link this with a noun: instead use the preposition *fuera de*
☐ *¡afuera!* out! get out!
☐ **las afueras** *nfpl* outskirts, suburbs (of a town): *vivimos en las afueras* we live in the (outer) suburbs

agarrar *vt* to grasp, seize, catch hold of
☐ stronger than cf *coger* in Spain
☐ often used in areas of Sp Am where *coger* has a rude meaning: *agarrar un taxi* to catch a taxi; *agarrar la gripe* to catch flu
☐ **agarrarse a algo alguien** *vr* to hold on to/grab sth/sb

agenda *nf* agenda; usual word for diary (into which you put your engagements)
☐ for diary in which you record past events, use *diario*

agitar *vt* has a wider meaning than 'agitate':
☐ to wave (hand, flag, etc); to shake (bottle)
☐ to excite; to worry (cf *preocupar*)
☐ **agitarse** *vr* to wave, flutter (flag)
☐ to get excited, worried, agitated
☐ to get rough (sea)
☐ **agitado** *adj* rough, choppy (sea)
☐ upset, anxious, agitated (person); excited
☐ **agitación** *nf* noun corresponding to all meanings of verb above: waving, worry, excitement, agitation, etc

agobiar *vt* to weigh down, overwhelm (in a negative sense): *estar/sentirse agobiado por el dolor* to be/feel overwhelmed by grief
☐ for 'overwhelmed with joy' use *rebosar*

agobiarse (*con/de*) *vr* to be weighed down (by/with)

agobio *nm* (noun for the effect of the verb!) burden, weight; anxiety: *siento mucho agobio* I feel very anxious

agotar *vt* to exhaust (in most senses)

agotarse *vr* to become exhausted (ie to reach that state)

to sell out (goods in a shop)

estar agotado to be exhausted (ie in that state)

agotador *agotadora, agotadores, agotadoras adj* exhausting

agotamiento *nm* exhaustion

agradar *vt* to please

stronger than *gustar: me agrada su comportamiento* I'm pleased/delighted by his behaviour

agrado *nm* liking: *¿Es de tu agrado?* Is it to your liking?; *con agrado* willingly

agradecer *vt -zc-* to thank, be grateful for

NB *agradecer algo a alguien:* to thank sb for sth: *agradecí a mis amigos su bondad* I thanked my friends for their kindness; *te lo agradezco* (I) thank you for it, I'm grateful to you

you can also use *estar agradecido* to be grateful: *le estoy muy agradecido* I'm very grateful to you

agradecimiento *nm* gratitude, thanks

agrandar *vt* to make bigger, enlarge

agrandarse *vr* to get bigger, larger

agrícola *adj* *mfsing agrícola, mfpl agrícolas* agricultural

NB yes, it does end in *-a* in masc!

agricultural not used in Sp

agua *nf* water

NB *el/un agua* because of the stressed *a-*

pl las aguas

if *adj* is interposed after article, this

reverts to *f: la bella agua* the beautiful water

aguantar *vt* to bear, endure, stand (in that sense), put up with: *no puedo aguantarlo* I can't bear/stand it; *no aguantamos más* we're not standing for/putting up with any more; *hay que aguantar* you've got to put up with (grin and bear) it

aguantable *adj* bearable, tolerable (cf *soportable*, also frequently used; negative: *inaguantable* intolerable)

aguante *nm* endurance, tolerance (in that sense)

aguardar *vti* to wait, wait for, expect

a rather less used alternative to *esperar*: handy when the latter could be ambiguous

agudo *adj* sharp (in most senses): *un punto agudo* a sharp point; acute (accent, angle, illness, pain, mind, intelligence); shrill (note, sound, voice, etc); witty

agudeza *nf* noun encompassing all the above qualities: sharpness, acuteness, shrillness, wit

agudizar *vt* *-ce-, -cé* to sharpen, make more acute; **agudizarse** *vr* to sharpen, in sense of become more sharp/acute

agujero *nm* hole

cf *hueco*

aguzar *vt -ce-, -cé* to sharpen

aguzar las orejas to prick up one's ears; *aguzar el apetito* to whet one's appetite (used rather more figuratively in these phrases than *agudizar* above)

ahí *adv* there

strictly 'there by you' (ie the person addressed), corresponding to *ese* 'that by you', but in practice the distinction is often somewhat blurred, though cf *allí* is usually further away

occurs in some set phrases: *de ahí que* that's why, hence; *por ahí* that way, over there (cf *por allí*); *salir por ahí* to go out and about; *ahí viene el tren* here comes the train

ahínco *nm*   earnestness, effort
- mainly occurs in **con ahínco** *adv* earnestly, hard: *trabajar con ahínco*   to work hard

ahogar *vt* -gue-, -gué   **ahogarse** *vr*   to suffocate cf *asifixiar(se), sofocar(se);* to drown
- **ahogo** or **ahogamiento** *nm* drowning; suffocation
- *perecer por ahogo/ahogamiento*   to drown

ahora *adv*   now
- occurs in numerous set phrases: *ahora mismo*   right now; *ahorita mismo* just now, a moment ago; *por ahora* for the time being, for now; *hasta ahora*   up to now; *desde ahora* from now on

ahorrar *vt*   to save (money, time, trouble): *ahorrarse tiempo*   to save oneself time
- for 'save (life)', 'rescue', see *salvar, rescatar*
- **ahorro** *nm*   saving; *ahorros*   savings: *caja de ahorros*   savings bank

airado *adj*   angry
- quite a strong word, as illustrated by its associated meaning of 'wild, violent'; perhaps rather like Eng 'wild' in that sense: *estaba airada*   I was wild/angry
- **airarse** *vr*   to get angry, get wild

aire *nm*   air (in most senses as in Eng) *aire acondicionado*   air conditioning; *tomar el aire*   to take the air
- appearance, bearing, 'airs', *darse aires* to give oneself airs
- resemblance: *tiene aire de su padre* he looks just like his father
- air (tune) *silbaba un aire alegre*   he was whistling a jolly tune
- worth further investigation in the dictionary

aislar *vt*   NB -í-: pi *aíslo, aíslas, aísla, aíslan*

and *ps aísle* etc   to isolate, cut off
- to insulate (with heat, electricity etc)
- **aislado** *adj*   isolated, cut off
- **aislamiento** *nm*   isolation; insulation

ajeno *adj*   belonging to sb else, other people's: *siempre está copiando ideas ajenas*   he's always copying other people's ideas; *no te metas en los asuntos ajenos*   don't get involved in other people's business, mind your own business
- alien, foreign, not belonging (*a*   to); *acceso prohibido a toda persona ajena a la obra*   no unauthorised admission; *es ajeno a mi modo de ver* it's not my way of thinking

al- *prefix*
- There are a great many words beginning with *al-* in Sp. They are mainly of Arabic origin, reflecting the Moorish occupation of Spain during the Middle Ages. They also reflect aspects of life at which the Moors excelled: irrigation (*aljibe*   water tank or cistern); building (*albañil*   mason, bricklayer), even the word for 'mayor' (*alcalde*). A browse in a dictionary will reveal many more. Unfortunately we only have room to list here those which are in common use and merit comment.

ala *nf*   wing (in most senses as in Eng: of bird, plane, political party, sports field, building, etc)
- NB *el ala* because of stressed *a*, but *las alas*
- also has wider meanings: blade (of eg propeller); brim (of hat); eave (of house)
- *nmf*   winger (in sport)

alabar *vt*   to praise
- **alabarse de** *vr*   to boast about, cf *jactarse*
- **alabanza** *nf*   praise: *en alabanza de* in praise of

alacena *nf* (food) cupboard
- □ use rather than *armario* for food

alargar *vt -gue-, -gué* to lengthen, extend, ie *hacer más largo*
- □ also used with the hand: *alargó la mano* he stretched out his hand; *alargó el papel* he handed over the piece of paper
- □ **alargarse** *vr* to lengthen, get longer: *los días empezaban a alargarse* the days were beginning to lengthen

alarma *nf* alarm (in most senses)
- □ for 'alarm clock' use *despertador*
- □ **alarmar** *vt* to alarm, frighten
- □ **alarmarse** *vr* to get/be alarmed, frightened
- □ **alarmante** *adj* alarming, frightening

albergue *nm* hostel, refuge, shelter: *albergue juvenil* youth hostel
- □ **albergar** *vt -gue-, -gué* to shelter, lodge, put up: **albergarse** *vr* to shelter, lodge, stay
- □ tends to suggest fairly basic accommodation (hostels, shelters, etc): some overlap with *alojamiento/ alojar(se),* which is more general in application; not really the equivalent of Fr *auberge,* as it doesn't mean 'inn' in that sense

alcalde *nm* mayor; **alcaldesa** *nf* mayoress
- □ even the smallest village in Spain has an *alcalde/sa*

alcanzar *vt -ce-, -cé* to catch up with
- □ to reach (especially of figures): *las cifras han alcanzado diez mil* the figures have reached ten thousand
- □ to hit, strike (bullets, shells etc): *la bala le alcanzó el brazo* the bullet hit him in the arm
- □ for 'reaching a place', use *llegar a: por fin llegamos a Córdoba* at last we reached Córdoba
- □ *alcanzar a + inf* to manage to, esp in

negative: *no alcanzamos a satisfacer la demanda* we didn't manage to satisfy demand
- □ **alcance** *nm* reach: *estar al alcance de alguien* to be within sb's reach; *estar fuera de alcance* to be out of reach

alcázar *nm* fortress, palace
- □ a Moorish word, which usually indicates a specific building which is neither a traditional castle nor necessarily a palace. There are *alcázares* in Sevilla, Toledo and Segovia – and they are all different!
- □ NB stress on 2nd syllable, where the accent is!

aldea *nf* small village, hamlet
- □ usually smaller than cf *pueblo*

alegre *adj* happy, merry, glad, gay, jolly
- □ used with *estar* to indicate a state arising from circumstances: *todo el mundo estaba muy alegre* everyone was very happy
- □ for 'happy' in the sense of 'having inner happiness' use cf *feliz*
- □ be a bit careful, too, as it can in some contexts verge on 'immoral', 'risqué', 'fast'!
- □ for 'gay' in the sense of 'homosexual' use *gay*
- □ **alegrar** *vt* to cheer (up), gladden (person, room, etc), please; often used 'back to front' with what you are glad about as the subject: *me alegra tu decisión* I'm pleased at your decision
- □ **alegrarse** *vr* to be happy, glad, pleased: *me alegro mucho* I'm very pleased
- □ *alegrarse de + inf* or *de que + subjunc* to be pleased to/that: *me alegro mucho de poder ayudarte* I'm very pleased to be able to help you; *nos alegramos de que vengas a vernos* we're glad you are coming to see us
- □ **alegría** *nf* joy, gladness, cheerfulness

alejar *vt* to remove, move sth away (*de* from)
- □ occurs frequently reflexively –
  alejarse *vr* to move away from, go away (*de* from): *se alejó hacia el horizonte* it moved away towards the horizon
- □ from *lejos* 'far', ie *hacerse más* cf *lejos*; its opposite *acercarse* and *cerca*
- □ **alejado** *adj* distant, remote, far-removed
- □ **alejamiento** *nm* removal, distancing
- □ can also be used to describe the state of remoteness, aloofness

alemán, *alemanes, alemana, alemanas* *adj* & *nmf* German
- □ NB accent in *m sing* but not in *f* or *pl*
- □ don't confuse with the country **Alemania** *nf* Germany

algo *pron* something
- □ can mean 'anything' in interrog phrases: *¿Necesitas algo?* Do you need anything?
- □ for 'not anything', 'nothing', see *nada*
- □ *adv* rather, somewhat: *estaba algo cansada* she was rather/a bit tired; cf *un poco*

alguien *pron* somebody, someone; anybody, anyone: *alguien tiene que saberlo* someone has to know; *si alguien lo sabe, será Carlos* if anyone knows, it will be Carlos
- □ 'anybody', 'anyone' in interrogative phrases: *¿Conoces a alguien aquí?* Do you know anyone here?
- □ for 'not anybody, not anyone', 'nobody', 'no-one' see *nadie*

alguno *adj* some, any
- □ *encontramos algunas faltas* we found some faults; *¿Has tenido algunas ideas?* Have you had any ideas?; *si tienes algún problema* if you have any problem
- □ NB drops *o* and takes accent on *ú* before *msing*: *tengo algún dinero –*

¡pero no mucho! I've got some money, but not much!
- □ NB *alguno que otro / alguna que otra* some … or other: *si encuentras alguno que otro problema* if you encounter some problem (or other). Used in this way, there is some overlap with cf *cualquier*: worth comparing uses
- □ more emphatic or more definite than cf *unos/as* (some, a few)
- □ also used after the noun in an emphatic negative sense: *¡no tengo idea alguna!* I have (absolutely) no idea! (stronger than *no tengo ninguna idea*)
- □ also used as *pron*: (in this case *msing* doesn't shorten) *alguno de mis amigos* one (or other) of my friends; *algunos de mis amigos* some of my friends
- □ *sing* can be used in the sense of *alguien; si alguno lo sabe* if anyone knows

aliento *nm* breath; courage, spirit: *cobrar aliento (de)* to take courage/heart (from)
- □ for breathing use *respiración*
- □ **alentar** *vt* -ie- to encourage, cheer
- □ *vi* breathe (*respirar* is more common)

alimento *nm* food, nourishment
- □ used mainly to refer to 'food' as the means of keeping you alive
- □ for 'food' in the sense of meals, prepared food, use and cf *comida*
- □ **alimentación** *nf* the act of feeding: *la alimentación de la familia* feeding the family; also occasionally used to indicate a food shop or department, as in Fr
- □ **alimentar** *vt* to feed, nourish (in the same sense as the nouns above); in a more routine sense use *dar de comer: ¿Has dado de comer al perro?* Have you fed the dog?
- □ can also mean 'to feed' in sense of 'support' (eg a family)
- □ **alimenticio** *adj* technical term

relating to food: *valor alimenticio* nutritional value

aliviar *vt* to relieve, ease (used of unpleasant sensations, esp pain, sorrow, etc)
- **aliviarse** *vr* to be relieved, lessen (eg pain)
- **alivio** *nm* relief
- fairly limited range of Eng 'relieve/relief': depends on precise meanings, but possible *syns* are *desahogar* and cf *tranquilizar*

allá *adv* there, over there
- more emphatic than *allí*: really means 'right over there away from both speaker and spoken to', maybe with a pointing gesture: *por allá* over there, thereabouts
- way back in time: *allá en el siglo 13* way back in the 13th century
- *más allá adv* further away, further over (there)
- **más allá de** *prep* beyond: *más allá de las montañas* beyond the mountains; *más allá de lo aceptable* beyond (the limit of) the acceptable
- worth further dictionary research!

allí *adv* there, ie away from both speaker and spoken to, further away than cf *ahí*, maybe not as far as cf *allá* above: *por allí* that way, over there

alma *nf* soul, spirit
- NB *f*, but *el alma* because of stressed *a*; *pl las almas*
- often used in expressions where Eng uses 'heart': *estar con el alma en la boca* to have one's heart in one's mouth; *con toda el alma* with all one's heart

almacén *nm* warehouse, store
- NB use of *pl almacenes* (no accent!): *(grandes) almacenes* department store
- **almacenar** *vt* to store

almendra *nf* almond

- **almendro** *nm* almond tree

almohada *nf* pillow; cushion

almorzar *vi -ue-, cé-* to have lunch
- *vt* to have for lunch: *almorzamos bistec* we had steak for lunch
- **almuerzo** *nm* lunch
- *comer* and *comida* are less formal and often preferred

alojar *vt* to lodge, accommodate, put up
- **alojarse** *vr* to lodge, stay, be accommodated; also 'to lodge', 'get stuck' (in sth): *la bala se le alojó en el pulmón* the bullet lodged in his lung
- **alojamiento** *nm* lodging, accommodation
- use these words for accommodate/accommodation, NOT cf *acomodar*

alquilar *vt* to hire, rent
- NB rent/hire in both directions, ie to offer for hire or to take on hire: *esta empresa alquila coches* this firm rents (out) cars; *alquilar a* to hire from: *alquilamos el coche a esta empresa* we hired the car from this firm
- *se alquila* for hire/rent: *se alquila piso* flat to rent
- **alquiler** *nm* hire, rent
- *de alquiler* hired, rented: *una bicicleta de alquiler* a hired bike
- also 'rent' (money): *pagar el alquiler del piso* to pay the rent for the flat

alrededor *adv* around, about: *a dos kilómetros alrededor* for two kms around
- **alrededor de** *prep* around, about: *alrededor de la casa* around the house
- NB does mean literally 'around', ie in a circle: but for eg 'a walk around the park', *por* would be better
- also 'about' (ie approximately): *había alrededor de mil personas* there were about a thousand people
- **alrededores** *nmpl* surroundings,

area: *en los alrededores de Málaga* in the Málaga area (can also mean 'suburbs' in this sense: in the suburbs of Málaga)

alterar *vt* **alterarse** *vr* to change, alter
- usually implies to change for the worse: safer to use *cambiar*
- often means 'to upset', 'get upset or angry'
- **alteración** *nf* (usually) upset, disturbance
- for 'alteration' use *cambio*

alternar *vt* to alternate
- **alternarse** *vr* to alternate, take turns
- **alternativa** *nf* alternative, option
- NB dual meaning of **alternativo** *adj* alternative; alternating; and **alternativamente** *adv* alternatively; alternately

alto *adj* high, tall (person, building, price, etc, covers most senses of the Eng words)
- NB *invariable* when giving dimensions: *esta torre tiene 25 metros de alto* this tower is 25 metres high/tall
- loud: *en voz alta* in a loud voice; *hable más alto, por favor* speak louder, please
- **altura** *nf* height
- can be used in dimensions: *esta torre tiene 25 metros de altura* this tower is 25 metres high/tall
- *a estas alturas* at this point/stage: *a estas alturas no vamos a volver* we're not going back at this stage
- **altitud** *nf* altitude, height: used in a technical sense as in Eng
- **alteza** *nf* highness (use it to address royalty!)
- **¡alto!** *nm, interj* nothing to do with 'high': it means 'halt'!
- *hacer un alto* to make a halt/stop

alubia *nf* bean (of the butter-bean type); for green bean, see *judía, haba*

alucinación *nf pl* *alucinaciones* hallucination
- **alucinar** *vt* to hallucinate
- **alucinarse** *vr* to hallucinate, ie be deluded
- **alucinante** *adj* hallucinatory – but can also be used as 'great, super'
- **alucinógeno** *adj* hallucinogenic
- NB all these words have no *h* and one *l*!

alumbrar *vt* to light (up)
- for 'switching on light' *encender* is more common
- **alumbrado** *nm* *el alumbrado público* street lighting

alzar *vt* -ce-, -cé to lift, raise
- **alzarse** *vr* to rise, stand up: *en el fondo se alza la torre* the tower rises up in the background
- to revolt, rise up (less commonly used alternative to *levantar/se*)
- for 'stand up' it's safer to use *levantarse*
- **alza** *nf* rise (eg of price, temperature); NB *el alza* because of stressed *a*, but *las alzas*
- **alzamiento** *nm* uprising, revolt

ama *nf* female owner, proprietress, mistress (in that sense)
- perhaps a rather old-fashioned word, now used mainly in *ama de casa* housewife, *ama de llaves* housekeeper
- NB *el ama* because of stressed *a*, but *pl las amas*
- **amo** *nm* owner, proprietor, master; 'boss', cf *jefe*

amable *adj* kind, nice: *(Vd es) muy amable* that's very kind of you

amanecer *vi* -zc- to dawn, get light
- can be used with personal subject in sense of to be somewhere at dawn: *amanecimos en la costa* we were on the coast when dawn broke; or to wake up + a complement: *amaneció rico* he woke up rich

◻ **amanecer** *nm* dawn; *al amanecer* at dawn

amargo *adj* bitter (taste, person, memory etc); sour, sharp (taste)
◻ **amargar** *vt -gue-, -gué* to make bitter, embitter
◻ **amargarse** *vr* to become/get bitter
◻ **amargura** *nf* bitterness (all senses); sharpness, sourness

ambiente *nm* atmosphere, environment – in the sense of 'surroundings', 'ambience': *un ambiente alegre* a happy atmosphere
◻ for atmosphere that you breathe, use *atmósfera* and for 'the environment' eg that you need to conserve, use *medio ambiente*

ambos *adj* or *pron* both: *ambos hermanos* both brothers; *conocemos a ambos* we know both (of them)
◻ you can also use *los/las dos: los dos hermanos* both brothers: *les conocemos a los dos* we know both (of them)
◻ for 'both … and …', see *tanto … como …*

amenazar *vti -ce-, -cé* to threaten, menace
◻ NB takes *de* with noun object: *nos amenazó de muerte* he threatened us with death; but *con* + verb: *amenazó con matarnos* he threatened to kill us
◻ it's regular apart from spelling change as indicated: don't confuse its parts with *amanecer* above!
◻ **amenaza** *nf* threat, menace (*de* of)

ameno *adj* pleasant, agreeable
◻ similar use to *agradable*, tends to be used of activities and situations rather than people

América *nf* America
◻ Be careful! From the Hispanic viewpoint 'America' is often Spanish-speaking America, so it does not necessarily mean USA: *Norteamérica* is safer, *Estados Unidos* safer still!
◻ **americano** *adj* same observations apply: use *norteamericano* for 'belonging to USA'; *estadounidense* also exists, but is a bit stilted and a mouthful to pronounce!
◻ **americana** *nf* jacket, esp sports jacket

amigo/a *nmf* friend: *hacerse amigo/a de* to make friends with; *un/a amigo/a mío/a* a friend of mine
◻ has numerous derivatives, depending on the type of friend: *amigacho, amigazo, amigote, amiguete, amiguito/a*: worth a browse in the dictionary!
◻ can be used as *adj*: *ser amigo de* to be fond of; *muy amigo/a mío/a* a close friend of mine
◻ **amistad** *nf* friendship: *hacer/trabar amistad con alguien* to strike up a friendship with sb
◻ **amigable, amistoso** *adjs* friendly, amicable; *amigable* a shade more colloquial

amor *nm* love
◻ *amor a* or *por* love for: *tiene tanto amor a/por su hija* he has so much love for his daughter
◻ *amor de* love of: *el amor de nadar* the love of swimming
◻ *amor mío* my love, darling
◻ for eg 'I love tennis', use *encantar: me encanta el tenis*
◻ **amoroso** *adj* loving, affectionate; amorous
◻ **amar** *vt* to love: perhaps a shade more emphatic and purposeful than cf *querer*
◻ **enamorarse** *vr* (*de alguien*) to fall in love (with sb); *estar enamorado (de alguien)* to be in love (with sb)

amparar *vt* to protect, shelter, support
◻ useful word covering areas of

meaning of *proteger, apoyar*
- **amparo** *nm* protection, shelter

ampliar *vt* -í-: *amplío, amplié* to enlarge, extend, make bigger (in most senses)
- wider sense than *amplificar* to amplify, which is used technically as in Eng
- **amplio** *adj* ample, spacious, wide
- **amplitud** *nf* spaciousness, ampleness

análisis *nm inv* analysis
- no plural form

anciano/a *adj* old, elderly
- for 'ancient' see *antiguo*
- can also be *nmf* old man/woman/person

ancho *adj* wide, broad
- invariable when used with *tener* in dimensions: *tiene dos metros de ancho* it's two metres wide
- with clothes, 'too big': *es muy ancho* it's too big
- *adv a sus anchas* at ease: *estaba a mis anchas allí* I felt quite at home there
- sometimes used as *nm* width, breadth: *el ancho de la vía* gauge (of railway track)
- **anchura** *nf* breadth, width: *tiene dos metros de anchura* it's two metres wide

andar *vi pret: anduve, anduviste, anduvo, anduvimos, anduvisteis, anduvieron; imp subj: anduviera/anduviese* to walk
- 'walk' in the sense of to propel oneself along: *no puedo andar* I can't walk; for 'go for a walk for pleasure', use *pasearse, dar un paseo*
- also has wider meaning simply of 'go', 'travel', 'wander': *andaba por estos sitios* I was travelling/wandering around those parts
- also 'go' in sense of 'work', 'function': *esa máquina no anda bien* that machine doesn't work very well

(cf *funcionar*)
- sometimes used in similar sense to *estar: tiene que andar por ahí* it must be around there; *no ando muy bien en estos momentos* I'm not very well at present
- *¡anda!* exclamation to express surprise or incredulity: Well I never!, Oh go on with you!
- for 'to walk somewhere' use *andando gerund* with *ir: vamos andando a la ciudad* we're walking into town; you cannot use the simple verb *andar* in this sense! (cf *correr* to run)
- can be used as *vt* with distance, road, etc: *anduvimos el Camino de Santiago entero* we walked the whole Camino de Santiago
- has many more idiomatic uses and is worth a further browse in the dictionary!

andén *nm pl andenes* platform (on a railway station)
- use *plataforma* in most other senses

anhelar *vt* to long for, yearn for: *anhelar la libertad* to long for freedom
- + *inf* to long to: *anhela salir* he's longing to go out
- + *por* + *inf* to aspire to: *anhela por encontrar la solución* he aspires to find the solution
- **anhelo** *nm* longing, yearning (*de/por* for)

anillo *nm* ring (that you put on your finger)
- for 'circle' use *círculo*

animar *vt* to animate; to liven up, cheer up: *su llegada animó la fiesta* her arrival livened up the party
- often also + *a* + *inf* to encourage to: *nos animó a continuar* he encouraged us to continue
- not same as cf *fomentar* encourage in sense of 'foster' eg a cause
- **animarse** *vr* to cheer up, brighten up:

¡vamos, anímate! come on, cheer up!
- + a + inf to make up one's mind to: *por fin se animó a ir* at last he made up his mind to go
- **ánimo** *nm* a noun with a wide range of meanings …
- mind (cf *mente*)
- soul, spirit (cf *alma*)
- courage (cf *valor*): *(no) tener ánimo de hacer algo* (not) to have the courage/heart to do sth
- intention: *con/sin ánimo de + inf* with/without the intention of; *con/sin ánimo de molestarle* with/without the intention of troubling him
- as encouragement: *¡ánimo!* cheer up! take heart!
- **animoso** *adj* lively; brave

anochecer *vi -zc-* to get dark
- can also be used with personal subject: to be (somewhere) at nightfall: *anochecimos en Santiago* we were in Santiago at dusk (cf its opp *amanecer*)
- *nm* nightfall, dusk: *al anochecer* at nightfall, at dusk

ansia *nf* **ansiedad** *nf* anxiety, worry (a shade stronger than *preocupación*)
- also 'anguish' (perhaps not quite as strong as *angustia*)
- **ansiar** *vt* (+ n) to long for; (+ inf) to long to: perhaps a shade stronger than *anhelar*
- **ansioso** *adj* anxious (stronger than *preocupado, inquieto*); eager (*de* to)

ante *prep* before (in place); in the presence of; faced with
- NB more limited in its meaning than cf *delante de*, usually implies some sort of confrontation or awe: *ante esta situación* faced with this situation; *compareció ante el juez* he appeared before the judge

antelación *adv* occurs as **con antelación** before *adv* in advance (eg when booking tickets): *reservar con antelación* to book in advance

anterior *adj* previous, earlier: *en la ocasión anterior* on the previous occasion; *sus problemas anteriores* his earlier problems
- also 'front': *la parte anterior* the front, front part (cf *delantero*)
- NB one of the comparative adjectives ending in *-or* with no *f* form
- **anteriormente** *adv* previously
- **con anterioridad** *adv* beforehand: *hacer algo con anterioridad* to do sth beforehand, in advance

antes *adv* before (in time): *nunca la había visto antes* I had never seen her before; *dos días antes* two days before
- can mean 'first(ly)' in the sense of 'before anything else': *antes tienes que decirme la verdad* first you've got to tell me the truth
- occurs in several set phrases: *nunca antes* never before; *lo antes posible* or *cuanto antes* as soon/quickly as possible
- can also mean 'rather' in sense of 'better': *yo tomo vino antes que cerveza* I drink wine rather than beer
- **antes de** *prep* before (+ n/pron or inf): *antes de las tres* before three o'clock; *antes de salir* before leaving
- **antes (de) que** *conj* + *subjunc* before + verb: *antes de que te vayas* before you go
- not same as cf *ante* above

anti- *prefix* against, anti-; can be put on beginning of almost any noun or adjective as in Eng

anticipar *vt* to bring forward, advance: *anticiparon la fiesta* they brought the party forward
- also: 'foresee': cf *prever*
- **anticiparse** *vr* to take place early: *se anticipó la fiesta* the party took place early
- **anticipación** *nf* anticipation

but NB also **con anticipación** and **anticipadamente** *adv* in advance, beforehand; similar to **con antelación** and **con anterioridad** above

antiguo *adj* old, ancient (objects rather than people)
- also 'former', 'one-time': *el antiguo capitán* the former captain: comes before n in this sense
- for 'antique' furniture etc, use *de época*
- **antigüedad** *nf* antiquity: *en la antigüedad* in antiquity, a very long time ago; **antigüedades** *nfpl* antiques (as noun)

antipático *adj* unpleasant, disagreeable (of people); opp of cf *simpático*

antojarse *vr* to take a fancy to: *se me antoja una copa* I fancy a drink
- NB used 'back to front' like *gustar* etc: what you fancy is the subject, and the fancier is the indirect object of the reflexive verb!
- can be used + *inf* in sense of 'fancy', 'have a mind to': *¿Se te antoja ir a la playa?* Do you fancy going to the beach?; *A mí se me antoja dormir un rato* I fancy/wouldn't mind sleeping for a while
- **antojo** *nm* whim, caprice

anuncio *nm* announcement
- also, commonly: advertisement, poster
- **anunciar** *vt* to announce; to advertise
- for 'advertising' use *publicidad*

añadir *vt* to add (in most senses)
- **añadidura** *nf* addition, in sense of 'thing added': **por añadidura** *adv* in addition
- NB for 'add up' use *sumar*, though 'addition', ie the maths term, is *adición nf*

año *nm* year
- NB to be x years old: *tener x años*

apagar *vt* -gue-, gué to extinguish, put out (fire, light, etc), turn off (radio, TV, etc)
- **apagarse** *vr* to go out (fire etc)

aparato *nm* apparatus, (piece of) equipment, device
- widely used for equipment and machinery of all sorts: *aparatos de mando* controls (eg in plane)

aparcar *vti* -que-, -qué to park (car etc)
- **aparcamiento** *nm* car park

aparecer *vi* -zc- to appear
- care is needed in the use of this and related words
- NB used in sense of 'come into sight', 'show up': for 'appear' in sense of 'seem', use *parecer*. Compare *apareció agotado* he appeared, ie turned up, exhausted; *pareció agotado* he appeared, ie seemed, exhausted.
- **aparente** *adj* apparent, seeming; **aparentemente** *adv* apparently, seemingly
- **aparición** *nf* appearance (act of coming into sight): *su aparición fue inesperada* his appearance (ie arrival) was unexpected; can also mean 'apparition' in Eng sense
- **apariencia** *nf* appearance (looks): *tenía una apariencia muy elegante* he had a very smart appearance (cf *aspecto*)
- **aparentar** *vt* to give the appearance of, feign: *aparentaba pobreza* he feigned poverty, gave the appearance of being poor
- + *inf*: *aparentaba ser pobre* he gave the impression of being poor

apartar *vt* to separate, take/move away, remove: *apartó los juguetes del niño* she moved the toys away from the child; *apartar los ojos* to look aside/away
- **apartarse** *vr* to move away: *apartarse del camino* to wander off the track
- **aparte** *adv* apart, aside; separately:

hacer algo aparte to do sth separately

- *punto y aparte* full stop, new paragraph
- **aparte de** *prep* apart from: *aparte de este problema* apart from this problem

apasionar *vt* to excite, thrill: used 'back to front' in expressions like *me apasionan las películas de Almodóvar* I'm dead keen on Almodóvar's films

- **apasionarse** *vr* to get excited, thrilled (*por* about): *me apasiono por las películas de Almodóvar* I'm dead keen on Almodóvar's films; *se apasiona por esa chica* he's mad about that girl
- **apasionante** *adj* exciting, thrilling: *es una película apasionante* it's an exciting film; use rather than *excitante* which tends to be used more in the medical sense of 'stimulating'

apellido *nm* surname, family name

- don't forget Sp people have two: from their father and their mother; use cf *nombre* for first name

apenas *prep* hardly, barely: *apenas cien personas* barely 100 people

- *conj* hardly, no sooner: *apenas oí el coche estaban en la casa* hardly had I heard the car than they were in the house
- should strictly be followed by past anterior tense: consult a grammar book for a full explanation

apetecer *vt* -zc- to appeal to, take one's fancy

- used 'back to front', the thing you fancy is the subject: *¿Te apetece la ensalada?* Do you fancy the salad?
- + *inf*: *no me apetece salir con el tiempo que hace* I don't fancy/feel like going out in this weather

aplazar *vt* -ce-, -cé to postpone, put off; *syn* also *posponer*

aplicar *vt* -que, -qué to apply (sth to sth): *me apliqué la crema bronceadora a los brazos* I applied the sun cream to my arms

- for 'apply for job' etc use *presentarse, solicitar*; see also *oposiciones*
- **aplicarse** *vr* to apply (*a* to): *esta regla se aplica a los conductores* this rule applies to drivers
- also, literally 'to apply oneself to' (+ *noun* or *inf*): *se aplica a ayudar a los enfermos* he applies/devotes himself to helping the sick
- **aplicación** *nf* application (in sense of *v* above); also in sense of 'industry', 'hard work'; for job etc use *solicitud*
- **aplicado** *adj* industrious, hard-working

apostar *vti* -ue- to bet

- *apostar a que* to bet that: *apuesto a que no vienen* I bet they don't come; *apuesto a que sí/no* I bet they do/don't (ie on a positive/negative outcome of whatever bet)
- **apuesta** *nf* bet, wager

apoyar *vt* to lean (eg head on sth, or sth against sth: *apoyó la cabeza contra la pared* he leaned his head against the wall); carries idea of support

- also 'to support' in both physical sense above, and abstract sense: *apoya ese partido* he supports that party
- **apoyarse** *vr* to lean (ie oneself) eg on/against sth: *me apoyaba contra la pared* I was leaning against the wall
- **apoyo** *nm* support (*dar apoyo a* to give support to)
- NB be careful over the Sp for 'lean': 'this word' essentially implies 'support'; for 'lean over', ie in a particular direction use *inclinarse*; for 'lean out' eg of window use *asomarse*

apreciar *vt* to appreciate

- used much as in Eng, however its meanings can be rather more intense

in the sense of 'value': *aprecio su interés*   I appreciate (ie value) your interest
- for 'increase in value' use *aumentar en valor*
- **aprecio** *nm*   appreciation, esteem: *tener algo/a alguien en gran aprecio* to have a high regard for sth/sb
- **apreciable** *adj*   appreciable (in sense of 'considerable', 'noticeable': *una cantidad apreciable*)
- can also have a stronger meaning of 'valuable' or 'much appreciated': *fue un regalo apreciable*   it was a much appreciated gift
- **apreciado** *adj past part*   used for politeness in letters: *Apreciado Señor Jiménez*   Dear Mr Jiménez

apresurar *vt*   to hurry (sb/sth); **apresurarse** *vr*   to hurry, to hasten (*a + inf* to): *me apresuré a terminar la redacción*   I hastened to finish the essay; *me apresuraba a terminar la redacción*   I was in a hurry to finish the essay
- although *apresúrate* can be used for 'hurry up!', *date prisa* is more common
- **apresurado** *adj*   hurried, hasty: *una despedida apresurada*   a hasty goodbye; **apresuradamente** *adv* hurriedly, hastily: cf *de prisa*
- perhaps implies greater haste and urgency than expressions containing *prisa*: refer to these for comparison

apretar *vt -ie-*   (basically) to tighten, but has a number of idiomatic meanings and uses …
- to press (down): *apretar el botón* press the button
- to be too tight: *estos zapatos me aprietan*   these shoes are too tight for me
- to squeeze: *le apretó la mano*   he squeezed her hand
- to tighten up: *van a apretar las reglas* they are going to tighten the rules
- to get more intense: *apretaba el sol*

the sun was getting hotter
- **apretarse** *vr*   to crowd together: *todos se apretaron contra el frío*   they all huddled together against the cold
- **apretado** *adj*   tight, dense, compact: basically describes the conditions brought about by the various meanings of the verb! *estar apretado* to be up against it/in difficulties
- **aprieto** *nm*   difficulty, fix: *estar en un aprieto*   to be in a fix/jam; *salir de un aprieto*   to get out of a jam
- impossible to give all uses here: merits further browsing in the dictionary!

aprobar *vti -ue-*   to approve (of)
- also, commonly 'to pass (an exam)': *¡aprobé!*   I passed!

apropiado *adj*   appropriate
- but NB *adecuado* is often more appropriate!; see also *apto* below

aprovechar *vt* or **aprovecharse de** *vr* to make good use of, take advantage of: *¿Porqué no (nos) aprovechamos (d)el buen tiempo?*   Why don't we take advantage of the good weather?
- *¡Que aproveche!*   Enjoy your meal!, Bon appétit!
- **provecho** *nm* advantage, benefit/profit: *sacar provecho de*   to get/derive benefit/advantage from; *buen provecho* means same as *¡que aproveche!* above

aproximar *vt*   to bring nearer
- used mainly as **aproximarse (a)** *vr* to approach; common alternative to *acercarse: se aproxima la primavera* spring is approaching
- also: to approximate
- **aproximado** *adj*   approximate
- **aproximadamente** *adv* approximately, about (cf *alrededor de*)

apto *adj*   apt, suitable: *no es muy apto para el trabajo*   he's not very suitable for the job
- another possible word for

'appropriate', in this sense: *esta palabra es muy apta* this word is very appropriate

apuntar *vt* to aim (eg gun)
- □ also: to point out
- □ but often: to jot down, note down
- □ **apunte** *nm* note, jotting: *hacer apuntes* to make/take notes

apuro *nm* to fix, jam
- □ often *pl*: *estar en apuros* to be in trouble, in a fix (cf *aprieto*)
- □ **apurarse** *vr* to get in a state, get upset: *¡No te apures!* Don't get upset!

aquel, aquellos, aquella, aquellas *demons adj* that, those
- □ always followed by noun: *aquella casa* that house
- □ strictly 'over there' ie away from both speaker and person addressed, compared with *ese* 'that near you', though there is often an overlap between the two words
- □ **aquél**, *aquéllos, aquélla, aquéllas demons pron* that, that one; those, those (ones): *esta casa y aquélla/s* this house and that one/those; same observations apply
- □ **aquello** *demons pron* note the neuter form used when the gender of the noun is not (yet) known or there is no noun: *¿Qué es aquello?* What's that?
- □ consult a grammar book for further details

aquí *adv* here
- □ *por aquí* round here, this way
- □ see other 'here/there' words for comparison *acá, ahí, allí, allá*

arder usually *vi* to burn
- □ similar to cf *quemar*, but perhaps rather less used in everyday speech and more figurative or abstract: *arder de amor* to burn (ie be consumed) with love

ardiente *adj* ardent (passion etc), but also 'burning' in all senses including 'shining', 'bright': *luz ardiente* bright/shining light

área *nf* area (eg of circle, field)
- □ NB *el área* because of the stressed *a*, but *las áreas*
- □ NB often means a demarcated area: *área de servicio* service area (on motorway); for 'district' of town, use *barrio* or *zona*; in country use *comarca, región* or *zona*
- □ also: are, as unit of area

argüir *vt* to argue
- □ NB -*uy*- and -*üi*-: *pi: arguyo, arguyes, arguye, argüimos, argüís, arguyen; ps: arguya; ger: arguyendo; pret: argüí, argüiste, arguyó, argüimos, argüisteis, arguyeron; imp subj: arguyera/arguyese*
- □ only 'argue' in the sense of 'to put forward an argument': *arguyó que era imposible* he argued that it was impossible
- □ for 'argue' in sense of 'disagree' use *discutir, disputar*
- □ **argumento** *nm* argument (in the above sense); also: plot (in play or novel); use *discusión, disputa* for 'disagreement'

arma *nf* weapon, arm
- □ NB *el arma* because of the stressed *a*, but *las armas*
- □ **armar** *vt* to arm
- □ also used in phrases like *armar un Belén/un lío* to cause, start up a row
- □ and as *vr armarse de valor* to pluck up courage
- □ **armada** *nf* 'Armada', yes, but nowadays simply 'navy', same as *marina!*

armonía *nf* harmony
- □ **armonioso** *adj* harmonious
- □ NB no *h* on these and other associated words

arquitectura *nf* architecture

□ NB **arquitectónico** *adj* architectural

□ **arquitecto/a** *nmf* architect

arrancar *vt* -que-, -qué to pull up, off or out, snatch away (eg flowers, teeth, hair, button, handbag, wallet: ie almost anything that can be removed by pulling!); stronger than cf *tirar*

□ *vi* to start off, move away (eg vehicle): *el tren arrancó de repente* the train suddenly moved away

□ *a + inf* to start doing sth(usually suddenly): *arrancó a correr* he started to run

□ **arranque** *nm* (sudden) start; outburst (of emotion); starter (on vehicle)

arrastrar *vt* to drag

□ **arrastrarse** *vr* can mean 'to drag oneself', but usually 'to crawl (along)'

□ **arrastre** *nm* drag, (action of) dragging

arreglar *vt* to arrange, fix

□ also often used in sense of 'repair': *arreglar un coche* to repair a car

□ **arreglarse** *vr* to come to an agreement

□ of hair: *arreglarse el pelo* to get one's hair done

□ to work out, be resolved: *todo se arregló* everything was sorted out

□ **arreglárselas** to get by, manage: *tendrás que arreglártelas* you'll just have to get by/get it sorted out

□ **arreglo** *nm* arrangement, agreement (in that sense); useful way of translating Eng 'compromise': *llegar a un arreglo* to come to an arrangement (ie to reach a compromise)

arrepentirse *vr* -ie-, -i- to be sorry, regret, repent (*de* for/about): *me arrepiento de haber causado un problema* I'm sorry I've caused a problem

□ it really means 'repent for' and is much stronger than *sentir* used in this sense: you could quite easily say *siento*

(mucho) haber causado un problema, and just to say 'I'm sorry', use *lo siento*; see *sentir* and also *perdón* for comparison

□ **arrepentido** *adj* sorry, regretful: *estar arrepentido de algo* to be sorry/regretful about sth

□ **arrepentimiento** *nm* regret, sorrow, repentance

arriba *adv* above, upstairs, up(wards) (ie position or direction)

□ *hacia arriba* upwards; *más arriba* further up; *calle arriba* up the street; *río arriba* upstream; *¡arriba los verdes!* up the greens!; *el pueblo de arriba* the upper part of the village

□ **arriba de** *prep* further up from: *arriba del castillo* up above the castle

arriesgar *vt* -gue-, -gué to risk (sth eg *la vida*)

□ **arriesgarse** *vr* to risk, take a risk (*a algo* or + *inf* doing sth): *te arriesgas a (coger) un catarro* you're risking (catching) a cold

□ **arriesgado** *adj* risky; **arriesgadamente** *adv* riskily, rashly

□ See also *riesgo* *nm* risk

arrodillarse *vr* to kneel down

□ this refers to the action of getting down on to your knees: when you are there use *estar arrodillado* or *estar de rodillas* to be kneeling, to be on one's knees

□ NB in common with most bodily positions, you use the past participle, which agrees with the subject: *las niñas estaban arrodilladas* the girls were kneeling

□ from (and see also) *rodilla*

arrojar *vt* to throw, fling, hurl: stronger than *tirar*

arruinar *vt* to ruin (eg a building); to ruin financially

□ for ruin in sense of spoil, use *estropear*

□ **arruinarse** *vt* to be ruined; **arruinado** *adj* ruined: same observations apply

arte *nmsing* and but *f* in *pl*! art: *las artes* the arts
□ NB gender above
□ most senses as in Eng, but 'art' loosely meaning 'painting' would be better as *pintura*
□ *las bellas artes* the fine arts
□ can also mean 'craft(iness)', 'knack'

artesano/a *nmf* craftsman/woman often a better translation than 'artisan'
□ **artesanía** *nf* craft, (in sense of) craftsmanship

asco *nm* disgust, revulsion: *me da asco* it disgusts me/I find it disgusting; *¡Qué asco!* How revolting!
□ **asqueroso** *adj* disgusting, revolting
□ **asquerosidad** *nf* loathsomeness

asear *vt* to adorn, embellish
□ often used as *vr* **asearse** to tidy/smarten oneself up
□ **aseo** *nm* neatness, tidiness, cleanliness (of person)
□ **aseos** *nmpl* toilet, loo, cloakroom

asegurar *vt* to make secure, safe
□ also, often: 'to assure': *te aseguro que es la verdad* I assure you it's the truth
□ and 'to insure'; for 'insurance' see *seguro*
□ **asegurarse** *vr* to assure oneself, ensure, make sure (*de* of, *de que* that): *nos aseguramos del premio* we made sure of the prize; *me aseguré de que vendrían* I made sure that they would come; see also *seguro*

asemejarse a *vr* to resemble, be like
□ from cf *semejante, semejanza*

asentir *vi* -ie-, -i- to assent, agree (*a* to)
□ similar to cf *consentir*

asequible *adj* available, obtainable (in that sense)

also 'reasonable': *a un precio asequible* at a reasonable price

asesinar *vt* to murder, kill
□ wider meaning than just 'to assassinate'
□ **asesino/a** *nmf* murderer, assassin
□ **asesinato** *nm* murder

así *adv* like that, thus, so (in that sense): *lo haces así* you do it like that
□ can also be used as *adj* in this way: *una persona así* a person like that
□ and with *de* in sense of 'this/that' + *adj*: *un pez así de largo* a fish this/that long
□ *así que conj* + *indic* (for known fact) as soon as: *así que nos vieron* as soon as they saw us; + *subjunc* referring to future: *así que nos vean* as soon as they see us (consult a grammar for further explanations)

asiento *nm* seat (ie in general)
□ see also *banco, butaca, silla, sillón* for specific kinds of seat

asignatura *nf* (school) subject
□ for subject in other senses, see *sujeto, súbdito*

asir *vt* *asgo, ases; asga* to seize, grab
□ **asirse de** *vr* to grab hold of
□ **asa** *nf* handle, grip (ie a handle that you grip)
□ NB *el asa* because of the stressed *a*, but *las asas*

asistir *vi* to attend, be present (*a* at)
□ can also mean 'attend' in medical sense, but for 'assist' in sense of 'help' use *ayudar*
□ **asistencia** *nf* attendance – ie presence at and also medical attendance
□ **asistente/a** *nmf* assistant; *adj los asistentes* those present
□ merits further research in the dictionary concerning meaning and function!

asomar *vt* to show, stick out: *asomar la cabeza por la ventana* to stick one's head out of the window
- **asomarse** *vr* to appear, show oneself (often above or through something): *los picos se asomaban por encima de la bruma* the peaks appeared/stood out above the mist; also 'to lean out': *es peligroso asomarse* it is dangerous to lean out
- NB like most of these reflexive verbs of getting into a position, once you are there, you use *estar asomado* to be leaning out

asombrar *vt* to amaze, astonish
- **asombrarse** *vr* to be amazed, asonished
- stronger than cf *sorprender, extrañar*
- **asombro** *nm* amazement, astonishment: *para mi asombro* to my astonishment
- **asombroso** *adj* amazing, astonishing

aspecto *nm* aspect (in all senses); look, appearance

áspero *adj* rough (in many of its senses, esp 'not smooth'); uneven; rugged; sour; gruff; harsh
- **aspereza** *nf* roughness (in all the above senses)

asunto *nm* subject, matter: *vamos al asunto* let's get to the point
- **al asunto de** *prep* on the subject of, about (in that sense)

asustar *vt* to frighten, scare
- **asustarse** *vr* to be frightened, scared (*de/por algo* at/by sth)
- see also *susto*

atacar *vt* -que-, -qué to attack
- **ataque** *nm* attack (in all senses, including eg *ataque cardíaco* heart attack)

atar *vt* to tie (up)
- in most senses, but use *amarrar* for boat

atardecer *vi* -zc- to get dark
- cf *anochecer*
- also as *nm*: *al atardecer* at dusk

atasco *nm* blockage (frequently used for traffic jam)
- **atascarse** *vr* -que-, -qué to get stuck (eg in traffic jam or mud)

atender *vt* -ie- to attend to (in most senses)
- for 'to attend' in the sense of 'be present' use *asistir*

atentar *vi* to commit an offence (*contra alguien* against sb)
- **atentado** *nm* offence (in that sense)

atento *adj* attentive (often with *estar*)
- polite, thoughtful, kind – usually with *ser*: *Vd ha sido muy atento con nosotros* you have been very kind/thoughtful towards us

aterrar *vt* to terrify
- **aterrorizar** *vt* -ce-, -cé- to terrify or terrorise
- both are based on cf *terror*

aterrizar *vi* -ce-, -cé to land (plane)
- don't confuse with *aterrorizar* above
- **aterrizaje** *nm* landing (of plane)

atleta *nmf* athlete
- always ends in -*a*
- **atletismo** *nm* athletics

atmósfera *nf* atmosphere (ie that you breathe)
- can be used for 'ambience', or you can use cf *ambiente*

atracar *vt* -que-, -qué to hold up, mug
- **atraco** *nm* hold-up, mugging
- don't confuse with *atacar, ataque* (attack), above, in spite of similarity of meaning

atraer *vt* to attract (in most senses)
- has all the irregularities of *traer*
- **attracción** *nf* attraction (in most senses): *parque de atracciones* funfair

□ **atractivo** *adj* attractive; also *n* attraction, esp appeal: *los atractivos de esta casa* the attractions/appeal of this house

atrapar *vt* to catch
□ more colloquial and suggests more effort involved than cf *coger*

atrás *adv* back
□ *hacia atrás* backwards; *más atrás* further back
□ can be used in time context in sense of 'ago': *siglos atrás* centuries ago
□ **atrasar** *vt* to slow down; also *vi* to lose time (clock)
□ **atrasarse** *vr* to be/lag behind
□ **atraso** *nm* delay: *este tren lleva 30 minutos de atraso* this train is 30 minutes late; see also *retraso*

atravesar *vt -ie-* to cross
□ same meaning as cf *cruzar*
□ also 'to pierce': *le atravesó una bala* he was hit by a bullet
□ *n* is cf *travesía*

atreverse *vi* to dare (*a* + *inf* to + verb)
□ same meaning as cf *osar*
□ **atrevido** *adj* daring, bold
□ **atrevimiento** *nm* boldness, daring

atribuir *vt* pi: *-uyo, -uyes, -uye, -uimos, -uís, -uyen; p.s.: -uya; pret: -uyó, -uyeron; imp subj: -uyera, -uyese; ger: -uyendo* to attribute (*a* to)

atropellar *vt* to knock over (usually violently, esp of vehicles); ride roughshod over
□ **atropello** *nm* act of knocking down

audiencia *nf* audience (senses as in Eng ie hearing, or people listening)
□ for audience at eg theatre you often use *público*; for radio audience, *oyentes*

auge *nm* peak, summit
□ commonly used in *estar en auge* to be doing well, to be at its peak

aumentar *vt* increase raise

□ **aumentarse** *vr* to increase, rise (in that sense)
□ **aumento** *nm* increase, rise

aun *adv* even: *aun tú* even you
□ cf *incluso, hasta*

aún *adv* still, yet: *aún no llegan* they still haven't arrived
□ means and has the same use as *todavía*
□ remember the accent and don't confuse with *aun* above (no accent)

aunque *conj* although, though
□ can take *indic* or *subjunc*: *indic* for statement of fact, *subjunc* when it means 'even though sth might happen'; consult a grammar for further explanation

ausente *adj* absent (use with *estar*)
□ **ausencia** *nf* absence
□ **ausentarse** to absent oneself, to absent (*de* from)
□ NB spelling *aus-*, no *b*!

auto- *prefix* auto- or self-: added to many words, eg *autoservicio* self-service

avanzar *vt -ce-, -cé* and **avanzarse** *vr* to advance, move forward
□ **avance** *nm* advance
□ can be used in sense of a money advance
□ cf *adelantar(se)*

ave *nf* bird (usually fairly large)
□ otherwise use *pájaro*
□ NB *el ave* in sing because of the stressed *a*
□ *el AVE (Alta Velocidad Española)* high-speed train: pun on *ave*

aventura *nf* adventure
□ **aventurero/a** *nmf* adventurer; also *adj* adventurous (NB not *-oso!*)
□ **aventurarse a** *vr* to venture to

avergonzar *vt -güe-; -ce-, -cé* to shame, embarrass
□ NB when stem change occurs, *u* is written *ü*: *avergüenzo*

□ **avergonzarse** *vr* to be ashamed, embarrassed

□ **avergonzado** *adj* ashamed, embarrassed (use with *estar*)

□ see also base word *vergüenza*

averiguar *vt* -güe-, -güé to find out, ascertain; verify, check (cf *comprobar*)

avión *nm* (aero)plane

□ NB: *pl aviones* and it's *m*, unlike most nouns ending in *-ión*

avisar *vt* to warn, inform

□ **aviso** *nm* warning; notice

B

B *(be)* has the same two sounds as cf: *v*: a 'b' sound at the beginning of a word, as in *baile*, though without expelling a puff of air, and a much lighter sound between vowels, where your lips just come together and part again, as in *haber*.

bachillerato *nm* school leaving certificate, roughly equivalent to GCSE

bajar *vi* to go/come down, descend; other meanings …

□ to get off or out of a means of transport

□ to fall, drop (prices etc)

□ *vt* to lower, put down (voice, hi-fi, hand, head, etc)

□ to get down (eg off shelf), carry, bring down(stairs) (eg suitcase)

□ **baja** *nf* drop, fall (in price, temperature, etc); casualty; *darse de baja* to be off work, drop out (of work, membership etc)

□ not the same as **bajada** *nf* slope; descent (ie action of going down)

□ **bajo** *adj* short (person), low (in most senses): *la planta baja* ground floor; *en voz baja* in a low voice, (speaking) quietly

□ also used as *adv*: *hablar bajo* to speak quietly

□ and *prep* under, below (meaning overlaps with *debajo de* but is used in a number of more abstract phrases:

bajo el reinado de under the reign of; *bajo la lluvia* under (in) the rain); *bajo Franco* under Franco

bala *nf* bullet

□ for 'ball', see *balón, bola, pelota* according to type

balancear *vt* to swing (eg arm), rock (eg boat)

□ **balancearse** *vr* to sway, swing, rock: *los árboles se balanceaban en el viento* the trees were swaying in the wind

□ better to use *equilibrar/se* for 'to balance'.

balbucear or **balbucir** *vt/vi* to stutter, stammer, babble
balbucir only has imperfect *balbucía* etc, preterite *balbucí* etc and imp subj *balbuciera/iese* etc.

balón *m pl balones* ball (large, inflated: football, rugby, beach ball etc)

□ 'a football' is *un balón de fútbol*

□ see also *bola, pelota* for comparison

banco *nm* bank (ie building where you make money transactions)

□ also 'bank' (for storage): *banco de datos* database/bank; *banco de sangre* blood bank

□ and 'bank' (of fog, sand, etc)

□ and, completely different meaning of 'bench' 'seat' (of that sort)

□ **banca** *nf* banking, 'the banks' (ie as a whole or group); not same as cf *banco* above

□ **bancario** *adj* (to do with) bank, banking: *cuenta bancaria* bank account

banda *nf* (music) band; but has various other common meanings…
- band (to wear), sash
- *banda sonora* soundtrack
- gang (cf *pandilla*)

baño *nm* bath, bathe
also used as euphemism for 'toilet', 'loo': *¿Dónde está el baño, por favor?* Where is the toilet, please?
- **bañar** *vt* to bath, to bathe (somebody/something)
- **bañarse** *vr* to have a bath, bathe (oneself), have a bathe
- **bañista** *nmf* bather; not **bañador** *nm* swimming costume, bathing trunks

barba *nf* beard; chin

barbaridad *nf* barbarity, barbarism, but often used in the expression *¡Qué barbaridad!* How dreadful!

barco *nm* boat (in general), ship; see also *buque*
- **barca** *nf* (small) boat (ie more limited meaning): *barca de remos* rowing boat

barman *nm pl barmans* or *barmanes* barman
- no *f*, use *camarera*

barra *nf* stick; small loaf (of bread)
- *barra de labios* lipstick
- bar (ie the counter) in a bar, pub

barrera *nf* barrier (in most senses)
- also translates 'gate', if this is, in fact, a barrier!

barrio *nm* district, quarter (of town)
- sometimes used to mean a 'suburb', but not 'the suburbs' (see also *afueras*)

barro *nm* one of several words for 'mud' (*syn fango, lodo*).
- also 'clay'

basar *vt* to base (*en* on)
- **basarse** *vr* to be based (*en* on)

base *nf* base, basis (in most senses)
- **a base de** on the basis of

bastante *adj* enough, sufficient
- as an adjective, it agrees with its noun: *¿hay bastantes tenedores?* are there enough forks?; (you can also use *suficiente*, especially with negative)
- *adv* enough, sufficiently: *es bastante inteligente para comprender* he's intelligent enough to understand
- quite, (in the sense of) fairly: *bastante bien, pero …* quite good, but …
- **bastar** *vi* to be enough, to be sufficient
- can be used to say 'that's enough' eg coffee: *basta, gracias,* or more emphatically to stop an action: *¡Basta ya!* That's quite enough of that!; *basta decir que …* suffice it to say that …

batería *nf* battery (usually a large one, eg for a car; see also *pila*)
- also: drums, drummer (in band, pop group)
- and 'set': *batería de cocina* set of kitchen utensils

batir *vt* to beat (in most senses)
- **batirse** *vr* to fight: *batirse con alguien* to fight someone
- **batido de leche** *nm* milk shake

bautizar *vt -ce-, -cé* to baptise, christen
- **bautismo** *nm* baptism, christening
- NB: note spelling, no *p*

bebé *nmf* baby; *bebé-probeta* test-tube baby

beber *vti* to drink
- **bebida** *nf* drink
- NB for 'Would you like a drink?' use *tomar: ¿Quieres tomar algo?*

belga *adj* Belgian (nationality)
- NB both *m* and *f* forms end in *-a*
- don't confuse with **Bélgica** *nf* Belgium

belleza *nf* beauty, loveliness
- can be applied to a person or object:

see also *hermosura*

□ **bello** *adj* beautiful, lovely (person or object); see also *bonito, hermoso, guapo* for comparison

beneficio *nm* benefit
□ but also: profit, earnings, gain

biblioteca *nf* library
□ don't confuse with *librería* bookshop!

bicho *nm* (small) animal, creepy-crawly

bicicleta *nf* bicycle
□ often abbreviated to *bici nf* bike; *ir en bici(cleta)* to ride a bike

bien a useful little word that has various uses and meanings:
□ *adv* well, properly (corresponding to the adjective *bueno* good): *lo hizo bien* he/she did it well/properly; *¡Qué bien hablas español!* How well you speak Spanish! *¿Cómo estás? ¿Bien?* How are you? Well? *¡Bien!* good! fine! OK!
□ also used (maybe by your teacher) to mean 'good' about a piece of work
□ *hacer bien en + inf* to be right in ...ing
□ see also *bueno*; and the opposite of *bien*, ie *mal*
□ *nm* (the) good (as a noun): *el bien público* the common good
□ *bienes nmpl* goods, property, wealth: *bienes de consumo* consumer goods
□ worth further investigation in a dictionary
□ **bienestar** *nm* welfare, well-being: *el estado de bienestar* the welfare state
□ **bienvenida** *nf* welcome (ie, as a noun): *dar una bienvenida caliente* to give a warm welcome
□ **¡bienvenido!** *adj* welcome! NB this agrees with the persons(s) you are welcoming: *¡Bienvenidos todos a esta ciudad!* Welcome everyone to this town!

billete *nm* ticket (especially for travel)
□ see also *entrada*, which is more commonly used for entry ticket

(cinema, sport etc), and *boleto* (Sp Am)
□ also banknote: *un billete de diez euros* a ten euro note

bizarro *adj* gallant, brave (*valiente* is more common)
□ for 'bizarre' use *raro, extraño*

blanco *adj* white
□ *nm* target

blando *adj* soft: *la droga blanda* soft drugs
□ see also *suave*, especially for Eng 'bland'

boca *nf* mouth (of person, animal, river etc)
□ used in some useful idioms: *boca abajo/arriba* face downwards/upwards; *boca de metro* tube station entrance
□ **bocadillo** *nm* sandwich
□ ie made with Sp style bread: 'flat' slices usually make *un sandwich*, which is usually toasted

boda *nf* wedding, marriage (ceremony, reception)
□ for the married state, see *matrimonio*
□ often used in the plural: *las bodas de plata* silver wedding, *Bodas de sangre* Blood Wedding (play by García Lorca)

bola *nf* ball
□ *bola de nieve* snowball, *bola de cristal* crystal ball
□ for ball used in sports see *pelota* and *balón*
□ **bolígrafo** *nm* ballpoint pen, biro; children often abbreviate it to *boli*

boleto *nm* ticket (used in most of Sp Am); see also *billete, entrada*

boletín *nm* bulletin: *boletín informativo/de noticias* news bulletin, *boletín meteorológico* weather report/forecast
□ also *boletín escolar* school report; some overlap with cf *parte*

bolsa *nf* bag (in most senses, but see also *bolso*)
- □ also: stock exchange/market
- □ **bolso** *nm* handbag (much more limited in meaning than *bolsa*)

bomba *nf* bomb
- □ *pasarlo bomba* to have a whale of a time
- □ also, rather disconcertingly, 'pump': *bomba de incendios* fire engine
- □ **bombero/a** *nmf* firefighter

bombón *nm pl bombones* chocolate (as a sweet)
- □ for 'sweets' in general use *caramelos; bombón helado* choc ice

bondad see under *bueno*

bonito *adj* pretty, nice, nice-looking
- □ used mainly to describe objects, but also of young, female persons; describes prettiness rather than loveliness or beauty
- □ See also for comparison *bello, guapo, hermoso, precioso, lindo*

borde *nm* edge, border, side, verge: *el borde de la carretera* roadside
- □ also used in a rather more abstract sense: *Mujeres al borde de una crisis nerviosa* Women on the Verge of a Nervous Breakdown (film by Pedro Almodóvar)

borracho/a *adj* drunk or *nmf* drunkard
- □ compare: *estar borracho* to be drunk, *ser borracho/a* to be a drunkard

bosque *nm* wood, forest (no real distinction in Sp, but see also *selva*); *el bosque pluvial* rainforest

bote *nf* can, tin
- □ also 'boat' (not ship): *bote de remos* rowing boat; *bote de salvavidas* lifeboat (see also *barco*)

botón *nm pl botones* button (on clothes); button, knob (on door, for bell, etc): *pulse el botón* press the button
- □ *botones* *nm inv* bellboy (in hotel)

bravo *adj* brave, but *valiente* is more usual; a variety of other common meanings:
- □ fierce, ferocious: *toro bravo* fighting (ie fierce) bull
- □ rough, rugged: *la Costa Brava* the Rugged Coast
- □ rough, stormy: *el mar estaba muy bravo* the sea was very rough

brazo *nm* arm (in most senses but for 'weapon' see *arma*)
- □ also 'hands', in sense of workers: *faltan brazos* more workers needed

breve *adj* short, brief (usually in a time context): *unas pocas breves palabras* a few brief words; *en breve* in brief, in short
- □ some overlap with, but not the same as cf *corto*, which is more physical in its application

brillante *adj* brilliant, bright, shining
- □ can be used metaphorically, as in English: *un estudiante brillante* a brilliant student
- □ **brillar** *vi* to shine

broma *nf* joke
- □ some useful phrases: *lo dije en broma* I said it as a joke; *fue en broma* it was (meant as) a joke; *gastar una broma a alguien* to play a joke on someone

bruma *nf* mist (not as thick as *niebla*; *syn* neblina)

bruto *adj* coarse, rough
- □ gross (financial): *el producto nacional bruto* gross national product

bueno *adj* good (in most senses)
- □ shortened form before a *m sing* noun: *un buen coche* a good car
- □ often heard as *interj* right! OK!: *bueno, vamos a ver ...* right, let's see ...

□ NB don't confuse with cf *adv bien:
su castellano es muy <u>bueno</u>* her
Spanish is very <u>good</u>, as against *habla
muy <u>bien</u> el castellano* she speaks
Spanish very <u>well</u>

□ **bondad** *nf* goodness, kindness;
tener la bondad de + inf to be
good/kind enough to …: *tenga la
bondad de llamarme mañana* would
you be kind enough to phone me
tomorrow

bulto *nm* size, bulk

□ also: package (especially in freight
terms)

buque *nm* boat, ship, vessel (used with
larger, mainly sea–going vessels): *buque
de guerra* warship

□ cf other words for 'boat': *barco,
barca, bote, embarcación*

burlar *vt* to deceive, trick: *nos burlaron*
they deceived us, we were tricked

□ **burlarse de** *vr* to make fun of,
mock: *no te burles de él* don't make
fun of him

buscar *vt -que-, -qué* to look for, search
for, seek: *'se busca'* 'wanted'

□ takes direct object: *estoy buscando mi
bolígrafo* I am looking for my pen

butaca *nf* armchair, easy chair (perhaps
more of an 'easy' chair than cf *sillón*)

□ *butacas* stalls (in cinema, theatre)

C (*ce*) is pronounced '-k-' before the
vowels *-a, -o, -u,* a consonant or on the
end of a word: *cara, copa, cura, claro,
creo, tecla, acne, ocre, doctor, coñac.*

♦ Before *-e* and *-i* it is 'softened' to 'th' as
in 'thin' in most parts of Spain, and 's'
in most of Spanish-speaking America.

♦ In the combination *-cc-,* the first *-c-* is
'hard' and the second 'soft', ie the
combined sound is 'kth', or 'ks' in Spanish
America: *acción, lección, restricción.* It is
not really a 'double c' since the sounds of
the two *c*s are different.

♦ The combination *ch* is pronounced
similarly to the 'ch' in 'church', but
English speakers must resist the
temptation to put a 't' before it, as in
'catch': *muchacha, chaqueta, chincheta.*
Note that until 1994, *ch* was treated as
a separate letter of the Spanish
alphabet, and had its own section in
the dictionary after *c.* Since then,
however, it has been incorporated in
the 'normal' place under **C**.

caballo *nm* horse; *montar/andar/ir a
caballo* to ride a horse; *ponerse/estar de
caballo de algo* to get/be astride sth

□ **caballero** *nm* gentleman:
'Caballeros' 'Gents' (loo); *sección de
caballeros* (gentle)men's department
(in store); rather more formal than cf
señor; also: knight; for horserider use
jinete nm

cabello *nm* hair: means exactly the same as
cf *pelo,* if slightly less used; usually used in
pl; esp used in fairy tales and popular
songs: *se cepillaba los cabellos con un peine
de oro* she combed her hair with a
golden comb; *con sus largos cabellos
dorados* with her long golden hair

caber *vi pi: quepo, cabes; ps: quepa;
fut/cond: cabré/cabría; pret: cupe, cupiste,
cupo, cupimos, cupisteis, cupieron;
imp subj: cupiera/cupiese*

□ to fit, have enough room, go
(*en* in(to)): *no sé si cabrá el equipaje
en el maletero* I don't know if the
luggage will fit in the boot;
no cabíamos todos en ese cuarto
there wasn't enough room for us all in
that room; *¿Cuántas veces cabe 19 en
57?* How many 19s in 57? *no cabe*

duda de que ... there's no (room for) doubt that ...; *no caber en sí* not to be able to contain oneself

□ this is quite a common verb, used in several more idiomatic phrases: worth further research!

□ **cabida** *nf* capacity, space/room (in that sense): *hay cabida para 20* there's room for 20

cabeza *nf* head: in most senses as Eng, including figurative uses

□ useful phrases: *caer de cabeza* to fall headfirst; *andar/estar de cabeza* to be snowed under, be up to the eyeballs; *decir que sí/no con la cabeza* to nod/shake one's head; *lavarse la cabeza* to wash one's hair; *a la cabeza de* at the head of; and many more ...

□ **cabezudo** *adj* big-headed;

□ **cabezota** *nmf* big/pig-headed person

□ **cabizbajo** *adj* crestfallen, dejected (ie with one's head lowered)

cabina *nf* cabin (in most senses); but not on ship: use *camarote*; *cabina telefónica* phone box/booth

cabo *nm* end

□ in both time and space concept: *al cabo de cinco minutos* at the end of (after) five minutes; *de cabo a rabo* from one end to the other; *dar cabo a algo* to finish sth off; *llevar algo a cabo* to carry sth out, see sth through; *estar al cabo de la calle* to be in the know

□ also 'cape' (in sense of) promontory: *cabo Trafalgar* Cape Trafalgar

□ and: (military) corporal

□ see also related verb **acabar** to finish, end

cacerola *nf* saucepan

□ **cazo** *nm* small saucepan

□ **cazuela** *nf* casserole (both receptacle and dish)

cada *adj* each, every

□ note *invariable* form ending in *-a*

□ *cada persona* each person; *cada noche* each night, *cada dos o tres días* every two or three days; *cada rato* every so often

□ *cada vez* each/every time; note use with comparisons: *cada vez más/menos* more and more/less and less; *cada vez más fuerte* louder and louder

□ NB *cada* puts some emphasis on individual item/person/grouping: eg *cada día* each/every day can be used as a simple alternative for *todos los días*, but there is an implied separation of each day into a unit. Compare *todos los días iba a verla al hospital* with *cada día fui a verla al hospital*: the first version simply indicates repeated action, the second, with the additional help of the verb in the preterite, separates each visit into an individual unit.

□ **cada uno/a** *pron* each (one), every one (used where the noun is not expressed or to achieve further individualisation): *cada uno recibió un regalo* each one received a gift; *cada una de estas casas tiene dos cuartos de baño* each/every one of these houses has two bathrooms

cadena *nf* chain

□ used figuratively much as in Eng: *cadena alimenticia* food chain; *cadena de supermercados* supermarket chain; *cadena montañosa* chain of mountains; and also *cadena perpetua* life imprisonment

□ note also verbs **encadenar** *vt* to chain (up), and **desencadenar** *vt* to unchain, unleash, let loose: *se desencadenó una tormenta* a storm broke

caer *vi pi: caigo, caes ... caímos; ps: caiga; pret: caí, cayó ... cayeron; imp subj: cayera/cayese;* NB needs accent on *í* of ending when stressed

□ to fall (in most senses), fall over: *las bombas cayeron en la plaza* the bombs fell in the square; *el árbol caerá por aquí* the tree will fall this way; *cayó enferma* she fell ill

□ **caerse** *vr* the reflexive form tends to be used when the falling is accidental: *el árbol se cayó en la tormenta* the tree fell down in the storm; *el libro se cayó del estante* the book fell off the shelf

□ NB the reflexive form is used with an indirect object when you accidentally drop sth: *se me cayó el reloj* I dropped my watch; *¡Cuidado! ¡Se te van a caer los platos!* Mind out! You're going to drop the plates! When the dropping is intentional, use *dejar caer: dejé caer la basura en el cubo* I dropped the rubbish into the bin

□ some useful expressions: *caer en la cuenta* to 'get it', catch on; *¡ya caigo!* got it! I see!; *no caigo* I don't get it; *los mejillones me cayeron mal* the mussels didn't agree with me; *las cortinas caen mal* the curtains don't hang properly; and many more: worth further research in the dictionary!

□ **caído** *adj* fallen: *un árbol caído* a fallen tree; *los Caídos* the Fallen (eg in war)

□ **caída** *nf* fall (in most senses): *una caída grave* a serious fall/drop (person, prices, etc); *caída libre* free fall; *la caída de Granada en 1492* the fall of Granada in 1492; *caída de la tarde* nightfall

café *nm* coffee

□ also 'café': NB serves all types of drink in Spain

□ **cafetería** *nf* coffee bar, café; NOT cafeteria in Eng sense of self-service (use *autoservicio*)

□ **cafetera** *nf* coffee pot; **cafetero/a** *nmf* café owner; **cafetal** *nm* coffee plantation

caja *nf* box (in most senses)

□ *caja de cambios* gearbox; *caja fuerte* or *de seguridad* safe, strongbox; *caja tonta/boba* 'goggle box' (TV)

□ also: till, checkout; window, counter (eg in bank); *pague Vd en caja* pay at the cash desk/checkout; *caja de ahorros* savings bank

□ **cajita, cajetilla** *nf* diminutives used for small boxes of things: *cajita de cerillas* box of matches

□ **cajón** *nm pl cajones* drawer

□ **cajero/a** *nmf* cashier (in bank); checkout assistant

calar *vt* to soak, drench

□ also 'to rumble', 'suss out': *ya te tengo calado* I've got you rumbled

□ as *vi* 'to catch on': *es una moda que va calando* it's a fashion which is catching on

□ **calarse** *vr* (of liquid) to soak (*en* into); (of person) to get soaked/drenched: *calarse hasta los huesos* to get soaked to the skin; *estar calado hasta los huesos* to be soaked to the skin

□ similar but more colloquial than *syn empapar(se)*, stronger than cf *mojar(se)*

calcular *vt* to calculate, reckon, estimate: *calculo que…* I reckon that; *se calcula que acudirán miles* it's estimated that thousands will attend

□ **cálculo** *nm* calculation (NOT calculación!): *según mis cálculos* according to my calculations; *hacer un cálculo aproximado* to make a rough estimate

□ **calculadora** *nf* calculator (NB it's *fem*!)

 Hot/heat, warm/warmth

Study these words and their differences carefully

calor *nm* heat, warmth: *no aguanto este calor* I can't stand this heat; *nos recibieron con mucho calor* they welcomed us very warmly

NB for weather use *hace (mucho) calor* it's

(very) hot; for persons feeling hot use *tener (mucho) calor* to be/feel (very) hot

calentar *vt* -ie- to heat (up), warm (up): *voy a calentar la sopa* I'll heat/warm up the soup; *esta estufa calienta muy pronto la habitación* this fire soon warms the room

calentarse *vr* to get warm, hot: *esta habitación se calienta muy pronto* this room gets warm very quickly; *el motor tarda en calentarse* the engine takes time to warm up; also to get het up: *¡No te calientes!* Don't get het up!

caliente *adj* hot, warm (used esp of liquids, with *estar*): *la sopa está caliente* the soup is hot; *tiene el temperamento muy caliente* he has a very hot temperament; see *calor* for 'feel hot'

cálido & **caluroso** *adj* hot, warm (fairly restricted use, mainly to describe climate): *un clima cálido/caluroso* a hot climate; also welcome: *una acogida cálida/calurosa;* or colour: *en colores cálidos/calurosos* in warm colours NB: Sp does not differentiate readily between 'hot' and 'warm': so to describe lukewarm or tepid liquids use: *tibio, templado;* to differentiate 'hot' as opposed to merely 'warm', it may be necessary to say *mucho calor* or *muy caliente/caluroso/cálido*, depending on the context

calefacción *nf* heating (ie apparatus): *calefacción central* central heating

calentador *nm* boiler, heater

calentamiento *nm* (ie act of) warming/heating (up) eg in sport; *calentamiento global* global warming;

calentura *nf* temperature (same sense as cf *fiebre*)

caloría *nf* calory; **calórico** *adj* caloric, to do with calories

calorífico *adj* calorific

calidad *nf* quality (grade, standard eg of product): *mercancías de alta/baja calidad* high/low quality goods; *calidad de vida* quality of life; *en calidad de* in the capacity of; *trabaja en calidad de ingeniero principal* he is working as chief engineer

- □ NB not the same as: **cualidad** *nf* quality (in sense of 'attribute', 'virtue'): *tiene muchas buenas cualidades* he has many good qualities/attributes; *la comprensión es una cualidad necesaria en este trabajo* understanding is a necessary attribute in this job

- □ **calificar** *vt* -que-, qué to describe, assess: *me calificaron de loco* they described me as mad, they thought I was mad; also to grade, give a mark (eg in exam)

- □ **calificarse (de)** to be considered (as): *se califica de obsoleto* it is regarded as obsolete

- □ **calificación** *nf pl* calificaciones noun for verb above: description, assessment; mark

- □ NB 'qualification(s)', eg academic, is best rendered by *título(s)*

- □ **cualificar** *vt* -que-, qué to qualify, in sense of prepare, **cualificarse** *vr* to become qualified (in that sense) for a particular purpose; often occurs as:

- □ **(estar) cualificado** *adj* to be qualified (*para* for/to) *esta persona está cualificada para realizar este trabajo* this person is qualified to carry out this work; BUT for sense of to be qualified with some sort of degree of diploma, use an expression based on *título: tiene título de ingeniero/es ingeniero titulado* he's a qualified engineer; see also *capacitarse/capacitado*

- □ **calificativo** *adj* qualifying, also as *nm* description: *sólo merece el calificativo de espantoso* it can only be described as frightful

callar *vi* or **callarse** *vr* to be/keep quiet,

remain silent, shut up: *¡Calla!* or *¡Cállate!* Shut up! Be quiet!; *de repente todos se callaron* suddenly everyone stopped talking

- □ can also be used as *vt* to keep quiet/not say anything about: *callaremos el asunto* we'll keep quiet about the matter
- □ **callado** *adj* silent, without saying anything: *me quedé callado* I remained silent; *¡Qué callado estás hoy!* How quiet you are today/You haven't got much to say for yourself today!
- □ **calladamente** *adj* silently, secretly, without telling anyone: *el veneno obraba calladamente* the poison was operating silently/without anyone being aware

calle *nf* street

- □ essentially a street in a town with houses and shops (not the same as *carretera* road, *camino* way, track): *en la calle* in/on the street; *por la calle* in/along the street
- □ *a/en/por la calle* can also mean 'outdoors', 'outside' (in that sense): *está en la calle* he's out(side); *no he salido a la calle en todo el día* I haven't been out(side) all day; *calle mayor* high street, main street
- □ **calleja, callejuela** *nf*; **callejón** *nm pl callejones* alley, narrow side street, *callejón sin salida* dead end, cul-de-sac
- □ **callejero** *adj* (to do with the) street: *vendedores callejeros* street vendors; *ser muy callejero* to be fond of going out

calma *nf* calm: *mantener la calma* to keep calm; *hacer algo con calma* to do sth calmly, unhurriedly; *¡Con calma!* Take your time!

- □ **calmar** *vt* to calm, soothe; **calmarse** *vr* to calm down; (similar to *tranquilizar(se)*)
- □ **calmante** *adj* soothing; *nm* sedative, tranquilliser

cama *nf* bed: *ir a la cama* to go to bed (same as cf *acostarse*); *guardar cama* to stay in bed (eg when ill); *cama individual/de matrimonio* single/double bed

cámara *nf* chamber (in most Eng senses except 'pot', use *orinal*): *cámaras reales* royal chambers; *cámara de comercio* chamber of commerce; *cámara de combustión* combustion chamber

- □ perhaps more commonly *cámara fotográfica* camera: *cámara de cine/cinematográfica* cinecamera

cambiar *vt* to change, alter (*a/en* into): *quisiera cambiar 50 libras a/en euros* I'd like to change £50 into euros; similar to cf *convertir*, and some overlap with cf *transformar*

- □ to exchange (*por* for): *cambié mis libras por euros* I exchanged my pounds for euros (same as cf *trocar*)
- □ as *vi* to change, alter: *¡Cómo ha cambiado la ciudad!* How the town has changed!
- □ + *de* + *n* to change (for sth new): *cambiar de ropa* to change one's clothes; *cambiar de trabajo* to change one's job; *cambiar de colegio* to change schools
- □ **cambiarse** *vr* to change clothes: *me voy a cambiar los zapatos* I'm going to change my shoes
- □ for to change into sth, better to use cf *convertirse, transformarse*
- □ **cambiante** *adj* changing, variable
- □ **cambio** *nm* change (in most senses): *¡Cuántos cambios han hecho!* What a lot of changes they've made!; *cambio de actitud* change of/in attitude; *cambio de velocidad* gear change (*caja de cambios* gearbox)
- □ also 'exchange': *cambio de moneda* money exchange; *tipo de cambio* exchange rate; *a cambio de* in exchange for
- □ and 'small change': *no tengo cambio*

I've no change (NOT change you get back from a larger sum: use *vuelta*)

camello *nm* camel
- □ but also: drug pusher

camino *nm* road, way (in that sense)
- □ NB originally the usual word for 'road': *camino real* (king's) highway; however, in modern Sp, it now means rather lane, track (meaning is nearer to *sendero* 'path', 'track' than *carretera*): *camino forestal* forest track
- □ can however be used in a general sense for 'road', 'way': *no hay otro camino* there's no other route; *camino de Avila* on the way to Avila; *ponerse en camino* to set off (on journey); *de camino* en route, on the way; *Camino de Santiago* Pilgrims' Way to Santiago; *el camino de la vida* life's way; and many more expressions – further research in the dictionary would be rewarding
- □ **caminar** *vti* to walk, travel: *pasa el domingo caminando en las montañas* he spends Sunday walking in the mountains; *puedes ir allí caminando* you can walk there; *ayer caminó veinte kilómetros* yesterday he walked 20 kilometres; similar to cf *andar*, but somehow more purposeful!
- □ **caminata** *nf* long walk, hike

camión *nm pl camiones* lorry, truck (in that sense); (large) van; *camión de bomberos* fire engine; *camión de la basura* dustcart; *camión de mudanzas* removal van
- □ one of the few words ending in *-ión* which is *m*!
- □ NB in Mexico it also means 'bus'

camisa *nf* shirt; *en mangas de camisa* in shirtsleeves; *cambiar de camisa* to change one's colours, change sides
- □ **camiseta** *nf* T-shirt; **camisón** *nm pl camisones; (de noche)* nightdress

campana *nf* bell (usually a big one eg in a church); not same as cf *campanilla* and *timbre*
- □ **campanilla** *nf* handbell
- □ **campanada** *nf* stroke, chime (of bell): *el reloj dio seis campanadas* the clock chimed six times
- □ **campanario** *nm* belfry, bell tower

campo *nm* country (as opposed to town), countryside: *vivimos en pleno campo* we live right out in the country; *vida del campo* country life
- □ also 'land': *trabajamos el campo* we work the land
- □ and 'field', 'ground', 'pitch' in various senses: *campo de fútbol* football ground/pitch; *campo de golf* golf course; *campo de batalla* battlefield
- □ 'sphere', 'area': *en el campo de la física* in the field of physics; *campo magnético* magnetic field
- □ NB *campo* is essentially a cultivated field, as opposed to *prado,* 'meadow', but many cultivated fields in Spain take the name from their specific crop: *trigal* wheatfield, *arrozal* ricefield, etc
- □ can also mean: 'camp' (but not for camping – use *camping*): *campo de concentración* concentration camp
- □ **campesino/a** *nmf* countryman/woman, farmer; can also be used meaning 'peasant' in derogatory sense

Canadá *nm* Canada
- □ NB it's *masc*!
- □ **canadiense** *adj* Canadian: no *fem* form

canguro *nm* kangaroo
- □ also 'babysitter': *hacer de canguro* to babysit

cansar *vt* to tire, make tired: *me cansa todo este trabajo* all this work makes me tired
- □ **cansarse** *vr* to get tired; *cansarse de algo* or + *inf* to get tired of/bored with sth or doing sth: *nos cansamos*

de esperar we got tired of waiting; *se cansó de sus juguetes* he got bored with his toys

- □ **(estar) cansado** *adj* (to be) tired (more common than *syn fatigado*); *(ser)* **cansado** to be tiring, tiresome (cf *molesto* in this sense): *es muy cansada esa música* that music is very tiresome
- □ **cansancio** *nm* tiredness: *causa cansancio* it causes tiredness

cantar *vti* to sing

- □ **canción** *nf pl canciones* song: ie a piece of music that you sing; (not same as cf *canto* below)
- □ **canto** *nm* song: ie action of singing, eg of bird: *el canto del ruiseñor* the nightingale's song; *canto del gallo* cockcrow; *canto llano* plainsong; **cante** *nm* used in very specialised flamenco context only: *cante jondo* 'deep song'
- □ **cantante** *nmf* (professional) singer; **cantador/a** *nmf* folk singer; flamenco singers are usually called *cantaores/as*

cantidad *nf* quantity, amount (used more often than English equivalent): *una gran cantidad de* a lot of, lots of; *tenemos cantidad de naranjas* we've got lots of oranges

- □ NB adverbial use in phrases like: *este pastel me gusta cantidad* I like this cake a lot

cantina *nf* canteen; but also buffet, refectory, refreshment room (eg on station, in college)

capa *nf* cloak, cape

- □ but also 'coat' (eg of paint): *primera capa* undercoat; and 'layer' *capa de ozono* ozone layer

capaz *adj pl capaces* capable, able: *es una persona muy capaz* he's a very capable person; *es capaz de hacer cualquier cosa* he's capable of doing anything; *no somos*

capaces de hacerlo we're not capable of doing it/able to do it

- □ NB *capable* doesn't exist, and if you made it up it would mean 'castratable', from *capar*!
- □ **capacidad** *nf* capacity (in most Eng senses)
- □ what sth will contain (same as cf *cabida*): *esta botella tiene una capacidad de dos litros* this bottle has a capacity of two litres; *el estadio tiene capacidad para 50.000* the stadium has a capacity of 50,000
- □ ability, competence, (same as *competencia* in that sense): *tiene una capacidad extraordinaria para divertirse* he has a great capacity for enjoying himself; *está fuera de mi capacidad* it's beyond my ability; *capacidad adquisitiva* purchasing power
- □ **capacitar** *vt* to make sb capable (ie *capaz*) of doing sth; to prepare, train: *todo esto me capacitó para el trabajo* all this prepared me for the job
- □ **capacitarse** *vr* (*para* for) to prepare oneself, get oneself qualified: *se capacitó para fontanero* he qualified as a plumber; **capacitado** *adj* qualified, trained
- □ see also its opposite *incapacitarse* to become incapacitated

capital *nm* capital (ie money)

- □ *nf* capital (ie city): *capital provincial* Sp equivalent of county town, ie regional administrative centre
- □ *adj* capital, but also broader meaning: *crimen capital* capital crime/offence; *punto capital* main/critical point; *importancia capital* extreme/utmost importance

cara *nf* face

- □ useful expressions: *cara a cara* face to face; *de cara al sol* with one's face towards/facing the sun; *hacer cara a algo/alguien* to face up to sth/sb; *poner mala cara* to pull a face (of displeasure)

- *tener cara de* + *inf* to look as if + verb: *tiene cara de no querer* he looks as if he doesn't want to
- NB *adjs* beginning *cari-* to describe types of face: *carilargo* long-faced; *carirredondo* round-faced; *cariacontecido* crestfallen, down-in-the-mouth
- also 'face', 'side', (eg of record or coin): *¿Cara o cruz?* Heads or tails?
- cheek, nerve: *¡Qué cara tienes!* What a cheek you've got/You've got a cheek!
- worth some research in the dictionary!

carácter *nm pl caracteres* character
- NB change of stress on to the first *e* in *pl*
- most senses as Eng, but use *personaje* for character in play, film etc
- **característico** *adj* characteristic (*de* of); **característica** *nf* characteristic, trait (much the same as cf *rasgo*)

carbono *nm* carbon: *monóxido de carbono* carbon monoxide; don't confuse with:
- **carbón** *nm* coal
- **carbonizar** *vt -ce-, -cé* to carbonise, char, reduce to ashes
- **carbonizarse** *vr* to be reduced to ashes; somewhat graphic journalistic word describing accidents: *todos los pasajeros murieron carbonizados* all the passengers were burnt to death

carcajada *nf* onomatopaeic word for 'laugh', 'guffaw', usually a loud one: *soltar una carcajada* to burst out laughing; *reírse a carcajadas* to roar with laughter
- much more hearty than cf basic *risa/reírse*

cárcel *nf* prison, gaol; perhaps more used than *syn prisión*
- **encarcelar** *vt* to imprison

carecer *vi -zc-* (+ *de* + *n*) to lack (sth);

carecen de comida they lack food; *carece de juicio* he lacks judgement
- **carencia** *nf* lack: *hay una gran carencia de agua* there's a big lack/shortage of water

cargar *vt -gue-, -gué* to load (*de* with), charge (in most Eng senses); **cargarse** *vr (de)* to be loaded, laden (with)
- mainly used as Eng 'charge' or 'load', but a look in the dictionary will reveal a fair list of other, often colloquial uses
- **estar cargado (de)** *adj* to be loaded/laden (with): *el árbol estaba cargado de manzanas* the tree was laden with apples; *cargado de años* very old
- **carga** *nf* load, cargo; also 'charge' (eg electrical, military); and 'burden'; not to be confused with:
- **cargo** *nm* responsibility, undertaking: *es un cargo difícil* it's a difficult undertaking; *estar a cargo de* to be in the charge/care of; also 'job', 'post': *cargo oficial* official post

caridad *nf* charity (in sense of) charitableness
- for a charity eg Oxfam, use *organización benéfica*

carne *nf* meat; types of meat in shop or on table are often described in full: *carne de cordero* lamb; *carne de vaca* beef; *carne de cerdo* pork, etc
- also 'flesh': *de carne y hueso* of flesh and blood
- often used in *pl* when referring to sb's appearance: *cobrar/echar carnes* to put on weight; *de carnes abundantes* plump; *de pocas carnes* thin, skinny;
- **carnero** *nm* sheep, ram; mutton; don't confuse with: **carnicero/a** *nmf* butcher; and **carnicería** *nf* butcher's shop/counter

caro *adj* (main use) dear, expensive: *las entradas son muy caras* the tickets are very expensive

- can also be used as *adv*: *te costará caro* it'll cost you dear
- NB also used in sense of 'beloved' in mainly literary contexts: *nos es tan caro* he is so dear to us; normally use cf *querido*
  - **carestía** *nf* high cost: *la carestía de la vida* high cost of living; can also mean 'scarcity': *en tiempos de carestía* in times of shortage

cariño *nm* affection, fondness, love (*a/por* for): *le tengo mucho cariño* I'm very fond of him
- also 'darling', 'love' (in that sense): *¿Adónde vas, cariño?* Where are you going, my love?
  - **cariñoso** *adj* affectionate, fond: *es un niño muy cariñoso* he's a very affectionate child; **cariñosamente** *adv* affectionately, fondly

carpeta *nf* folder, file (for paper)
- for 'carpet' use *alfombra*

carrera *nf* race, in competitive sense: *carrera de caballos* horse race; *carrera de armamentos* arms race
- also: chase, (act of) running: *a la carrera* at full speed
- career, profession: *médico de carrera* career doctor
- university course: *elegir una carrera universitaria* to choose a university course

carretera *nf* road, esp main road; *carretera nacional* 'N' road
- equivalent of Eng 'A' road; not same as cf *camino*

carril *nm* lane (ie division of road): *carril de bus* bus lane

carro *nm* cart
- NB 'car' in most of Sp Am

carta *nf* letter (correspondence)
- for letter of alphabet use *letra*
- also 'card' (with limited application): *jugar a las cartas* to play cards (but

cf *naipe*); for post-, visiting-, identity- etc card, see *tarjeta*
- 'chart' (geographical/nautical); for 'map' use *mapa*
- **cartero/a** *nmf* postman/woman

cartel *nm* poster, placard: *prohibido fijar carteles* stick no bills
- use *póster* for the type you stick on your bedroom wall!

cartera *nf* wallet; briefcase; portfolio (esp in politics: *ministro sin cartera* minister without portfolio)

casa *nf* house
- also 'home', ie the place where you live, often used without *def art*: *ir/volver a casa* to go (back) home; *estar en casa* to be at home; *salir de casa* to leave home (go out from). NB use of *a* for 'to' home, and *en* for 'at' home; also difference between *en casa* at home, and *en la casa* in the house; *a/en casa de* to/at the house of, to/at …'s: *vamos a casa de Pepe* we're going to Pepe's (house); *Vd está en su casa* make yourself at home; *¿Vas a pasar por casa?* Are you going to pop in to see us? For 'home' in sense of focal point of family life, or eg 'old people's home' see *hogar*
- 'company', 'firm': *es una casa bien conocida* it's a well-known firm; *especialidad de la casa* speciality of the house
- NB derivative words: **casita** *nf* small house, cottage; **casuca, casucha** *nf* hovel, slum; **caserón** *nm* pl *caserones* large (rambling) house; **caserío** *nm* country house, farmhouse esp in N Sp; **caseta** *nf* (market) stall; (exhibition) booth; (beach) hut; **casilla** *nf* can mean 'hut'; but commonly 'pigeon-hole' (ie for papers)
- **casero** *adj* homemade, household: *productos caseros* homemade produce; homeloving: *es muy casero*

he likes staying at home

casar *vt* to marry (ie what the priest or registrar does): *el párroco les casó* the parish priest married them
  □ **casarse** *vr* to marry, get married (*con* to) (ie what the couple do): *Pablo se casó con Lucinda* Pablo married Lucinda; *se casaron por la iglesia* they got married in church
  □ **casamiento** *nm* (act of) marriage (cf *matrimonio* for resultant state); wedding (ie ceremony, cf *boda*)

casi *adv* almost, nearly
  □ NB use with negative words: *casi nunca* hardly ever; *casi nada* almost nothing; a mere trifle
  □ *casi no* + *v* hardly: *casi no le veía* I could hardly see him

caso *nm* case
  □ in many senses as Eng: *en este caso* in this case; *dos casos de gripe* two cases of flu; *esto ocurre en muchos casos* this happens in many cases; *en último caso* in the last resort; *según el caso* as the case may be; *vamos al caso* let's get to the point; *hacer caso a algo/alguien* to take notice of sth/sb: *no le hagas caso* don't take any notice of him
  □ NB *en caso de* in the event of: *en caso de incendio* in the event of; or: + *que* + *subjunc*: *en el caso de que no contesten* in the event of them not answering. (NOT 'in case (something happens)' – this is *por si acaso* + *indic*: *por si acaso no contestan* in case they don't answer; NOT 'in any case', use *de todos modos/de todas maneras*; and NOT 'suitcase', use *maleta*.)
  □ there are many more expressions in which *caso* is used: research in the dictionary would be rewarding!

Castilla *nf* Castile (or Castille): the central area of Spain, now consisting of the *autonomías* of *Castilla-la Mancha*, *Castilla-León* and *Madrid*

castellano *adj* Castilian: ie from, belonging to, of Castile, the central area of Spain
  □ as *el castellano nm* it is often used in both Spain and Sp Am to mean 'Spanish', ie the Spanish language; this is because there are three other full-blown languages spoken within Spain: Catalan, Basque and Galician (*gallego*): *¡Qué bien hablas el castellano!* How well you speak Spanish!

casual *adj* chance: *un encuentro casual* a chance meeting
  □ **casualmente** *adv* by chance, as it happens/happened: *casualmente le vi ayer* I happened to see him yesterday
  □ **casualidad** *nf* chance, accident (in that sense); *por (pura) casualidad* by (pure/sheer) chance; *da la casualidad que* it just happens that
  □ NB these words are connected to *caso* above and DO NOT translate Eng 'casual' meaning 'informal' etc: refer to a dictionary for specific examples; for 'casualty/ies' see: *herido(s), lesionado(s), víctima(s)*

catar *vti* to look (at); to try (out): useful colloquial alternative to *mirar* or *probar*: *¡cata esto!* look at this!; try this!

catarro *nm* catarrh, but also 'cold': *coger/pescarse un catarro* to catch a cold

categoría *nf* category, class (in that sense); *de tercera categoría* third-rate; *de categoría* first-rate, classy: *un servicio de categoría* a top-class service

causa *nf* cause (as in Eng, but often wider meaning, eg) reason, motive (*de* for): *la causa de mis dificultades* the cause of/reason for my difficulties
  □ **a/por causa de** *prep* because of + *n* or *pron*, do not confuse with *porque* + *v* because + verb: *a causa de esto* because of this; *a causa del tiempo que*

hacía because of the weather

□ **causar** *vt* to cause, give rise to

cautela *nf* caution: *hay que obrar con cautela* we must act cautiously

□ **cauteloso** *adj* cautious; **cautelosamente** *adv* cautiously

cautivo/a *adj* or *nmf* captive

□ **cautivar** *vt* to capture; also captivate; **cautiverio** *nm* captivity

□ NB spelling: *caut-* not *capt-*

caza *nf* hunt, hunting

□ wider meaning also includes 'shoot', 'shooting' (as sport): *caza del zorro* fox-hunt(ing); *caza del faisán* pheasant shoot(ing); *caza furtiva* poaching; *ir de caza/a la caza* to go hunting/shooting; also 'chase', 'pursuit': *ir a la caza de alguien* to go in pursuit of sb

□ **cazar** *vt -ce-, -cé* to hunt, shoot (in this sense)

□ **cazador/a** *nmf* huntsman/woman, hunter; *cazador furtivo* poacher

ceder *vt* to give (sth) up, hand over; yield: *ceda el paso* give way (road sign)

□ *vi* to give in, surrender; give way (eg roof, ground)

celebrar *vt* to celebrate: *mis padres celebran sus bodas de plata* my parents are celebrating their silver wedding; similar to cf *festejar*

□ also: 'to be pleased', 'welcome' (an event): *lo celebramos mucho* we're very pleased (about it)

□ **celebrarse** *vr* to take place (esp of events of a positive, celebratory nature)

□ **celebración** *nf pl celebraciones* celebration(s)

□ **célebre** *adj* famous, celebrated (*por* for): *es célebre por sus platos de pescado* she's famous for her fish dishes; NB *superlative*: *celebérrimo* very famous

□ **celebridad** *nf* celebrity (NB always

fem); can also mean 'celebrations', 'festivity'

celo *nm* zeal

□ but **celos** *nmpl* jealousy: *tener celos de alguien* to be jealous of sb; *No me tienes celos, ¿verdad?* You're not jealous of me, are you?

□ **celoso** *adj* zealous, keen (*de* for, on, to) (usually with *ser*): *es muy celoso* he's very keen; jealous (*de* of, with *estar*): *está celoso* he's jealous

□ NB **celosía** *nf* shutter

celda *nf* cell (eg in prison, monastery)

□ not same as **célula** *nf* cell (scientific, eg of battery, tissue, etc)

centro *nm* centre: many uses same as Eng

□ **central** *adj* central, as Eng in many cases

□ *nf* several common applications: headquarters, head office; (telephone) exchange or switchboard; *central eléctrica* power station

□ **céntrico** *adj* central, (more limited application than cf *central*), in centre (usually of town): *las calles céntricas de la ciudad* the streets in the city centre; *mi piso es muy céntrico* my flat is very central

□ **centrar** *vt* to centre, focus; **centrarse** *vr* to be centred/focussed (*en* on): *las discusiones se centraron en el hambre* the discussions focussed on hunger

□ **Centroamérica** *nf* Central America

cerca *adv* near, nearby, close: *hay muchos restaurantes ahí cerca* there are lots of restaurants nearby

□ **cerca de** *prep* near/close (to): *cerca de mi casa* near my house; also 'about', 'approximately': *hay cerca de veinte restaurantes en esa calle* there are about 20 restaurants in that street

□ **cerca** *nf* or **cercado** *nm* fence, wall

□ **cercanías** *nfpl* neighbourhood,

surroundings; suburbs, outskirts: *trenes de cercanías* suburban trains
- see also **acercarse** to approach, get nearer, closer

cero *nm* nought, zero
- used for most words in sport meaning 'nil', 'love' (no score): *estamos a 3 contra cero/a 15 contra cero* the score is three-nil/fifteen-love; *ser un cero a la izquierda* to be useless, a dead loss (of person) (because if you add a nought to the left of the number it has no effect …)

cerrar *vti* -ie- to shut, close: *cerré las ventanas* I closed the windows; *las tiendas cierran a las 20* the shops close at 8 pm; *cerrar con llave* to lock
- also: to turn off (eg tap)
- **cerrarse** *vr* to shut up, close (doors, windows etc when they shut (themselves)): *la puerta se cerró de un golpe* the door shut with a bang
- **cerrado** *adj* closed, shut (use *estar*): *el castilla está cerrado* the castle is closed; also, (of person) 'reserved', (use *ser*): *los ingleses son muy cerrados* the English are very reserved
- **cierre** *nm* (act of) closing, closure; locking; **cerradura** *nf* lock

certificar *vt* -que-, -qué to certify
- NB also 'to register' (post); **certificado** *adj* registered (post)

cesar *vti* to cease, stop (*de + inf* –ing): *cesó de llover* it stopped raining
- also, in formal or journalistic language 'to sack', 'fire': *le cesaron* they sacked him (same as cf *despedir*), can be used intransitively in similar sense of ending eg a job, to resign: *el jefe cesó* the boss resigned (cf *dimitir* is more usual).
- **cese** *nm* cessation, ending eg of hostilities; also sacking, dismissal (in that sense)

césped *nm* grass, lawn
- NB ends in -*d*, but is *masc* !

cesta *nf* basket (of most kinds, esp for shopping); **cesto** *nm* (large, eg clothes) basket, less common than *cesta*

chaleco *nm* waistcoat; also used in *chaleco salvavidas* lifejacket

champú *nm* NB *pl champús* or *champúes* shampoo

charca *nm* pond, pool (in that sense)
- **charco** *nm* puddle, pool (in that sense), ie *charco* is much smaller than *charca*; also used in: *cruzar el charco* to cross the 'pond' (ie the Atlantic)

charlar *vi* to chat, chatter
- **charla** *nf* chat
- **charlatán/ana** *adj pl charltanes/as* chatty, talkative, or *nmf* chatterbox; also 'charlatan', as in Eng

chaval *nm* lad, kid; *los chavales* the lads; **chavala** *nf* girl, kid; colloquial, but not slang, refers to late teenage or early twenties

chico/a *nmf* boy, girl
- can be used of any age up to early twenties: cf *niño/a* for a very young boy/girl/child up to, say, 8; also cf *muchacho/a*
- *adj* small, small-sized: *esta camisa es muy chica* this shirt is very small *dame un trozo muy chico* give me a very small slice
- NB diminutives: **chiquito/a** *nmf* little boy/girl; *adj* very small, tiny
- **chiquitín/ina** *adj pl chiquitines/as* very tiny, teeny-weeny
- **achicar** *vt* -que-, -qué to make smaller (from *chico*)
- **achicarse** *vr* to get smaller, shrink

chiflar *vt* to drive mad, crazy: *me chifla el chocolate* I'm crazy about/dead nuts on chocolate; also to boo, hiss (eg theatre)
- **chiflarse** *vr* to go mad, crazy (*por*

about): *me chiflo por el chocolate*

□ **chiflado** *adj* nuts, barmy, crazy: *estará chiflado* he must be barmy; *está chiflado por esa chica* he's crazy about/nuts over that girl

□ colloquial but not slang

chillar *vti* to screech, squeal, squeak (noise appropriate to animal which makes it); to scream, shriek (person)

□ **chillido** *nm* screech, squeal, squeak, shriek, scream

□ NB shriller than cf *gritar/grito*

□ **chillón/ona** *adj pl chillones/as* shrill, piercing; also used of colours: *viste de colores chillones* she dresses in loud colours

chimenea *nf* chimney

□ in house also includes the fireplace and mantelpiece: *el sofá está delante de la chimenea* the settee is in front of the fireplace

chocar (contra/con) *vi -que, -qué* to crash (into/with), collide (with): *chocó contra el muro* he crashed/bumped into the wall; *choqué con el camarero* I bumped into the waiter

□ also as *vt* conveys surprise, at about level of 'take aback': *me chocó su respuesta* his answer took me aback

□ **choque** *nm* crash, collision, bump; shock, surprise: *fue un gran choque* it was a big shock (ie unpleasant surprise)

□ **chocante** *adj* startling, surprising, shocking

□ these words have a stronger connotation than *sorprender*, with some suggestion of a perhaps unpleasant surprise (eg take sb aback), but are not so strong as those associated with cf *escándalo*

chófer *nmf* driver, especially professional one (otherwise much the same as cf *conductor/a*)

c(h)rismas *nm no pl form* Christmas card

(only): for Christmas use *Navidad*

ciego *adj* blind: *quedar ciego* to go blind; *hacer algo a ciegas* to do sth blindly

□ **ciego/a** *nmf* blind person

□ **cegar** *vt -ie-; -gue-, gué* to blind

cien/ciento *adj* hundred

□ *cien* is used before a noun or where one is understood: *cien palabras* 100 words; *una moneda de cien* a 100 (peseta) coin

□ *ciento* is used when followed by another number: *ciento uno* 101; *ciento noventa* 190; unlike hundreds from 200 to 900, it does not agree with its noun

□ *cientos (de)* *nmpl* hundreds (of): *había cientos de pájaros* there were hundreds of birds

□ **centenar** *nm* hundred: limited use as collective number, mainly in: *un centenar (de + n/pron)* about a hundred: *había un centenar de animales* there were about a hundred animals; *centenares (de)* hundreds (of); in *pl* alternative to *cientos*

□ **céntimo** *nm* originally 100th of a peseta, but disappeared with inflation in the seventies; will be resurrected as 100th of the euro, ie cent

ciencia *nf* science; tends to be *pl* as school subject: *ciencias naturales* natural science; *saber a ciencia cierta* to know for certain; *ciencia-ficción* science fiction

□ **científico/a** *adj* scientific; *nmf* scientist

cierto *adj* certain, sure, (use *estar*): *no estoy cierto* I'm not sure (same as cf *seguro* in this sense)

□ also: 'so', 'right', 'true', 'the case', (use *ser*): *¿No es cierto?* Isn't that so/right?; (sometimes used rather like cf *¿verdad?*) *Es una chica guapa, ¿no es cierto?* She's a good-looking girl, isn't she?; *es cierto que ...* it's true/certain that ...; *por cierto* of course (+ following comment); *¡cierto!* of course! (when agreeing with a statement)

☐ before noun with no *indef art*: a certain: *cierto día de cierto mes* on a certain day of a certain month

☐ **certeza** *nf* or **certidumbre** *nf* certainty (little difference between them): *tengo la certeza/certidumbre de que ...* I'm certain that ...; but for 'it's a certainty' use *es seguro* or *es cosa segura*

cifra *nf* figure, number (in sense of both symbol and quantity): *las cifras no mienten* the figures don't lie

cima *nf* top, summit eg of mountain (cf *cumbre* in this sense)

☐ also 'top', 'height' (eg of powers, career, etc): *estaba en la cima de su poder* he was at the height of his power

☐ see also **encima (de)** *adv/prep* on top (of)

cinta *nf* ribbon, tape; audio/video tape: *cinta magnética* recording tape; *cinta de vídeo* videotape; *cinta en blanco* blank tape

cintura *nf* waist, waistline

☐ **cinturón** *nm pl cinturones* belt: *cinturón de seguridad* safety belt; *apretarse el cinturón* to tighten one's belt; *cinturón verde* green belt

círculo circle (in most Eng senses); ring (in that sense): *pónganse en círculo* stand in a ring

☐ **circular** *vti* to circulate; in more general sense, to walk, go, drive, move around: *¡Peatones, circulen por la izquierda!* Pedestrians, please walk on the left!; *en Gran Bretaña se circula por la izquierda* in Britain one drives on the left; run (eg bus, train): *no circula los festivos* doesn't run on bank holidays

☐ **circulación** *nf pl circulaciones* circulation (in most Eng senses); can

also mean 'traffic', but *tráfico* is at least as common

☐ **circular** *adj* circular, round (on flat plain, not spherical); see also *redondo*

circunstancia *nf* circumstance

☐ note spelling with *-n-*

cita *nf* arranged meeting, equivalent of appointment, rendezvous, date (in that sense): *darse cita* to arrange to meet each other

☐ also 'quotation' (eg from text)

☐ **citarse** *vr* to make an appointment/date (*con* with), arrange to meet: *nos hemos citado para las ocho* we've got a date for 8 o'clock

☐ **estar citado** to have an appointment (*con* with): *estoy citado con el médico para las 10* I've got an appointment with the doctor for 10 o'clock

☐ **citar** *vt* to quote (eg from text); to fix sb an appointment: *me citaron para las 3* they arranged to meet me at 3 o'clock

ciudad *nf* city, town

☐ NB spelling *C-I-U ...* NOT *c-u-i ...*; don't confuse with *c-u-i-d-a-d-o* which means care!

☐ NB also no distinction between city/town through having a cathedral or certain population: can be used of any town from above say 5,000; below that, use cf *pueblo* or *población*

☐ **ciudadano/a** *nmf* citizen (of town in question or in general): *ciudadano de la tercera edad* senior citizen; *adj* civic, belonging to a/the town: *seguridad ciudadana* public safety

claro *adj* bright, light: *habitación clara* bright/light room; *camisa azul claro* light blue shirt (*claro* agrees with *azul* not *camisa*, so not *fem*!)

☐ also 'clear' (liquid, thought, explanation etc): *agua clara* clear water; *una declaración clara* a clear statement; *está muy claro que …* it's very clear that; *¡claro!* of course! agreed! *claro que sí/no!* of course/not!

- can be used as *adv*: *tienes que hablar más claro* you must speak more clearly
- *nm* clearing (eg in wood)
- **claridad** *nf* brightness; clarity: *hablar con claridad* to speak clearly
- **clarificar** *vt* -que-, -qué to clarify; **clarificarse** *vr* to become clear: *ahora todo se ha clarificado* now all has become clear
- **clarificación** *nf pl clarificaciones* clarification

clase *nf* class (in most Eng senses): *billete de segunda clase* second–class ticket; *clase obrera* working class

- sort: *¿qué clase de zapatos quieres?* what sort of shoes do you want?
- NB use in school context: *voy a clase* I'm going to school; *las clases terminan a las cinco* lessons/school end/s at 5; *clase de matemáticas* maths lesson (ie often used in these contexts in preference to cf *escuela/colegio* and *lección*)

clave *nf* key

- NB limited range of meaning: key (to problem etc); (music) clef (for music key, use *tono*)
- NB for 'door key' etc use *llave*
- *punto clave adj* key point
- **clavo** *nm* nail
- **clavar** *vt* to hammer, nail (*en* into)
- NB wider meaning: *clavar los ojos/la mirada en algo/alguien* to fix one's eyes on/stare at sth/sb; *tenía una navaja clavada en el pecho* he had a knife stuck in his chest

clima *nm* climate

- NB it's *masc*!
- **climatizado** *adj* air–conditioned

club *nm pl clubs* or *clubes* club (of the kind you join)

cobrar *vt* to charge, collect, earn

- NB common use in contexts involving money: *¿Cuánto cobran para limpiar un traje?* What do they charge to clean a suit? *¿Me cobra, por favor?* (eg in restaurant) How much do I owe you?, Can I pay?
- common alternative to cf *ganar* to earn: *¿Cuánto cobras al mes?* How much do you earn per month?
- also 'to take on', 'acquire': *el asunto cobra importancia* the matter is gaining in importance; *el tren cobraba velocidad* the train was picking up speed
- **cobrador/a** *nmf* (bus) conductor/tress (NB *conductor/a* is 'driver')
- **cobro** *nm* recovery, collection, payment (of money)

cocer *vt* -ue- and -z-: *cuezo, cueces; cueza:* to cook

- used transitively, 'to cook sth', equivalent of 'boil' and 'bake', depending on method: *cocer en el horno* bake in the oven
- can be used in English sense of 'cook up' (plot) *¿Qué estáis cociendo aquí?* What are you cooking/hatching up here?
- **cocerse** *vr* cook, ie what the food does: *la cena se está cociendo* supper's cooking
- **cocido** *nm* stew, casserole; *adj* cooked, 'done': *bistec bien cocido* a 'well–done' steak
- **cocción** *nf* (act or time of) cooking: *durante la cocción* while (it is) cooking; *dale media hora de cocción* give it half an hour's cooking
- **cocina** *nf* three straightforward meanings: kitchen; cooking (art and process of); and cooker, stove
- **cocinar** *vti* to cook (in general sense of prepare food, do the cooking): *no me gusta cocinar* I don't like cooking; to cook sth: *estoy*

cocinando una paella I'm cooking a paella
- □ **cocinero/a** *nmf* cook
- □ NB *cocer* is more specific than *cocinar*, although there is an overlap when used to cook a dish; cf *preparar*, also often used in this sense

coche *nm* car: *ir a alguna parte en coche* to drive somewhere, go somewhere by car
- □ carriage, coach (road or rail): *coche de línea* long–distance coach; *coche restaurante* dining car

cocodrilo *nm* crocodile
- □ watch that *-r-*!: *c-o-c-o-d-r̠-i-l-o*

coger *vt -j-: cojo, coges; coja* to catch, take (take/grab hold of): *¡cógele!* catch him!; *cogí un resfriado* I caught a cold; *se puede coger el autobús* you can catch the bus; *me cogió por las solapas* he took hold of me by the lapels; *cogidos de la mano* hand in hand, holding hands
- □ **cogerse** *vr* to take, grab hold (*de* of): *se cogió del asa* he grabbed the handle
- □ NB considerable overlap with cf *tomar* in sense of 'take hold of' and 'take/catch' a form of transport; not so vigorous as cf *asir*
- □ NB also: avoid use of this verb in polite company in parts of Sp Am because of its common crude sexual connotation! *agarrar* and *tomar* are useful alternatives, depending on sense
- □ worth further research in the dictionary

cohibir *vt* to inhibit, embarrass
- □ **cohibirse** *vr* to feel inhibited, shy, embarrassed (a useful way of expressing embarrassment, shyness, awkwardness): *siempre se cohibía/se sentía cohibida en esta situación* she always felt awkward/embarrassed in this situation
- □ cf *tímido, violento, vergüenza* for other ways of expressing this

cola *nf* tail (of most animals, though cf *rabo* is sometimes preferred)
- □ also queue: *hacer cola* to queue (up)

colapsar *vt colapsar el tráfico* to bring traffic to a standstill
- □ NB NOT 'to collapse': use *derrumbarse, desplomarse* for eg building
- □ **colapso** *nm* collapse (of person): *sufrir un colapso* to collapse; (of traffic): standstill

coleccionar *vt* to collect, ie make a collection of: *colecciona sellos* he collects stamps
- □ for 'collect' in sense of 'pick up' use *recoger;* for 'gather together' use *reunir(se)*
- □ **colección** *nf pl colecciones* collection, in above sense
- □ **coleccionismo** *nm* (act of) collecting (as eg hobby): *coleccionismo de monedas* coin collecting

colega *nmf* colleague, workmate (either gender ends in *-a*)

colegio *nm* school, college: used specifically of private schools, but distinction between cf a state *instituto* is often blurred; children often shorten it to *cole*
- □ **colegial/a** *nmf* schoolboy/girl

colgar *vti -ue-; -gue-, -gué* to hang (up): *voy a colgar mi chaqueta* I'm going to hang up my jacket; *colgué el teléfono* I put the phone down, hung up (cf opp *descolgar*); *este cuadro cuelga en el Prado* this picture hangs in the Prado
- □ **colgado** *adj* hanging (use *estar*): *estaba colgado de las puntas de los dedos* I was hanging by my fingertips (NB use of *past part* for bodily position)

colina *nf* hill (usually a complete hill with two sides); for hill in sense of slope, and up/downhill, see *cuesta*

colocar *vt* -que-, -qué   to put, place
- NB more limited and specific in scope than cf *poner*: means 'to place' eg on a shelf, in a job, (money) into a bank
- **colocación** *nf pl colocaciones* placing, placement

color *nm*   colour
- NB **colorado** *adj*   red: *ponerse colorado*   to go red, blush
- for 'coloured' use *en colores*: *televisión/fotos en colores*   colour TV/photos
- **colorido** *nm*   (act or effect of) colouring: *no me gusta el colorido* I don't like the (eg combination of) colours

collar *nm*   necklace
- NOT normally 'collar', except for animals; use *cuello* for people

coma *nf*   comma; *punto y coma*   semi-colon
- also decimal point: *tres coma dos (3,2)* three point two (3.2); don't confuse with **coma** *nm*   coma
- **comillas** *nfpl*   quotation marks, inverted commas, often appearing as « »

comarca *nf*   region, area; usually rural or provincial; similar to *región* but not same as cf *barrio, área*

comentar *vt*   to comment, remark (on); takes dir obj: *comentó mi aspecto*   s/he commented on my appearance
- **comentario** *nm*   comment, commentary: *no hizo comentario* s/he made no comment
- **comentarista** *nmf*   commentator (in media)

comenzar *vti* -ie-; ce-, -cé   begin, start, commence; meanings exactly same as cf *empezar*
- NB *comenzar a + inf*   to begin to; *comenzar por + inf* or *comenzar + ger* to begin by ...ing

comienzo *nm*   beginning, start, commencement: *al comienzo*   at first, in the beginning; *al comienzo del programa*   at the start of the programme

comer *vt*   to eat
- **comerse** *vr*   to eat up; more emphatic than basic verb: *se comió todas las galletas*   s/he ate up all the biscuits
- **comida** *nf*   food (in general sense), less clinical than *alimento(s)*: *les falta comida*   they lack food; *la comida española*   Sp food; *comida y bebida* food and drink
- also 'meal': *está preparando la comida* s/he's preparing the meal
- and 'lunch', 'midday meal': *tomamos la comida a las dos*   we have lunch at two o'clock; cf *almuerzo/almorzar*
- **comedor** *nm*   dining room, refectory
- **comestible** *adj*   edible; **comestibles** *nmpl*   food: *tienda de comestibles*   food shop; **comilona** *nf* feast, 'blow-out'

comercio *nm*   commerce, trade, business: *hay mucho comercio entre los dos países* there's a lot of trade between the two countries; considerable overlap with cf *negocio*
- also 'shop': *esta calle contiene varios pequeños comercios*   this street contains several small businesses/shops
- **comerciante** *nmf*   shopkeeper, trader

comisión *nf pl comisiones*   commission (all senses); committee

como *prep*   as, like: *se tenía como una estatua*   she was standing like a statue; *quiero un ordenador como el tuyo*   I want a computer like yours; *me habló como amigo*   he spoke to me as/like a friend
- occurs as second element of *tanto/tan ... como ...* as (much/many) ... as ...

- *conj* as/since (in that sense): *como no me has escrito* as/since you haven't written to me; *como te quiero tanto* as/since I love you so much
- *como si + subjunc* as if: *como si supiera* as if s/he knew
- *adv* about, approximately: *tendrá como unos 20 años* s/he'll be about 20
- NB no accent!

¿cómo? *adv* how?: *¿cómo se hace?* how is it done?
- NB accent, as on all interrog words, even in 'indirect' questions: *no sé cómo se hace* I don't know how it is done; see a grammar book for details on indirect questions
- NB differentiate *cómo + ser* – *¿Cómo es el hotel?* What's the hotel like?; and *cómo + estar* – *¿Cómo estás?* How are you?
- used in some vigorous questions or reactions: *¿cómo?* what?, how do you mean?; *¿cómo que no?* why not?; *¿cómo así?* how come?
- **¡cómo!** (in exclamations + *v*) how…!: *¡cómo has crecido!* how you've grown!

cómodo *adj* comfortable; same as, but sounds more natural Sp than cf *confortable*
- **comodidad** *nf* comfort, convenience: *a tu comodidad* at your convenience; *pl comidades* comforts, amenities; for 'commodity' use *producto* or *artículo*
- see also related words under **acomodar**

compañero/a *nf* companion, pal, mate
- also 'partner' (ie you live with)
- and 'comrade' (political)

compañía *nf* company (in all senses): *en compañía de* in the company of; in sense of 'firm' cf also *empresa, firma, casa*
- see also **acompañar** *vt* to accompany

comparar *vt* to compare (*con* with);

comparado con compared with
- **comparación** *nf pl comparaciones* comparison: *en comparación con* in comparison with; NB spelling
- **comparativo** *adj* and *nm* comparative

comparecer *vi -zc-* to appear; NB specific limited use: *comparecer ante el tribunal/juez* to appear before the court/judge; cf *parecer, aparecer*

compartir *vt* to share (out): *compartir un piso* to share a flat; *compartir las ganancias* to share (out) the profits; not same as cf *repartir*

competir *vi* to compete
- **competencia** *nf* competition: *hacer competencia con alguien* to compete with, be in competition with sb; also 'competence', though *aptitud* might be better, depending on the context; and 'field', 'domain': *eso es de la competencia de mi colega* that's the responsibility of my colleague, that's my colleague's specialism; NB for eg a sports competition, better to use cf *concurso* or *certamen*; see also *rivalidad*
- **competición** *nf* competition (less common)
- **competitivo** *adj* competitive

completo *adj* complete; full (transport, hotels etc): *los hoteles estaban completos* the hotels were full

componer *vt pi: compongo, compones; ps: componga; tú imperative: compón; fut/cond: compondré/ía; pret: compuse, compusiste, compuso, compusimos, compusisteis, compusieron; past part: compuesto; imp subj: compusiera/compusiese* to compose, make up: *el grupo estaba compuesto de peruanos* the group was made up/composed of Peruvians
- **componerse** *vr* to be composed, made up (*de* of): *el agua se compone de oxígeno e hidrógeno* water is composed/made up of oxygen and hydrogen

□ **composición** *nf pl composiciones* composition (all senses)

comprar *vt* to buy
- □ remember that to buy sth FROM sb is *comprarle algo A alguien: le compré esta bicicleta A mi compañero* I bought this bike FROM my pal

comprender *vt* to understand
- □ much the same as cf *entender*
- □ can also mean 'include': *en el precio se comprende la comida* food included in the price
- □ **comprensión** *nf* understanding, comprehension
- □ **comprensible** *adj* understandable, comprehensible; **comprensivo** *adj* understanding; less likely to mean 'comprehensive' (all-embracing); better to consult a good dictionary for the word to suit your exact context

comprobar *vt -ue-* to check: *comprobar el aceite* to check one's oil; more used than cf *verificar*
- □ also 'to prove': *¿puedes comprobar que es verdad?* can you prove that it's the truth?
- □ and 'to realise': *comprobé que ya no me amaba* I realised that s/he no longer loved me
- □ **comprobación** *nf* check(ing): for 'proof', use *prueba*

compromiso *nm* commitment, obligation: *sin compromiso* without obligation
- □ also 'engagement': *tengo muchos compromisos esta semana* I've a lot of engagements this week
- □ and 'awkward spot': *¡qué compromiso es éste!* what a difficult situation this is!
- □ NB NOT usually the equivalent of Eng 'compromise': use *acuerdo mutuo*; you can say *llegar a un compromiso* to reach an agreement (but one that may not necessarily be a compromise – eg meeting halfway – as in Eng)

□ **comprometer** *vt* to commit (sb): *no quiero comprometerte* I don't want to commit you; to put at risk: *esto compromete mi reputación* this puts my reputation at risk
- □ **comprometerse** *vr* to promise, commit oneself (*a + inf* to): *me he comprometido con mi tía a visitarla* I've committed myself to visit my aunt/promised my aunt I'll visit her
- □ NB these words and most of their meanings carry the sense of the base word 'promise'

común *adj pl comunes* common (by/of/for everybody): *un acuerdo común* a common agreement; *en común* in common; *no tienen nada en común* they have nothing in common
- □ also 'common', in sense of 'ordinary', 'usual', 'widespread': *es un problema común* it's a common problem; cf *corriente; común y corriente* common or garden
- □ for 'common' in sense of 'vulgar' use *ordinario*

comunicar *vt -que-, -qué* to communicate
- □ NB formal use in sense of to inform: *tengo que comunicarle(s) la muerte del Sr X* I have to inform you of the death of Mr X
- □ NB: on phone: *están comunicando* the line is engaged
- □ **comunicarse** *vr* (*con alguien* with sb) to get in touch with sb

con *prep* with; used with noun, pronoun or infinitive of verb
- □ NB special forms *conmigo, contigo* with me, with you: *ven conmigo* come with me; also *consigo*, the reflexive 3rd person form, which must refer back to the subject of the verb: with him/her/one/yourself (*Vd*), them/yourselves (*Vds*): *¿Lo han traído Vds consigo?* Did you bring it with you?; *se lo llevó consigo* s/he took it away with her/him

concentrar *vt* to concentrate (eg sth somewhere): *van a concentrar sus actividades en Barcelona* they are going to concentrate their activities in Barcelona
- NB **concentrarse en** *vr* to concentrate on: *se concentraba en su trabajo* he was concentrating on his work

concertar *vt* -ie- to arrange, set up: *concertamos un proyecto* we set up a project
- + *inf* to agree to: *concertamos reunirnos otra vez* we agreed to meet again

conciencia *nf* conscience
- also 'awareness': *tener conciencia de algo* to be aware of sth: *tengo conciencia de que no todos estáis de acuerdo* I'm aware that you don't all agree
- **consciente** *adj* conscious, aware: *estar consciente* to be conscious, aware (*de algo*, of sth; *de que* that)
- **concienzudo** *adj* conscientious
- **concienciar** *vt* to make aware; *estar concienciado de que* to be aware that

concluir *vti pi*: concluyo, -uyes, -uye, -uyen; *ps*: concluya; *ger*: concluyendo; *pret*: concluyó, concluyeron; *imp subj*: concluyera/concluyese to conclude, in both senses of 'finish' (cf *terminar, acabar*); and 'decide' (cf *decidir, resolver*)
- *concluir + de + inf* to finish doing: *concluyó de leer el párrafo* s/he finished reading the paragraph (denotes completion of reading, not just leaving off)

concretar *vt* to fix, settle: *concretamos el trato* we settled the deal; define, make clear: *¿puede concretar?* can you be more specific?; *vamos a concretar los detalles* let's clarify the details
- **concreto** *adj* specific: *dame un ejemplo concreto* give me a specific example; *en concreto* specifically

- **concretamente** *adv* specifically: *quisiera saber concretamente cuántos* I'd like to know exactly how many
- 'concrete' as building material is *betún*

concurso *nm* competition, contest (ie the meeting: for the concept see *competencia*); much the same as cf *certamen*
- **concursar** *vi* to take part (in a *concurso*); **concursante** *nmf* competitor (in this sense)

condición *nf pl* condiciones condition (in most senses)
- 'stipulation': *con una condición* with/under one condition
- often used *pl* in sense of 'state': *está en buenas condiciones* it's in good condition; *estar en condiciones para* to be in the right state to/for
- *en su condición de* in one's position/role of: *lo hizo en su condición de alcalde* he did it in his role as mayor
- *a condición de que + subjunc* on condition that

conducir *vti pi*: conduzco, conduces; *ps*: conduzca; *pret*: conduje, condujiste, condujo, condujimos, condujisteis, condujeron; *imp subj*: condujera/condujese to lead: *¿adónde conduce todo esto?* where does all this lead to? this use similar to this sense of *llevar*
- also 'to drive': *¿sabes conducir (un coche)?* can you drive (a car); For 'we drove to Dover' use *fuimos en coche a Dover*, or if you know from the context you are in a car, just say *fuimos a Dover*
- also 'to conduct' (electricity)
- **conductor/a** *nmf* driver (of car, bus, etc); possibly more common nowadays than cf *chófer*; also (electrical) conductor; for bus conductor/tress use *cobrador/a*
- **conducta** *nf* conduct, behaviour; useful alternative to cf

comportamiento

- □ **conducción** *nf* conduction; (action of) driving: *clases de conducción* driving lessons

conferencia *nf* conference (although *congreso* is often preferred)
- □ also (eg university) lecture
- □ and long-distance phone call
- □ **conferenciante** *nmf* lecturer

confesar *vt -ie-* to confess, admit (in this sense)
- □ **confesarse** *vr* to confess, go to confession (in church)

confianza *nf* confidence, trust: *poner su confianza en algo/alguien* to put one's trust in sth/sb; *tener confianza en sí mismo/a* to be self-confident; *tener confianza de (que)* to be confident of/that
- □ also 'intimacy', 'familiarity': *tener confianza con alguien* to be close friends with sb
- □ NB not same as **confidencia** *nf* confidence (sth you confide to sb, ie a secret)
- □ **confiar** *vi -í-: confío, confías; confíe* to trust (*en algo/alguien* sth/sb): *confiamos en tus conocimientos* we trust your knowledge; *confío en mi jefe* I trust my boss
- □ *en algo; en + inf* or *en que + subjunc* to be confident of/that: *confiamos en nuestros jugadores* we're confident of our players; *ellos confían en ganar* they are confident of winning; *confiamos en que ganen la copa* we're confident of them winning the cup
- □ *vt* to confide: *confió el secreto a su novia* he confided the secret to his girlfriend
- □ **confiarse** *vr* to confide (*a alguien* in sb)
- □ **confiado** *adj* trusting; for 'be confident' use *tener confianza;*
- □ **confiable** *adj* reliable, trustworthy

confitería *nf* patisserie and confectionery; cake and confectioner's shop (ie sells both cakes and sweets)
- □ **confitero/a** *nmf* confectioner/cake seller
- □ NB **confección** *nf* tailoring, dressmaking

conflicto *nm* conflict
- □ **conflictivo** *adj* difficult, troubled: *zona conflictiva* trouble spot; *clase conflictiva* difficult class (ie in behaviour)
- □ **conflictividad** *nf* tendency to dispute

conforme *adj* agreed, satisfied: *¿Estáis conformes?* Do you agree?, Are you happy with that?
- □ *conj* as, (in sense of in proportion, at the same time as): *conforme te vayas haciendo mayor, comprenderás estas cosas* as you grow up you will understand these things; *conforme recibas tu salario, es mejor ahorrar una proporción* as you receive your salary it's best to save some
- □ **conforme a** *prep* in accordance with, in keeping with: *conforme a las situación* in keeping with/according to the situation

confort *nm* comfort
- □ **confortable** *adj* comfortable
- □ often occurs in modern Sp: *confort* especially is a gallicism, ie import from French: purists would prefer cf *comodidad* and *cómodo*!

confuso *adj* confused; often used for 'embarrassed': *estaba todo confuso* he was all embarrassed

congelar *vt* to freeze (sth); **congelarse** *vr* to freeze (over): *el río se congeló* the river froze (over); also used figuratively: *¡me estoy congelando!* I'm freezing!; and of assets etc: *congelar los salarios* to freeze wages
- □ some overlap with cf *helar*, which

tends to have a narrower meaning, more confined to the weather

□ **congelado** *adj*   frozen (esp foods);

□ **congelador** *nm*   freezer, deep-freeze;

□ **congelación** *nf*   (act of) freezing; *morir por congelación*   to die of exposure

congreso *nm*   congress; often equivalent of 'conference'

conjunto *nm*   collection: *un conjunto magnífico de trajes de época*   a magnificent collection of period costumes

□ also: (pop) group, (classical) ensemble

□ and: outfit, ensemble: *conjunto de invierno*   winter outfit

□ *en conjunto*   as a whole: *si lo consideramos en conjunto*   if we consider it as a whole/all together

conllevar *vt*   to entail, bring with: *las responsabilidades que conlleva un bebé*   the responsibilities a baby brings (with it)

conmover *vt -ue-*   to move (emotionally): *estaban todos muy conmovidos*   they were all very moved

□ **conmovedor** *adj f -edora; pl -edores, -edoras*   moving: *una historia conmovedora*   a touching story

□ **conmoción** *nf pl conmociones*   NB shock, upset; NOT commotion, use *alboroto* or similar

□ NB spelling: *c-o-n-m;* not as Eng c-o-m-m-

conocer *vt -zc-*   to know, be acquainted with

□ NB not same as cf *saber*   know, be aware of (eg a fact)

□ *no conozco Salamanca*   I don't know Salamanca; *¿Conoces a mi prima?*   Do you know my cousin?, often used in sense of 'Have you met my cousin?'; *no conozco la solución del problema*   I don't know the answer to the problem

□ NB use of *pret* meaning 'got to know': *sí, la conocí el año pasado*   yes, I met her last year

□ **conocido** *adj*   well-known, famous: *futbolista conocido*   famous footballer

□ **conocimiento** *nm*   knowledge, often used in *pl conocimientos* in this sense: *tiene tantos conocimientos*   he has so much knowledge; some overlap with cf *saber*, which however tends to lean towards 'wisdom'

□ *venir en/hacer conocimiento de algo*   to learn about sth

□ also 'understanding' (esp of children): *es muy joven para tener conocimiento de eso*   he's very young to understand about that

□ and 'consciousness': *perder conocimiento*   to lose consciousness

conque *conj*   (and) so, so then, well then; used at beginning of sentence only, usually to introduce a comment, perhaps as result of previous discussion: *conque ¿te vas?*   so, you're off?; *conque, ¿no me quieres?*   so, you don't love me?

□ cf *entonces*

consecuencia *nf*   consequence: *a consecuencia de*   as a consequence of; *en consecuencia*   in consequence, therefore

□ **consiguiente** *adj*   consequent: *el resultado consiguiente*   the consequent result; *por consiguiente*   consequently, therefore

□ NB **consecuente** *adj*   consistent: *ser consecuente*   to be consistent, although **consecuentemente** *adv* consequently!

conseguir *vt -i-, -g-: consigo, consigues; consiga*   to obtain, (manage to) get, achieve: *hemos conseguido las entradas* we've got (managed to get) the tickets; *consiguió el rango de oficial*   he achieved the rank of officer

□ + *inf*   to manage to: *conseguimos atraparle*   we managed to catch him

□ + *que* + *subjunc*   to manage to get

sth to happen (implies effort or persuasion): *conseguí que le escribiesen* I managed to get them to write to him
- very similar to cf *lograr*

consejo *nm* piece of advice: *un último consejo* one last piece of advice; so 'advice' in general usually needs *pl*: *gracias por tus consejos* thanks for your advice; can also be translated by 'counsel'
- also 'council', 'board': *Consejo de Europa* Council of Europe
- **concejo** *nm* is also used, esp *Concejo Municipal* Town Council
- **consejero/a** *nmf* adviser; or sb who is a member of a *consejo,* councillor; a member of a *concejo* is **concejal/a** *nmf* (town) councillor
- see also **aconsejar** *vt* to advise

consentir *vti -ie-, -i-* to allow, permit: *mi madre no consiente que lo haga* my mother doesn't allow me to do it; *no se consiente* it's not permitted; similar to cf *permitir, tolerar* in this sense
- + *en* + *n* or *inf* to agree to sth/to do sth: *no consiento en esto* I'm not agreeing to this; *todos consintieron en ayudarle* everyone agreed to help him; similar to cf *ponerse de acuerdo* but the agreement must carry the element of consenting
- **consentimiento** *nm* consent
- NB **consentido** *adj* spoiled: *un niño consentido* a spoilt child; *syn mimado*

consistir *vi* to consist (*en* of); *¿en qué consiste?* what does it consist of?; *su día consiste en levantarse, trabajar y acostarse* his day consists of getting up, working and going to bed: cf *constar de*
- can also be used in sense of 'involve', 'be all about': *¿en qué consiste el problema?* what's the problem all about?
- **consistente** *adj* consistent; also, esp in cooking 'firm', 'stiff'; *consistente en* consisting of; *una familia consistente*

en padres y dos niños a family consisting of parents and two children
- **consistencia** *nf* consistency

constar *vi* (*de* of) to consist of (in sense of be composed/made up of): *la novela consta de 20 largos capítulos* the novel consists of 20 long chapters; cf *consistir*
- otherwise used rather formally with meaning of 'to be stated', 'appear'; mainly in legal use, and in *(no) me consta que* I am (not) sure that

constiparse *vr* to catch a cold; **constipado** *adj* *estar constipado* to have a cold in Sp – but to be constipated in Sp Am
- use *estar estreñido* in Sp for to be constipated

constituir *vt -y- pi: constituyo, -uyes, -uye, -uyen; ps: -uya; ger: -uyendo; pret: -uyó, -uyeron; imp subj: -uyera/-uyese* to constitute
- in formal language can be used for *ser: esto constituye su cualidad principal* this is its main attribute

construir *vt -y- pi: construyo, -uyes, -uye, -uyen; ps: -uya; ger: -uyendo; pret: -uyó, -uyeron; imp subj: -uyera/-uyese* to build, construct
- **construcción** *nf pl construcciones* building (act of); construction (act of or finished job)
- **constructor/a** *nmf* builder; or *adj* building; *industria constructora* building industry

consultar *vt* to consult, but NB: *consultar algo con alguien:* to consult sb about sth: *consulté el asunto con mi hermano* I consulted my brother about the matter
- **consultorio** *nm* (eg doctor's) consulting room, surgery

contaminar *vt* to contaminate, pollute
- **contaminación** *nf pl contaminaciones* contamination, pollution
- **contaminante** *nm* contaminant, pollutant

□ preferable words for pollute/pollution rather than cf *polucionar/polución*

contar *vti -ue-* to count (most senses as in Eng): *cuenta hasta diez* count up to 10; *somos veinte sin contar a la profesora* there are twenty of us not counting the teacher; *no cuenta para tus notas* it doesn't count towards your marks; *al contado* in cash

□ also 'to tell', 'relate', 'recount': *cuéntame lo que pasó* tell me what happened; *se cuenta que …* it is told that …, the story goes that …

□ **contar con algo/alguien** to rely on sth/sb: *todos contamos contigo* we're all relying on you

□ also 'to have', 'possess': *el hospital cuenta con 1.000 camas* the hospital has 1,000 beds

□ **cuenta** *nf* various meanings: account, eg in bank; bill, in restaurant; sum, (in sense of) calculation; count: *perder la cuenta* to lose count; and in phrase *darse cuenta de/de que* to realise sth/that: *me di cuenta di que estaba oscuro* I realised it was dark; and many other useful expressions: look in the dictionary!

□ **cuento** *nm* tale, short story; can also be used in sense of 'fib'

contener *vt pi:* contengo, -tienes, -tiene, -tienen; *ps:* contenga; *tú imperative:* contén; *fut/cond:* contendré/ía; *pret:* contuve, -tuviste, -tuvo, -tuvimos, -tuvisteis, -tuvieron; *imp subj:* contuviera/contuviese to contain: ;used mainly as Eng: *esta caja contiene libros* this box contains books; *se ha contenido la epidemia* the epidemic has been contained; *no pudimos contener la risa* we couldn't contain our laughter

□ **contenerse** *vr* to contain oneself

□ **contenido** *nm* contents

□ **contenedor** *nm* container, rubbish bin, 'wheelie bin'

contento *adj* happy, pleased, content

□ normally used with *estar* to express happiness as the result of circumstance: *estoy muy contento con/de mi nuevo coche* I'm very pleased with my new car; *estaremos muy contentos de recibirles* we'll be very happy to welcome them; (*de que + subjunc* that): *tu tía está muy contenta de que vayas a verla* your aunt is very pleased that you are going to see her; similar to cf *alegrarse (de que)*; cf for contrast *feliz*, which might be used with *ser* to express a more profound, inner happiness

□ **contentar** *vt* to please, make happy

□ **contentarse** *vr* to content oneself, make do, be satisfied (*con algo* with sth, *con + inf*, or simply + *ger. se contenta leyendo* he's happy (ie just) reading); for 'to be pleased with' use *estar contento de* as above

contestar *vti* answer, reply

□ can be used with *dir obj* or + *a* + *obj:* *no contestaron (a) mi carta* they didn't answer my letter

□ **contestación** *nf pl* contestaciones answer, reply

□ much the same as cf *responder/respuesta*

□ **contestador automático** *nm* answering machine, answerphone

continuar *vti* continúo, -úas, úa, -úan; -úe, -úes, -úe, -úen to continue, go on

□ NB followed by *ger* not *inf:* *continuaron peleándose* they continued fighting; cf this use of *seguir*

□ **continuación** *nf pl* continuaciones continuation; *a continuación* next, below: *como se describe a continuación* as described below

□ **continuo** *adj* continuous; continual: NB stress is on *-i-: contInuo*

□ **continuidad** *nf* continuity

contra *prep* against: *estaba contra la puerta* it was against the door; *el Real Madrid* *contra el Barcelona* Real Madrid v Barcelona

- NB *estar en contra (de algo)* to be (ie have opinion) against sth: *están en contra del aborto* they are against abortion; *yo estoy en contra* I'm against (it)
- **contra-** *prefix* has meaning of 'counter–': *contraataque* counterattack

contrario *adj* opposite, contrary: *opinión contraria* opposite opinion; *sentido contrario* opposite direction

- 'opposing': *equipo contrario* opposing team
- *al contrario/por el contrario* on the contrary; *al contrario de* unlike: *al contrario de Londres, Madrid tiene …* unlike London, Madrid has …; *al contrario de lo que piensas tú, yo …* unlike what you think, I …
- NB for physically opposite, ie in place: use *enfrente (de)*
- **contrariedad** *nf* obstacle, setback: *fue una contrariedad* it was a significant setback

contribuir *vi* to contribute

- same *-y-* irregularities as cf *constituir* above

convencer *vt -z-* convenzo, convences; convenza to convince

- *a alguien de algo* sb of sth: *me convenció de su sinceridad* he convinced me of his sincerity; *a alguien para* or *de que* + *subjunc* to persuade sb to do sth: *le convencí para que viera al médico* I persuaded him to see the doctor; *no me convences* I'm not sure (ie whether I believe what you're saying)
- **convencerse** *vr* to be convinced
- **convencimiento** *nm* (act of) convincing; conviction: *tener el convencimiento de que* to have the conviction/be convinced that

convenir *vi pi:* convengo, -vienes, -viene, -vienen; *ps:* convenga; *ger:* conviniendo; *fut/cond:* convendré/ía; *pret:* convine, -viniste, -vino, -vinimos, -vinisteis, -vinieron; *imp subj:* conviniera/conviniese

- 'to be suitable': *¿Te conviene la fecha?* Is the date all right for you?; *rellena los espacios en blanco con la palabra que más convenga* fill the gaps with the most suitable word
- 'to be advisable': *no conviene fumar tanto* it's not wise to smoke so much
- 'to agree' (*en* to/on), usually in sense of two or more persons reaching an agreement: *todos convinimos en mandar dinero* we all agreed to send money; *convinieron en la hora y fecha* they agreed on the time and date
- **convenio** *nm* agreement (esp in labour relations)
- **conveniente** *adj* convenient: *su llegada fue poco conveniente* their arrival was not very convenient; NB the *adj* takes its main meaning from *v* convenir
- 'suitable': *será conveniente para los niños* it will be useful/handy for the children
- also 'advisable': *es conveniente que no salgas* it's advisable you don't go out
- **conveniencia** *nf* suitability, advisability, as for the above *adjs*; for 'convenience', the best equivalent would depend on the context: a good dictionary will provide several suggestions!

convertir *vt -ie-, -i-* to convert, change (*en* into): *la rana convirtió a la bruja en princesa* the frog turned the witch into a princess

- **convertirse** *vr* (*en*) to change (into), become: *la bruja se convirtió en princesa* the witch changed into/became a princess; cf *transformar(se)*, *cambiar(se)* for 'change'
- 'become', used with noun

complement: *la calle se convirtió en zona peatonal* the street became a pedestrian area; see also *hacerse, llegar a ser*

- □ **conversión** *nf* conversion, change

copa *nf* glass (with a stem); not same as cf *vaso; tomarse unas copas* to have a few drinks; *vamos a tomar una copa* let's go for a drink

- □ cup (in competition): *copa mundial* world cup

copia *nf* copy, (ie that you made, eg of papers); *fotocopia* photocopy; not quite same as cf *ejemplar* copy of eg book, record

- □ **copiar** *vt* to copy (in all senses)

corazón *nm pl corazones* heart; *ataque al corazón* heart attack; *corazones* glossy (society) magazines, eg *'¡Hola!'*

correcto *adj* correct, (in sense of polite): *es muy correcto* he's very correct/polite

- □ correct (in sense of right): *una respuesta correcta* a correct answer; to say a person is right use *tener razón*
- □ **corregir** *vt -i-, -jo, -ja- corrijo, corriges; corrija* to correct, mark (in that sense); to rebuke, reprimand
- □ **corrección** *nf pl correcciones* correction (in most senses)

correo *nm* post, mail: *por correo* by post; *correo aéreo* airmail; *correo electrónico* e-mail; *Correos* post office

correr *vti* to run

- □ NB this verb only denotes the manner of propelling yourself along: it doesn't actually get you anywhere (cf *andar/andando* walk)! So, for run somewhere, and run in/out/up/down use *corriendo* with the verb of direction: *ir/venir/entrar/salir/subir/bajar corriendo: iba corriendo por la calle* s/he was running down the street; *bajó corriendo la escalera* s/he ran downstairs

- □ also 'to flow' (eg river): *el río corre muy rápido* the river's running/flowing very fast
- □ and, as Eng 'run' (eg risk): *correr un riesgo* to run a risk; *correr peligro* to risk dangers
- □ and *correr las cortinas* to draw the curtains
- □ worth further investigation in the dictionary!

corresponder *vi* to correspond (*a* to), but with wider meanings

- □ to fit, match: *estos calcetines no corresponden* these socks don't match
- □ to be sb's job, lot: *todo esto te corresponde a ti* all this is your job; (similar to cf *tocar*)
- □ **corresponderse** *vr* to tally (*con* with); also correspond with (write to)
- □ **correspondencia** *nf* correspondence; also interchange station in metro
- □ **correspondiente** *adj* corresponding, relevant; NB this is NOT a noun!
- □ **corresponsal** *nmf* correspondent (ie for TV, paper, etc); for penfriend, use *amigo/a por correspondencia*

corriente *adj* common, ordinary, usual: *vino corriente* ordinary wine, cf Fr vin ordinaire; *es muy corriente por aquí* it's very common around here; cf also *normal, usual, ordinario, común* for similarities and contrasts of use; *estar al corriente de algo* to be up to date/au fait with sth

- □ current: *el mes corriente* the current month
- □ *nf* current: *la corriente está muy fuerte por ahí* the current is very strong around there; *corriente de aire* draught; *cortar la corriente* to cut off the (ie electric) power/current

cortar *vt* to cut (in most senses)

cut off: *cortar el agua* to cut off the water; cut down: *cortar un árbol* to cut down a tree; cut out: *cortar un anuncio* to cut out an advert

☐ **cortarse** *vr* to cut oneself (NB use with part of body and def art, not possessive): *me corté el dedo* I cut my finger

☐ **corte** *nm* cut (in most senses, esp as *n* for above); *¿Te gusta mi nuevo corte?* Do you like my new (hair) cut?; don't confuse with *corte nf* (royal) court, esp *Las Cortes* Spanish Parliament!

cortés *adj* polite, courteous; no *f* form: **cortésmente** *adv* politely

☐ **cortesía** *nf* politeness, courtesy; *tener la cortesía de* to have the courtesy to

cortijo *nm* farm, farmhouse; usually large ranch-style farm in S of Spain; not same as cf the smaller *granja*

corto *adj* short (ie opp of *largo* long)

☐ can also be used in sense of 'lacking': *corto de edad* not very old; *andar corto de dinero* to be short of money; *ser corto de vista/oído* to be short-sighted/hard of hearing; *corto de luces* dim, not very bright (person)

☐ some overlap with cf more limited *breve*

☐ for 'short' as opp of 'tall', use *bajo*

☐ **cortometraje** *nm* short (film)

cosa *nf* thing: *otra cosa* something/anything else; *cualquier cosa* anything; *es poca cosa/no es gran cosa* it's nothing much, nothing to worry about; often used in *pl* as in Eng: *así están las cosas* that's how things are, that's the way it is

☐ dictionaries have long lists of expressions: worth a look!

cosecha *nf* harvest, crop (in that sense): *tuvimos una buena cosecha de coliflores* we had a good crop of cauliflowers; for crop in sense of what you grow use *cultivo*

costar *vti* -ue- to cost (in most senses as Eng)

☐ useful idiom: *me cuesta trabajar* I have a job to work, I find it hard to work; *te cuesta, ¿no?* you're finding it hard, aren't you?

☐ **costa** *nf* mainly used in **a costa de** *prep* at the cost/expense of: *a costa nuestra* at our expense; *a toda costa* at all costs

☐ as opposed to the more general **coste** or **costo** *nm* cost: *coste/o de la vida* cost of living; *costes/os de producción* production costs

☐ **costoso** *adj* expensive, costly

costumbre *nf* habit, custom: *tener la costumbre de* to be in the habit of

☐ see also **acostumbrar(se)** *vtr* to accustom/be accustomed (*a* to)

crear *vt* to create

☐ entirely regular: don't confuse its parts with *creer* and *criar*!

crecer *vi* -zc- to grow (get bigger): *¡Cómo has crecido!* Haven't you grown! *nuestros ahorros han crecido* our savings have grown

☐ for 'grow' in sense of 'cultivate' (eg crops) use *cultivar: las flores que cultivamos crecen bien* the flowers we grow, grow well

☐ **crecimiento** *nm* growth

☐ **creciente** *adj* growing, increasing: *un número creciente* a growing number; **crecido** *adj* full grown, with growth: *tener la barba crecida* to have a full-grown beard

creer *vti* -y-: *creyendo; creyó, creyeron; creyera/creyese* to believe: *no te creo* I don't believe you; *creer en Dios* to believe in God

☐ think (in sense of believe): *creo que sí/no* I (don't) think so: interchangeable with cf *pensar* in this sense

☐ NB *no creer que* not to believe that usually takes subjunc: *no creemos que*

sea así we don't think so
- don't confuse parts with *crear, criar*
- **creencia** *nf* belief; **creyente** *nmf* believer
- **creíble** *adj* credible (opp *increíble* incredible)

criar *vt* -í-: *crío, crías; críe* to bring up (children), to rear (animals)
- **criarse** *vr* to grow up (in sense of pass one's formative years) *me crié en Cádiz* I grew up in Cádiz
- don't confuse parts with *crear, creer*
- **crío/a** *nmf* kid, child
- **cría/crianza** *nf* raising, rearing (animals)
- **criatura** *nf* creature; *todos somos criaturas de Dios* we're all God's creatures; often used for 'baby', 'small child'
- **criado/a** *nmf* servant, maid (*f*)

crimen *nm* NB *pl crímenes* crime
- **criminal** *adj nmf* criminal
- **criminalidad** *nf* criminality; crime rate

crisis *nf inv* crisis
- invariable – no plural form

cristal *nm* crystal, but often used for 'glass', esp in windows: *los cristales de la ventanas* the window panes; cf *vidrio*

crudo *adj* raw, uncooked: *carne cruda* raw meat
- harsh, severe: *un clima crudo* a harsh climate
- for 'crude', use *grosero* meaning rude, *rudimentario* for lacking refinement
- **crudeza** *nf* harshness, severity

cruz *nf pl cruces* cross
- **cruzar** *vt* -ce-, -cé to cross (in most Eng senses); go across; same as cf *atravesar* in this last sense
- **cruzarse** *vr* to meet, pass (going in opposite directions): *nos cruzamos en la carretera* we passed each other on the road
- **cruce** *nm* crossing, crossroads: *cruce*

de peatones pedestrian crossing; *cruce giratorio* roundabout; *luces de cruce* dipped headlights;
- **encrucijada** *nf* crossroads

cuaderno *nm* notebook, exercise book (ie for writing in)

cuadra *nf* stable; cf *establo* means cowshed

cuadrar *vti* to tally (*con* with): *mis cálculos no cuadran con los tuyos* my calculations don't tally with yours; *si te cuadra así* if that suits you (same as cf *convenir*); to square (maths)
- **cuadro** *nm* painting, picture (in general sense): *los cuadros de Goya* Goya's paintings/pictures; *¡Qué cuadro me pintas!* What a picture you paint!
- square, check (in that sense): *camisa de cuadros* check shirt; *ponga una X en uno de los cuadros* put a cross in one of the squares
- **cuadrado** *adj* square: *una habitación cuadrada* a square room; also as *nm* square: *el cuadrado de 9 es 81* the square of 9 is 81
- NB square in a town is *plaza*
- all these words have other specialised applications

cual *pron* which, who; used as relative pronoun in *el cual, la cual, los cuales, las cuales*, as alternative to cf *quien* or *el que* mainly after *prep*: *las calles por las cuales pasamos* the streets along which we passed; has neuter form *lo cual*, referring back to an idea to which no gender can be attached: *dimitió, lo cual no les gustó a sus colegas* he resigned, which didn't please his colleagues; *cada cual* each/every one
- NB no accent
- **¿cuál?** *pron pl ¿cuáles?* which one(s)?: *¿He aquí unas manzanas. ¿Cuál/Cuáles quieres?* I've got some apples here. Which one/ones do you want?

- for 'which' + noun use cf *¿qué?*
- NB in common with all interrog words, *cuál(es)* needs an accent!

cualidad see under **calidad** (they are NOT the same)

cualquiera *adj pl cualesquiera* any (ie offering the widest choice)
- NB shortens to *cualquier* before noun: *si hay cualquier razón* if there is any reason (ie at all): *puedes venir cualquier día* you can come on any day; *si vienes en cualquier momento* if you come at any time; *de cualquier manera/forma* in any case
- can come after noun, but sense tends to imply no choice or no desire to choose: *veremos una película cualquiera* we'll watch any old film
- as *pron* either (of two), any one (of more): *¿cuál te gusta? cualquiera* which do you like? either/any one
- NB both *adj* and *pron* can be used + *que* + *subjunc* meaning 'whatever', 'whichever' *cualquier moto que compres* whichever motorbike you buy; *cualquiera que compres* whichever (one) you buy; *cualesquiera que compres* whichever ones you buy; also 'whoever': *cualquier que lea esto* anyone who reads this
- for further explanation, examples and practice, consult a grammar book!

cuando *adv* when (no accent): *cuando llegué a casa* when I arrived home; *de vez en cuando* from time to time
- NB takes subjunc when referring to future: *cuando llegue mi primo* when my cousin arrives (he hasn't arrived yet); study this further in a grammar book!
- don't confuse with **¿cuándo?** when? asking a question; NB in common with all interrogative words, needs an accent, even in indirect questions! *¿Cuándo te vas?* When are you going? *no sé cuándo me voy* I don't know when I'm going

¿cuánto? *interrog adj* and *pron* how much? how many?; *pl ¿cuánto dinero tienes?* how much money have you got?; *¿cuántas mesas necesitamos?* how many tables do we need?; *no sé cuántas personas vienen* I don't know how many people are coming
- NB needs accent, including in indirect questions
- also used in exclamations meaning 'what a lot (of)!': *¿Cuántos regalos has tenido!* What a lot of presents you've had!; and also 'how (much)': *¡Cuánto valoro tu amistad!* How (much) I do value your friendship!
- **cuanto** *adj* and *pron* (NB without accent) as much/many as, in sense of *todo lo que/todos los que/todas las que: toma cuanto necesites* take as much as you need; *toma cuantos/as necesites* take as many as you need
- *cuanto más/menos … más/menos …* the more/less … the more/less …; *cuanto más trabajamos, menos ratos libres tenemos* the more we work the less free time we have
- *cuanto antes* as soon as possible; *en cuanto a* as for; *en cuanto* (+ *subjunc* if referring to future, cf *cuando* above) as soon as

cuarto *nm* room (mainly in house)
- *cuarto de estar* lounge; *cuarto de baño* bathroom; *el cuarto de mi hermano* my brother's (bed)room; not same as cf *sala*, except in *cuarto/sala de estar*; some correspondence with cf *habitación*
- also 'quarter', see under *cuatro* below

cuatro *num* four
- NB don't confuse *cuatro (-t-r-o)* with *cuarto (r-t-o)* a quarter, or fourth
- NB all '4' numbers begin with *cu-*, NOT *qu-*!: *cuatro, cuarto, cuarenta, cuatrocientos*

cubrir *vt* NB *past part* **cubierto** to cover (*de* with) (in most senses as Eng) *el* *suelo estaba cubierto de hojas* the ground was covered with/in leaves

cuchillo *nm* knive of most kinds, esp for eating/cooking with; some overlap with cf *navaja* for the more vicious kind!

cuello *nm* neck
- □ also 'collar' (of shirt, dress, etc)
- □ not same as cf *collar* necklace, (animal's) collar

cuenta, cuento see **contar**

cuerda *nf* rope, string, cord: *dar cuerda a un reloj* to wind up clock/watch; *cuerda floja* tightrope
- □ also 'chord' (musical)

cuesta *nf* slope, hill (in that sense): *cuesta arriba/abajo* up/downhill
- □ some overlap with cf *colina* hill, which however can have two or more sides!
- □ *llevar a cuestas* to carry on one's back

cuestión *nf pl cuestiones* question
- □ NB one you consider or discuss (cf *tema, problema*), but not ask: that's *pregunta: es una cuestión que me preocupa* it's a question/matter that worries me; *es cuestión de* it's a matter of; *poner en cuestión* to call into question
- □ **cuestionar** *vt* to question (in sense of) dispute: *cuestiono sus motivos* I question/dispute his reasons

cuidado *nm* care *¡cuidado!* careful! mind! watch out!
- □ *tener cuidado de + n* or *+ inf* take care of/to: *tuvimos cuidado de no pisar las plantas* we took care not to tread on the plants
- □ NB DON'T confuse it with *c-i-u-d-a-d* town: this is spelt *C-U-I*!
- □ **cuidar** *vt* or **cuidar de** *vi* to take care of, look after: *los vecinos me cuidan el piso* the neighbours look after my flat; *hay que cuidar de la piel* you have to look after your skin

- □ *cuidar de que + subjunc*: take care that, make sure that: *yo cuidaré de que no surjan problemas* I'll make sure no problems arise
- □ **cuidadoso** *iadj* careful: *es un trabajador cuidadoso* he's a careful workman

culpa *nf* blame, fault
- □ note how it is used: *echar la culpa a alguien* to put the blame on sb: *tener la culpa de algo* to be to blame for sth; *la culpa (no) es mía* it's (not) my fault
- □ **culpar** *vt* to blame (*de* for)
- □ **culpable** *adj* guilty (*de* of): *eres (el/la) culpable* you're (the one) to blame; *sentirse culpable de algo* to feel guilty/to blame for sth
- □ **culpabilidad** *nf* guilt, guiltiness

cultivar *vt* to cultivate (in most senses)
- □ also 'grow' (in sense of what you do to plants): for what they do, ie grow, get bigger, use *crecer*
- □ **cultivo** *nm* crop (in sense of what you grow); use *cosecha* for what you harvest

cumbre *nf* summit, height, top (in that sense): *la cumbre de la montaña* the top/summit of the mountain; *reunión cumbre* summit meeting; *en la cumbre de sus poderes* at the height of his powers; similar to but with wider application than cf *cima*

cumplir *vti* to fulfil, carry out: *cumplir una promesa/deseo* to fulfil a promise/wish; sometimes used with *con*, but some authorities regard this as incorrect
- □ to do the right thing, to fulfil an understood eg social obligation: *fue sólo para cumplir* it was just to do the right thing/only to do what we had do
- □ also 'to complete', 'attain': *ayer cumplió 18 años* s/he was 18 yesterday
- □ hence **cumpleaños** *nm* birthday (no *pl* form)

curar *vt*   to cure
- NB also 'to treat': *le curaron las heridas*   they treated his wounds
- *vi*   (of sick person) get better, (of wound) to heal, or use:
- **curarse** *vr*   to recover, get better
- **cura** *nf*   cure, treatment: *cura de urgencia*   first aid
- don't confuse with **cura** *nm*   priest!

curioso *adj*   curious (in both senses as Eng)
- inquisitive: *esa situación me tiene curioso*   this situation makes me curious; *estar curioso por* + *n* or *inf* to be eager for/to: *están curiosos por saber lo que pasa*   they are eager to know what's going on
- strange: *es una situación curiosa*   it's a curious situation
- also *nmf*   onlooker
- **curiosidad** *nf*   curiosity (*por*   for)
- **curiosear** *vi*   to pry (*en*   into), rummage (eg in drawer to find sth)

curso *nm*   course (in most senses): *el curso del río*   the course of the river); *en el curso del programa*   in the course of the programme
- in academic context 'year': *curso escolar*   school year; *¿En qué curso estás?*   Which class are you in? also 'course': *curso de inglés*   English course (classes or book)
- **cursillo** *nm*   short (eg holiday) course

cuyo *relative adj*   whose, of which: *la chica cuyos zapatos se encontraron en el patio* the girl whose shoes were found in the playground; *la palabra cuya sentido no se conoce*   the word whose meaning is not known
- NB agrees with thing possessed, not possessor
- NB you CANNOT use it to ask questions; use *¿De quién?*: *¿De quién son estos zapatos?*   Whose are these shoes?

D (*de*) is pronounced with the tongue against the back of the top teeth: *de, dar, diez, día.*
- ◆ When it occurs between vowels or at the end of a word, it is pronounced rather like English 'th' in 'then': *ciudad, cuidado, hablado, hablad, comido, comed, vivid, césped, Valladolid;* this happens therefore in most past participles (ending in -*ado, -ido*), *vosotros* imperatives (ending in -*ad, -ed, -id*), and the many words ending in -*ad -ed, -id* and -*ud.*
- ◆ In southern Spain, although not regarded as 'accepted' pronunciation, be prepared to find that the final or intervocalic (between vowels) -*d*- has disappeared altogether: *verdá, llegao.*

dañar *vt*   to damage, (harm) (used of goods, health, reputation) *estas mercancías se dañaron en tránsito*   these goods were damaged in transit; *si sigues fumando así te vas a dañar la salud*   if you go on smoking like that you'll damage your health
- **daño** *nm*   damage, harm, hurt: *la ciudad sufrió muchos daños*   the town suffered a lot of damage; *hacerle daño a alguien*   to hurt sb: *al placarme me hizo daño en el pie*   when tackling me he injured my foot; *hacerse daño (a algo)*   to hurt oneself (somewhere): *se ha hecho daño a la rodilla*   he has hurt his knee; *¡Cuidado, no te hagas daño!* Careful, don't hurt yourself!
- **dañino** or, less commonly, **dañoso** *adj*   harmful (*para*   to): *efectos dañinos*   harmful effects, *sustancia dañina*   harmful substance; *dañino para la salud*   harmful to health
- this group means 'hurt/harm' in sense

of 'damage'; not as severe as cf
herir/herida, lesión/lesionar; similar to
cf *lastimar(se);* for 'hurt' in sense of
'give pain', see *doler/dolor*

dar *vt pi: doy, das* etc; *ps: dé, des, dé, demos,
deis, den; pret: di, diste, dio, dimos, disteis,
dieron; imp subj: diera/diese* to give (in
most senses as in Eng)

□ also occurs in a number of
expressions, sometimes where you
might expect another verb: *dar los
buenos días/buenas noches* to say
good morning/night; *dar las gracias a
alguien por algo* to thank sb for sth;
dar miedo to frighten; *dar un susto a
alguien* to give sb a fright; *dar pena
(a alguien)* to make one feel sorry;
da pena verle así it makes you sorry
to see him like that; *dar de comer a*
to feed; *dieron las ocho* the clock
struck 8; *dar clase* to teach; *dar por*
to consider as; *le dieron por muerto*
they assumed he was dead; *dar con
alguien* to bump into, run across sb
(ie meet by chance); *dar contra* to
knock/bump into (literally); *dar en*
to hit (eg target); *dar a* (of
door/window) to look on to

□ dictionaries devote a whole page to
this verb: worth further research!

□ **dado** *adj/past part* given: *dadas las
circunstancias* given the
circumstances; *dado que* given that;
dado que no ha estado bien de salud
given that she hasn't been well

dato *nm* fact (piece of information):
necesitamos todos los datos we need all
the facts; *datos* data

□ some overlap but not necessarily same
as cf *hecho,* fact in sense of something
that has happened, an established truth

debajo *adv* underneath, below, sometimes
occurs as *por debajo: ¿Qué hay (por)
debajo?* What is there underneath?

□ **debajo de** *prep* under, underneath,
below: *debajo del suelo* under the floor

deber *vt* to have to, must + *inf: debes
hacerlo* you must do it

□ if there is any difference of emphasis
from cf *tener que/hay que, deber*
expresses moral duty (cf *noun* below),
but there is considerable overlap; in
neg *deber* means 'must not', whereas
no tener que can suggest merely 'no
obligation to'

□ condit *debería* etc means 'ought to':
deberías ir a verle you ought to go
and see him; 'ought to have (done)' is
debería or *debía haber* + *past part:
debería/debías haber ido a verle* you
ought to have gone to see him; you
can also use condit perfect of *deber* +
inf: habrías/hubieras debido ir a verle:
see a grammar for full explanation

□ can also express supposition or
probability, often followed by *de:
deben (de) estar en el cajón* they
must be in the drawer

□ also means 'to owe': *¿Cuánto le debo?*
How much do I owe you?

□ **deber** *nm* duty: *cumplir con su deber*
to carry out/fulfil one's duty

□ **debido** *adj* owing, due (*a* to):
debido a las circunstancias owing to
the circumstances; *debido a que*
owing to the fact that; *hacer algo con
debido cuidado* to do sth with due
care; *hacer lo debido* to do what
one ought, what is expected

decaer *vi decaigo, decaes; decaiga;
decayendo; decayó, decayeron;
decayera/decayese* to flag, wane,
decline: *le decaían las fuerzas* his
strength was flagging;

□ for 'decay' in sense of 'rot', use
pudrir(se) descomponer(se)

□ **decaído** *adj* low (in spirits): *se
encontraba muy decaída* she was
very low/depressed/despondent

decente *adj* decent (used similarly to Eng,
ie respectable or acceptable)

decepción *nf pl decepciones*

disappointment, let-down: *te vas a llevar una decepción enorme* you're going to have a great disappointment, be extremely disappointed

- □ for 'deception', use *engaño*
- □ **decepcionar** *vt* to disappoint, let down: *estar/quedar decepcionado* to be disappointed
- □ **decepcionante** *adj* disappointing
- □ similar to cf *desilusión/desilusionar, desengaño/desengañar*

decidir *vti* to decide

- □ **decidirse** *vr* to decide, make up one's mind; a shade more emphatic than straight *decidir*: *¿Te has decidido?* Have you made up your mind?
- □ NB *decidir* + *inf* or *decidirse a* + *inf* to decide to, make up one's mind to; cf *resolver, determinar*
- □ **decisión** *nf pl decisiones* decision (*de* + *inf* to): *tomaron la decisión de volver* they took/made the decision to go back
- □ **decisivo** *adj* decisive

decir *vt pi: digo, dices, dice, decimos, decís, dicen; ps: diga; tú imperative: di; ger: diciendo; fut/cond: diré/ía; past part: dicho; pret: dije, dijiste, dijo, dijimos, dijisteis, dijeron; imp subj: dijera/dijese* to say, tell

- □ a common but very irregular verb: ensure you know all parts, and don't confuse *pret* with that of *dar: dijo* s/he said, *dio* s/he gave; *dijeron* they said, *dieron* they gave
- □ occurs in many expressions, of which here are some of the most important: *¡di!, ¡dime!, ¡diga!, ¡dígame!* tell me!; formal form used as 'hello?' when answering phone; *se dice que* or *dicen que…* it is said, they say that…; *¿Cómo se dice…?* How do you say…? *decir que sí/no* to say yes/no; *querer decir* to mean: *¿Qué quieres decir?* What do you mean? *¿Qué quiere decir esta palabra?* What does this word mean?
- □ NB important difference between

decir que + *indic*, which just reports what sb says: *le dije que lo haría* I told him (that) I would do it; and *decir que* + *subjunc*: which tells sb to do sth: *le dije que lo hiciera* I told him to do it; (see a grammar for further explanation)

- □ **dicho** and *adj/past part* this, (in sense of said, aforesaid, aforementioned): *en dichas circunstancias* in these (ie the aforesaid circumstances; *en dicho caso* in this case
- □ NB some other uses: *¿Qué te tengo dicho?* What have I told you?, What have I just said?; *dicho y hecho* no sooner said than done; *dicho de otra manera* to put it another way
- □ dictionaries devote almost a page to this verb: worth further investigation!

declarar *vt* to declare, but also useful equivalent of 'to state'

- □ **declaración** *nf pl declaraciones* declaration, statement

dedicar *vt -que, -qué* to dedicate

- □ also devote, give eg time (*a* + *n* or *inf* to): *dedicó muchas horas a esta tarea* he devoted many hours to this task; *se dedicó a terminar el proyecto* he devoted himself to finishing the project
- □ **dedicación** *nf pl dedicaciones* dedication, devotion

dedo *nm* finger

- □ also toe (*dedo del pie* if clarification is needed!)
- □ NB *señalar algo con el dedo* to point to sth

deducir *vt pi: deduzco, deduces; ps: deduzca; pret: deduje, dedujiste, dedujo, dedujimos, dedujisteis, dedujeron; imp subj: dedujera/dedujese* to deduce; deduct

- □ **deducción** *nf pl deducciones* deduction (all senses)

defecto *nm* defect, but has wider meaning

of fault, flaw, shortcoming

- **defectuoso** *adj* defective, faulty, flawed: don't use *defectivo*, which is a grammar term (eg *verbo defectivo*)

defender *vt -ie-* to defend

- **defenderse** *vr* to defend oneself, but NB also to manage, get along: *se defiende en español* she gets along in Spanish
- **defensa** *nf* defence: *en defensa de* in defence of; also *nm*: defence, back (football etc)
- **defensivo** *adj* defensive; *nf* defensive: *estar a la defensiva* to be on the defensive

deficiencia *nf* deficiency

- also: handicap: *deficiencia física* physical handicap
- **deficiente** *adj* deficient, handicapped (*en* in); inadequate (used as school mark): *muy deficiente* very poor (about 3/10!)
- **déficit** *nm* deficit

definir *vt* to define

- **definido** *adj* (well!-)defined
- **definitivo** *adj* definitive, definite (though you might consider *firme* or *confirmado* for 'definite', depending on context)
- **definitivamente** *adv* definitely, once-and-for-all
- **definición** *nf pl definiciones* definition (all senses)

dejar *vt* to leave

- to leave sth (eg somewhere, or in some state): *dejé mi paraguas en el autobús* I left my umbrella on the bus; *deja un olor muy dulce* it leaves a very sweet smell; *siempre dejas la puerta abierta* you always leave the door open
- to abandon, go away from: *dejó a su marido* she left her husband; *dejó la casa a las ocho* s/he left the house at 8
- to leave sb (eg in a state): *le dejaron*

maltrecho they left him in a bad way

- NB: *dejar* must always have an object. For 'leave' in sense of 'depart' see *salir, partir, irse*
- also means 'to let', 'allow': usually + *inf*: *no le dejes entrometerse* don't let him interfere; *dejar caer* to let fall, drop; or can take *subjunc*: *deja que pasen* let them come through
- **dejar de** to stop, leave off (+ *inf* doing sth): *dejó de hablar* he stopped talking; *¿Cuándo va a dejar de llover?* When is it going to stop raining?; means the same as cf *cesar de*
- **dejarse** *vr + inf* to let oneself be + *past part*: *se deja dominar por los demás* he lets himself be dominated by the others; *no se deja aconsejar* she doesn't let herself be advised, ie she won't take advice
- **dejo** *nm* trace, hint: *con un dejo de ajo* with a hint of garlic
- **dejado** *adj* slovenly, unkempt (eg appearance); lazy, slack (person)
- **dejadez** *nf* slovenliness, laziness

delante *adv* in front (sometimes *por delante*): *yo me pongo (por) delante* I'll stand in front; *la parte de delante* the front (ie noun)

- **delante de** *prep* in front of: *delante del colegio* in front of the school; not exactly the same as cf *ante*
- **delantero/a** *adj* front: *rueda delantera* front wheel; also as *nmf* forward (football, hockey etc)
- **delantera** *nf* lead: *tomar la delantera* to take the lead; also forward line
- see also **adelante** forwards and **adelantar(se)** to advance, move forward

deleite *nm* delight (in the sense of amusement or pleasure); more abstract, less sensual than cf *delicia/delicioso*

- **deleitar** *vt* to delight (in this sense)
- **delicia** *nf* delight, usually in the sense of something you taste or

appreciate in a physical sense: *el cálido sol andaluz fue una delicia* the warm Andalusian sunshine was a delight/delightful

- **delicioso** *adj* delicious: *la comida está deliciosa* the food's delicious
- also 'delightful': *es una chica deliciosa* she's a lovely girl (implying good looks as well as other positive characteristics)
- produces a rather more sensual reaction than cf *deleite/deleitar*

deletrear *vt* to spell (out): *¿Quiere Vd deletrear su nombre?* Will you spell your name?; though for 'How do you spell it?' you usually say *¿Cómo se escribe?*

delgado *adj* thin (slim, slender); has positive connotation; cf more formal *esbelto*; not the 'skinny' connotation of cf *flaco*

- **delgadez** *nf* thinness, slimness, slenderness
- see also **adelgazar** to slim, to lose weight

delicado *adj* delicate (in most senses as in Eng)

- also used for 'sensitive', 'tricky': *es una situación delicada* it's a tricky situation; *es una cuestión delicada* it's a sensitive question
- and 'fussy': *es muy delicada con la comida* she's very fussy over her food
- **delicadeza** *nf* delicacy, daintiness; also sensitiveness, tact; fussiness: to correspond to the adjectival meanings above
- worth a further look in the dictionary at some of the more idiomatic meanings

delito *nm* crime, offence (don't confuse with *deleite* delight!)

- **delictivo** *adj* criminal: *actividades delictivas* criminal activities
- **delincuente** *nmf* delinquent, offender
- **delincuencia** *nf* delinquency

demanda *nf* demand (ie forceful request or claim)

- **demandar** *vt* to demand, request, stronger than cf *pedir*. Some overlap with cf *exigir, reivindicar*.

demás *adj inv* other, remaining, rest of: *¿Qué hacemos con las demás cosas?* What do we do with the other/remaining/rest of the things? *los demás miembros de la familia* the other members/rest of the members of the family

- also *pron lo demás* the rest; in *pl* the others: *y lo demás, ya lo sabes* and the rest you already know; *¿qué hacen los demás?* what are the others/rest doing?
- refers to what or who remains out of eg a quantity or group; often used as alternative to cf *el resto (sing)* or *los otras/las otras (pl)*
- other expressions: *por demás* excessively, extremely; *por lo demás* as for the rest, apart from that; *por lo demás está bien* apart from that, he's well
- **demasiado** *adv* too: *es demasiado lejos* it's too far
- NB the idea of 'too' (eg tight, big etc) when trying clothes is often contained in cf *muy: estos zapatos son muy grandes*, though *demasiado grandes* is perfectly correct
- NB when used as *adj* 'too much', 'too many', agreement is necessary: *había demasiadas urbanizaciones en la costa* there were too many building developments on the coast

demora *nf* delay; *sin demora* without delay; *una demora de media hora* half an hour's delay; means same as *retraso*

- **demorar** *vt* to take time in: *demoró tres meses en contestar* he took 3 months to reply (used in same way as cf *tardar*)

□ used in Sp, but more common in Sp Am

demostrar *vt -ue-* to demonstrate, show, prove: *eso demuestra que tengo razón* that shows/proves I'm right; *demostrar sentido común* to show common sense; *demostrar cómo hacer algo* to show/demonstrate how to do sth; used in this sense rather than 'point out', for which use *mostrar, indicar, señalar*

□ **demostración** *nf pl demostraciones* proof, demonstration, display; for eg political demonstration, use *manifestación*

□ NB no *n*: dem<u>o</u>stración!

dentro *adv* inside, within; *aquí/allí dentro* in here/there; *¿Qué hay dentro?* What's inside?

□ **dentro de** *prep* inside, within: *dentro de la caja* inside the box

□ also used in time context: *dentro de una semana* within a week, in a week's time; *dentro de poco* soon

□ See also *v adentrar*

denuncia *nf* denunciation, but also commonly 'report' (on accident): *hacer una denuncia* to make a report (for police)

□ **denunciar** *vt* denounce; report (in above sense)

departamento *nm* department (in many of English senses); but use *sección* for department in a store: *sección de caballeros* men's department

□ also compartment (in train)

depender *vi* to depend (NB *de* on): *depende* it depends; *depende de lo que diga mi madre* it depends on what my mother says

□ also 'to rely on': *no podemos depender de él* we can't rely on him; similar to cf *contar con*

□ and 'to be dependent on': *depende de su padre* he's dependent on his

father

□ **dependencia** *nf* dependence, dependency (*de* on)

□ **dependiente** *nm* **dependienta** *nf* shop assistant

deporte *nm* sport

□ **deportista** *nmf* sportsman/woman/person; can also be used as *adj*: *es muy deportista* s/he's very sporty/sporting

□ **deportivo** *adj* (to do with) sports: *revista deportiva* sports magazine; *zapatos deportivos* trainers; *coche deportivo* or just *deportivo nm* sports car; note also *polideportivo nm* sports centre

deprimir *vt* to depress (in sense of press down): *deprima la palanca* hold the handle down

□ to depress mentally: *esa película me deprimió* that film depressed me

□ **deprimirse** *vr* to get depressed: *siempre me deprimo en el invierno* I always get depressed in the winter; NB distinguish between this action of *becoming* depressed, and *being* depressed, ie in that state: use *estar deprimido*

□ **depresión** *nf pl depresiones* depression (all senses)

derecho *adj* right: *brazo derecho* right arm; *a mano derecha* on the right-hand side

□ straight, vertical, upright: *tu corbata no está derecha* your tie isn't straight; *en línea derecha* in a straight line; also used in this sense as *adv*: *siga todo derecho* carry straight on; in this use identical with cf *recto*

□ *nm* right (*a* to, *de* of): *¿Qué derecho tienes a hacer esto?* What right have you to do this? *derecho de asilo* right of asylum; *derechos humanos* human rights; *¿No hay derecho!* It's not fair!

□ also 'Law' (as a subject): *estudiar*

Derecho to study/read Law

- **derecha** *nf* right, right-hand side: *tuerza a la derecha* turn (to the) right; NB in directions don't confuse *a la derecha* to/on the right with *todo derecho* straight on: it could make quite a difference!
- also 'the (political) right': *la derecha ha ganado 50 escaños* the right have gained 50 seats
- **derechista** *adj* of the (political) right, right-wing: *tiene inclinaciones derechistas* s/he has rightist leanings, s/he inclines to the right
- also: *nmf* right-winger
- **derechismo** *nm* right-wing outlook or tendencies; cf opp *izquierdista/ismo*

derramar *vt* to spill, pour (a liquid accidentally): *derramé café sobre mi vestido* I spilled coffee over my dress (similar in this sense to cf *verter*); also used for 'shed' eg tears; and 'scatter' *derramó los papeles por el suelo* s/he scattered the papers over the floor

- **derramarse** *vr* to spill, pour, spread (in that sense): *el agua se derramaba por el suelo* the water was pouring/spreading over the floor
- **derramamiento** *nm* (action of) spilling, pouring, spreading: *derramamiento de sangre* bloodshed

derretir *vt -i-* to melt

- **derretirse** *vr* to melt, thaw: *el hielo se derritió* the ice melted/thawed; also to go crazy, go weak at the knees (*por alguien* over sb)

derribar *vt* to knock down, demolish (used mainly of buildings, but can mean: bring down (eg plane, government) or knock down (person))

- **derribarse** *vr* to tumble, fall down (esp of buildings)
- **derribo** *nm* demolition, knocking/ bringing down (in above senses)

derrochar *vt* to squander, waste (money, resources, etc); much the same as cf *malgastar,* cf *despilfarrar*

- **derroche** *nm* waste

derrotar *vt* to defeat, beat, esp in military or sporting context: *el Barcelona derrotado por el Real Madrid* Barcelona defeated by Real Madrid

- **derrota** *nf* defeat
- **derrotado/a** *adj* beaten; *nmf* loser: *los derrotados* the losers
- some overlap with cf *vencer*

derrumbar *vt* to knock/throw down (person); demolish (building etc); knock over (eg receptacle)

- **derrumbarse** *vr* to fall down, collapse (building); can also be used of hopes, ambitions, prices; has general idea of coming to an end, 'biting the dust!'!
- **derrumbamiento** *nm* collapse, demolition
- considerable overlap with cf *derribar/derribo* above

desafiar *vt -í-* to challenge: *desafiar a alguien a algo* to challenge sb to sth; *les desafió a otro partido* he challenged them to another match; *desafiar a alguien a + inf* to challenge sb to + verb: *te desafío a comprobarlo* I challenge you to prove it

- also to defy
- **desafío** *nm* challenge, defiance

desarrollar *vt* and **desarrollarse** *vr* to develop

- note difference between transitive use: *desarrolló su proyecto* he developed his project, and reflexive/intransitive: *el proyecto siguió desarrollándose* the project continued to develop
- can also have its literal meaning of 'unroll', 'unfurl' (ie *des-arrollar*)
- NB for developing a film, use *revelar*
- **desarrollo** *nm* development

des- = 'dis' or 'un-'

des- *prefix* gives negative meaning to verbs, adjectives, adverbs and nouns; corresponds largely to English 'dis-' or 'un-'; the following is a list of some common examples of its use in practice; please note that these are all straightforward examples of the opposite of the positive form, with no more observations to be made, except that ★ means see positive form in main text for full details of irregularities. Otherwise, if there is anything significant to say about a word beginning with *des-*, it is listed separately in the main text below.

des-	positive word	meaning
desabrochar *vt*	*abrochar*	unfasten
desacuerdo *nm*	*acuerdo*	disagreement
desafortunado *adj*	*afortunado*	unfortunate
desagradable *adj*	*agradable*	unpleasant
desagrado *nm*	*agrado*	displeasure
desaparecer *vi -zc-*	*aparecer*	disappear
desaprobar *vti -ue-*	*aprobar*	disapprove
desatar *vt*	*atar*	untie
descargar *vt -gue-, -gué*	*cargar*	unload
descomponer(se)★ *vt/vr*	*componer*	decompose, rot
desconectar *vt*	*conectar*	disconnect
descontento *adj*	*contento*	unhappy, discontent
desembarcar(se) *vt/vr -que-, -qué*	*embarcar(se)*	disembark
desigual *adj*	*igual*	unequal, uneven
desobedecer *vti -zc-*	*obedecer*	disobey
desocupado *adj*	*ocupado*	unoccupied, vacant
desorden *nm*	*orden*	disorder
desplegar(se) *vt/vr -ie-, -gue-, gûe*	*plegar(se)*	unfold
desventaja *nf*	*ventaja*	disadvantage but see also *inconveniente*
desventajoso *adj*	*ventajoso*	disadvantageous

desastre *nm* disaster; used much as Eng but NB *des-* not 'dis-'
- □ **desastroso** *adj* disastrous

desatender *vt -ie-* to disregard, neglect
- □ **desatendido** *adj/past part* neglected: *un aspecto desatendido* a neglected appearance

desayunar *vi* to have breakfast
- □ can be used as *vt*: *desayunamos tostadas* we had toast for breakfast
- □ cf similar use of *almorzar, cenar*
- □ lit means 'to un-fast', ie break-fast: *des-ayunar (ayunar/ayuno* fast)

- □ **desayuno** *nm* breakfast

descansar *vi* to rest, relax (in that sense), lit 'to un-tire': *¡Que descanses bien!* Sleep well!; *que en paz descanse* (may s/he) rest in peace
- □ can be used as *vt*: *descansaba la mano en la barrera* he was resting his hand on the barrier
- □ **descanso** *nm* rest, repose; *tomarse un día de descanso* to take a day off; interval, half-time (eg in theatre or match)
- □ **descansillo** *nm* landing (on stairs)

descartar *vt* to put aside, rule out: often occurs in useful phrase *descartar la posibilidad de/de que* (+ *subjunc*) to rule out the possibility of/that

descender *vi -ie-* to descend, go/come down, fall (in that sense); means much the same as cf *bajar*, just a bit more formal
- **descenso** *nm* descent, fall, drop: *un descenso de temperatura* a drop in temperature

descifrar *vt* to decipher, make out (eg writing)

descolgar *vt -ue-; -gue-, -gué* to take down (eg off hook), unhook
- NB used in sense of 'pick up', 'answer the phone'; cf opp *colgar* hang up

desconcertar *vt -ie-* to disconcert, take aback, bewilder
- **desconcertarse** *vr* to be disconcerted, taken aback, bewildered
- **desconcierto** *nm* bewilderment

desconfiar *vi -í- de algo/alguien* to mistrust sth/sb
- **desconfianza** *nf* mistrust, distrust, lack of confidence
- **desconfiado** *adj* distrustful, suspicious (*de* of)

desconocer *vt -zc-* to not know, be unaware of: *se desconocen sus motivos* his reasons are unknown; tends to be neg of *conocer*, whereas the similarly used cf *ignorar* is rather more the neg of *saber*, though there is a considerable overlap
- **desconocido/a** *adj* unknown; also *nmf* stranger

descontar *vt -ue-* to discount (eg a %)
- also to discount, in sense of 'leave out': *si descontamos a los demás* if we leave out the others, not counting the others
- **descuento** *nm* discount, reduction (eg in price): *descuentos de 20%* 20% off

describir *vt past part descrito* to describe (all senses)

descubrir *vt past part descubierto* to discover
- can also mean uncover
- **al descubierto** *adv quedar/ponerse al descubierto* to come to light, be revealed
- **descubrimiento** *nm* discovery
- **descubridor/a** *nmf* discoverer

descuido *nm* lack/lapse of attention; *en un momento de descuido* in a moment of inattention; *hacer algo con descuido* to be slapdash
- **descuidar** *vt* to neglect
- **descuidarse** *vr* to not pay attention, let one's attention stray
- **descuidado** *adj* careless
- all denote lack of *cuidado* care

desde *prep* (in a time context) since: *desde 1975* since 1975; *desde su niñez* since his childhood; *desde entonces* since then; *desde … hasta …* from … until: *desde 1975 hasta 2000* from 1975 until 2000
- NB when used in conjunction with verb need for present/imperfect tense if action is/was still continuing: *desde entonces ya no fuma* since then he hasn't smoked; *desde entonces ya no fumaba* since then he hadn't smoked
- also means 'for' in combination *desde hace/hacía: espero desde hace media hora* I've been waiting half an hour; *esperaba desde hacía media hora* I had been waiting half an hour; consult a grammar for a full explanation of these last 2 points
- also (in a space context) 'from'; often emphasises the distance more than merely using *de: hemos venido desde Cádiz* we've come (all the way) from Cádiz; *conozco el texto desde aquí* I know the text from here (on); *los tenemos desde 12 euros para arriba*

we have from 12 euros upwards; *desde
… hasta …* from … to/as far as …;
*fuimos andando desde la plaza hasta la
estación* we walked from the square
to the station

desdén *nm pl desdenes* disdain, scorn
(*por* for)
- **desdeñar** *vt* to disdain, scorn
- **desdeñoso** *adj* disdainful, scornful

desear *vt* to desire, wish, want
- similar to cf *querer* in its meaning of
'want/wish', but slightly more
polite/formal: *¿Qué desea?* What
would you like? ie can I help you?
- preferred where *querer* would be
ambiguous: *embarazo no deseado*
unwanted pregnancy
- used to wish sb sth: *os deseamos buen
viaje* we wish you a good trip
- NB 'to want sb to do sth' needs
subjunc: *deseamos que lo hagan
cuanto antes* we want them to do it
as soon as possible
- **deseo** *nm* wish, desire: (*de* to) *el
deseo de tener éxito* the wish/desire
to succeed; *que + subjunc* that: *es
nuestro deseo que tengas éxito* it's
our wish that you are successful
- **deseoso** *adj* longing, eager (*de*
for/to) (often stronger than just
'wanting'): *estar deseoso de ayudar*
to be longing/eager to help

desempeñar *vt* to fulfil, carry out, play:
desempeñar un papel/una función to
play a role/fulfil a function (you can also
use *jugar un papel*)
- **desempeño** *nm* fulfilment,
performance (of function or role etc)

desempleo *nm* unemployment
- **desempleado/a** *adj* or *nmf*
unemployed (person)
- means exactly same as cf *paro/parado*
in this sense

desengañar *vt* to disillusion, disappoint;
- **desengañarse** *vr* to be

disillusioned, disappointed
- **desengaño** *nm* disillusionment,
disappointment: *llevarse un desengaño*
to have a disappointment
- see also *decepcionar/decepción,
desilusiónar(se)/desilusión*

desenvolver *vt* -ue-, *past part: desenvuelto*
to unwrap
- **desenvolverse** *vr* to cope,
perform: *¿Cómo se desenvolvió en la
entrevista?* How did s/he
cope/perform in the interview?; *se
está desenvolviendo estupendamente*
s/he is managing superbly well
- **desenvuelto** *adj* self-assured,
confident

desesperar *vt* to drive to despair: *me
desespera su actitud* his attitude makes
me despair
- perhaps more often used as *vi* 'to
despair', 'lose hope' (*de* of):
desespero de volver a verle I
despair/give up hope of seeing him
again
- **desesperarse** *vr* to despair, get
exasperated (*de* of/with): *me
desespero de su comportamiento* I
despair of/am exasperated with his
behaviour
- **desesperación** *nf* despair,
desperation
- **desesperado** *adj* desperate;
desesperadamente *adv*
desperately
- **desesperante** *adj* exasperating,
maddening
- all based on the negative of *esperar*
'hope', so meanings indicate loss of
hope in some form

desgastar *vt* to wear out (clothes etc)
- **desgaste** *nm* wear, wear and tear;
also waste (in this sense): *un desgaste
de recursos* a waste of resources
- NB prefix *des-* intensifies rather than
contradicts meaning of *gastar*!

desgracia *nf* misfortune, piece of bad

luck: *por desgracia* unfortunately

- **desgraciado** *adj* unfortunate, hapless; can be used as *nmf* hapless, wretched person
- **desgraciadamente** *adv* unfortunately
- NOT 'disgrace' in sense of something disgraceful: use *vergüenza* or *escándalo*; you can, however, *caer en la desgracia* to fall into disgrace

deshacer *vt* (has all irregularities of cf *hacer*) to undo, unpick, take apart: *deshizo todo lo que había logrado* he undid all that he had achieved

- **deshacerse** *vr* to come undone, come apart, disintegrate: *el motor se deshizo en mil fragmentos* the engine disintegrated into 1,000 pieces
- NB also *deshacerse de algo/alguien* to get rid of sth/sb: *nos deshicimos de nuestro viejo coche* we got rid of our old car
- **deshecho** *adj/past part* undone; broken, in pieces (eg apparatus, limb); also (person): *estar deshecho* to be exhausted, shattered

desierto *nm* desert, but also used as *adj* deserted: *la playa estaba desierta* the beach was deserted

desilusionar *vt* to disillusion, disappoint

- **desilusionarse** *vr* to be(come) disillusioned, disappointed
- **desilusión** *nf pl desilusiones* disappointment, disillusion
- cf *decepcionar(se), decepción* and *desengañar(se), desengaño*: there is little difference between the three words in the sense of 'disappoint(ment)'

deslizar *vt -ce-, -cé* to slip (ie to slip sth eg somewhere) *deslicé el papel debajo del libro* I slipped the paper under the book

- **deslizarse** *vr* to slide, glide, slither: *los patinadores se deslizaban sobre el hielo* the skaters slid/glided over the ice

- also 'slip (up)', ie by accident
- similar to cf *resbalar* but perhaps has a wider more positive sense of smooth movement, than the more limited accidental or involuntary slipping or sliding!

desmayarse *vr* to faint, swoon (nothing to do with dismay, see *asombrar(se), asombro*)

desnudar *vt* to undress (sth/sb); **desnudarse** *vr* to undress (ie oneself)

- **desnudo** *adj* naked, nude, bare; **desnudez** *nf* nakedness, nudity
- NB the prefix *des-* is meaningless here: *nudo* means 'a knot'!

desorden *nm pl desórdenes* disorder, but often just means untidiness; *dejar algo en desorden* to leave sth in a mess

- **desordenado** *adj* disorderly, untidy, in a mess
- **desordenadamente** *adv* in a disorderly manner/fashion, untidily

despacho *nm* office; little different from *oficina*, though tends to be smaller, more intimate; can also mean study

despacio *adv* slowly; more common than cf *lentamente*; NB it's an adverb, not an adjective: slow is *lento*

despedir *vt -i-* to dismiss, fire, sack (from job)

- to see off: *vamos a despedirte a la estación* we're coming to the station to see you off
- **despedirse** *vr* to say goodbye, take one's leave (*de* to/of): *se despidió de nosotros y subió al tren* he said goodbye to us and got on the train
- **despedida** *nf* (act of saying) goodbye, farewell: 'send-off'
- **despido** *nm* dismissal, sacking

despegar *vt -gue-, -gué* to unstick, peel (sth) off

- but most frequent use as *vi* to take off (of plane)

- **despegarse** *vr* to come unstuck, peel off
- **despegue** *nm* take-off

despertar *vt -ie-* to wake (sb) up;
- **despertarse** *vr* to wake up (ie oneself)
- **despierto** *adj* awake: *quedarse despierto* to stay awake
- **despertador** *nm* alarm clock

despistarse *vr* to get confused, muddled: *estar/sentirse despistado* to be/feel confused (ie you are somehow off *la pista*)

desplazarse *vr -ce-, -cé* to move/get around, travel (surprisingly common, perhaps a shade journalistic, alternative to *ir, viajar*, etc)
- **desplazamiento** *nm* movement, journey, trip (in sense of above)

desprenderse *vr* to come away, come loose (eg of paint, tiles etc); also to let go of: *no quiere desprenderse de su dinero* he won't let go of his money

después *adv* (ie when not attached to another part of speech) after, afterwards, later: *eso ocurrió después* that happened afterwards/later
- *prep después de* after (+ *n, pron* or *inf*): *después de la guerra* after the war; *después de esto* after this; *después de llegar* after arriving
- *conj* (ie before verb in tense) *después (de) que: después de que llegaron* after they arrived; *después de que lleguen* after they arrive; NB need for subjunc when referring to a future event
- NB *yo llegué después que usted* I arrived after you (arrived): *que* not *de* when a clause is understood
- see a grammar for a full explanation of these last 2 points

destacar *vt -que-, -qué* to emphasise, stress, bring out, enhance (ie to make stand out in some way)

- **destacarse** *vr* to stand out: *la torre se destacaba contra el cielo* the tower stood out against the sky; *se destaca por su hermosura* it stands out for its beauty
- **destacado** *adj* prominent, outstanding

destino *nm* destiny, fate
- also destination: *el tren con destino a Córdoba* the train going to Córdoba

destreza *nf* skill: *tener mucha destreza* to be very skilful
- NB a skill you have to learn is best translated by *técnica*
- **diestro** *adj* skilful, dextrous (ie clever in manipulating eg hands, brain etc)

destrozar *vt -ce-, -cé* to destroy, shatter, smash (sth/sb)
- **destrozarse** *vr* to be shattered, destroyed (ie to break into *trozos*): more specific and graphic than all-purpose *destruir* below
- **destrozado** *adj/past part* shattered, smashed: *tengo los nervios destrozados* my nerves are in shreds/tatters
- **destrozo** *nm* damage (often pl): *los destrozos del tiempo* the ravages of time

destruir *vt pi: destruyo, -uyes, -uye, -uyen; ps: destruya; ger: destruyendo; pret: destruyó, destruyeron; imp subj: destruyera/destruyese* to destroy
- **destrucción** *nf pl destrucciones* destruction

desvelar *vt* to keep awake, prevent from sleeping: *nos desvelaba el ruido de la calle* we were kept awake by street noise
- **desvelarse** *vr* to stay awake, be unable to sleep: *me desvelé toda la semana* I couldn't sleep all week
- **desvelo** *nm* sleeplessness

desventaja *nf* disadvantage: *estar en desventaja* to be at a disadvantage
- can be used in all senses, though

when talking of the disadvantages of sth, *los inconvenientes* is often used

desviar *vt -í-* to divert

- **desviarse** *vr* to branch off, turn off: *se desvió de la carretera* he turned off the main road; *desviarse del tema* to stray off the subject
- **desviación** *nf pl desviaciones* or **desvío** *nm* diversion, detour (eg on road)

detener *vt pi*: *detengo, detienes, detiene, detienen*; *ps*: *detenga*; *tú imperative*: *detén*; *fut/condit*: *detendré/ía*; *pret*: *detuve, detuviste, detuvo, detuvimos, detuvisteis, detuvieron*; *imp subj*: *detuviera/detuviese* (use *tener* for model) to stop, detain; *le detuve para hablarle* I stopped him in order to speak to him

- also: to arrest
- **detenerse** *vr* to stop: *el autobús se detuvo* the bus stopped; *me detuve para hablarle* I stopped (ie myself) to speak to him
- NB difference between transitive and intransitive use, ie bringing sb/sth else to a halt, and stopping yourself; meaning is much the same as cf *parar(se)* used in this sense
- **detenido** *adj* arrested, detained; also has useful meaning lengthy, thorough: *hizo un examen detenido* he made a thorough examination
- **detenidamente** *adv* lengthily, thoroughly, at length: *examinó detenidamente la respuesta* he examined the reply at length

deteriorar *vt* to spoil, damage (cause) wear: *el temporal ha deteriorado la carretera* the bad weather has damaged the road

- **deteriorarse** *vr* to become damaged/worn; to deteriorate
- **deterioro** *nm* damage, wear (and tear), deterioration (in above sense)
- NB wider meaning and use than Eng deteriorate/deterioration, and

that the verb can and often does have a direct object

determinar *vti* to determine (in most senses)

- NB *determinar* + *inf* or *determinarse a* + *inf* to decide/determine/make up one's mind to + verb; similar to cf *decidir(se), resolver(se)*
- **determinado** *adj* determined, but NB also particular, certain: *en determinados casos* in certain cases

detrás *adv* behind: *los otros seguían detrás* the others were following behind; sometimes used with *por* to mean 'from behnd', 'at/from the rear': *por detrás hay otra puerta* there's another door at the back; *atacaron por detrás* they attacked from behind

- **detrás de** *prep* behind, at the back of; use this form to link to a noun: *estaban detrás de la barrera* they were behind the barrier
- NB not same as cf *atrás, tras*, though *atrás* is used with this meaning in Sp Am

devolver *vt -ue-, past part: devuelto* to give back, return (in that sense): *me devolvió el dinero* he gave the money back to me

- NB 'return' in sense of go/come back is *volver*

día *nm* day (NB it's *masc*); NB also *pl buenos días* good morning; *todos los días/cada día* every day; *día tras día* day after day, day in, day out; *un día de éstos* one of these days; *el día que …* the day that/when (+ *subjunc* if referring to future): *el día que te cases* the day you get married

- **diario** *adj* daily: *hay un vuelo diario* there's a daily flight
- *nm* daily paper; diary (ie record of events past); but use *agenda* for diary of future engagements!; *telediario* television news
- **diariamente** *adv* daily, every day: *se vacía el buzón diariamente* the

letter box is emptied every day/daily

diente *nm* tooth: refers to tooth/teeth in general, though cf *muela* is as commonly used in this sense

dieta *nf* diet (much the same as alternative *régimen*): *ponerse/estar de dieta* to go/be on a diet

diferencia *nf* difference; *a diferencia de* unlike, in contrast to: *a diferencia de su hermano, Merche estudia mucho* unlike/in contrast to her brother, Merche studies a lot
- **diferente** *adj* different; see also *distinto*
- **diferenciar** *vt* to differentiate; **diferenciarse** *vr* to differ, be different (*de* from): *¿En qué se diferencian estas imágenes?* How do these images differ/are these images different?
- **diferir** *vi -ie-, -i-* to differ (*de* from) (perhaps more formal than *diferenciarse*); can also mean 'to defer', 'postpone': *se ha diferido una decisión* a decision has been deferred/postponed (see also *aplazar*)

difícil *adj* difficult
- NB stress is on the middle *-í-*, not the last one!
- can also mean unlikely, improbably: *veo muy difícil que tenga éxito* I think it very unlikely s/he'll succeed
- **difícilmente** *adj* (NB handy word with an idiomatic use) with difficulty, hardly: *se ve difícilmente* you can see it with difficulty, you can hardly see it; *difícilmente vamos a caber aquí todos* we're all going to have a job to get in here
- **dificultad** *nf* difficulty
- **dificultar** *vt* to make difficult, obstruct (in that sense): *la lluvia dificultaba el juego* the rain was making play difficult, was obstructing play

dimitir *vi* to resign (*de* from)
- NB not 'dismiss': this is an intransitive verb, used by person who leaves job, post etc; for 'dismiss' in sense of 'sack' use *despedir*
- **dimisión** *nf pl dimisiones* resignation (in above sense); 'dismissal' is *despido*

dirección *nf pl direcciones* direction (in most senses); cf *sentido*, which is also used for direction of movement: *dirección única/sentido único* one-way; *dirección Madrid* in the Madrid direction
- also 'address' (*señas* is a common alternative)
- and 'management' (refers to the people who run an organisation or the act of doing so)
- and 'steering' (of vehicle)
- **directo** *adj* direct: *tren directo* direct/through train; *en directo desde* (broadcast) live from
- **director(a)** *nmf* director, manager, headteacher: in general, the person in charge of an organisation (cf however *gerente*)
- **dirigir** *vt -jo, -ja-; dirijo, diriges; dirija* to direct, manage (in that sense)
- also 'to address' (sth to sb), 'direct': *la publicidad va dirigida a los niños* the advertising is directed/aimed at children; *dirigir la palabra a alguien* to address/speak to sb; *dirigir la mirada a alguien* to look/glance at sb
- **dirigirse** *vr* (*a/hacia* to/towards) to make for, head for sth/somewhere: *se dirigió hacia el puente* he made for the bridge: implies more determination or purpose than just *ir*; *dirigirse a alguien* to address, talk/write to sb: *Vd tendrá que dirigirse al director* you'll have to talk/write to the manager

disculpa *nf* excuse, apology: *pedir disculpas a alguien* to make an apology to sb; *¡No valen disculpas!* No excuses!
- **disculpar** *vt* to excuse: *¡Disculpen*

los errores! Excuse the mistakes!
¡Discúlpeme! I'm sorry!, I do
apologise!

- **disculparse** *vr* to apologise (*con
  alguien por algo* to sb for sth): *me
  disculpé con ellos por haber llegado
  tarde* I apologised to them for
  arriving late
- NB points to watch: the imperative
  ending (*-a, -ad, -e, -en*), depending on
  the form of 'you' you are using;
  similar in use to cf *excusa/excusar(se)*
  and *perdonar*, but the correspondence
  is not total, so check against these
- for 'sorry' see *perdón/perdonar* and
  sentir

discurso *nm* speech (wider meaning than
Eng 'discourse')

discutir *vt* to discuss

- NB also **discutir** *vi* to argue,
  quarrel (*de/sobre* about/over):
  discutieron de la religión they argued
  over religion; *¡No (me) discutas!*
  Don't argue (with me)!; cf also *reñirse,
  disputar(se)*; not *argüir* to argue in
  sense of 'to form an argument'
- **discusión** *nf pl* discusiones
  discussion; argument (in that sense)

disfrutar *vti* to enjoy oneself, have fun:
estoy disfrutando I'm enjoying myself
(similar to cf *divertirse*); *disfruta viendo la
televisión* s/he enjoys watching
television; *¡que disfrutes!* enjoy yourself!

- also 'to enjoy' (benefit from) (either +
  dir obj or *de algo* sth): *la casa disfruta
  (de) una buena situación* the house
  enjoys a good position; cf also *gozar*
- **disfrute** *nm* enjoyment; use, benefit

disgusto *nm* upset, ie sth that causes
displeasure, dislike or annoyance: *¡Qué
disgusto!* How annoying/upsetting!; *se
va a llevar un disgusto enorme* s/he's
going to be extremely upset, s/he's not
going to like it at all

- **disgustar** *vt* to upset: *eso me
  disgustó mucho* that upset me a lot/

I was very upset by that
- for 'disgust(ing)', see *repugnar/
  repugnancia*, and phrases using
  asco/asqueroso

disminuir *vti pi:* disminuyo, -uyes, -uye,
-uyen; *ps:* diminuya; *ger:* disminuyendo;
pret: disminuyó, disminuyeron; *imp subj:*
disminuyera/disminuyese to diminish,
lessen, reduce; fall, drop, get smaller: *la
cantidad de atracos ha disminuido* the
number of muggings has reduced/
fallen/decreased; *disminuyó la velocidad*
s/he reduced speed/slowed down

- **disminución** *nf pl* disminuciones
  diminution, lessening, fall/drop (in
  that sense): *una disminución de los
  precios* a fall/reduction in prices

disolver *vt* **disolverse** *vr* -ue-, *past part*
disuelto to dissolve (in most senses)

disparar *vt* to fire, shoot (eg a gun, an
arrow); also *vi disparar sobre alguien/algo*
to fire at sb/sth

- NB for 'to shoot a person or animal',
  see *fusilar, matar a tiros*
- **disparo** *nm* shot (ie action or noise
  of firing)

disponer *vi* (has all the irregularities of
poner + tú *imperative:* dispón) *disponer de
algo* to have sth at one's disposal: *no
dispongo de tanto dinero* I don't have so
much money available

- for 'to dispose of sth', use *deshacerse
  de*
- **dispuesto** *adj* (*a* to) *estar dispuesto
  a* to be disposed, ready, prepared to
- **disposición** *nf* disposal: *tener algo a
  su disposición* to have sth at one's
  disposal; NB when 'disposal' means
  'getting rid of' it may be better to
  reconstruct sentence to use verb
  deshacerse de

disputa *nf* quarrel, argument (in that
sense)

- **disputar** *vt* (*algo a alguien*) to
  dispute sth with sb, to challenge sb

about sth

- □ **disputarse** *vr* to quarrel, argue (see also *discutir*)

distancia *nf* distance

- □ NB used in asking 'how far?' *¿A qué distancia está Avila de Segovia?* How far is Avila from Segovia?

distinguir *vt* -go-, -ga-: *distingo, distingues; distinga* to distinguish (in most senses)

- □ **distinto** *adj* distinct: NB used as synonym for *diferente* different: *Carlos es muy distinto* Carlos is very different
- □ **distinción** *nf pl distinciones* distinction; but also difference: *hay una gran distinción entre los dos* there's a big difference between the two

distraer *vt* (has all irregularities of *traer*) to distract

- □ **distraerse** *vr* to be distracted, let one's attention wander; also to amuse oneself: *¿Cómo te distraes en tus ratos libres?* How do you relax in your spare time?
- □ **distraído** *adj* absent-minded, vague (use *ser*); distracted (use *estar*)
- □ **distracción** *nf pl distracciones* entertainment; distraction

distribuir *vt* -y- *distribuyo, -uyes, -uye, -uyen; distribuya; distribuyendo; distribuyó, -uyeron; distribuyera/-uyese* to distribute

- □ **distribución** *nf pl distribuciones* distribution, allocation

disuadir *vt* to dissuade (*a alguien de algo* sb from sth): *me disuadió de mi proyecto* he dissuaded me from/talked me out of my plan; *a alguien de + inf* or *de que + subjunc* sb from doing sth; *me disuadió de hacerlo* or *me disuadió de que lo hiciera* he dissuaded me from doing it

diverso *adj* diverse

- □ NB use in *pl*: several, various: *el público constaba de diversas nacionalidades* the audience was

made up of various nationalities; *se encuentra en diversas ciudades* you can find it in various towns

- □ some overlap with cf *varios*

divertir *vt* -ie-, -i- to amuse: *me divirtió mucho su respuesta* his reply amused me a great deal/I was very amused by his reply

- □ **divertirse** *vr* to amuse oneself, enjoy oneself, have a good time: *te divertirás mucho en Beniform* you'll have a very good time in Benidorm
- □ **diversión** *nf pl diversiones* fun, amusement, entertainment: *hay muchas diversiones* there's lots of entertainment; for 'diversion' in traffic sense, use *desviación* or *desvío*
- □ **divertido** *adj* amusing, funny (use *ser*): *la película fue muy divertida*; NB when used with *estar* means amused (often used ironically): *estaba muy divertido* I was very amused (but not really!)

doblar *vti* to double (basically): *el gobierno ha doblado el impuesto* the government has doubled the tax; but has various other common meanings:

- □ to fold (ie in two, eg paper), bend: *doblar el papel aquí* fold the paper here
- □ to turn (corner): *doblamos la esquina* we turned the corner
- □ to dub (film): *una película doblada al catalán* a film dubbed into Catalan
- □ **doblarse** *vr* intransitive use of above meanings: *se ha doblado el impuesto* the tax has doubled; *los árboles se doblaban en el viento* the trees were bending in the wind
- □ **doble** *adj* or *nm* double: *una ración doble* a double portion; *pagamos el doble del precio* we paid double the price; also used in scoring in various games and sports; and *pl dobles* doubles

doler *vi* -ue- to hurt; the most common way to say that a part of your body hurts or that you have a pain in it: *¿Dónde te duele?* Where does it hurt?; *me duele la cabeza* I've got a headache; NB if what hurts is plural, so is the verb: *le duelen las piernas* his legs ache

□ can also be used to express emotions of hurt or sorrow: *me duele mucho decirte esto* it hurts me a great deal/I'm very sorry to tell you this

□ **dolor** *nm* pain, can be used as an alternative way to express aches and pains: *tengo dolor de cabeza/muelas* etc I've got a headache/toothace, etc; also 'grief', 'sorrow': *me da mucho dolor decirte esto* it gives me great pain/sorrow to tell you this

□ NB neither the verb *doler* nor the noun *dolor* by themselves can make the Eng distinction between 'pain/hurt', which is usually sharper, and 'ache', which can be a duller but perhaps more continuous sensation, and to explain the exact sensation eg to a doctor, it may sometimes necessary to qualify these with an adjective or adverb: *es un dolor agudo* it's a sharp pain; *es un dolor sordo y continuo* it's a dull, nagging ache

□ **doloroso** *adj* painful: *es una enfermedad dolorosa* it's a painful illness

□ **dolorido** *adj* in pain, aching: *estar todo dolorido* to be all aches and pains

domicilio *nm* address; mainly used on official forms for more common *dirección* or *señas*; *sin domicilio fijo* of no fixed abode

don *m* **doña** *f* title used with first name or first name plus surname, never with surname alone; spelt with small *d*, though the abbreviation uses a capital: *don Federico/don Federico Blásquez; doña Carmen, doña Carmen Blásquez; D. Federico, Dª. Carmen*

□ used as a respectful form of address between the over-familiar (for the

situation) straight first name and the over-formal *Sr/Sra* + surname

□ that said, given the tendency to familiarity and the common use of *tú/vosotros* in Spain, this form of address is becoming somewhat old-fashioned; not so in Sp Am

donde *adv* where: *el pueblo donde nací* the village where I was born

□ **¿dónde?** *interrog adv* where?: needs accent whenever it is asking the question 'where?': *¿dónde vives?* where do you live?; even if the question is indirect: *no sé dónde vives* I don't know where you live; see a grammar for a full explanation of indirect questions

□ both statement and question form link with *a* and *de*: *adonde/adónde* to where(?), *de donde/de dónde* from where(?)

□ **dondequiera que** *conj* wherever (+ *subjunc*): *dondequiera que esté lo encontraré* wherever it is, I'll find it

dormir *vi* -ue-, -u- to sleep

□ **dormirse** *vr* to go to sleep, fall asleep

□ **dormitorio** *nm* can mean dormitory, but is the usual word for bedroom; for hotel room use *habitación*

□ **dormido** *adj* asleep: *estar dormido* to be asleep

droga *nf* drug; often used in *sing* to refer to 'drugs', ie the drug problem: *el problema de la droga*

□ **drogar** *vt* -gue-, -gué to drug; **drogarse** *vr* to take drugs

□ **droguería** *nf* shop selling hardware, household goods and cleaning materials, NOT a chemist, NOR a drugstore in American sense

duda *nf* doubt: *no cabe duda* there's no (room for) doubt; *sin duda* without doubt, doubtless

□ **dudar** *vti* to doubt: *lo dudo* I

doubt it; NB *dudar que* doubt whether needs subjunc: *dudo que lo sepan* I doubt whether they know
- also 'to hesitate': *¿Por qué dudas?* Why do you hesitate?; *dudar en + inf* to hesitate to/in: *dudaron en responder* they hesitated in replying (cf *vacilar* in this sense)
- **dudoso** *adj* doubtful: *ver dudoso que + subjunc* to think it doubtful whether; dubious: *de aspecto dudoso* of dubious appearance; hesitant

dulce *adj* sweet (sugary); *este postre está muy dulce* this dessert is too sweet
- also suggests softness, gentleness: *una persona muy dulce* a very gentle/kind/sweet person; *música dulce* soft/sweet music; *agua dulce*

fresh (as opposed to salt) water
- **dulces** *nmpl* sweets
- **dulzura** *nf* sweetness, softness, ie quality described by *dulce*

durante *prep* during
- means 'for' a completed period of time usually in the past: *vivimos allí durante seis años* we lived there for 6 years; *no se movió durante todo el día* he didn't move all day long; emphasises the time span more than cf *por*
- **durar** *vi* to last
- **duración** *nf* duration

duro *nm* often-used expression meaning a 5-peseta coin; *veinte duros* 100 pesetas; can it survive the introduction of the euro …?

E

E is one of the five Spanish vowels.
- ◆ It always has the same full value wherever it occurs: *el, este, elemento, pensé, leyese.*
- ◆ It forms diphthongs both ways round with -*i*- (-*y* on the end of a word) and -*u*-: *seis, ley; siete, metieron; nueve, vuelve; Europa.*
- ◆ It does not form diphthongs with -*a*- and -*o*- or itself, which are pronounced separately: *lea, leo, lee; cae, roe, roer.*

echar *vt* basically: to throw (in most general sense, less specific than cf *arrojar, tirar, lanzar*), but a word that has numerous idiomatic uses:
- to add, put in (eg in recipe): *echar la sal* put in the salt
- to pour out: *echó el café* s/he poured out the coffee

- to give off, emit: *echar gases nocivos* to give off noxious fumes
- to throw/chuck out: *el profesor le echó de la clase* the teacher chucked him out of the class
- to post: *voy a echar estas cartas (al correo)* I'm going to post these letters
- as *vi + a + inf* to begin to (usually suddenly): *echó a llorar* s/he burst out crying/into tears
- **echarse** *vr* literally to throw oneself, but frequently to lie down, stretch out: *se echó en el sofá* s/he lay down on the settee; cf *tumbarse*
- NB **estar echado** to be lying down; cf *estar tumbado*
- *echar(se)* has quite a number of other uses: impossible to list them all here, so follow it up in a dictionary!

economía *nf* economy (in general sense)
- NB *hacer economías* to economise, make savings
- economics (the subject): *estudiar economía* to study economics
- **económico** *adj* economical, but

also 'cheap' in the sense of 'costing less': *es más económico así* it's cheaper that way
- **economizar** *vti -ce-, -cé* to save (on), economise: *economizar el esfuerzo* to save effort

edad *nf* age
- how old: *¿qué edad tiene Vd?* how old are you?; *a la edad de* at the age of; *de edad avanzada* of advanced age
- period of history: *la Edad de Oro* the Golden Age; *la Edad Media* (NB *sing*) the Middle Ages

educación *nf* education (in general); often includes idea of 'upbringing', ie the whole formation of the young person, as opposed to cf *enseñanza* which basically means education in the narrower sense of 'teaching'
- **educar** *vt -que-, -qué* to educate, bring up (in same sense)
- **educado** *adj* educated, brought up, but also often well–mannered, cultured; *mal educado* ill-mannered, 'rude' in that sense

efecto *nm* effect: *hacer efecto* to have an effect; *efecto invernadero* greenhouse effect
- *nmpl efectos* property, goods: *efectos de consumo* consumer goods
- **en efecto** *adv* in fact, indeed, actually
- don't confuse with *afecto* affection!
- **efectivo** *adj* effective; also *nm* cash: *pagar en efectivo* to pay cash
- **efectivamente** *adv* effectively; in fact, indeed, actually; often used as an emphatic affirmative answer: – *Entonces ¿tú le crees? – ¡Efectivamente!* – 'So you believe him?' – 'Indeed I do!'
- **efectuar** *vt -ú-: efectúo, efectúas; efectúe* to carry out, put into effect: *efectuar una visita* to carry out/make a visit
- **eficaz** *adj pl eficaces* efficacious; ie

effective (cf *efectivo*): rather than efficient (cf *eficiente*)
- **eficacia** *nf* efficacity, effectiveness (*efectividad*)
- **eficiente** *adj* efficient, ie works well, without problems or fuss
- **eficiencia** *nf* efficiency
- there is clearly some overlap between these concepts but perhaps **eficaz/-cia** put more emphasis on the end product and **eficiente/-cia** on the process of reaching it

ℹ *NB: these words begin ej- not ex-* **❗**

ejecutar *vt* to execute, carry out (used much as in Eng)
- **ejecutivo** *adj* executive (as Eng); urgent, pressing: *negocio ejecutivo* urgent business

ejemplo *nm* example: *por ejemplo* for example
- **ejemplar** *adj* exemplary; also *nm* copy (of book, magazine, etc); (for 'copy' as result of copying, use *copia*)

ejercer *vt -zo, -za-: ejerzo, ejerces; ejerza, ejerzas* to exercise (in its wide sense, as in Eng): *ejercer su autoridad/profesión/influencia* to exercise one's authority/profession/influence
- **ejercicio** *nm* exercise (in most Eng senses: physical, educational, and practice of profession etc)

ejército *nm* army
- not cf *armada*: that's the navy!

elaborar *vt* to elaborate; sometimes used for cf *fabricar* to manufacture
- **elaboración** *nf* elaboration; also manufacture
- for *adj* 'elaborate' use *complicado, detallado*

elegante *adj* elegant
- but also has wider sense 'smart', 'stylish', 'tasteful' (esp clothes); used of

both women and men: *¡qué elegante estás!* how smart you look!
- **elegancia** *nf* elegance; smartness, stylishness, tastefulness

elegir *vt -i-; -jo, -ja-: elijo, eliges; elija* to choose, select (in this sense, same as cf *escoger*)
- also: elect
- **elección** *nf pl elecciones* election; selection, choice

elemento *nm* element (in most Eng senses)
- also chap, bloke, guy: *es un buen elemento* he's a good bloke
- NB **elemental** *adj* elementary

elevado *adj* elevated, high
- often used of prices: *un precio muy elevado* a very high price
- and of thoughts: *tener pensamientos elevados* to have lofty thoughts
- **elevar** *vt* to raise (eg prices): *han elevado el precio de la electricidad* they have raised/increased the price of electricity
- **elevarse** *vr* to rise, go up (eg prices or buildings); *la torre se elevaba en el horizonte* the tower rose on the horizon
- **elevación** *nf pl elevaciones* elevation (in all Eng senses); also act of rising or raising corresponding to the associated words above

eliminar *vt* to eliminate
- also sometimes used in sense of 'remove', 'get rid of', 'shut down': *se ha eliminado el servicio de trenes* the train service has been shut down/removed
- 'to knock out' (in competitions): *se eliminaron en la semifinal* they were knocked out in the semi-final
- **eliminación** *nf pl eliminaciones* elimination; (act of) removal, shutting down, knocking out (as *v* above)

embarazar *vt -ce-, -cé* to obstruct, hinder
- but more often: to make/get (sb) pregnant
- **embarazarse** *vr* to get (become) pregnant
- **embarazada** *adj f* pregnant: *quedar embarazada* to get/become pregnant; *dejar embarazada a alguien* to get (= make) sb pregnant
- **embarazo** *nm* pregnancy: *embarazo no deseado* unwanted pregnancy
- **embarazoso** *adj* awkward (inconvenient): *un momento embarazoso* an awkward moment; embarrassing (see note following)
- NB: with the exception of the *adj embarazoso*, NONE of these words has any meaning of 'embarrass/ing/ment': there are various words for embarrass/ment, see eg *desconcertar/desconcierto, turbar/turbación, molesto, vergüenza, violento*, but remember, if you are *embarazada*, there's no embarrassment about it: you're pregnant!

embarcar *vt -que-, -qué* to embark, ie a transitive verb; to put sth or sb on to a boat
- **embarcarse** *vr* to embark, get on to a boat (ie use this *vr* if you are getting on to it yourself)
- **embarco** *nm* embarkation
- **embarcación** *nf pl embarcaciones* boat, ship, vessel; cf *barco, buque*; better to use *embarco* (above) for act of embarkation
- opps: *desembarcar(se)/desembarco* disembark/ation

emblema *nm* emblem; NB it's *masc*!

emigrar *vi* to emigrate
- ie to migrate *out*, don't confuse with cf *inmigrar* to immigrate, or migrate *in*
- **emigración** *nf* emigration
- **emigrante** *nmf* or **emigrado/a** *nmf*

emigrant: strictly *un emigrante*
(present participle), is a person in the
process of emigrating, while *un
emigrado* (past participle) is an
emigrant who has already settled
- remember also this term is used for
internal 'emigrants' within Spain, eg
out of Andalucía to other regions

emitir *vt* to emit (sound, vapour etc)
- also to broadcast
- and to issue (stamps, money, etc)
- **emisión** *nf pl emisiones*; emission;
issue (as *v* above); broadcast
- **emisora** *nf* broadcasting station

emoción *nf pl emociones* emotion
- also excitement, thrill
- **emocionar** *vt* to excite, thrill;
emocionarse *vr* to get excited,
thrilled
- **emocionante** *adj* exciting, thrilling
- NB use this rather than *excitar* and
associated words when the meaning is
'thrill/ing': *estaba muy emocionado/a*
I was very excited/thrilled

empeñarse *vr* literally to pledge oneself
- often used as **empeñarse en** + *n*
to insist on + *noun*: *se empeñó en una
respuesta* he insisted on a reply; or
+ *inf*: to insist/persist in + *verb*: *se
empeñó en escribir* he persisted in
writing
- can suggest more willpower, possibly
obstinacy, than cf *insistir, determinar*,
but not as strong as cf *obstinarse*
- **empeño** *nm* insistence, persistence,
determination: ie the noun for the
action explained above: *tener empeño
en hacer algo* to be bent on doing
sth

empezar *vti -ie-; -ce-, -cé* to begin, start,
commence
- + *a* + *inf* to begin to: *empecé a
aprender el español* I began/started
to learn Spanish
- this is the most common 'beginning'
verb but cf the others; all take *a* + *inf*:

comenzar, principiar; NB *ponerse a*
and *echar a* can only be used in this
sense with an infinitive
- NB *empezar por* + *inf* or + *ger* to
begin by …ing: *empezó por
agradecernos/empezó agradeciéndonos
nuestra acogida* he began by
thanking us for our welcome
- NB the *noun* for 'beginning' is
comienzo or *principio*, not *'empiezo'*!

emplear *vt* to employ (in work)
- also to use; in this sense it can be used
in the same way as cf *utilizar, usar*:
emplea muchas palabras extranjeras
he uses a lot of foreign words
- **empleado/a** *nmf* employee; also
esp clerk in office, bank etc
- **empleo** *nm* employment; work, job
(in that sense): *está buscando empleo*
he's looking for work/a job; *es un
empleo que me gusta mucho* it's a
job I like very much; *(estar) sin
empleo* (to be) out of work, jobless;
cf also *puesto, trabajo*

emprender *vt* to undertake, tackle (job,
problem, journey etc) NB *emprenderla
con alguien* to tackle/set about sb
- **emprendedor/a** *adj pl
emprendedores, emprendedoras*
enterprising, go-ahead; *nmf*
entrepreneur
- **empresa** *nf* enterprise, undertaking:
empresa privada private enterprise;
una empresa arriesgada a risky
undertaking/venture
- also frequently 'firm', 'company'; cf
compañía, firma
- **empresario/a** *nmf* businessman/
woman/person

empujar *vti* to push
- **empuje** *nm* push, thrust (ie general
force)
- **empujón** *nm* push, shove (ie on
one occasion): *hacer algo a empujones*
to do sth by pushing/shoving or in
fits and starts

en *prep* (before *noun* or *pronoun*) in, on; when 'on' usually interchangeable with *sobre*
- + *inf* often 'in/on/ …ing' eg *insistir en* to insist on, but does not always correspond literally
- detailed uses are dealt with in full by most grammar books

enamorarse see **amor**

encantar *vt* to enchant, charm, delight
- NB used like *gustar*, with a rather stronger meaning, when you love sth or (+ *inf*) love doing sth: *me encanta el tenis* I love tennis; *me encanta jugar al tenis* I love playing tennis
- **encanto** *nm* charm, enchantment, delight: *es un encanto* it's a delight; *por encanto* by magic
- **encantado** *adj* charmed, enchanted, delighted; *el bosque encantado* the enchanted forest *¡encantado/a!* pleased to meet you! (agrees with person who is pleased)
- **encantador/a** *adj pl* encantadores, encantadoras enchanting, charming, delightful: *es un sitio encantador* it's a delightful spot; *es una mujer encantadora* she's a charming/delightful woman

encargar *vt* -gue-, gué to entrust: *encargo todo esto a mi hijo* I entrust all this to my son
- also(+ *inf*): to recommend, advise: *te encargo hacerlo pronto* I advise you to do it soon
- and (in commerce) to order: *encargamos dos toneladas* we order 2 tons
- **encargarse** *vr* (*de* + noun) to take charge of sth, look after sth: *nos encargaremos de la casa* we'll take charge of/look after the house
- (+ *inf*) to see about doing: *nos encargaremos de limpiar la casa* we'll see about cleaning the house

- **encargado/a** *nmf* person in charge (in business context – 'foreman/woman' or similar suitable title, but not usually 'boss' in sense of owner or manager)
- **encargo** *nm* undertaking, job (in that sense, ie what you have undertaken to do); order (commercial)

encender *vt* -ie- to light (fire, match, cigarette, etc); switch on (light, TV, radio etc)
- **encenderse** to catch fire, light up; can be used of face: turn red
- **encendido** *adj estar encendido* to be on fire, burning; to be alight, lit up
- **encendedor** *nm* lighter

enchufar *vt* to plug in (electrical apparatus)
- *estar bien enchufado* to be well connected (ie able to 'pull strings' to get job etc)
- **enchufe** *nm* (electrical) plug/socket; *conseguir algo por enchufes* to get sth by 'pulling strings'

encima *adv* above, overhead, on top
- *por encima* over the top (more emphatic and can be used with motion: *pasar por encima* to pass over the top)
- can mean 'on one's self or person': *es un problema que me he quitado de encima* that's a problem I've got rid of; *¿tienes dinero encima?* have you got any money on you?
- **encima de** *prep* on top of, above (+ *n* or *pron*); **por encima de** over (the top of): *el avión pasó por encima de nosotros* the plane passed over the top of us
- can be used in sense of 'in addition to': *por encima de todos estos problemas* in addition to/on top of all these problems

encoger *vt* -jo, -ja- and **encogerse** *vr* to shrink, contract
- mainly used in *encogerse de hombros* to shrug one's shoulders

□ **encogido** *adj* shrunken, but often timid, shy

encontrar *vt* -ue- to find; at least as common and used in same way as cf *hallar*

□ also to meet, encounter sth or sb
□ **encontrarse** *vr con alguien* to meet, run into sb (usually by chance)
□ also to be (situated) (used like *estar*): *Toledo se encuentra sobre el río Tajo*

Toledo is (situated) on the River Tagus; *¿Te encuentras mejor?* Are you better?

□ **encuentro** *nm* encounter, meeting: *salir al encuentro de algo/alguien* to go out and meet sb/sth; also (vehicle) crash; and (opinion) clash

enderezar *vt* and **enderezarse** *vr* -ce-, -cé to straighten (out/up), stand up straight

---

 Verbs beginning with **em-** *and* **en-**

There are many verbs beginning with **em-** (before *b* and *p*) and otherwise **en-**, which are derived from an adjective and which mean to give or to take on the quality described by that adjective. Others derive from nouns and often have the idea of getting or being put into that noun. Here are a few: you will find many more if you look in the dictionary!

□ NB those ending in **-ecer** have the *-zc-* change

em-/en- verb	base word	English
embellecer(se)	**bello**	to make/become beautiful, embellish
emborrachar(se)	**borracho**	to make/get drunk
empeorar	**peor**	to make/get worse
empequeñecer	**pequeño**	to make/get smaller
enajenar(se)	**ajeno**	to alienate/become alienated
enamorarse	**amor**	to fall in love
encajar(se)	**caja**	to fit into (not necessarily a box!)
encaminar(se)	**camino**	to make for/set out
encarcelar	**cárcel**	to imprison
endurecer(se)	**duro**	to harden, make/become hard
enflaquecer(se)	**flaco**	to make/become thin
enfriar	**frío**	to cool down, freeze
enfurecer(se)	**furia**	to infuriate/become furious
enganchar(se)	**gancho**	to hook/get hooked
engordar	**gordo**	to fatten/get fat
engrasar/engrase	**grasa**	to grease/greasing, servicing (of car)
enloquecer(se)	**loco**	to drive/become mad
ennegrecer(se)	**negro**	to blacken/become black
enorgullecerse	**orgullo**	to become proud, pride onself
enriquecer(se)	**rico**	to enrich/become rich
enrojecer(se)	**rojo**	to turn red/blush
ensordecer	**sordo**	to deafen/go deaf
ensuciar	**sucio**	to make dirty, soil
enternecer(se)	**tierno**	to make/become tender, soften
enterrar	**tierra**	to bury, inter
entristecer(se)	**triste**	to sadden, make/become sad
envejecer(se)	**viejo**	to make/grow old

enemigo *nm* enemy
- □ can also be *adj*: *tierra enemiga* enemy soil
- □ **enemistad** *nf* enmity

energía *nf* energy
- □ NB **enérgico** *adj* energetic: *una vida enérgica* an energetic life; and **energético** *adj* relating to energy in sense of 'power': *fuentes energéticas* energy sources

enfadar *vt* to make angry, annoy
- □ **enfadarse** *vr* to get angry/annoyed
- □ expresses annoyance rather than mere irritation, ie stronger than cf *fastidiarse*, about same level as cf *enojarse*; but not so strong as cf *airarse, enfurecerse*
- □ *estar enfadado* to be annoyed
- □ **enfado** *nm* anger, annoyance: *reaccionar con enfado* to react angrily
- □ bother, nuisance; *es un enfado* it's a bother
- □ **enfadoso** *adj* annoying, irksome

enfermo/a *adj & nm* ill, sick; sick person, patient
- □ NB used with *estar* to be ill: *estoy enfermo de gripe* I'm ill with flu
- □ NB used with *ser* to be an invalid (ie permanently ill): *su padre es enfermo* his father is an invalid (ie ill and not going to get better)
- □ **enfermar(se)** *vi/vr* to fall ill, go down (*de* with): *se enfermó de sarampión* he went down with measles
- □ **enfermedad** *nf* disease, illness
- □ **enfermero/a** *nmf* nurse
- □ **enfermería** *nf* infirmary, sickbay
- □ **enfermizo** *adj* sickly, weak (in that sense)

enfrente *adv* opposite, facing (for 'in front', use *delante*): *el edificio que está enfrente* the building which is opposite; or, more simply *el edificio de enfrente* the building opposite
- □ **enfrente de** *prep* prepositional form used when followed by a noun: *enfrente del edificio* opposite the building; see also *frente a*

engañar *vt* to deceive, cheat, trick
- □ **engañarse** *vr* to deceive onself; to be wrong, mistaken: *te engañas si crees eso* you're mistaken if you believe that
- □ **engaño** *nm* deceit; trick, swindle; *es un engaño* it's a trick/swindle; can mean 'misunderstanding', esp with neg: *no queremos engaños* we don't want misunderstandings
- □ **engañoso** *adj* deceitful, dishonest

¡enhorabuena! *nf* used as *interj* good luck! or all right!, usually implying 'that's all right, but …', or 'that'll do!'
- □ also: congratulations! *dar la enhorabuena a alguien* to congratulate sb

enjugar *vt* -gue-, -gué; not stem-changing: *enjugo*, etc to wipe, dry, (esp sweat, eyes): *enjugarse las lágrimas* to dry one's tears
- □ less common than cf *secar*
- □ NB: there is no one Sp verb for 'wipe': use *enjugar(se)*, or more commonly *secar(se)* if wipe means 'dry', and *limpiar(se)* if it means 'clean'
- □ don't confuse with *enjuagar* *vt enjuagarse* *vr* -gue-, gué to rinse, get soap out of: *enjuagarse el pelo* to rinse one's hair

enlace *nm* link, connection, tie-up (in that sense)
- □ used in transport, esp rail, for 'connection'
- □ also rather formally for 'marriage' eg in newspaper announcements: *el próximo enlace* the forthcoming marriage
- □ see also *vínculo*
- □ **enlazar** *vt* -ce-, -cé to link, connect; **enlazarse** *vr* to be(come) linked, connected

enojar *vt* to annoy, anger, upset, vex
- **enojarse** *vr* to get angry, annoyed, upset
- in degree of annoyance/anger, tends to be nearer cf *enfadarse* than cf *fastidiar(se)*
- **enojo** *nm* annoyance, anger
- **enojoso** *adj* annoying, irritating

enorme *adj* enormous; huge, vast
- also monstrous: *¡fue una acción enorme!* it was a monstrous thing to do!
- **enormidad** *nf* both 'enormousness', ie 'hugeness', and 'enormity' in Eng sense of 'monstrousness'

ensalada *nf* salad (type is usually specified): *ensalada de tomates* tomato salad
- **ensaladilla** *nf* 'Russian salad', (ie a mixed salad with mayonnaise)

ensanchar *vt* to enlarge, widen, ie *hacer más ancho*
- **ensancharse** *vr* to become wider, expand (in that sense)
- **ensanche** *nm* widening
- based on cf *ancho*

ensayar *vt* to test, try (in that sense) (*probar* is more common)
- **ensayo** *nm* test, trial (in that sense), but *prueba* is more used except in some set phrases: *vuelo de ensayo* test flight
- also 'essay', (though tends to be more literary): what you write for an exam is *una redacción*
- and: rehearsal (of play etc)

enseñar *vt* to teach; (+ *a* + *inf*): *me enseñaron a hablar español* they taught me to speak Spanish
- also, frequently, to show: *enséñame tus dibujos* show me your drawings (same meaning as cf *mostrar*); to point out: *enséñame dónde está la oficina de turismo* show me where the tourist office is (cf *señalar*)

enseñanza *nf* education, teaching; as 'education', tends to have emphasis towards processes of teaching/being taught; cf *educación*

entender *vti* -ie- to understand, comprehend
- **entender de** *vi* to be an expert on: *no entiendo de ordenadores* I don't know anything about computers
- **entenderse** *vr* (*con* with) to get on with each other: *no me entiendo con mi hermano* I don't get on/hit it off with my brother
- **entendido/a** *adj* often used as question or exclamation in sense of *de acuerdo: ¿entendido? ¡sí, entendido!* agreed? yes, agreed!
- also as *nm/f* 'expert', 'versed in' (use *ser*): *es un entendido en los ordenadores* he knows all about computers
- **entendimiento** *nm* understanding: both in sense of 'comprehension' and 'intelligence'
- further dictionary study of this range of words would be rewarding

enterar *vt* to inform (*de algo* about sth)
- **enterarse** *vr* to be informed, find out (*de algo* about sth), enquire (in that sense): *sólo me enteré ayer de tu accidente* I only found out yesterday about your accident; *nos enteramos de la hora del tren* we enquired about the time of the train
- NB also: *¿te enteras?* do you understand? got that?
- *estar enterado de algo* to be in the know, well informed about sth

entero *adj* entire, whole: *la clase entera* the whole class
- follows noun and tends to be slightly more positive/emphatic than cf *todo*, eg *toda la clase*; NB and cf *todo el mundo* everybody and *el mundo entero* the whole world
- **entereza** *nf* entirety, wholeness; also: integrity

entonces *adv* then, (in sense of) at that time
- *en aquel entonces* (ie *en aquella época*) at that time (ie a period in the past)
- also 'then' (next): *entonces me compré un vestido* then I bought myself a dress; similar to cf *luego* in this sense
- and also, frequently 'and so', 'then' (in that sense): *Entonces, ¿qué vas a hacer?* So what are you going to do?, What are you going to do then?; similar to cf *pues* and *conque* in this sense

entrar usually *vi* to enter, go/come into, (always + *en* + *noun*): *entraron en el museo* they went into the museum
- can be used as *vt*, ie with an object: *¿quieres entrar el equipaje?* will you bring in the luggage?
- **entrada** *nf* entrance (in both senses: way in or action of going in)
- also frequently (admission) 'ticket': *¿Cuánto cuestan las entradas al fútbol?* How much are the football tickets? (use *billete* for bus, train etc ticket)
- entrance hall (of a house)
- **entrado** *adj* used in expressions like *muy entrada la noche* very late at night; *ser entrado en años* to be very elderly
- there are several more specialised meanings worth further investigation in a dictionary!

entre *prep* between, among
- NB *entre tú y yo* between you and me

entregar *vt* -gue-, -gué to deliver
- also 'to hand' (over, in), 'give' (but more deliberate than cf *dar*)
- **entrega** *nf* (action of) handing over, delivery
- usual words for delivering of single letter, parcel etc, but use *repartir/reparto* for paper round type of distributed delivery
- **entregarse** *vr* to surrender, give oneself up

entrenar *vt* to train, coach; **entrenarse** *vr* to train, be in training (for sporting activities: use *formar(se)* for education or business context)
- **entrenamiento** *nm* training, coaching
- **entrenador/a** *nmf* trainer, coach

entretener *vt* (see *tener* for irregularities) to entertain, amuse (slightly less common than cf *divertir*)
- also to delay, detain: *nos entretuvieron hablando de su hijo* they kept us back talking about their son
- **entretenerse** *vr* to amuse oneself, keep oneself occupied (+ *ger* doing sth): *se entretuvo haciendo crucigramas* he amused himself/kept himself occupied doing crosswords
- **entretenimiento** *nm* entertainment, amusement; also maintenance, upkeep (of machinery)
- **entretenido** *adj* entertaining, amusing (cf *divertido*)

entrometerse (or **entremeterse**) *vr* to meddle, interfere (*en* in)
- **entrometido** or **entremetido** *adj* meddlesome, interfering

entusiasmar *vt* to thrill, excite, make sb keen on
- NB often used like *gustar*, eg in the following example, the idea thrills you: *¿Te entusiasma la idea de ir a Italia?* Are you keen on the idea of going to Italy?
- or you can use **entusiasmarse** *vr* (*por/con algo*) to be keen on, enthusiastic about sth, with a personal subject: *me entusiasmo mucho con la idea de ir a Italia* I'm very keen on the idea of going to Italy
- **entusiasmo** *nm* enthusiasm (*por* for)
- **entusiasta** *adj* enthusiastic; *nmf* enthusiast; both *adj* and *n* always end in *-a* (*-as* in pl)

enviar *vt* -í-: envío, envías; envíe to send

□ alternative to *mandar* used in this sense

envidiar *vt* to envy; **envidia** *nf* envy
□ don't confuse with parts of *enviar* above!

envolver *vt* like *volver: -ue-; past part: envuelto* to wrap up (parcel etc)
□ can sometimes mean 'involve', but *implicar, involucrar* are safer
□ **envoltura** *nf* wrapping

época *nf* time, (in sense of 'period'): *en la época de Cervantes* in Cervantes' time; can mean 'season': *la época de la vendimia* the season of the grape harvest
□ also 'epoch', but is used much more than this and with a less momentous meaning!

equilibrar *vt* and **equilibrarse** *vr* to balance
□ better to use this than cf *balancear(se)* which means 'swing', 'sway'
□ **equilibrio** *nm* balance

equipo *nm* equipment (ie the tackle etc you need to perform a function): *el equipo de pesca* fishing tackle
□ also, frequently 'team' (both sporting and in sense of gang eg of workers)
□ **equipar** *vt* to equip
□ **equipaje** *nm* luggage; *bagaje* exists, but this is more usual

equivocarse *vr -que-, -qué* to be mistaken, to be wrong
□ this is the most common way of saying sb is wrong, as there is no literal opposite of *tener razón* to be right
□ also in the sense of doing the wrong thing: *nos equivocamos de autobús* we got on the wrong bus; *se equivocó de puerta:* he went to/through the wrong door
□ **equivocado** *adj* mistaken: *estar equivocado* to be mistaken/wrong; *es una opinión equivocada* it's a mistaken opinion
□ **equívoco** *nm* ambiguity: *para evitar equívocos* to avoid ambiguities/ misunderstandings; also *adj* ambiguous, equivocal

esbelto *adj* slim, slender: more positive and complimentary ('svelte') than cf *delgado, flaco*

escala *nf* ladder
□ also 'scale' (of map etc)
□ and in *hacer escala (en)* to call into, stop over (ships, planes, etc)
□ **escalera** *nf* stairs, staircase; NB *sing* and refers to whole flight of stairs, staircase
□ **escalón** *nm* pl *escalones* (a single) step, stair

escándalo *nm* scandal
□ has wider meaning of 'outrage', 'shock', 'scene': *¡Es un escándalo!* It's an outrage! *claro que armó un escándalo* of course she caused a scene
□ **escandaloso** *adj* scandalous, outrageous; also often 'shocking'
□ **escandalizar** *vt -ce-, -cé* to scandalise; often 'to shock': *la película escandalizó al público* the film shocked the audience
□ **escandalizarse** *vr* to be shocked (*de* by/at): *el público se escandalizó de la película* the audience was shocked by the film
□ **escandaloso** *adj* scandalous, outrageous; or, perhaps a shade stronger:
□ **escandalizante** *adj* shocking

escapar *vi* to escape; more often used reflexively
□ **escaparse** *vr* to escape; (*de* + *noun* or *inf* from + noun or verb): *escaparse de la pobreza* to escape from poverty
□ also used as in Eng when you can't remember sth: *se me escapa el número de la casa* the number of the house escapes me

- □ 'to leak' (from eg pipes)
- □ **escapada** *nf* escape, flight; can mean 'escapade', as Eng
- □ **escape** *nm* escape, as *escapada*; also 'leak' (in pipe), and '(vehicle) exhaust': *tubo de escape* exhaust pipe

escaso *nm* scarce, scant: it means there isn't much of whatever it is applied to!
- □ NB tendency to precede noun: *dados sus escasos recursos* given their scarce/scant resources; *de escasa edad* not very old; *existe la escasa posibilidad de que …* there exists the remote possibility that …
- □ also used with *estar/andar* in sense of 'to be short of': *estar/andar escaso de fondos* to be short of funds
- □ also used in sense of 'only just': *tenían un kilo escaso de patatas* they only just had a kilo of potatoes
- □ **escasamente** *adv* barely, hardly (more emphatic than cf *apenas*)
- □ **escasez** *nf pl escaseces* shortage, scarcity
- □ **escasear** *vi* to be/become scarce, be in short supply

escena *nf* scene (ie what you see: not in sense of 'scandal', see *escándalo* above)
- □ also: stage (in theatre); *poner en escena una obra* to perform a play
- □ **escenario** *nm* stage setting, scenery (in that sense)
- □ also scenery, setting, scenario

escoger *vt -jo, -ja-* to choose; alternative to *elegir* but not 'elect' in political sense

esconder *vt* to hide; when you hide (yourself), use **esconderse** *vr* to hide, be hidden (*de* from): rather more common than cf *ocultar(se)*
- □ **a escondidas** *adv* secretly: *siempre obra a escondidas* he always operates in secret
- □ **escondite** *nm* hiding place

escribir *vti past part: escrito* to write
- □ NB *¿Cómo se escribe?* How do you spell it?; *escribirse con alguien* to correspond with sb; *por escrito* in writing
- □ **escritor(a)** *nmf* writer; **escritorio** *nm* bureau, writing desk/table (domestic not school: use *pupitre*)
- □ **escritura** *nf* writing; also 'scripture'; and 'deeds' (of house): those buying a property in Spain will need it!

escuchar *vti* to listen (to)
- □ NB takes *dir obj*: *escuchar la radio* to listen *to* the radio
- □ cf *oír*: the distinction between *escuchar* and *oír* is nowhere near as clear as 'listen'/'hear' in Eng
- □ **escucha** *nf* (act of) listening: *estar a la escucha (para)* to be listening (for)
- □ for 'listening' as adjective, use *auditiva*: *comprensión auditiva* listening comprehension

escuela *nf* school (in education system, usually primary; see *colegio, instituto* for 'secondary')
- □ used also in most other senses: *escuela automovilista* driving school; *escuela de geografía* school of geography (ie in university); *escuela clásica* classical school (eg of painting)
- □ **escolar** *adj* (to do with) school: *las vacaciones escolares* the school holidays; also as *nmf* schoolboy/girl/pupil
- □ **escolaridad** *nf* schooling

ese *demons adj ese, esa, esos, esas* that (by you, ie near the person addressed)
- □ **ése** *demons pron ésa, ésos, ésas*; NB accent, needed on this pronoun form when not followed immediately by noun
- □ NB *neuter pron* form *eso* (no accent) when gender is not known: *¿Qué es eso?* What's that?
- □ cf *este, aquel*

esforzarse *vr -ue-; -ce-, -cé* to strive, make an effort, try hard (*en/por* + *inf* to +

verb): *se esforzó por ganar el concurso*
he strove to win the competition

- much stronger than other 'trying' verbs cf *tratar de, intentar, probar*
- **esfuerzo** *nm* effort: *hacer un esfuerzo por + inf* to make an effort to + verb

espacio *nm* space (in most senses as in Eng)

- slot (advertising, TV etc)
- **espacial** *adj* (to do with) space: *exploración espacial* space exploration
- **espacioso** *adj* spacious, roomy

espalda *nf* back (ie of human body)

- NB dictionaries also give 'shoulder': only refers to shoulder blade area of back; for top of shoulder use *hombro*
- *de espaldas a* with one's back to

espantar *vt* to frighten, scare;
espantarse *vr* to be/get frightened, scared

- much the same as *asustar(se)*: perhaps a slightly more immediate reaction than cf *dar/tener miedo*
- **espanto** *nm* fright cf *susto, miedo*; can mean 'amazement' cf *asombro*
- **espantoso** *adj* frightful, dreadful; also 'appalling', 'shocking': *la subida de los precios es espantosa* the rise in prices is shocking

especie *nf* kind, sort: *es una especie de cesta* it's a sort of basket cf *tipo* in this sense; *cosas de esta especie* things of this sort

- species

especial *adj* special; especial

- can also mean 'fussy', 'pernickety': *es muy especial en su comida* he's very fussy about his food
- **especialmente** *adv* specially, especially

espectáculo *nm* spectacle, show (in that sense)

- **espectador/a** *nmf* spectator: used in *pl los espectadores* spectators, or

collectively, the audience (where the audience views as well as hears); cf *público*; not same as cf *oyentes* listeners (only)

esperar *vti* wait (for): *¡espérame!* wait for me; *yo te esperaré aquí* I'll wait for you here; more often used than cf *aguardar*

- can mean 'meet' (at a rendezvous): *te esperaré a las 8 delante del cine* I'll meet you at 8 outside the cinema
- also, often 'to hope (for)', 'expect': *es precisamente lo que esperaba* it's exactly what I expected/hoped for; *esperar que* (usually + *subjunc*) to hope that: *esperamos que vuelvan pronto* we hope they'll come soon (consult a grammar about when and when not to use subjunctive!)
- NB not used for 'expect' in eg 'I expect that …', ie when it means 'suppose' – use *supongo que: supongo que volverán pronto* I expect they'll come back soon; or 'future of supposition' where feasible – *habrán vuelto ya* I expect they are already back
- **espera** *nf* wait: *una larga espera* a long wait; used in phrases eg *sala de espera* waiting room, and in letters: *en espera de su respuesta* awaiting your reply
- **esperanza** *nf* hope, expectation

espeso *adj* thick

- **espesor** *nm* thickness (used for dimensions): *este libro tiene dos centímetros de espesor* this book is 2 cm thick
- **espesura** *nf* thickness

espíritu *nm* spirit (in most Eng senses – religious, supernatural, ghost); driving force: *el espíritu de la época* spirit of the time; *Espíritu Santo* Holy Spirit/Ghost; for 'ghost' not same as cf *fantasma*

- also 'mind', 'intelligence', with much same meaning as cf *mente; tiene el espíritu agudo* he has a sharp mind/intelligence

- □ **espiritual** *adj* spiritual
- □ for 'spirits' (drinks), use *licores*

esposo/a *nmf* husband/wife; spouse; *los esposos* the married couple, husband and wife

- □ more formal and polite than *marido/mujer* and should be used when referring to sb else's husband or wife; cf also *señora*
- □ *esposas* can also mean 'handcuffs'!

esquema *nm* scheme, but *proyecto* is often used when a scheme is a project

- □ NB *masc*
- □ also means 'diagram', 'plan', 'sketch'

esquí *nm pl esquís* ski or skiing: *hacer el esquí* to go skiing

- □ **esquiar** *vi -í-: esquío, esquías; esquíe* to ski
- □ **esquiador/a** *nmf* skier
- □ **esquiable** *adj* skiable, suitable for skiing

esquina *nf* (outside) corner, ie more than 180°, not same as cf *rincón* (inside) corner

establecer *vt -zc-* to establish

- □ **establecimiento** *nm* establishment

establo *nm* cowshed; for stable, use *cuadra*

estación *nf pl estaciones* station (in many of same senses as Eng): *estación de ferrocarriles/autobuses* railway/bus station; *estación de servicio* service/petrol station but cf *gasolinera*; *estación de esquí* ski station/resort

- □ also 'season (of year)'; cf *temporada*
- □ **estacional** *adj* seasonal; **estacionalidad** *nf* seasonal nature (eg *del empleo*)
- □ **estacionar** *vt* to park (alternative to cf *aparcar*); **estacionamiento** *nm* parking, car park (ie both action and place)

estadística *nf* statistic, statistics (usually *sing*)

estado see **estar** below

estar *vi pi:* estoy, estás, está, estamos, estáis, estáis, están; *ps:* esté, estés, esté, estemos, estéis, estén; *pret:* estuve, estuviste, estuvo, estuvimos, estuvisteis, estuvieron; *imp subj:* estuviera/estuviese to be

- □ NB not alternative to cf *ser*; see below; note also connection with *estado* 'state', below, a further clue to its use
- □ summary of main uses, but consult a grammar for full details:
- □ circumstantial state: *estaban cansados y enfermos* they were tired and ill
- □ situation: *la puerta está a la izquierda* the door is on the left
- □ price: *las manzanas están a un euro el kilo* apples are 1 euro a kilo
- □ continuous tenses: *estamos aprendiendo el español* we're learning Spanish
- □ **estado** *nm* state (in most senses as in Eng):
- □ condition: *¿En qué estado le encontraste?* What state did you find him in?; *en buen/mal estado* in a good/bad state/condition; *estado de ánimo* state of mind
- □ country or component of country: *Estados Unidos* United States
- □ status: *estado civil* marital status
- □ **estatal** *adj* (to do with the) state: *colegio estatal* state school
- □ **estancia** *nf* stay (in a place)

este *demons adj esta, estos, estas* this (near the speaker)

- □ *demons pron: éste, ésta, éstos, éstas;* NB accent: needed on this pronoun form, when not followed immediately by noun
- □ NB *neuter* form *esto* (no accent) when gender is not known: *¿Qué es esto?* What's this?
- □ cf *ese, aquel*

este *nm & adj* east; *adj* is invariable: *la zona este* the eastern region

estimar *vt* to estimate

□ also: to esteem, respect
□ **estimado** and **estimable** *adjs* NB
use in formal correspondence:
Estimado Sr Pérez Dear Mr Pérez;
recibimos su estimable carta we
received your esteemed letter
□ **estimación** *nf pl estimaciones*
estimate; esteem

estrecho *adj* narrow
□ also 'tight' (clothes): *un vestido estrecho*
a tight dress; *esta falda me viene muy
estrecha* the skirt is very tight on
me (cf *apretar*)
□ used with similar meaning of 'tight',
'close', 'restricted' in various contexts
eg money: *andamos estrechos de
dinero* money is very tight; *una
amistad estrecha* a close friendship;
tiene la vista estrecha he has a
narrow view/outlook
□ *nm* strait(s): *El Estrecho de Gibraltar*
the Straits of Gibraltar
□ **estrechez** *nf* narrowness, tightness;
noun for all qualities described above
by *estrecho*
□ **estrechar** *vt* to (make) narrow; to
squeeze: *estrechar la mano a alguien*
to shake sb's hand; to hug, embrace
(same as *abrazar*)
□ **estrecharse** *vr* to become narrow;
to become tight(er); *estrecharse la
mano* (of 2 people) to shake hands
□ worth further study in the dictionary

estrella *nf* star (both in sky and in films etc)
□ remains *f* when referring to any
person
□ **estrellar** *vt* to smash, shatter
□ **estrellarse** *vr* to be smashed,
shattered; often used of cars, planes etc
in sense of to crash (*contra algo*
against something)

estremecerse *vr* -zc- to shake, tremble,
shiver, shudder – (*de* with) cold,
emotion, horror, fright, etc: the cause is
often expressed: *se estremeció de miedo*
he trembled with fear; *nos estremecíamos*

de frío we were shivering
□ **estremecido** *adj* shaking, trembling
□ **estremeciento** *nm* shake/shaking,
shiver/ing, shudder/ing
□ **estremecedor** *adj estremecedora,
estremecedores, estremecedoras*
alarming, disturbing (ie causing alarm)

estreno *nm* first performance or showing
(of play/film); début, first appearance (of
eg actor/sportsperson)
□ **estrenar** *vt* to put on/show for
first time; also used of clothes: *estrenar
un vestido* to wear a dress for the
first time

estropear *vt* to spoil, damage, ruin (in
that sense)
□ **estropearse** *vr* to get damaged,
spoiled; to deteriorate
□ **estropeado** *adj* damaged, spoiled
□ **estropicio** *nm* damage, breakage;
also 'harmful effects': *los estropicios de
la droga* the harmful effects of drugs

estudio *nm* study (act of studying or
room in which you do it)
□ also studio or studio flat/bedsitter
□ **estudios** *nmpl* studies (ie course in
education)
□ **estudiar** *vti* to study
□ **estudiante** *nmf* student (either
sex); **estudianta** *nf* female student
(form used but not necessarily
'officially' accepted!)
□ **estudiantil** *adj* student, ie to do
with students and their life: *vida
estudiantil* student life
□ **estudioso** *adj* studious

estufa *nf* heater, fire (limited use, usually
electric or gas: *estufa eléctrica/de gas*)
□ for 'open fire', see *fuego, hogar*; for
'stove' for cooking, see *cocina, horno*

estupefaciente *adj* stupefying, but
commonly used meaning 'narcotic'; also
used as *nf (sustancia) estupefaciente*
narcotic
□ **estupefacto** *adj* astonished (cf

asombrado, syn atónito), speechless: *quedé estupefacto* I was speechless

etapa *nf* stage (of a journey, race, project, etc)

Europa *nf* Europe
- □ **europeo** *adj* European
- □ **europeo** *nm* European (man); **europea** *nf* European (woman)
- □ don't mix them up!!

evaluación *nf* evaluation
- □ also, usually *pl evaluaciones* periodic assessment (in school)
- □ **evaluar** *vt; -ú-: evalúo, evalúas; evalúe* to evaluate, assess

eventual *adj* possible (but see explanation below)
- □ NB not 'eventual' in Eng sense of 'in the end': the thrust of the meaning is 'depending on the circumstances'; study these examples to get a feel for the meaning
- □ *un encuentro eventual* a possible /chance meeting; *un conflicto eventual* a possible conflict; *la dimisión eventual del jefe* the possible resignation of the boss (all examples would be as result of certain circumstances, so meaning is usually more specific than simply *posible*): *en el caso eventual de que llamen* in the event of them phoning; *busco algún trabajo eventual* I'm looking for a temporary/casual job
- □ **eventualmente** *adv* by chance; depending on the circumstances
- □ **evento** *nm* contingency, eventuality, unexpected incident (rather than merely 'event': use *acontecimiento, suceso*)

evidente *adj* evident, but also 'obvious', 'clear': *es evidente que no lo sabes* it's obvious you don't know
- □ **evidencia** *nf* evidence, proof, obviousness
- □ **evidenciar** *vt* to prove, show, demonstrate: *evidencia una falta de preocupación* he shows a lack of concern

exacto *adj* exact, but also 'right', 'correct': *¡Exacto!* Right!, I agree!; *hay que tenerlo exacto* you've got to have it right

exagerar *vti* to exaggerate
- □ NB one *g*!
- □ also 'to overdo it': *siempre exageras* you always overdo it
- □ **exagerado** *adj* exaggerated, but also 'excessive', given to overdoing things: *¡Eres una exagerada!* You're always overdoing it!
- □ **exageradamente** *adv* exaggeratedly; excessively, overmuch

examen *nm pl exámenes* examination (mainly in education context; for medical use *reconocimiento*)
- □ **examinar** *vt* to examine, inspect, check (in that sense); in sense of search (eg luggage), inspect: *syn inspecciones*; cf *registrar* and (medically) *reconocer*
- □ **examinarse** *vr* to take an exam (in educational context)
- □ **examinador/a** *nmf* examiner

excepto *prep* except (for), excepting
- □ **excepción** *nf pl excepciones* exception: *a excepción de* with the exception of

exceso *nm* excess
- □ used in phrases which indicate too much of sth: *exceso de plantillas* overmanning; *exceso de velocidad* speeding
- □ *en/por exceso* in excess: *comer en exceso* to overeat
- □ **excesivo** *adj* excessive; **excesivamente** *adv* excessively
- □ **exceder** *vt* to exceed, surpass

excitar *vt* to excite, in most senses, but see also *apasionar, emocionar*
- □ **excitarse** *vr* to get excited
- □ **excitante** *adj* stimulating (rather than 'exciting': use *apasionante, emocionante*)
- □ **excitación** *nf* excitement, stimulation; or act of exciting

excluir *vt* -y-: *pi: excluyo, excluyes, excluye, excluyen; ps: excluya* etc; *ger: excluyendo; pret: excluyó, excluyeron; imp subj: excluyera/excluyese* to exclude (*de* from)
- □ **exclusión** *nf pl exclusiones* exclusion

excursión *nf pl excursiones* excursion, but also wider sense of 'trip', 'outing': *ir de excursión* to go out for/on a trip
- □ **excursionista** *nmf* tripper, esp day-tripper; also often 'rambler', 'hiker'
- □ **excursionismo** *nm* rambling, hiking

excusa *nf* excuse, but also 'apology': *hacer sus excusas* to make one's apologies (*pretexto* can also often be used for 'excuse' as a reason eg not to have done sth); cf *disculpa*
- □ **excusar** *vt* to excuse
- □ can be used in sense of 'avoid': *si queremos excusar problemas* if we want to avoid problems
- □ **excusarse** *vr* to excuse oneself, but more often 'to apologise' (*de* + *noun* for): *me excuso del retraso* I apologise for the delay; to decline to (*de* + *inf*): *se excusó de acompañarnos* he declined to go with us; cf *disculparse* for apologise

exigir *vt* -jo, -ja-: *exijo, exiges; exija* to require, demand (in that sense): *este trabajo exige mucha paciencia* this work requires/demands a lot of patience
- □ **exigencia** *nf* requirement, demand
- □ for vocal demands, eg rights, use *reclamar/reclamación, reivindicar/reivindicación;* see also *requerir;* stronger than *necesitar* need; cf also *demandar*
- □ **exigente** *adj* demanding

éxito *nm* success (never 'exit'!): *tener (mucho) éxito* to be (very) successful; *ser un éxito* to be a success; *tener éxito en* (+ *noun*) to be successful in; (+ *inf*) to succeed in
- □ for 'succeed in' + verb see also

conseguir, lograr
- □ **exitoso** *ad* successful: *una carrera exitosa* a successful career

explicar *vt* -que-, -qué to explain
- □ **explicarse** *vr* to explain onself; *no me explico* means 'I don't understand': *no me explico por qué* I don't understand why
- □ **explicación** *nf pl explicaciones* explanation

exponer *vt pi: expongo, expones; ps: exponga;* tú *imperative: expón; fut/cond: expondré/expondría; past part: expuesto; pret: expuse, expusiste, expuso, expusimos, expusisteis, expusieron; imp sub: expusiera/expusiese* to expose
- □ also 'to exhibit', 'show' (in that sense)
- □ **expuesto** *adj (past part)* exposed (*a* to)
- □ **exposición** *nf pl exposiciones* exhibition (rather than *exhibición* in most cases)

exprimir *vt* to squeeze out (eg extract liquid from fruit, washing, etc)
- □ NB don't confuse with Fr *exprimer:* 'express' is *expresar*, which gives no problems!

extender *vt* -ie- to extend (in most senses)
- □ **extenderse** *vr* to extend, stretch: *los Pirineos se extienden del Atlántico al Mediterráneo* the Pyrenees stretch from the Atlantic to the Mediterranean
- □ **extenso** *adj* extensive, vast

exterior *adj* exterior, (as *adj*) outside, outer: *puerta exterior* outside/outer door
- □ no *fsing* form, *mfpl* **exteriores**
- □ also 'foreign', in sense of outside the country: *Ministerio de Asuntos Exteriores* Ministry of Foreign Affairs, Foreign Office
- □ *nm* (the) outside, exterior: *al exterior* on the outside
- □ **externo** *adj* external

extinguir *vt -go, -ga- extingo, extingues; extinga*
to extinguish, put out: less common in
everyday context than cf *apagar*

extra *adj inv* extra; often suggests higher
quality rather than Eng 'additional': *pan
extra* good-quality bread
- NB invariable

extraer *vt* (has all irregularities of cf *traer*)
to extract

extranjero *adj* foreign
- *nm* foreign country, abroad: *ir al
extranjero* to go abroad; *estar en el
extranjero* to be abroad
- **extranjero/a** *nmf* foreigner

extraño *adj* strange, odd (in that sense);
much same as cf *raro*
- **extrañar** *vt* to surprise: *me extraña
su actitud* his attitude surprises me
- **extrañarse** *vr* to be surprised (*de*
at/by): *me extraño de su actitud*

I'm surprised by his attitude

extremo *nm* end, furthest point
(in any dimension): *al extremo de la
península* at the end of the
peninsula
- also 'wing(er)' (in sport): *extremo
derecho* right wing
- *adj* extreme, furthest (ie mainly
in geographical/dimensional
context): *el punto extremo* the
furthest point
- not same as **extremado** *adj*
extreme, excessive: *el calor extremado
del desierto* the extreme heat of the
desert
- **extremadamente** *adv* extremely,
excessively
- **extremarse** *vt* to make every effort
(*en + inf* to + verb)

extrovertido/a *adj nmf* extrovert
- note extra syllable *-id-*

F

F (*efe*) is pronounced as in English. It
never occurs as a double letter.
- It always replaces *ph* in the many
words of Greek origin which are
spelt with *ph* in English and other
languages: *fotografía, filósofo.*

fabricar *vt -que-, -qué* to manufacture
- also, as in Eng 'to fabricate', 'invent'
(eg a story)
- **fábrica** *nf* factory; **fabricante** *nmf*
manufacturer; **fabricación** *nf*
manufacture: *de fabricación española*
made in Spain

facción *nf* faction (eg political); also esp in
pl: *facciones* features (of face)

fácil *adj* easy (NB stress on the *á*: that's
what the accent is there for!)

- **facilidad** *nf* ease, easiness, facility
- fluency: *hablar el español con facilidad*
to speak Spanish fluently;
- *las facilidades* facilities (in most
senses), although *instalaciones,
prestaciones* are often used in context
of buildings, campsites, etc
- **facilitar** *vt a* to facilitate; to
provide, supply: cf *proporcionar,
proveer, suministrar*

factura *nf* invoice, bill (mainly as business
term, for restaurant bill etc, use *cuenta*)
- **facturación** *nf* check-in, checking-
in (of baggage); also (in business sense)
invoicing
- **facturar** *vt* to check in (baggage);
to invoice

faena *nf* task, chore: *las faenas
domésticas* household chores; more of a
chore than cf *tarea*, 'task' in a general
sense

fallar *vi* to fail, give way (machinery,

structures, etc): *los frenos fallaron* the brakes failed

- □ don't confuse with *faltar, fracasar* below
- □ **fallecer** *vi -zc-* to die, pass away: formal and rather euphemistic alternative for cf *morir*
- □ **fallecimiento** *nm* death, passing (in that sense)
- □ **fallo** *nm* defect, fault: *un fallo de fabricación* a manufacturing fault; failure (of eg machine); not same as cf *fracaso*

falso *adj* false, untrue: 'false' in most senses, but for 'teeth' use *postizo*

falta *nf* lack: *una falta de compasión* a lack of compassion

- □ fault, mistake: *esta redacción tiene muchas faltas* this essay has many mistakes
- □ NB its use in the following expressions:
- □ *hacer falta + inf* to be necessary to: *hace falta pagar ahora* it's necessary to (we must) pay now
- □ *hacer falta + noun* to be necessary, needed: *nos hace falta un coche* we need a car
- □ **faltar** *vi* to be lacking, missing, short: *falta una persona* there's one person missing; *nos faltan mil pesetas* we're 1,000 pesetas short
- □ NB the person to whom sth is missing is the indirect object: *a Miguel le faltan dos puntos* Miguel has two points missing, two points too few
- □ it is also used in idioms such as: *faltan diez días para la Navidad* there are 10 days to go to Christmas; *¡No faltaba más!* That's all we needed!

fama *nf* fame

- □ reputation: *tener buena/mala fama* to have a good/bad reputation
- □ **famoso** *adj (por)* famous (for)
- □ see also *célebre*, and *conocido* for 'well-known'

familia *nf* family

- □ **familiar** *adj* familiar (well-known, recognisable, as in Eng)
- □ but also frequently '(to do with the) family': *problemas familiares* family problems
- □ and also as *nmf* 'relative', 'family member': *Carmen tiene muchos familiares* Carmen has lots of relatives

fantasma *nm* ghost

- □ NB masculine (ends in *-ma*), regardless of sex of ghost! Not exactly same as cf *espíritu*

farmacia *nf* pharmacy, chemist's shop

- □ NB stress on *-acia*, not *-ía*, unlike most shop names
- □ **farmacéutico/a** *nmf* pharmacist, chemist (in that sense); *adj* pharmaceutical; not same as *químico* chemist/chemical (related to chemistry)

fastidio *nm* annoyance

- □ **fastidioso** *adj* annoying, irksome
- □ NOT 'fastidious', which might be *meticuloso*, depending on the exact context of the Eng word
- □ **fastidiar** *vt* to annoy, upset; **fastidiarse** *vr* to get annoyed, upset, cross
- □ not so strong as cf *enojo/enojar*

fatal *adj* fatal

- □ but commonly also 'awful', 'dreadful': *me siento fatal* I feel awful; *fue un partido fatal* it was a dreadful match

fatiga *nf* fatigue, weariness (stronger and less common than: *cansancio*)

- □ **fatigar** *vt -gue-, -gué* associated with *fatiga* above, 'to weary', 'fatigue' (stronger than *cansar*)
- □ also 'to annoy', 'irritate'
- □ **fatigarse** *(de) vr* to become weary, tired (of … –ing)

favor *nm* favour

- □ used in a number of useful idioms: *haga(n) el favor de no fumar* please do not smoke; *estar a favor de algo* to be in favour of something

☐ **favorito** *adj* favourite

☐ cf *predilecto, preferido* (little difference in usage)

fax *nm* fax (message or machine)

☐ NB **faxear** *vt* or *mandar por fax* to fax: *te lo faxearé, te lo mandaré por fax* I'll fax it to you

fecha *nf* date: *¿Qué fecha es?* What's the date?; *fecha de caducidad* expiry/sell-by date; *fecha de nacimiento* date of birth

feliz *adj pl felices* happy

☐ tends to be used with *ser*, expressing a deeper and more permanent happiness than cf *contento*, which tends to be used with *estar* and more transient states

☐ can also mean 'successful', 'felicitous': *un resultado feliz* a successful outcome

☐ **felicidad** *nf* happiness

☐ NB *felicidades (por)* congratulations (on)

☐ **felicitar** *(a alguien por algo) vt* to congratulate (sb on sth)

femenino *adj* feminine; NB spelling: *feme-*

fenomenal *adj* phenomenal

☐ also colloquially 'super', 'great': *marcó un gol fenomenal* he scored a super goal

feo *adj* ugly (persons and things)

☐ nasty (smell, situation, etc)

feria *nf* market, show, fair (of that sort)

☐ 'bank' (one-day) holiday (cf *fiesta*, not same as cf *vacaciones*)

feroz *adj pl feroces* fierce, ferocious

festejar *vt* to celebrate (eg birthday)

☐ often better than *celebrar* in this sense

festivo see **fiesta**

fiarse de *vr -í- (me fío, te fías, etc; me fíe,*

etc) to trust, rely on: *¿Podemos fiarnos de ti?* Can we trust/rely on you?

fiebre *nf* fever

☐ *tener fiebre* usual phrase for 'to have/run a temperature'

fiesta *nf* party, celebration

☐ holiday (religious Feast or single day): *día de fiesta* holiday (eg bank holiday)

☐ **festivo** *adj* festive, holiday: *día festivo* ('bank') holiday

☐ some overlap with cf *feria*, not same as cf *vacaciones*

figura *nf* figure (in most senses)

☐ for 'number' use *cifra*, for shape of body, use *línea*

☐ **figurarse** *vr* to imagine, suppose, figure (in American sense): *¡Figúrate!* Just imagine!; *no te puedes figurar lo que pasó* you can't imagine what happened

☐ cf *imaginar(se), fijarse*

fijar *vt* to fix, stick (stamp etc): *fijar la mirada en algo/alguien* to stare at sb/sth

☐ **fijarse** *vr* to notice, pay attention (*en algo* (to) sth): *no me fijé en lo que pasaba* I didn't notice what was happening; *¡fíjate!/¡fíjese!* just imagine!

☐ not 'fix' in the sense of repair: use *arreglar, reparar*

☐ **fijo** *adj* fixed: *a precio fijo* (at a) fixed price; *mirar fijamente* to stare (at)

film or **filme** *nm* film ('movie')

☐ see also *película*, which is the more 'purist' word; see this also for camera film

☐ **fílmico** *adj* film, to do with films: *la técnica fílmica* film(ing) technique

☐ **filmar** *vt* to film (but see also *rodar*)

fin *nm* end (esp in a time context): *al fin del año* at the end of the year

☐ *en/por fin* at last; *al fin y al cabo* in

the end, finally
- □ NB *pl* form in *a fines de* at/around the end of (used with months, seasons, etc): *a fines de agosto* around the end of August
- □ end (purpose): *¿con qué fin?* with/to what purpose?; *con el fin de + inf* with the purpose of ...ing
- □ not entirely the same as cf *final* below
- □ **final** *adj* final, last
- □ also *nm* end (usually of something physical): *al final de la calle* at the end of the street
- □ and *nf* final (match): *la final de copa* cup final
- □ **finalidad** *nf* aim, goal, purpose
- □ overlap of meaning with *fin* in this sense
- □ also means, of course, 'finality'
- □ **finalizar** *vt -ce-, -cé* to end, conclude (in this sense), same as but less common than: *terminar, concluir*
- □ also 'finalise', as in Eng
- □ **finalizarse** *vr* to end, conclude (ie to come to an end)

financiero *adj* financial
- □ NB not *financial*!

fingir *vt -jo, -ja-* to sham, fake: *fingir la identidad* to fake one's identity
- □ *+ inf*: to feign, pretend: *fingir no escuchar* to pretend not to be listening
- □ **fingirse** *vr + noun/adj*: to pretend to be: *fingirse rico* to pretend to be rich
- □ **fingido** as *adj/past part* feigned, pretended, false: *bajo identidad fingida* under false identity
- □ NB not same as cf *pretender* to claim

fino *adj* fine (in most senses)
- □ use *bueno* for weather: *hace buen tiempo* the weather's fine

firma *nf* signature
- □ also firm, company (cf also *compañía, empresa*)
- □ **firmar** *vti* to sign

firme *adj* firm (in most senses)
- □ **firmeza** *nf* firmness (in most senses): *con firmeza* firmly

física *nf* physics (NB *sing* and spelling)
- □ **físico/a** *adj* physical; *nmf* physicist

flaco *adj* thin
- □ NB means 'skinny', 'lean': often has somewhat derogatory/negative meaning, as opposed to cf *delgado, esbelto* slim
- □ also 'weak', 'feeble': *es mi punto flaco* it's my weak point
- □ **flaqueza** *nf* thinness; weakness (in above sense)

flan *nm* crème caramel (dessert)
- □ not a 'flan' in the British sense

flojo *adj* loose, slack, limp
- □ *cuerda floja* tight(!)rope
- □ also 'weak', 'feeble': *es un estudiante muy flojo* he's a very weak student; *Ana se siente floja después de la gripe* Ana feels weak/feeble after the flu
- □ **flojedad** *nf* looseness, slackness; weakness (in above sense)

flor *nf* flower, blossom
- □ *a flor de prep* on the level with: *a flor del agua* at water level
- □ **florecer** *vi -zc-* to flower, bloom
- □ also 'to flourish'

fluctuar *vi -ú- fluctúo, fluctúas, fluctúe* to fluctuate, vary (cf *oscilar, variar*); also 'to hesitate' (cf *vacilar, ducar*)

fluido *adj* fluid; fluent
- □ *nm* fluid
- □ also (electric) current
- □ **fluidez** *nf* fluidity; fluency; *con fluidez* fluently: *habla español con fluidez* he/she speaks Spanish fluently
- □ **fluir** *vi -y-*: *pi: fluyo, fluyes, fluye, fluyen; ps: fluya* to flow

fomentar *vt* to promote, foster, encourage (a cause, not a person – use *animar*): *fomentar la enseñanza del castellano* to

encourage the teaching of Spanish
- **fomento** *nm* fostering, encouragement (in above sense)

fondo *nm* has a variety of meanings and idioms:
- back, (in the sense of far end), background (on horizontal plane): *en el fondo había unos pocos árboles* in the background there were a few trees
- bottom, depths (ie far end on vertical plane): *en el fondo del pozo* at the bottom of the well
- **a fondo** (*adv* used as *adj*) in-depth, thorough: *una investigación a fondo* a thorough/an in-depth investigation
- *en el fondo* at bottom, basically: *en el fondo me parece buena persona* deep down s/he seems a good person

forastero see under **fuera**

forma *nf* form, shape: *estar/mantenerse en forma* to be/keep fit, in good shape
- way, means (used in same way as cf *manera, modo*): *es la única forma de hacerlo* it's the only way to do it; *de esta forma* in this way; *de todas formas* anyway, in any case
- *de (tal) forma que* (*conj*) so that ... + *subjunc* to indicate purpose: *lo repararé de tal forma que no se note* I'll repair it in such a way that you won't notice it
- or + *indic* to indicate result: *lo reparó de tal forma que no se notaba* he repaired it in such a way that you couldn't notice it
- **formar** *vt* to form (in most senses)
- to train, educate
- **formarse** *vr* to form, take shape; to train, get trained (as above)
- to train for sports etc use *entrenar(se)*
- **formación** *nf pl formaciones* formation (in most senses)
- but also, in an educational sense, 'training': *formación profesional* vocational training; see also *formar*
- for sports training use *entrenamiento*

formal *adj* formal
- but also 'serious', 'earnest', 'reliable': *es un chico formal* he's a serious/reliable lad
- similarly **formalidad** *nf* formality, but also 'seriousness', 'earnestness', 'reliability'

fortalecer, forzar, forzoso see **fuerte**

fortuna *nf* fortune, chance
- often implies good luck (much the same as cf *suerte*)
- *adj* is *des/afortunado* un/lucky

fotografía *nf*, **foto** *nf* photo(graph)
- **fotógrafo/a** *nm/f* photographer (NB stress and don't confuse with *fotografía*!)

fracaso *nm* failure, flop
- opp. of *éxito*, not same as cf *fallo; un fracaso escolar* a school drop-out
- **fracasar** *vi* to fail, flop, come to grief
- not same as cf *fallar*

frase *nf* sentence
- for 'phrase', as a meaningful group of words use *locución*

frecuente *adj* frequent
- **frecuencia** *nf* frequency: *con frecuencia* often, frequently (useful alternative to cf *frecuentemente, a menudo, muchas veces*)

fregar *vt* -ie-; -gue-, -gué to scour, wash (dishes): *fregar los platos* to wash up
- **fregadero** kitchen sink

freír *vt* -i-; *frío, fríes; fría; past part: frito* to fry; *patatas fritas* chips

frente NB different meaning depending on gender:
- *nf* forehead, brow
- *nm* front (esp in military, political or weather): *frente nacional* national front; *frente frío* cold front
- **frente a** *prep* opposite (slightly less common than *enfrente de*)

- □ NB can also have a more specific meaning – 'face to face with', 'in the face of', 'confronted by/with': *frente a esta decisión* in the face of this decision; *se encontró frente al enemigo* he found himself face to face with the enemy

fresco *adj* cool, fresh (in most senses): *¡qué fresco hace!* isn't it fresh!

- □ cheeky: *¡qué fresco eres!* you've got a cheek!
- □ **frescura** *nf* freshness, coolness; cheek

frío *nm* (the) cold: *no me gusta el frío* I don't like the cold

- □ NB when used with *tener* and *hacer*, it is a noun and is qualified by *mucho* not *muy*, and is invariable: *hace mucho frío* it's very cold; *Isabel tiene mucho frío* Isabel is/feels very cold!,
- □ used as *adj*, it agrees in the usual way and is qualified by *muy*: *una cerveza muy fría* a very cold beer
- □ as *adj* tends to be used with *estar*: *¡mi sopa está fría!* my soup is cold!, unless it indicates a natural characteristic: *no me gusta ese profesor, es muy frío* I don't like that teacher, he's very cold (ie has a cold character)
- □ **friolero/a** *adj* or *nmf* subject to cold; *es una friolera* she's a chilly mortal

fruta *nf* (usual word for) fruit

- □ **fruto** *nm* fruit, but tends to be used more in the sense of 'result(s)': *el fruto de todo nuestro trabajo* the fruit of all our labour

fuego *nm* fire (in general sense)

- □ also, in cooking, 'heat': *a fuego lento* on a (s)low heat
- □ 'a light' (for cigarette): *¿tienes fuego?* do you have a light?
- □ NB not same as cf *incendio*, for which you would need the fire brigade!

fuente *nf* fountain, spring

- □ source (eg of material)
- □ serving dish or bowl

fuera *adv* outside, out: *¡fuera!* out! get out!; *por fuera* on the outside; *estar fuera* to be away (ie somewhere else)

- □ **fuera de** *prep* out of, outside (of): *fuera de moda* out of fashion
- □ NB not 'outside the shop' in the sense of 'in front of': use *delante de; nos veremos delante del cine* we'll see each other outside (ie in front of) the cinema
- □ **forastero/a** *nmf* stranger, outsider
- □ implication is sb who is 'from outside', who 'doesn't belong', 'alien': not same as cf *desconocido*, or quite as definite as *extranjero*
- □ can also be used as *adj*

fuerte *adj* (basically) strong, tough, but with a much wider range of meaning:

- □ widely used in phrases such as: *un golpe fuerte* a heavy/hard blow
- □ *un dolor fuerte* an intense pain
- □ *lluvia fuerte* heavy rain
- □ also 'loud': *un ruido fuerte* a loud noise
- □ often used as *adv* 'loudly': *¡más fuerte!* speak up! louder!
- □ worth further research in a dictionary!
- □ **fuerza** *nf* strength, force
- □ *(no) tener fuerzas para* (not) to have the strength to/for; *(no) sentirse con fuerzas para algo* (not) to feel up to something; *con fuerza* strongly
- □ **a fuerza de** *prep* by dint of: *a fuerza de mucho trabajo* by dint of a lot of hard work
- □ **forzar** *vt* -ue-; -ce-, cé to force (in most senses)
- □ *forzar a alguien a hacer algo* to force sb to do sth: *le forzaron a confesar* they forced him to confess
- □ **forzoso** *adj* necessary, compulsory
- □ *es forzoso que* + *subjunc* it's necessary that …
- □ **fortalecer** *vt* -zc- to strengthen, fortify

fumar *vti* to smoke (tobacco etc)
- NB *fumar en pipa* to smoke a pipe (generally), *fumar una pipa* to smoke a (= one) pipeful
- not same as cf *humear* to (give off) smoke

función *nf pl funciones* function (in most senses)
- **en función de** *prep* according to, depending on, in relation to (has a more limited usage than cf *según*):

rellena los espacios en blanco en función del significado del texto fill the gaps according to the meaning of the passage
- **funcionar** *vi* to function, work (in that sense): *no funciona* out of order

fusilar *vt* to shoot (somebody), execute
- not same as cf *disparar* to shoot (ie fire) a gun

fútbol *nm* football (the game)
- for the ball, see *balón*

G

G *(ge)* there are a number of points to watch in the way this letter is pronounced:
- it is pronounced similarly to English when 'hard', before *a, o, u,* although it tends to be sounded further down the throat, especially between vowels and in the combination *gua* (eg *agua*).
- it is pronounced the same as Spanish *j* before *-e* and *-i-* (*gesto, giro*).
- it is pronounced 'gw' in combinations *gua, guo,* but *u* is silent in *gue* and *gui* where it separates the g from the vowel to keep it 'hard': *guerra, guisar.*
- to get the sound 'gw' before *e/i,* you need the diaeresis on the *ü,* as in *vergüenza, argüir.*

gabinete *nm* study (room)
- used in some professional contexts as office or room where the profession is practised: *gabinete de consulta* consulting room; *estudio* is often used for a study in private house
- also political 'cabinet'

Gales *nm* Wales
- don't confuse with, and note different stress of: **galés** (*galesa, galeses,*

galesas) *adj/nmf* Welsh, Welshman/woman

galleta *nf* biscuit
- NB some American dictionaries give *bizcocho,* which is a sponge cake or sponge finger, not a 'biscuit' in the British sense

gallina *nf* hen, chicken (ie a live female chicken)
- use *pollo* for chicken to eat
- **gallo** *nm* cockerel, rooster

gamberro *nm* lout, hooligan, yob
- can also be *adj*: loutish
- these types indulge in **gamberrismo** *nm* loutishness, hooliganism

gana *nf* desire, inclination
- mainly used in a number of common idioms, sometimes in *pl*: *tener ganas de + inf* to wish to, feel like ...ing, have a mind to; *de buena gana* willingly; *de mala gana* unwillingly, reluctantly; *me entró la gana de + inf* I felt the urge to; *se me fue/quitó la gana de + inf* I lost the urge to; *lo hice sin ganas* I did it without really wanting to, reluctantly; *hazlo como te dé la gana* do it as you wish

ganado *nm* cattle, livestock
- general word, can be used for livestock other than bovine if specified: *ganado lanar* woollen livestock, sheep

ganar *vti* 3 main meanings:
- to win (game, points, respect, etc): *el Real Madrid ganó tres a uno* Real Madrid won 2–1
- to earn (money) cf *cobrar*: *gana x euros al año* he earns x euros a year
- to reach (usually after some effort): *por fin ganamos la otra orilla* we finally reached/made the other bank; cf *alcanzar*
- **ganador/a** *adj* winning: *el billete ganador* the winning ticket
- *nmf* winner
- also *nmf* earner (see *ganar* above)
- **ganancia** *nf* gain, profit (especially in commercial context): *ganancias y pérdidas* profit and loss; cf *beneficio*

gansa/ganso *nf/m* goose/gander
- *m* often used (especially in *pl*) loosely meaning 'goose/geese'

garaje *nm* garage (ie where a car is kept)
- NB for place to get car repaired use *taller (mecánico)*, for place to buy petrol use *estación de servicio, gasolinera*, for place to buy car use *concesionario*

garantizar *vt* -ce-, -cé to guarantee
- **garantía** *nf* guarantee
- NB spelling: no *u*

gas *nm* gas
- *gas invernadero* greenhouse gas; *gases de escape* exhaust fumes
- **gasolina** *nf* petrol
- **gasolinera** *nf* petrol station (often small, without services – a bigger one would be *estación de servicio*)

gastar *vt* several common meanings:
- to spend (money, effort; not time, use *pasar*)
- to waste: *gastar palabras* to waste words
- to wear out (especially clothes)
- to wear, sport (clothes, accessories, often with some emphasis on conspicuousness): *gastaba una corbata amarilla brillante* he was sporting a bright yellow tie
- *gastar una broma* to play a trick
- **gastado** *adj (past part)* spent, (of clothing) worn out
- **gasto** *nm* expenditure; occurs especially in *pl*: *los gastos* expenses, costs

gato/a *nmf* cat
- *m* or *f* form used depending on sex of cat

gemelo/a *nmf* or *adj* twin; *gemelos* twins (one of each sex or both male)
- strictly 'identical' twin: cf *mellizo*
- also *pl*: cufflinks
- and *pl*: binoculars
- NB use *hermano* *adj/hermanar(se)* *vt/r* for twin(ning) towns

gemir *vi* -i- to groan, moan (in that sense)
- **gemido** *nm* groan, moan

general *adj* general (in most senses)
- *adv* **en general/por lo general** in general, generally, as a general rule
- **general/a** *nmf* (military) general

género *nm* kind, sort, type, genre (see also *clase, tipo*, which can be used in much the same way): *no me gusta este género de película* I don't like this sort of film
- also: gender (in grammatical sense, not used to mean 'sex' ie male/female as is modern tendency in Eng – use *sexo*)
- in *pl los géneros* goods, merchandise

generoso *adj* generous (*con/para* to/towards)

genio *nm* temperament, nature, character: *de buen genio* good-natured; *de mal genio* bad-tempered
- can mean 'bad-tempered' without the *mal*: *tiene genio* he/she's quick-tempered
- also 'genius': *es un genio* he's a genius
- **genial** *adj* brilliant, having genius
- less frequently, can also mean 'genial' in Eng sense, though *simpático, amistoso* would be safer

gente *nf* people, folk
- NB usually singular, with singular

verb: *la gente dice que …* people say that …
- □ can also mean 'people' in the sense of 'race', 'nation': *la gente británica* the British people (similar here to cf *pueblo*, though without any of the 'plebeian' implications of the latter)

gentil *adj* elegant, graceful, courteous
- □ not as English 'gentle', use *suave, amable*, nor as Fr 'kind', use *amable*!
- □ **gentileza** *nf* elegance, gracefulness, courtesy (as above)

geografía *nf* geography;
- □ **geográfico** *adj* geographic(al)
- □ note spelling: accents and *f* not *ph*!

gerente *nmf* manager (of factory, hotel, etc)
- □ a little more limited in scope and status than *director(a)*
- □ **gerencia** *nf* management: ie organisation which manages, cf *dirección*, not same as *gestión* below
- □ **gestión** *nf* management (ie act of managing, not same as *gerencia* above)
- □ also 'measure', 'step' (in that sense): *haremos las gestiones necesarias* we'll take the necessary steps
- □ **gestionar** *vt* to manage

gesto *nm* (facial) expression: *hacer un gesto* to pull/make a face; *poner mal gesto* to scowl
- □ also: sign, gesture

girar *vti* to turn, (in sense of) to rotate, spin: *la tierra gira alrededor del sol* the earth revolves around the sun
- □ also used in such phrases as *gire a la izquierda* turn left; *girar alrededor de* to be approximately; *el total giraba alrededor de los mil* the total was around a thousand
- □ **giro** *nm* turn, revolution
- □ also 'turn' (change): *el asunto tomó un giro desfavorable* the matter took a turn for the worse
- □ *giro postal/bancario* postal/banker's order

gira *nf* tour, trip
- □ especially of entertainment or sports groups, etc *el conjunto hizo una gira por Sudamérica* the group did a tour of South America
- □ more limited in application than cf *vuelta* and *syn viaje*

globo *nm* globe, sphere
- □ balloon

gobierno *nm* government (in most senses)
- □ guidance, control: *el gobierno de la casa* housekeeping, household management
- □ **gobernar** *vti -ie-* to govern

gol *nm* goal (ie what is scored); goalmouth is *meta* or *portería*

golpe *nm* blow, hit, knock
- □ has a number of idioms: *dar golpes a* to hit (an object); *golpe de estado* coup d'état; *cerrar algo de golpe* to slam something shut; *de un golpe* suddenly
- □ **golpear** *vt* to strike, knock, hit cf *pegar*

gordo *adj* fat; *el Gordo* lottery jackpot

gorra *nf* (peaked) cap
- □ cf **gorro** *nm* cap, bonnet (less restrictive than *f* form): *gorro de baño* bathing cap

gozar *vti -ce-, -cé* to enjoy
- □ used transitively or followed by *de*: *gozar buena salud* or *gozar de buena salud* to enjoy good health
- □ also: to enjoy oneself (cf *divertirse*)
- □ **gozo** *nm* enjoyment, pleasure: *da gozo/es un gozo verlo* it's a pleasure to see it; *para nuestro gozo, vino a vernos* to our pleasure, she came to see us
- □ cf *disfrutar/disfrute*

gracia *nf* grace, gracefulness
- □ *tener gracia* to be funny (of joke, person, etc); *¡qué gracia!* how amusing!
- □ *pl (muchas) gracias* (many) thanks, thank you (very much); *dar las gracias*

a alguien por algo to thank someone for something; *gracias a* thanks to
- □ merits further research in a dictionary
- □ **gracioso** *adj* graceful
- □ also 'funny', 'amusing': *¡qué gracioso es!* isn't he funny!

grado *nm* degree, stage, grade: *de primer grado* first grade; *por grados* by degrees; *en sumo grado* in the highest degree; *grado universitario* university degree (but see also *título*)
- □ degree (heat or geometrical): *veinte grados* 20°
- □ *de buen/mal grado* (un)willingly

grande *adj* big, large
- □ tall: *es un hombre grande* he's a tall man
- □ grand, grandiose
- □ great, ie through fame or achievement, when it precedes the noun: *un gran escritor* a great writer
- □ NB drops -*de* before any singular noun: *un gran problema* a big problem
- □ when it means 'big', 'large' it can come before or after the noun, though the bigness is more emphatic when it is placed after: *un gran árbol/un árbol grande* a big tree
- □ **grandeza** *nf* bigness, greatness: noun for the qualities listed under *grande*

granja *nf* farm
- □ tends to be used for small farm, not the much larger *cortijo* of S Spain

grano *nm* seed, grain
- □ also: pimple, spot

gratis *adv* free, for nothing: *no lo hacen gratis* they don't do it for nothing
- □ **gratuito** *adj* free, gratis
- □ same meaning as *gratis*, but this is the adjectival form normally used with a noun: *comida gratuita* free food/meals
- □ also means 'gratuitous': *una*

observación gratuita a gratuitous/uncalled-for remark

grato *adj* pleasing, pleasant, agreeable
- □ emphasises the pleasant effect or acceptability to the receiver: *fue una acción muy grata para nosotros* it was a very welcome action for us
- □ in eg business correspondence: *nos es grato mandarle …* we have pleasure in sending you …

grave *adj* grave, serious, critical (in that sense)
- □ perhaps more likely to be used than *serio* in the sense of 'grave': *una enfermedad grave* a serious illness
- □ **gravedad** *nf* gravity (in all senses); graveness, seriousness

gritar *vti* shout, cry, scream, shriek
- □ for 'cry' in sense of 'weep' use *llorar*; see also *chillar* for scream, shriek (rather shriller)
- □ **grito** *nm* shout, cry, scream, shriek; *a voz en grito* at the top of one's voice

grosero *adj* rude, crude, coarse, gross (in that sense)
- □ covers 'rude' in most senses, though *descortés* or *mal educado* might be better for 'impolite'

grueso *adj* thick, stout, solid (applied to objects): *un árbol grueso* a stout/solid tree
- □ applied to a person: stout, thickset, (NB not 'fat', use *gordo*)

gruñir *vi ger: gruñendo; pret: gruñó, gruñeron; imp subj: gruñera/gruñese* to grunt, growl
- □ also: to grouse, grumble
- □ **gruñido** *nm* grunt, growl
- □ **gruñón** *adj gruñona, gruñones, gruñonas* grumpy, grumbling

grupo *nm* group
- □ has a wider meaning than Eng equivalent: 'party': *un grupo escolar* a school party; 'squad': *grupo de*

estupefacientes drug squad; 'cluster': *un grupo de árboles* a cluster of trees

guapo *adj* used mainly to describe people rather than objects: good-looking, pretty (*f*), handsome (*m*)
- □ also: smart, elegant
- □ NB use with *estar* to indicate impression made: *¡Qué guapa estás!* How elegant you look!

guarda *nmf* guard, keeper (ie someone who looks after something)
- □ not a policeman/woman, ie don't confuse with *guardia*
- □ **guarda-** *prefix* there are quite a number of words beginning with this prefix, which means 'guard' or 'protector', eg **guardabosque** *nmf* gamekeeper; **guardarropa** *nm* cloakroom; wardrobe
- □ **guardar** *vt* to guard, watch over, protect
- □ also: to keep (back), retain, hold on to
- □ *guardar la ley* to observe the law; *guardar respeto a alguien* to have/show respect for sb
- □ **guardarse** *vr* to be on one's guard
- □ *guardarse de hacer algo* to be careful not to do sth
- □ **guardia** *nf* care, custody, guard: *estar de guardia* to be on guard; *farmacia de guardia* duty chemist
- □ also, perhaps more frequently as *guardia nf* guard: *la Guardia Civil* Civil Guard
- □ *nmf* NB either gender when it means 'policeman/woman'
- □ **guardián/guardiana** *nmf mpl* *guardianes* guardian, usually in sense of warden, keeper, eg in zoo; also (legal) guardian of a child

guerrilla *nf* not 'guerrilla' as used in Eng:
- □ the diminutive of the Sp word *guerra*, 'little war' means 'guerrilla warfare', or guerrilla band; 'guerrilla' is **guerrillero/a** *nmf*

guía *nf* guide (in sense of) guidebook

- □ also: guidance
- □ *nmf* guide (person who shows you round)
- □ **guiar** *vt -í-: guío, guías,* etc; *guíe* etc to guide (in most senses)

guisar *vt* to cook, prepare food
- □ especially : to stew

gustar *vi* to please
- □ NB the person who likes is the indirect object and what or who is liked is the subject: *a Javier le gustó mucho la película* Javier liked the film a lot
- □ remember if you like something plural, the verb is plural: *no me gustan las zanahorias* I don't like carrots
- □ without an indirect object, it expresses general pleasure or displeasure: *las obras de X ya no gustan* X's works are no longer liked/popular
- □ *gustar más* can be used with same meaning as cf *preferir* to prefer: *me gusta más ése* I prefer that one
- □ it is used with a personal subject in some set phrases: *¿Usted gusta?* Would you like some? *como usted guste* as you please/wish
- □ as *vt* it can also mean 'to taste', 'try': *¿Has gustado este vino?* Have you tried/tasted this wine? (but *probar* is more common in this sense)
- □ **gusto** *nm* taste, (flavour) (*a* of): *tiene gusto a limón* it has a lemon flavour, it tastes of lemon: in this sense cf *sabor*
- □ also 'taste' (style): *de buen/mal gusto* in good/bad taste
- □ and 'pleasure': *con mucho gusto* with great pleasure; *mucho gusto – el gusto es mío* pleased to meet you – the pleasure's mine (when two people are introduced)
- □ used in quite a number of idioms: *tener gusto por* to have a liking for; *a gusto* as you fancy, to taste
- □ would reward further research in a dictionary

H (*ache*)

- It is never sounded, whether on the beginning of a word or in the middle: as in *hacer, prohibir*.
- It combines with *c* to make the sound *ch*, as in *muchacho*, which was listed in dictionaries as a separate letter until 1994.
- Another interesting point is the number of words beginning with *h* which at one time in their passage from Latin to Spanish began with *f*. If you put the *f* back, you will recognise words which begin with *f* and are very similar in French and other Latin languages, and sometimes even English! There are several examples of words of this type in the following list, incuding: *haba*, as in *fabada asturiana* a bean stew, *hacer* (Fr *faire*), *hambre* (Fr *faim*, Eng *famine, famished*), *hembra* (Eng *female*), *hijo/a* (Fr *fils/fille*, Eng *filial*), *hila* (Eng *file*).
- These words are marked ⋆, for interest's sake, but also to help you develop a strategy for more easily recognising Spanish words.

haba⋆ *nf* bean; NB *el/un haba* because of stressed *ha-*; *pl* is *las habas*; usually means a 'broad' or 'butter' bean, see also *alubia*; see *judía* for 'green' bean

haber *v pi: he, has, ha, hemos, habéis, han; ps: haya* etc; *fut/condit: habré/habría; pret: hube, hubiste, hubo, hubimos, hubisteis, hubieron; imp subj: hubiera/hubiese.* A common verb with a number of idiomatic uses:
- □ 'to have', used only as auxiliary verb to form compound tenses (perfect, pluperfect, future and conditional perfect, past anterior): *hemos llegado* we've arrived; *habrían visto* they would have seen; don't confuse with *tener*, which is used for 'have' in the sense of 'possess'
- □ *haber de* 'to be to', used to express mild obligation, necessity, or an emphatic future ('shall' rather than 'will'): *¿qué hemos de hacer?* what are we to do?; *has de ver* you shall see
- □ *hay* there is/are: a special 3rd pers sing of present indic, which is invariable. Other tenses use the normal 3rd pers sing form *había, hubo*, etc: *no hay muchos verbos como éste* there aren't many verbs like this one; *hubo un accidente* there was an accident
- □ *hay que + inf* it is necessary to (another of the several ways of expressing obligation): *hay que estudiar mucho* it's necessary/you have to study a lot; see also *tener que, deber*
- □ *habérselas con* to be up against, to have to contend with: *tendrás que habértelas con el campeón mundial* you'll be up against the world champion

hábil *adj* clever, able
- □ also 'skilful', though *diestro* might be better if the meaning leans towards 'dextrous'
- □ **habilidad** *nf* cleverness, ability
- □ skill (cf *destreza* and observation re *diestro* above)

habitación *nf pl habitaciones* room (in hotel, in house): *habitación doble/individual* double/single room
- □ room as unit in house: *la casa tiene cinco habitaciones*
- □ see also for comparison: *cuarto, dormitorio, sala*

habitante *nmf* inhabitant (NB NOT *inhabitante*!)
- □ **habitar** *vt* to inhabit, live in; not used so frequently as *vivir en*

hábito *nm* habit, custom
- □ much the same as *costumbre* in sense of 'habit', 'custom'
- □ also 'habit', as Eng in sense of eg a monk's habit

hablar* *vti* to speak, talk: *hablar de algo con alguien* to talk to/with somebody about something
- □ *hablar castellano* to speak Spanish; but *hablar bien el castellano* to speak Spanish well (ie no definite article unless *hablar* is qualified by an adverb); *aquí se habla español* Spanish spoken here; *¡ni hablar!* no way!, not likely!, not on your life!
- □ **habla*** *nf* speech (ie act of speaking): *de habla española* Spanish-speaking
- □ NB *el habla* because of stressed *ha*

hacer* *vt pi:* hago, haces etc; *ps:* haga etc; *tú imperative:* haz; *fut/condit:* haré/haría: *past part:* hecho; *pret:* hice, hiciste, hizo, hicimos hicisteis, hicieron; *imp subj:* hiciera/hiciese, a common verb with multiple uses:
- □ to make, do: *¿qué estás haciendo?* what are you doing?; *estoy haciendo la cama* I'm making the bed
- □ *hacer + inf* to get/have something done: *hice construir una casa* I had a house built
- □ *hacer que + subj* to make something happen: *hicimos que terminaran la casa* we made them finish the house
- □ *hace + length of time:* ago; used as follows: either *llegaron hace media hora* or *hace media hora que llegaron* they arrived half an hour ago; consult a grammar book for a full explanation of this use of *hacer* and of *desde hace* (see under *desde*) 'for a period of time'
- □ *hace + weather expression* it's + weather expression: *hace frío/viento/sol* it's cold, windy, sunny
- □ **hacerse** *vr* to become (used with nouns, not adjectives): *se hizo veterinario* he became a vet
- □ **hecho*** *nm* fact

- ie a reality: *es un hecho ineludible* it's an unavoidable fact; not quite the same as cf *dato* (fact in sense of thing that has happened)
- □ *adj* (*past part* of *hacer*) ready-made, done: *un vestido hecho* a ready-made dress; *¡hecho!* done!, agreed! (eg a deal); *¡trato hecho!* it's a deal! *dicho y hecho* no sooner said than done

hacia *prep* towards
- □ in both space (*hacia mí* towards me) and time (*hacia medianoche* towards midnight) contexts
- □ used in equivalents of phrases ending in '-wards': *hacia abajo/arriba* downwards/upwards, *hacia adelante/atrás* forwards/backwards; *hacia casa* homewards

hallar *vt* to find
- □ often used reflexively **hallarse** *vr* to be found, to be situated: *Sitges se halla al sur de Barcelona* Sitges is situated south of Barcelona
- □ much the same meaning as cf *encontrar(se)* used in these senses

hambre* *nf* hunger
- □ *el/un hambre* because of stressed *ha-*; *sufrieron un hambre indescriptible* they suffered indescribable hunger
- □ NB *tener (mucha) hambre* to be (very) hungry
- □ *pasar hambre* to starve (in sense of) go hungry; *morir de hambre* to starve to death; *me muero de hambre* I'm starving
- □ note also **hambriento*** *adj* usually used to qualify noun: *la gente hambrienta del tercer mundo* the hungry/starving people of the third world; not used to say 'I'm hungry', see above

harina* *nf* flour
- □ *eso es harina de otro costal* that's another matter, that's a different kettle of fish

harto* *(de) adj*   fed up (with); use with *estar*: *estoy harto de este trabajo*   I'm fed up with this work
- **hartarse* (de)** *vr*   to eat one's fill (of)
- also, quite frequently: to get fed up (with)

hasta   a word with numerous functions and meanings:
- *adv*   even: *hasta nos invitaron a cenar* they even invited us to supper; cf *aun, incluso*
- *prep*   (in place) as far as, up to: *¿Puede llevarnos hasta Segovia?*   Can you take us as far as Segovia?; *hasta cierto punto, estoy de acuerdo*   up to a certain point, I agree
- *prep*   (in time) until, till, up to: *esperaremos hasta las tres*   we'll wait until three o'clock; *hasta ahora*   up to now; *hasta luego*   see you soon; *hasta sábado*   until/see you Saturday; see also *desde … hasta* under *desde*
- *hasta que conj*   until/till (+ *verb*): take care here!: to report a fact or an event taken place use *indicative*: *me quedé hasta que llegaron*   I stayed until they arrived (fact – they arrived); to talk about an action not yet taken place use *subjunctive*: *me quedaré hasta que lleguen*   I'll stay until they arrive (not fact – they haven't yet arrived); *dije que me quedaría hasta que llegasen*   I said I would stay until they arrived (not fact – they hadn't yet arrived at the time of speaking); consult a grammar book for further clarification

hay see **haber**

he aquí *adv*   here is, here are
- somewhat formal, and used mainly in written Sp: *he aquí las razones*   here are the reasons

hecho* see **hacer**

helar *vt* **helarse** *vr* -ie-   to freeze: *el río se heló*   the river froze up/over
- **helada** *nf*   frost, freeze(-up); **helado** *nm*   ice cream (don't confuse them!)
- **hielo** *nm*   ice
- some overlap with cf *congelar*

hembra* *nf*   female
- used, especially, with animals, where there is no specific feminine: eg *el conejo hembra*   the female rabbit
- NB it is a noun, so there is no agreement; *conejos hembra*   female rabbits

herir* *vt* -ie-, -i-   to wound, hurt, injure
- **herido/a*** *nmf*   wounded person, casualty
- often occurs in plural: *hubo muchos heridos*   there were many casualties/wounded/injured
- *adj/past part*   wounded, injured
- don't confuse with **herida** *nf* wound, injury: *tenía muchas heridas* he/she had many wounds
- injuries usually more severe than cf *lesión/lesionar*

hermano/hermana* *nm/f*   brother/sister
- NB *hermanos nmpl* in the sense of 'brothers and sisters': *¿Tienes hermanos?*   Have you any brothers and sisters?
- *hermano menor*   younger/est brother; *hermana mayor*   elder/est sister
- *nuestra ciudad hermana*   our twin town (for 'twins', see *gemelo*)
- **hermanar*** *vt* **hermanarse** *vr*   to twin (of eg towns)

hermoso* *adj*   beautiful, lovely, handsome
- used with both people and objects: *es una chica muy hermosa*   she's a very beautiful girl; *¡Qué día tan hermoso!* What a beautiful/lovely day!
- see also for comparison of degree of loveliness: *bello, guapo, lindo, precioso*
- **hermosura*** *nf*   beauty, loveliness, handsomeness; cf *belleza,*

lindeza/lindura, preciosidad

héroe *nm* hero
- **heroína** *nf* heroine (female hero)

heroína *nf* heroin (drug)
- **heroinómano/a** *nmf* heroin addict

herramienta* *nf* tool (rather more heavy-duty than cf *utensilio*)

hervir* *vti -ie-, -i-* to boil
- NB: *agua hirviendo* boiling water

hielo see **helar**

hierba *nf* grass
- in sense of 'lawn' use *césped*
- *malas hierbas* weeds; *hierbabuena* mint

hierro* *nm* iron
- ie the metal; you iron (*planchar*) clothes with *una plancha*

higo* *nm* fig
- **higuera*** *nf* fig tree

hijo/hija* *nm/f* son/daughter
- NB *pl hijos* in sense of 'children', 'offspring', collectively: *¿Cuántos hijos tiene Vd?* How many children have you got?; in this sense, it is used in preference to cf *niños*

hila or **hilera*** *nf* row, line: *en la tercera hilera* in the third row
- **hilo*** *nm* thread

hincapié* *nm* useful in the expression *hacer hincapié en* to emphasise, make a special point of: *hay que hacer hincapié en sus actividades políticas* we must emphasise his political activities

hinchar *vt* to inflate (tyre, etc)
- reflexive form often used –
  hincharse *vr* to swell (up): *se me hinchó la rodilla* my knee swelled up; *(estar) hinchado* (to be) swollen; *tengo la rodilla hinchada* I've got a swollen knee

historia *nf* history
- also 'story', 'tale': some overlap with cf *cuento*, though the latter tends to be shorter

hogar* *nm* hearth, fireplace
- and by extension, 'home': *hogar de ancianos* old people's home; *los sin hogar* the homeless
- *related to cf *fuego*, in case you hadn't realised!

hoja* *nf* leaf (of plant, tree, etc)
- leaf, page (of book), sheet (of paper, metal)
- blade (of knife, razor)
- **hojear** *vt* to flick/leaf through (the pages of a book, magazine)

holgarse* *vr -ue-; -gue-, -gué* to enjoy oneself, have a good time
- *huelga decir que …* it goes without saying that …
- **huelga*** *nf* strike
- interestingly derived from *holgarse** above!
- *huelga de hambre* hunger strike; *ir a la huelga/ponerse en huelga* to go on strike
- **huelguista** *nmf* striker

hombre *nm* man; *el hombre* mankind
- *interj ¡hombre!* expresses surprise: 'good heavens!', 'well, well!', or protest: 'come come!', 'now then!'

hombro *nm* shoulder
- essentially top of shoulder(s), NB not same as cf *espalda(s)* 'back', 'shoulder blade(s)'

hondo* *adj* deep, profound
- tends to be used more to describe feelings/emotions, use cf *profundo* for more physical concepts – sea etc

honesto *adj* decent
- rather than 'honest': use *honrado*
- **honestidad** *nf* decency
- rather than 'honesty': use *honradez*

honor *nm* honour (in general sense)
- also especially in C16/17 Sp literature: virtue, good name

□ *tener el honor de* + *inf* to have the honour to + verb

honrado *adj* NB honest
□ but can, of course, mean 'honoured' as *past part* of *honrar*
□ **honradez** *nf* honesty, integrity
□ **honrar** *vt* to honour

hora *nf* hour: *esperamos dos horas* we waited two hours
□ time by the clock or calendar: *¿Tiene hora, por favor?* Do you have the time, please?; *¿A qué hora llegaste?* At what time did you arrive?; *la una, hora peninsular* one o'clock, mainland Spanish time; *horas punta* peak time
□ time to do sth: *es hora de decidirnos* it's time to make up our minds
□ occurs in other idioms: *en mis horas libres* in my spare time; *a última hora* at the last moment; *¿Puede darme hora con el dentista?* Can you give me an appointment with the dentist?; *coger hora* to make an appointment
□ cf and contrast in sense of 'time' the different applications of: *época, rato, tiempo, vez*

horror *nm* horror, dread
□ *¡qué horror!* how dreadful!, how ghastly!
□ there are various *adjs* based on it, as in Eng: **horrendo** *adj* horrendous, hideous, dire; **horrible** *adj* horrible, dreadful, ghastly; **horroroso** *adj* horrifying, horrible, ghastly; **horripilante** *adj* horrifying, enough to make your hair stand on end

hortaliza *nf* mainly used in *pl* vegetables, greenstuff
□ especially as garden produce; cf *legumbres, verduras*

horizonte *nm* horizon
□ **horizontal** *adj* horizontal; NB across (in crosswords)

horno* *nm* oven
□ *horno microondas* microwave oven; *alto horno* blast furnace

hospedar *vt* to lodge, put up (in that sense), receive as guest
□ **hospedarse** *vr* to stay, to lodge (as guest)
□ **hospedaje** *nm* lodging; *tenemos que incluir el hospedaje* we have to include the (cost of) lodging

hospital *nm* hospital
□ yes, there is an *s* in it – *hôpital* is French!
□ **hospitalizar** *vt* -ce-, *cé* to send to/put into hospital
□ **hospitalizarse** *vr* to go into hospital

hotel *nm* hotel
□ **hotelero** *adj* (to do with) hotel(s): *la industria hotelera* the hotel industry
□ **hotelero/a** *nmf* hotel keeper, hotelier

hoy *adv* today; note useful phrases:
□ *hoy (en) día* nowadays; *de hoy en ocho/quince días* a week/fortnight today; *por hoy* for the present

hueco *adj* hollow, empty (in that sense)
□ also as *nm* hollow, hole: (golf) hole
□ not same as cf *agujero* for hole in eg clothes or ground

huelga see **holgarse**

huella *nf* trace, mark, footprint: *sin dejar huella* without leaving a trace
□ ie the mark made by foot etc; not same as cf *paso*

huerta *nf* vegetable garden
□ some overlap with **huerto** *nm* vegetable garden, orchard
□ also cf *jardín*

hueso *nm* bone
□ also: stone (of fruit)
□ *ser de/estar hecho de carne y hueso* to be made of flesh and blood

huésped/a *nmf*   an odd word, in that it can mean:
- guest (of any kind, but not quite same as *invitado/a*, who, logically, has to have been invited; could be guest at eg hotel)
- host(ess) (you can also use *anfitrión/anfitriona*)

huir* *vt* or **huirse de** *vr* -y-: *huyo, huyes; huyas; huyendo; huyó, huyeron; huyera/ese* to flee, run away (*de* from)
- **huida*** *nf*   flight, ie act of fleeing; not same as *vuelo*!

húmedo *adj*   humid
- but NB also: damp, moist
- note this range of meaning also in **humedad** *nf* humidity but also: dampness, moisture; **humedecer** (*-zc-*) *vt* to dampen, moisten; **humedecerse** *vr* to become damp/moist

humo* *nm*   smoke
- **humear*** *vi*   to smoke
- ie give off smoke: not same as cf *fumar*!

humor *nm*   humour, mood

- occurs in useful phrases: *estar de buen/mal humor* to be in a good/bad mood; *el sentido del humor* sense of humour
- **humorístico** *adj*   humorous, ie relating to humour: *la literatura humorística* humorous literature
- to describe a person, better to use *divertido, chistoso: es muy divertido/chistoso* he's very humorous/funny

hundir *vt*   to sink: *el huracán hundió el buque* the hurricane sank the ship
- **hundirse** *vr*   to sink: *el buque se hundió a causa del huracán* the ship sank because of the hurricane
- also 'to collapse': *la casa se hundió* the house collapsed; *se hundió la economía* the economy collapsed
- **hundimiento** *nm*   sinking, collapse (in above senses)

hurtar* *vt*   to steal
- less common and maybe a shade stronger than *robar*
- **el hurto*** *nm*   theft, robbery
- *a hurto/a hurtadillas*   stealthily, by stealth

I is one of the five Sp vowels and is pronounced the same wherever it occurs in a word: *sin, insistir, mismo, así, crisis, invisible.*
- It forms diphthongs either way round with -a – *hacia, Jaime;* -e – *siete, seis;* -o – *radio, oigo;* and -u – *diurno, ruido.* If the vowel + -i- diphthong occurs on the end of a word, the -i- is replaced by -y-: *hay, ley, hoy, muy.*
- You cannot begin a word with -ie-: you put an *h-* on the beginning – *hielo;* stem-change verbs are prone to this eg *hiela, huele.*

- If the -i- combined with another vowel needs to be separated and stressed, it has an accent: *panadería, comisaría, veía, vería* (and in all -ía type imperfect and all conditional endings) *ríe, río, tío.*

Iberia *nf*   Iberia: refers to the whole of the 'Spanish' peninsula, including Portugal
- **ibérico** *adj*   Iberian: *la Península Ibérica* Iberian Peninsula
- **ibero/a** *nmf* and *adj*   Iberian: these were the early pre-Roman inhabitants of the peninsula

idea *nf*   idea (used mostly as in Eng)
- some common phrases: *no tengo la menor/la más mínima idea* I haven't the slightest idea; *¡ni idea!* no idea!;

idea fija fixed idea; *cambiar de idea* to change one's mind; *se me ocurrió la idea de + inf/de que …* the idea occurred to me to/that …

☐ **idear** *vt* to devise, think up: *idear un nuevo método* to think up a new method

identidad *nt* identity: *tarjeta de identidad* identity card

☐ **idéntico** *adj* identical

☐ **identificación** *nf pl identificaciones* identification

☐ **identificar** *vt -que-, -qué* to identify (*como* as, *con* with)

☐ **identificarse** *vr* to identify (*con* with): *¿Puedes identificarte con alguno de los personajes?* Can you identify with any of the characters?

idioma *nm* language (NB it's *masc*!); same as cf *lengua* in this sense

☐ NOT 'idiom', in the Eng sense, as used in explanations in this book: use *modismo*

☐ **idiomático** *adj* idiomatic: is however used in same sense as Eng

idiota *nmf and adj* idiot, fool; idiotic, foolish, silly; either gender ends in *-a*; *pl -as*; means much the same as cf *tonto*: *¡No seas idiota!* Don't be silly!

ignorar *vt* to not know, be unaware (of) *lo ignoro* I don't know, I've no idea; *ignoramos las circunstancias* we're not aware of the circumstances; basically, negative of *saber*; some overlap with, but not exactly the same as cf *desconocer*

☐ sometimes used in Eng sense of 'ignore', but advisable to use *no hacer caso* for this

☐ **ignorante** *adj* ignorant; **ignorancia** *nf* ignorance

igual *adj* equal

☐ often means 'same': *todos los chicos sois iguales* all you boys are the same; *(me) es igual* it's all the same to me, I don't mind; *y tu madre, ¿sigue igual?* and your mother, is she still the same? (ie in health, appearance etc)

☐ also 'level' (eg surface, temperature)

☐ can be used as *adv*: *me pasó igual* it happened to me like that, the same thing happened to me;

☐ **al igual que** just like, in the same way as: *yo, al igual que todos mis colegas, pienso …* I, just like all my colleagues, think …

☐ **igualar** *vt* to even up (eg surface), equalise (score, etc)

☐ **igualdad** *nf* equality: *igualdad de oportunidades* equality of opportunity; NB no *i* after the *l*

☐ **igualmente** *adv* equally; often used in reciprocal wishes: – *¡que lo pases bien!* – *¡y tú igualmente!* – 'have a good time!' – 'you as well!'

☐ all these forms and other derivative words are used in a number of useful and interesting idioms: worth some research in the dictionary!

❗ *Words beginning with* **il-, im-, inm-, in-** **❗**

The prefix **in-** is used to make words (mainly but not always adjectives) negative, or to reverse their meaning; it therefore often corresponds to Eng 'in-', or 'un-'.

NB before *-l-* the *-n-* disappears, and Eng words beginning 'imm–' become *inm-* in Sp; the *-n-* becomes *-m-* before *-p-* and *-r-*; before *-nn-* is also possible if the positive word begins with *n-*.

Here is a list of some of the most common of these negative words (whose positive may not appear in this book if the meaning and use are obvious); for words marked ★, please refer also to important notes in the main text on the word indicated.

ilegal *adj* illegal

ilegítimo *adj* illegitimate

imperfecto *adj* imperfect

★imposible *adj* impossible (**★posible**)

improbable *adj* improbable (***probable**)

inadecuado *adj* inadequate, unsuitable: (***adecuado**)

inaguantable *adj* intolerable, unbearable (***aguantar**)

incalculable *adj* incalculable

*incapaz *adj* incapable, unable (***capaz**)

incesante *adj* unceasing, ceaseless, unending (***cesar**)

incierto *adj* uncertain; **incertidumbre** *nf* uncertainty (***cierto**)

incómodo *adj* uncomfortable, inconvenient; **incomodidad** *nf* discomfort, inconvenience (***cómodo**)

incompetencia *nf* incompetence (***competencia**)

incompleto *adj* incomplete

incomprensible *adj* incomprehensible (***comprender**)

*inconveniente *adj* inconvenient; *nm* inconvenience; (***conveniente**)

increíble *adj* incredible, unbelievable (***creer**)

indeciso *adj* undecided, hesitant (***decidir**)

indefinido *adj* indefinite

indirecto *adj* indirect

indudable *adj* undoubted, doubtless (***duda**)

ineficaz *adj* ineffective, inefficacious; **ineficacia** *nf* ineffectiveness (***eficaz**)

inesperado *adj* unexpected (***esperar**)

inevitable *adj* inevitable, unavoidable (**evitar**)

inexacto *adj* inexact

infeliz *adj* unhappy (***feliz**)

infiel *adj* unfaithful; **infidelidad** *nf* infidelity, unfaithfulness (**fiel**)

informal *adj* informal (***formal**)

ingrato *adj* ungrateful

inhumano *adj* inhuman; **inhumanidad** *nf* inhumanity

injusto *adj* unjust, unfair; **injusticia** *nf* injustice (***justo**)

immediato *adj* immediate; **inmediatamente** immediately, cf **al instante**, **en seguida**

inmigrar *vi* to immigrate;

inmigración *nf* immigration

inmoderado *adj* immoderate; **inmoderación** *nf* immoderation

inmoral *adj* immoral; **inmoralidad** *nf* immorality (***moral**)

inmotivado *adj* unmotivated

inmóvil *adj* motionless, still (***mover(se)**)

innecesario *adj* unnecessary (***necesario**)

inolvidable *adj* unforgettable (***olvidar**)

inseguro *adj* unsure, unsafe, insecure (***seguro**)

insensato *adj* senseless, foolish (in that sense) (***sentir**)

insensible *adj* insensitive; unconscious; **insensibilidad** *nf* insensitivity; unconsciousness (***sentir**)

insignificante *adj* insignificant (***significar**)

insoportable *adj* intolerable, unbearable (***soportar**)

insufrible *adj* insufferable, intolerable (***sufrir**)

interminable *adj* interminable, unending (***terminar**)

intolerable *adj* intolerable, unbearable (***tolerar**)

inútil *adj* useless (***útil**)

irresponsable *adj* irresponsible (***responsable**)

ilusión *nf* illusion, but NB frequent use with the following meanings:

- □ hope, dream – but often unfounded or wishful thinking: *era su ilusión conocer al Rey* it was her dream to meet the King: *se está haciendo ilusiones* she's kidding herself; *no me hago ilusiones* I'm not that hopeful
- □ also 'thrill': often used as a fairly close equivalent of 'look forward to': *a mi padre le hace mucha ilusión tu visita* my father is very much looking forward to your visit; *tu visita le hizo mucha ilusión* your visit thrilled him a great deal/gave him a great thrill
- □ **ilusionar** *vt* used similarly to *noun* – to thrill, make excited: *le ilusiona tu visita* he's thrilled by/looking forward to your visit
- □ **ilusionarse** *vr* to build one's hopes up (often false ones): *no te ilusiones* don't count on it; to get excited (*con* about)
- □ worth further investigation in the dictionary

imagen *nf pl imágenes* image (sense largely as Eng)

- □ **imaginar** *vt* or **imaginarse** *vr* to imagine
- □ if there is any difference between these two forms, the transitive form is used more in the sense of 'think up': *imagina la escena* imagine/visualise the scene, *imagina que eres ministro* imagine you are a minister, whereas the reflexive is used more in the sense of 'suppose', 'fancy', but any distinction is somewhat blurred: *¡imagínate!* just imagine! *me imagino que tienes razón* I imagine/suppose you're right
- □ **imaginación** *nf pl imaginaciones* imagination: *(no) se me pasó por la imaginación + inf/que* it passed/didn't pass through my mind to/that

- □ **imaginario** *adj* imaginary; **imaginativo** *adj* imaginative

impaciencia *nf* impatience; **impaciente** *adj* impatient

- □ NB useful *verb* **impacientarse** *vr* to get impatient or to lose one's patience: *empiezo a impacientarme con él* I'm beginning to lose my patience with him

impacto *nm* impact

- □ NB *verb* **impactar** *vi* (*en/contra*) to hit, strike: *la pelota impactó en contra la pared* the ball struck the wall; also 'to shock', 'strike' (in that sense): *lo hace para impactar* he does it to shock/make an impression

impedir *vt -i-* to prevent, stop (in that sense)

- □ NB + *subjunc*: *quería impedir que lo vieran* I wanted to prevent/stop them (from) seeing it
- □ also 'to block': *la grúa impedía la salida* the crane was blocking the exit
- □ **impedimento** *nm* impediment; or disability

imponer *vt* has all the irregularities of *poner + tú imperative: impón;* to impose (in most senses as Eng)

- □ **imponente** *adj* imposing, impressive; **imposición** *nf pl imposiciones* imposition

importar *vi* to matter, be important: *no importa* it doesn't matter; *lo que importa es que estén seguros* what matters/is important is that they are safe

- □ useful equivalent of 'mind': + *inf* or + *que + subjunc*: *¿Te importa ayudarme?* Do you mind helping me?; *¿Te importa que yo te ayude?* Do you mind me helping you?
- □ also: *vt* to import
- □ **importante** *adj* important; can also mean 'significant', 'considerable': *la empresa sufrió pérdidas importantes*

este año the company suffered considerable losses this year
- □ NB various derivative nouns
- □ **importancia** *nf* importance
- □ **importe** *nm* amount (money): often used on invoice forms, bills etc; NOT 'import', that's:
- □ **importación** *nf pl importaciones* import

imposible *adj* impossible
- □ NB + *inf* or + *que* + *subjunc*: *es imposible solucionar este problema* it's impossible to solve this problem; *es imposible que lo solucionen ellos* it's impossible for them to solve it
- □ NB also with noun/pronoun subject: *este problema es imposible de solucionar* this problem is impossible to solve
- □ NB useful verb **imposibilitar** *vt* to make impossible: *esto imposibilita la solución del problema* this makes the solution of the problem impossible
- □ **imposibilidad** *nf* impossibility

imprescindible *adj* indispensable, essential, 'undowithoutable' (if such a word existed!)
- □ see also **prescindir de** to do without

impresionar *vt* to impress
- □ but does have rather wider meaning of 'to make an impression on' (ie to shock): *me impresionó el estado en que le encontré* I was shocked by the state I found him in; or 'affect'/'move': *me impresionó su discurso* I was affected/moved by his speech
- □ **impresionarse** *vr* to be impressed; shocked, affected etc as above
- □ **impresión** *nf pl impresiones* impression (used as in Eng, but with wider implications as with verb above)
- □ **impresionante** *adj* impressive,

amazing; can also mean 'awesome','moving' (in line with *v* above)
- □ **impresionable** *adj* impressionable; also 'easily affected'

impropio *adj* inappropriate; cf also *inadecuado*
- □ **impropiedad** *nf* inappropriateness, unsuitability; also 'impropriety'
- □ **improperio** *nm* insult: *lanzar improperios* to hurl insults
- □ for improper in sense of 'indecent', use *indecente*

improviso occurs as **de improviso** *adv* unexpectedly, out of the blue; more dramatic than other words for 'suddenly'

incapaz *adj pl incapaces* incapable, unable (*de* of/to): used similarly to positive *capaz*
- □ **incapacitar** *vt* to incapacitate, render incapable
- □ **incapacitarse** *vr* to become incapacitated, incapable
- □ **incapacitado** *adj* disabled, handicapped
- □ **incapacidad** *nf* incapacity; also 'disability', 'handicap'

incendio *nm* fire, ie accidental, for which you need the fire brigade! not same as cf *fuego*
- □ **incendiar** *vt* to set fire to, burn down; **incendiarse** *vr* to catch fire, burn down
- □ NB usually conveys idea of fire as a destructive force: cf *arder, quemar* for other senses of burn

inclinar *vt* to tilt, bow, bend downwards: *inclinar la cabeza* to tilt, nod one's head (meaning 'yes')
- □ **inclinarse** *vr* various uses with the basic meaning of adopting a position out of the vertical; to tilt, lean: *el edificio se inclina por 5 grados* the

building leans through 5 degrees; 'to stoop': *se inclinó a recoger el papel* he stooped down to pick up the paper; 'to bow': *se inclinó ante el altar* he bowed before the altar

- also 'to be inclined' (*a + inf* to): *me inclino a pensar que ...* I'm inclined to think that ...
- **inclinación** *nf pl inclinaciones* (noun for the meanings explained above) inclination (in most senses as Eng), slope, stoop, bow, etc
- **inclinado** *adj* sloping, leaning: *estar/sentirse inclinado a* to be/feel inclined to

incluir *vt -y- pi: incluyo, incluyes, incluye, incluyen; ps: incluya; ger: incluyendo; pret: incluyó, incluyeron; imp subj: incluyera/incluyese* to include; *todo incluido* everything included, 'all in'

- **incluso** *adj or adv* even, including: NB *invariable: todos, incluso mi madre* everyone, including my mother
- **inclusive** *adj inv* inclusive: used mainly with days/dates: *hasta el viernes próximo inclusive* up to and including next Friday

inconveniente *nm* problem, drawback, difficulty: *las ventajas e inconvenientes de algo* the advantages and drawbacks of sth; *¿Cuáles son los inconvenientes de la propuesta?* What are the drawbacks of the proposal?; another possible equivalent of 'mind': *¿Tendría Vd inconveniente en llamarme?* Would you mind phoning me?

- as *adj* 'inconvenient', though *incómodo* is more usual; also 'unsuitable', 'inappropriate', ie similar to *inadecuado, impropio*
- **inconveniencia** *nf* unsuitability, inappropriateness (cf *impropiedad*); also 'inconvenience'; can also mean 'tactless remark'
- NB no verb; for 'to inconvenience' the best verb will usually be *incomodar* or possibly *molestar*

incorporarse *vr* to sit <u>up</u>: ie from a lying or slouched position: don't be tempted by any form of *sentarse* to sit <u>down</u>!

incrementar *vt* to increase, ie make larger; **incrementarse** *vr* to increase ie become larger

- **incremento** *nm* increase
- used esp with figures; similar to, perhaps slightly more formal than cf *aumentar(se), aumento*

incurrir *vi en algo* to fall into sth, incur sth

- NB followed by *en: incurrir en gastos* to incur costs; *incurrir en la ira de alguien* to incur sb's wrath

independiente *adj* independent (*de* of/from); **independencia** *nf* independence (*de* of/from)

- NB useful verb **independizarse** *vr -ce-, -cé* to become, make oneself independent (*de* of/from): *los jóvenes se independizan poco a poco de sus padres* youngsters gradually become independent of their parents

India *nf* India; **indio/a** *adj or nmf* Indian (of India or America)

- NB **indiano/a** *nmf* NOT 'Indian': means an emigrant who has returned to Spain from Sp Am, usually having made fortune

indicar *vt -que-, -qué-* to indicate, show (point out) *el reloj indicaba las once* the clock was showing/pointing to 11; *nos indicó las ruinas* she pointed out the ruins to us; cf *señalar*

- **indicación** *nf pl indicaciones* indication; but has wider range of use — 'instructions': *según las indicaciones del paquete* according to the instructions on the packet; 'suggestion', 'guideline' — *según tus indicaciones* according to your suggestions/guidelines
- **indicado** *adj* suitable, proper, right (in this sense), esp with *más* or

menos: *es el candidato más indicado*
he's the most suitable candidate; *es la
menos indicada para el puesto* she's
the least suitable/last person for the
job

□ **indicador** *nm* indicator, gauge,
sign: *siga los indicadores* follow the
road signs

□ **índice** *nm* index (in most senses as
Eng)

□ **indicio** *nm* sign, trace: *había
indicios de sabotaje* there were signs
of sabotage; some overlap with cf
huella in this sense

indiferente *adj* indifferent (much as
Eng)

□ NB also use with indir obj: *me es
indiferente* it's immaterial to me,
I don't mind (cf similar use of *igual*)

indígena *adj* or *nmf* native, indigenous;
NB either gender ends in *-a*

indigno *adj* unworthy (*de* of)

□ **indignarse** *vr* to become angry,
indignant, outraged (*por*
about/over)

□ **indignado** *adj* indignant,
outraged: *estaba indignada por el
trato que recibió* she was indignant
at the treatment she received

□ **indignación** *nf* indignation

□ **indignidad** *nf* indignity; also
'unworthiness'

□ NB meaning of this group can be
rather stronger than indignant etc in
Eng, and can go as far as 'outrage'

individuo *nm* individual (often used
pejoratively rather as in Eng in sense of
guy, bloke, woman): *no me gusta aquel
individuo/aquella individua* I don't like
that individual

□ **individual** *adj* individual (used
largely as Eng *adj*; also single room or
bed: *cama individual*; as *nm* in
sport: singles

□ **individualizar** *vt* -ce-, -cé to
individualise, single out

infante *nm* prince; **infanta** *nf* princess
(limited application to king or queen's
children)

□ NOT usually 'infant': use *niño/a*

□ **infantil** *adj* does, however, mean
'children's', 'to do with children':
juegos infantiles children's games

inferior *adj mfpl inferiores* lower, bottom
(in that sense): *vivimos en la parte
inferior de la ciudad* we live in the
lower part of the town; **inferior a**
below, under: *una cifra inferior a 1.000*
a figure below 1,000

□ also 'inferior': *de calidad inferior* of
inferior quality

□ NB one of the series of comparative
adjs that do not have a separate *fem*
form; cf its opp *superior*

□ **inferioridad** *nf* inferiority

influir *vi* -y- *pi*: influyo, influyes, influye,
influyen; *ps*: influya; *ger*: influyendo; *pret*:
influyó, influyeron; *imp subj*:
influyera/influyese to influence, have
influence (*en/sobre algo/alguien* on
sth/sb): *eso influyó en mis acciones* that
influenced my actions

□ can also be used as *vt*: *no me influyó*
it didn't influence me

□ **influenciar** *vt* to influence: use
similarly to cf *influir en* above

□ **influencia** *nf* or **influjo** *nm*
influence (*en/sobre* on); *tener
influencias* to have contacts

informar *vt* to inform; **informarse** *vr*
to find out (*de/sobre algo/alguien*
about sth/sb, *de que* that); similar to cf
enterar(se)

□ **información** *nf* information; also:
news, sometimes used in *pl* eg
informaciones extranjeras foreign
news

□ **informado** *adj* informed; *estar
bien informado sobre* to be 'clued
up' about

□ **informes** *nmpl* information; also
'reference' eg for job: *pedir informes*

to ask for references

- **informativo** *adj* informative; also 'of information': *boletín informativo* news bulletin
- **informática** *nf* computer science, computing; **informatizar** *vt -ce-, -cé* to computerise

Inglaterra *nf* England: but often used by Sp speakers to mean the whole of the UK *Reino Unido* or Great Britain *Gran Bretaña*

- **inglés/inglesa** *nmf* and *adj pl ingleses, inglesas*: Englishman/woman, English, but often used loosely for British person, British person, British *británico*
- also *nm* English (ie the language)

ingresar *vi* (*en*) to join (eg club), enter (eg school, prison), gain access

- *vt* to put into eg money in bank, person in hospital/prison
- **ingreso** *nm* action of above: entry, joining, deposit (of money), depending on context
- NB rather limited and specialised range of meanings

iniciar *vt* to initiate, begin/start (in that sense) (sth): *iniciaron la manifestación* they began the demonstration

- **iniciativa** *nf* initiative, enterprise
- **iniciación** *nf* initiation, beginning
- **inicial** *adj* initial; *nf* initial (letter), but use *sigla* for 'acronym'

inmueble *nm* property, building: NB *inm*

inquieto *adj* anxious, worried, uneasy: use *estar*: cf *preocupado*

- restless: *espíritu inquieto* restless mind/spirit
- **inquietar** *vt* to worry, make anxious; **inquietarse** *vr* to get worried, anxious (*por* about): *se inquieta por su hijo* she worries about her son; *¡No se inquiete!* Don't worry!
- **inquietud** *nf* anxiety, worry (*por*

about): *siente inquietud por su hijo* she's worried about her son

- **inquietante** *adj* worrying, disturbing: *es una situación inquietante* it's a disturbing/worrying situation
- large amount of overlap with cf *preocupar* and its derivative words, but also carries idea of opp of cf *quieto*, ie the idea of unease, restlessness

inscribir *vt past part: inscrito* to inscribe: *estar inscrito en letras doradas* to be inscribed in gilded letters

- also, commonly: to enrol, register (eg *a alguien* sb on course)
- **inscribirse** *vr* to enrol (oneself) eg on course
- **inscripción**, *nf pl inscripciones* inscription, enrolment

insistir *vt* to insist (*en* on): *insiste en su derecho* she insists on her right; *en + inf* insist on …-ing; *en que + subjunc* if action involves influencing sb else: *insiste en que lo tomes tú* she insists on you taking it; *en que + indic* if stating a supposed fact: *ella insiste en que lo hizo él* she insists that he did it

- **insistencia** *nf* (*en* on, *en que* as above that); *con insistencia* insistently

instalar *vt* to install

- **instalarse** *vr* to install oneself, often in sense of settle: *¿Te has instalado en tu nuevo piso?* Have you settled in your new flat?
- **instalación** *nf pl instalaciones* installation (action and) equipment: *instalaciones deportivas* sports facilities

instante *nm* instant, moment; often much the same as *momento*: *cada instante del día* every single moment of the day; *al instante* instantly, immediately, cf *inmediatamente, en seguida*; NOT used as *adj*, see *instantáneo* below

- **instantáneo** *adj* instant, instantaneous: *café instantáneo* instant coffee
- **instar** *vt* to urge: *a alguien a hacer algo* or *a alguien para que* + *subjunc* to urge sb to do sth
- **instancia** *nf* fairly formal for 'request', most commonly used in *a instancia de* at the request of: *a instancia de las autoridades* at the request of the authorities

instituto *nm* institute, institution
- but also 'secondary school': some overlap with cf *colegio*

instruir *vt* -y- *pi: instruyo, instruyes, instruye, instruyen; ps: instruya; ger: instruyendo; pret: instruyó, instruyeron; imp subj: instruyera/instruyese* to instruct, teach (in that sense), train (*de/sobre* about, *en* in)
- **instruirse** *vr* to learn, teach oneself (*de/sobre* about, *en* in)
- **instrucción** *nf pl instrucciones* instruction (in both senses: ie teaching/training, and indication of how to): *instrucciones para el uso del aparato* instructions on how to use the equipment; cf *indicaciones* above in latter sense
- **instructor/a** *nmf* instructor, teacher, coach, trainer
- some overlap with *entrenar(se)/entrenamiento* for train(ing), but *instrucción* suggests more emphasis on the learning process and *entrenar/entrenamiento* more on the physical tuning

insuficiente *adj* insufficient; of person: incompetent, not up to the job
- also *nm* fail: in exam or school *evaluaciones* (about 4/10)
- **insuficiencia** *nf* insufficiency, but also 'inadequacy', 'incompetence'

intención *nf pl intenciones* intention: *con la intención de* + *inf*/*de que* + *subjunc*

(if influence involved) with the intention to/that; *tener la intención de* + *inf* to have the intention of, intend to: NB don't use *intentar* (see below) for 'intend', use *pensar*
- intent, purpose, motive: *decir algo con intención* usually implies: to say sth deliberately, meaningfully, or with intent to provoke; *segunda intención* ulterior motive
- **intencionado** *adj* tends to have above meaning of 'deliberate', 'meaningful': *fue una observación intencionada* it was a meaningful observation (ie designed to provoke); however *bien/mal intencionado* simply mean 'well/ill-intentioned'
- **intencional** *adj* **intencionalmente** *adv* intentional(ly), ie intended, on purpose
- this group is worth further investigation in the dictionary

intentar *vt* to try, attempt: *intentar algo* to attempt sth: *intentó otro vuelo* he attempted another flight; + *inf* to try, attempt, endeavour to: *intentó batir el récord* he tried to beat the record
- **intento** *nm* (*de* to) attempt: *otro intento de batir el récord* another attempt at the record/to beat the record
- also 'intention', 'intent' (cf *intención* above)
- *intentar/intento* suggest an attempt/endeavour, ie something a shade stronger than just try, than cf *tratar de*; also not 'try (to do) sth' in sense of try out/test: use cf *probar* in this case

intercambiar *vt* to exchange, swap (ideas, collector items, words, etc)
- **intercambio** *nm* exchange, swap (in that sense); also exchange of students, language exchange; for money use *cambio*
- **intercambiable** *adj* interchangeable

interés *nm pl intereses*   interest (meanings much as in Eng): *interés en* or *por algo* interest in sth; *intereses creados*   vested interests

- □ **interesar** *vt*   to interest
- □ **interesarse** *vr*   to be interested
- □ NB to be interested in: either use *interesar* with the thing you are interested in as subject, or *interesarse en/por* + item of interest; so, for 'Are you interested in bullfighting?', you can say: *¿Te interesan los toros?* or *¿Te interesas en/por los toros?*
- □ also *vi* 'to be of interest': *el asunto no interesaba*   the matter was of no interest
- □ **interesado/a** *nmf* or *adj*   interested (party/person): *los interesados*   those interested, concerned
- □ NB **estar interesado en** is another way of saying 'to be interested in', though it may still be regarded as something of an anglicism: *estoy interesado en la situación económica* I'm interested in the economic situation
- □ **interesante** *adj*   interesting
- □ this group is worth further investigation in the dictionary

interior *nm* and *adj no fem form*   interior, inside, inner, internal

- □ useful phrases: *en el interior (de)* inside (of); *habitación interior* inward facing room; *la parte interior*   (the) inside; *paredes interiores* inner/interior walls; *ropa interior* underclothes; *asuntos interiores* internal matters; *Ministerio del Interior* Home Office; cf *dentro* and opp *exterior*
- □ **interiormente** *adv*   inwardly

interlocutor/a *nmf*   interlocutor (ie the person you are speaking to)

- □ quite common in Sp, though direct Eng equivalent seldom used: *mi interlocutora respondió que …*   the woman I was speaking to replied that …

intervenir *vi*   (has all the irregularities of cf *venir* + the imperative *intervén*) to intervene

- □ also 'to take part', 'appear', 'contribute': *quería intervenir en la discusión*   he wanted to take part in the discussion; *intervinieron en el concierto*   they appeared/took part in the concert
- □ can be used as *vt*   to operate (on): *le intervinieron por una hernia*   he was operated on for a hernia; cf *operar*
- □ **intervención** *nf pl intervenciones* intervention; participation, appearance, operation corresponding to above verb meanings

íntimo *adj*   intimate, but also simply 'private', 'close': *amigos íntimos*   close friends; *agenda íntima*   private diary; *persona íntima*   private person

- □ **intimidad** *nf*   privacy, private life: *en la intimidad*   in private/privacy
- □ **intimarse** *vr*   to become friendly (*con alguien*   with sb)
- □ this group of words does not necessarily convey the idea of sexual intimacy of its Eng equivalent: often 'private' rather than 'intimate', for which *personal* might be a better translation

introducir *vi pi: introduzco, -duces; ps: introduzca; pret: introduje, -dujiste, -dujo, -dujimos, -dujisteis, -dujeron; imp subj: introdujera/-dujese*   to introduce, bring in: *se introdujo el tabaco en Europa desde América*   tobacco was introduced into Europe from America

- □ NB can be used in sense of introduce sb to sth: *me introdujo a la música española*   she introduced me to Spanish music, but NOT introduce sb to sb: use cf *presentar*
- □ also 'to insert': *introduzca la moneda en la ranura*   insert the coin into the slot
- □ **introducirse** *vr*   often used in sense of 'get into', 'gain access to': *se introdujo por la ventana abierta*   he

got in through the open window; *el aire se introducía por el ventilador* the air was coming in through the ventilator

- **introducción** *nf pl introducciones* introduction, insertion (in senses of verb above); for 'making acquaintance', use *presentación*
- **introductorio** *adj* introductory

intruso/a *nmf* intruder: *¿cuál es el intruso?* which is the odd one out?

inútil *adj* useless

- also 'vain', 'futile': *un intento inútil de* a vain attempt to
- **inutilizar** *vt -ce-, -cé* to make/render useless, put out of action; **inutilizarse** *vr* to become useless; **inutilidad** *nf* uselessness

invertir *vti –ie-, -i-* to invest (time/money *en* in)

- also 'to invert', 'reverse', 'turn upside down/the other way round'
- **invertido** *adj* inverted, reversed; wrong way round
- **inverso** *adj* reverse, inverse: *a la inversa* the other way round, vice versa
- **inversión** *nf pl inversiones* investment; also: reversal

invitar *vt* to invite *a alguien a hacer algo* or + *subjunc: a que haga algo* sb to do sth

- used when eg buying a round of drinks: *os invito yo* it's my turn, it's on me
- **invitado/a** *nmf* guest; ie one you've invited eg to a party; NOT paying, in eg hotel, use *cliente*
- **invitación** *nf pl invitaciones* invitation (*a* to); **invite** *nm* also used colloquially: invitation, invite

involucrar *vt* to involve (*a alguien en algo* sb in sth)

- **involucrarse** *vr* to get involved, mixed up; or 'meddle' (*en algo* in sth)

ir *vi pi: voy, vas, va, vamos, vais, van; ps: vaya; tú imperative: ve; ger: yendo; imperf: iba, ibas, iba, íbamos, ibais, iban; pret: fui, fuiste, fue, fuimos, fuisteis, fueron; imp subj: fuera/fuese* to go

- also + *a* + *inf* to be going to: *¿Qué vamos a hacer?* What are we going to do?; or 'to go and': *fue a llamar a la puerta* he went and knocked on the door
- 'to suit': *esta camisa no me va* this shirt doesn't suit me
- 'to be' (health etc): *¿Cómo te van las cosas?* How are things (going)?
- used with *ger* to form a 'supercontinuous' tense in place of *estar* esp where motion is involved: *iban andando por la calle* they were walking along the street; *la noche iba cayendo* night was falling
- some parts are commonly used as interjections and other set phrases: *¡Vaya!* Well I never!, Well, Well!; *¡Vamos!* Come on!; *¡Qué va!* Oh yeah?, Not on your life!
- **irse** *vr* NB *vosotros imperative idos* to go away: *¡No te vayas!* Don't go away!
- NB this is a verb which has a large number of idiomatic uses and meanings: large dictionaries devote more than a whole page to it – worth a look at further uses!
- **ida** *nf* (action of) going; outward journey: *billete de ida* single ticket, *billete de ida y vuelta* return ticket

itinerario *nm* itinerary, route: better for route eg that you are planning or that you took, than cf *ruta*

IVA (Impuesto al Valor Agregado/ Añadido) *nm* VAT (Value Added Tax)

izquierdo *adj* left; *brazo izquierdo* left arm; *a mano izquierda* on the left-hand side

- **izquierda** *nf* left, left-hand side; *tuerza a la izquierda* turn left; *a la izquierda* to/on the left

□ also 'the (political) left': *la izquierda ha ganado 50 escaños* the left have gained 50 seats

□ **izquierdista** *adj* of the (political) left, left-wing: *tiene inclinaciones izquierdistas* s/he has leftist

tendencies, inclines to the left; also: *nmf* left-winger

□ **izquierdismo** *nm* left-wing outlook or tendencies, cf opp *derechista/ismo*

□ **J** (*jota*) is always pronounced as a guttural sound, stronger than *h*, but be careful not to say *k*; it's like the *ch* in the Scottish word *lo<u>ch</u>*.

jactarse *vr* to boast, brag (+ *de* + or *inf* of, about): *se jacta de poder levantar grandes pesos* he boasts that he can lift great weights

jamás *nf* never
□ like all negatives, needs *no* when it follows the verb: *no vamos jamás allí* we never go there
□ often rather stronger than cf *nunca*; *nunca jamás* is very emphatic: 'never ever'

jamón *nm pl jamones* ham
□ there are two main types in Spain: *jamón de York* or *jamón dulce* sweet ham, boiled ham; and *jamón serrano* cured ham

Japón *nm* Japan
□ NB *en el Japón*: *masc* article usually used

jardín *nm pl jardines* garden
□ essentially for flowers, ornament or pleasure: see also *huerta/o*

jarra *nf* jar; mug, tankard (for beer)
□ *estar en/de jarras* to stand with arms akimbo/on hips
□ **jarro** *nm* jug: don't confuse with *jarra*!

jefe *nm* **jefa** *nf* boss, chief

jeringa *n* syringe
□ but use *dim* **jeringuilla** for hypodermic (cf *aguja* needle, also used in this sense)

jersey *nm pl* usually *jerseys* jersey, sweater, pullover
□ *syn* **suéter**

Jesucristo *nm* Jesus Christ
□ **Jesús** Jesus, but note spelling of full name without final -s
□ abb. *J.C.; antes de Jesucristo/J.C.* B.C; *después de Jesucristo/J.C.* A.D.
□ *¡Jesús!* Bless you! (when someone sneezes)

joven *adj pl jóvenes* (NB accent) young
□ *nm* youngster, youth

joya *nf* jewel
□ *pl joyas* jewellery
□ **joyería** *nf* jewellery (jewels)
□ also: jewellery (jeweller's shop)

jubilación *nf* retirement
□ NB 'jubilation' would be *júbilo* or *regocijo*
□ **jubilarse** *vr* to retire; *estar jubilado* to be retired
□ **jubilado/a** *nmf* retired person

judía *nf* (green) bean (not same as cf *haba, alubia*)

juego *nm* game, play: *juego de roles* role-play(ing); *estar fuera de juego* to be offside, out; *los Juegos Olímpicos* Olympic Games; for theatre play see *obra*
□ set, service: *un juego de café* a coffee

set/service

□ **jugar** *vti ue; -gue-, gué: juego, juegas; juegue, juegues; jugué, jugaste* to play

□ NB *jugar a un juego* to play a game: *los niños juegan al fútbol* the children are playing football

□ NB NOT to play an instrument/music, use *tocar*

□ NB as *vr jugarse el dinero* to gamble (away) one's money

□ **juguete** *nm* toy: *un tren juguete* a toy train

juerga *nf* binge, spree: *ir/estar de juerga* to go/be out on a binge

juez, juicio see **juzgar**

jugo *nm* juice; same as cf *zumo*

jungla *nf* jungle

□ used in metaphorical sense as well as literal: *una jungla de asfalto* a concrete jungle

□ see also *selva*

juntar *vt* to join, put together

□ **juntarse** *vr* to join/come together, unite; *unir(se)*

□ **junto a** *prep* next to, near/close to; cf *al lado de, cerca de*

□ **juntos** *adj* together

□ NB it's an adjective, so it agrees with its noun: *las dos hermanas hacían todo juntas* the two sisters did everything together

□ *junto con* together with

□ **junta** *nf* council, assembly, committee

□ used in a number of Sp *autonomías* for 'parliament': *la Junta andaluza*, occuring in *gallego* as *Xunta*

□ *junta militar* military junta

jurar *vti* to swear (most senses)

□ though *decir/soltar palabrotas* is often used for using bad language

justo *adj* just, fair, right (in that sense)

□ also, of clothes 'tight': *esta falda me viene muy justa* this skirt is tight on me

□ **justamente** *adv* precisely, exactly: *es justamente lo que decía yo* that's exactly what I was saying

□ and, of course: justly, fairly (in that sense)

□ **justicia** *nf* justice, fairness

□ can also mean 'the law' in the sense of 'the police'

juvenil *adj* youthful, to do with youth, juvenile: *albergue juvenil* youth hostel; *sección juvenil* youth section; *delincuente juvenil* juvenile delinquent

□ but for 'juvenile' in derogatory sense of 'childish', use *pueril: no seas pueril* don't be juvenile

□ **juventud** *nf* young people, youth (in that sense): *la juventud de hoy* the youth of today

□ for 'a youth' use *un joven*

juzgar *vti gue-, -gué* to judge; *a juzgar por* to judge by

□ **juez** *nm, mpl -ces* **jueza** *nf* judge

□ **juicio** *nm* judgement (in all senses); *a mi juicio* in my opinion/judgement; *estar fuera de juicio* to be out of one's mind

K *(ka)* This letter only occurs in words of foreign origin, and nowadays is often converted to *c* or *qu: quiosco* kiosk. It is however used in *kilo* compounds for 'x 1000' measures of Greek origin: *kilogramo, kilómetro, kilométrico, kilometraje, kilovatio* (kilowatt), etc.

There are no words beginning with *k* deserving of further comment!

L

L *(ele)* and **Ll** *(elle)* were treated as separate letters until 1994, and are listed as such in dictionaries and vocabularies published before then. They are now integrated and listed alphabetically.

◆ Single **i** is always pronounced clearly, and does not get 'swallowed' as it sometimes does in English (eg 'principal' pronounced 'principaw').

◆ Double **ll** is sounded rather more strongly than the *ll* in English 'mi<u>lli</u>on', and in some parts of Spain or Spanish-speaking America, like y or even an English j.

labor *nf* labour, work (in general)
- also: job, piece of work
- and: needlework, sewing
- NB it's *fem*!
- **laborable** *adj* used in *día laborable* working day (as opposed to cf *festivo*)
- **laboral** *adj* (to do with) work, labour: *problemas laborales* labour problems

lado *nm* side (in most senses)
- used in several adverbial and prepositional phrases: *al lado (de)* at the side (of), beside, next to; *al otro lado (de)* on the other side (of); *la casa de al lado* the house next door; *por el lado de* in the direction of, towards: *por el lado de Toledo* in the direction of Toledo

ladrón *nm mpl ladrones* **ladrona** *nf* thief, robber: *¡Al ladrón!* Stop thief!

lamentar *vt* to be sorry about/to regret: *lamento tener que decirles esto* I'm sorry/I regret to have to tell you this
- **lamentarse** *(de/por)* *vr* to lament, moan, complain (about): *se lamenta por la falta de clientes* he's moaning/complaining about the lack of customers
- **lamentable** *adj* regrettable
- can mean 'lamentable' but usually not as strong: *su ausencia es lamentable* his absence is regrettable

lámpara *nf* lamp, light (in that sense), torch
- cf also *linterna, luz, lumbre* for different sorts of light

lana *nf* wool
- NB no adj equivalent of 'woollen' – use *de lana*: *un suéter de lana* a wool(len) sweater

lancha *nf* launch, small boat: *lancha salvavidas* lifeboat; cf *barco, barca, buque*

lanzar *vt -ce-, -cé* to throw
- used literally, and also in *lanzar una mirada* cast a glance, *lanzar un grito* to let out a yell/shout
- also: to launch (boat, campaign, etc)
- **lanzarse** *vr (a, en, sobre)* to throw oneself (into, on, on to)
- **lanzamiento** *nm* throw (act of throwing); launch (of boat, campaign etc)

lápiz *nm pl lápices* pencil
- *lápiz de labios* lipstick

largo *adj* long (in distance or time)
- NB: not 'large'!
- *¡largo!* scram!, hop it!
- also occurs in a number of prepositional and adverbial phrases: *a lo largo de* along, alongside; *a la larga* in the long run; *hace largo rato* a long time ago
- used in dimensions with *tener*, it is invariable: *esta calle tiene 500 metros de largo* this street is 500 metres long
- **largamente** *adv* for a long time, at length
- **largura** *nf* length
- used in dimensions *esta calle tiene*

500 metros de largura this street is 500 metres long

- □ **largometraje** *nm* full-length feature film; cf opp *cortometraje*
- □ **largarse** *vri -gue-, -gué* to beat it, 'hop it': *¡Lárgate!* Scram!, Clear off!

lástima *nf* pity, shame (in that sense): *¡Qué lástima!* What a pity/shame!; *es una lástima* it's a pity/shame; *dar lástima* to arouse pity: *da lástima verle en ese estado* one feels very sorry (ie it makes one feel pity) to see him in that state; much the same as cf *pena*

- □ **lastimar** *vt* to hurt, harm, injure
- □ also: to pity, feel pity for
- □ **lastimarse** *vr* to hurt/injure oneself: *me lastimé el pie* I hurt my foot: cf *(hacerse) daño*

lata *nf* tin, can

- □ also 'nuisance': *¡Qué lata!* What a nuisance!, What a bind!; *dar la lata a alguien* to be a nuisance to/to annoy someone

lateral *adj* lateral, the *adj* form of 'side': *las puertas laterales* the side doors

- □ *nm* winger (in football etc)

latín *nm* Latin (language)

- □ **latino/a** *nmf/adj* Latin, ie from a 'Latin' country
- □ and as *adj* for *latín: una palabra latina* a Latin word
- □ **Latinoamérica** *nf* **latinoamericano** *adj* Latin America(n)

lavar *vt* to wash

- □ **lavarse** *vr* to wash (oneself): *lavarse la cara* to wash one's face; *lavarse la cabeza* to wash one's hair
- □ **lavado** *nm* wash (ie act of washing): *lavado de coches* car wash; *lavado de cabeza* shampoo (in hairdresser's)
- □ **lavadora** *nf* washing machine
- □ **lavaplatos** *nm inv* dishwasher
- □ **lavabo** *nm* washbasin
- □ sometimes used euphemistically for 'toilet', 'washroom'

lazo *nm* bow, knot

- □ also 'bond', 'tie': *lazos culturales* cultural ties/links; similar to cf *vínculo* in this sense

lección *nf pl lecciones* lesson (in educational sense, though *clase* is used more frequently)

leche *nf* milk

- □ also used in a number of colloquial expressions, some quite crude: look in a big dictionary!

lechuga *nf* lettuce (ie the plant)

- □ on the menu you are more likely to see *ensalada verde*

lector, lectora, see **leer** below

leer *vti ger: leyendo; pret: leyó, leyeron; imp subj: leyera/leyese* to read

- □ **leíble** *adj* legible
- □ **lector/a** *nmf* reader (of book, paper)
- □ also: mf language 'assistant(e)' in school or university
- □ and: *m* electronic scanner
- □ **lectura** *nf* (act of) reading
- □ NB not 'lecture': use *conferencia*
- □ **leyenda** *nf* legend
- □ also: heading, caption, footnote (eg to describe a picture)

legumbre *nf* vegetable (cf *hortaliza, verdura*)

lejos *adv* far, far away: *no está lejos* it's not far (away); *a lo lejos* in the distance

- □ **lejos de** *prep* far from, a long way from
- □ **lejano** *adj* distant; as in *truenos lejanos* distant rumbles of thunder
- □ see also *alejar(se)*

lengua *nf* tongue (in mouth): *sacar la lengua* to put one's tongue out

- □ also 'language' (eg Spanish): same as cf *idioma* in this sense
- □ **lenguaje** *nm* language
- □ NB in the sense of type or style of

language: *lenguaje periodístico*
journalistic language, 'journalese';
lenguaje literario literary language:
NOT used in sense of 'Spanish',
'French' – use *lengua* or *idioma*

lento *adj* slow
- can be used adverbially, for *lentamente*: *el tren iba muy lento* the train was going very slowly
- **lentamente** *adv* slowly; cf *despacio*

león *nm pl leones* lion
- **leona** *nf* lioness

lesión *nf pl lesiones* wound, injury (often used in accident reports, perhaps a little more formal or journalistic – and less grave – than cf *herida*)
- **lesionar** *vt* to hurt, injure (cf *herir*)
- **lesionarse** *vr* to get hurt, injured
- **lesionado/a** *nmf* casualty, wounded/injured person
- *adj/past part* hurt, wounded, injured

letra *nf* letter (of alphabet, not one you write – use *carta*)
- also: handwriting: *de mi propio puño y letra* in my own fair hand
- and: lyrics, words (of song)
- **letrero** *nm* sign, notice

levantar *vt* to raise, lift (up): *levantar la mano/voz* to raise one's hand/voice; also: *levantar la mesa* to clear the table
- **levantarse** *vr* to rise (up), stand up, get up: *¡No se levante Vd!* Don't get up!; *el viento se levantó de repente* the wind got up suddenly

ley *nf* law
- ie in the sense of what you obey; use *Justicia* for 'the Law', ie police, and *Derecho* for the subject studied

liar *vt* -í-: *lío, lías, etc; líe, líes, etc* to tie, bind
- **liarse** *(con) vr* to get tied up, involved (with sth/sb), get oneself into *un lío* (see below)
- **lío** *nm* (basic meaning) bundle

- occurs frequently as 'fuss', 'mess', 'mix-up': *armar un lío* to create a fuss; *estar hecho un lío* to be/feel all mixed up; *¡qué lío!* what a fuss!, what a mess (depending on context)

libra *nf* pound (sterling or weight)
- NB: don't confuse with *libre* or *libro*!

libre *adj* free (in most senses except 'without payment' – see *gratuito*)
- don't confuse with *libra* or *libro*!
- has a number of idiomatic meanings: 'vacant' (toilet, bathroom etc)
- *al aire libre* in open air
- **liberar** *vt* to free, liberate; **liberarse** *vr* to be freed, liberated (*de* from)
- **libertad** *nf* freedom, liberty: *libertad de prensa* freedom of the press
- **libertar** *vt* to set free, release; NB used mainly in captivity context: more limited in meaning than *liberar*
- **librar** *vt* to free (similar meaning to *libertar*); **librarse** *vr* to free oneself, escape (*de* from)

libro *nm* book
- don't confuse with *libra* or *libre*!
- **librería** *nf* bookshop
- NB not library – use *biblioteca*!
- also: bookcase

REMINDER: *librA* = pound; *librE* = free; *librO* = book!

licencia *nf* licence, permission (but *permiso* is more usual for eg driving licence)
- also: leave (of absence)
- **licenciado/a** *nmf* graduate

líder *nmf* leader (usually political or sporting)

ligar *vt* -gue-, -gué to tie, bind
- also, *vi* to flirt, look for a pick-up
- **ligarse** *vr (con alguien)* to get off (with sb): careful! – it's rather slangy
- **ligue** *nmf* now has slang use amongst young people meaning boyfriend/girlfriend, though

previously had more dubious meaning
of 'pick-up'; careful where and how
you use it!

ligero *adj*   light (ie not heavy): *un
ferrocarril ligero*   a light railway; *una
comida ligera*   a light meal; *ligero de pies*
light-footed
- also 'slight': *una tos ligera*   a slight
cough
- use *claro* for light colour

limitar *vt*   to limit, restrict
- can be used reflexively: *limitarse (a)*
to limit oneself (to)
- **límite** *nm*   limit (most senses as in
Eng): *límite de velocidad*   speed limit;
como límite   at the most/latest; *voy
hasta 20 como límite*   I'll go up to 20
at most/and that's the limit; *tengo que
recibirlo el jueves como límite*   I must
get it by Thursday at the latest

limón *nm pl limones*   lemon
- **limonero** *nm*   lemon tree

limpio *adj*   clean; pure, clear (in sense of
being clean); usually used with *estar*:
¡Qué limpia está la casa!   Isn't the house
clean!
- **limpiar** *vt*   to clean, cleanse
- also 'to wipe', if this means 'to clean';
use reflexively when action is
performed to part of body or
clothing: *limpiarse las narices*   to
wipe one's nose, *limpiarse los zapatos*
to clean/wipe one's shoes
- **limpia-** *prefix* forms a number of
compound *m inv* nouns which clean
things: *limpiaparabrisas*   windscreen
wiper; *limpiabotas*   bootblack;
limpiaventanas   window-cleaning
fluid; you can find more in a
dictionary
- **limpieza** *nf*   cleanness, cleanliness
- (act of) cleaning: *hacer la limpieza*   to
do the cleaning, clean up; *limpieza en
seco*   dry cleaning

lindo *adj*   pretty, elegant, lovely

- doesn't go as far as 'beautiful', but
usually imples a degree of refinement:
cf and contrast *bonito, guapo, bello,
hermoso, precioso* for degrees of
prettiness and beauty
- applied to a man, means 'good-
looking'
- can also be used ironically: *¡Qué
situación tan linda!*   Here's a pretty
situation!
- **lindeza/lindura** *nf*   prettiness etc
(qualities described under *lindo* above)

línea *nf*   line (in most senses)
- also (bodily) 'figure': *cuidarse la línea*
to watch one's figure

linterna *nf*   torch, lamp (of that sort, cf
lámpara)

líquido *adj/nm*   liquid
- also 'cash': *pagar en líquido*   to pay
(in) cash

liso *adj*   smooth (mainly used to describe a
surface): *pelo liso*   straught hair
- *liso y llano*   straightforward, plain and
simple: *ahora todo va a ser liso y llano*
from now on everything will be plain
sailing

lista *nf*   list: *lista de esperas*   waiting list;
lista de correos   poste restante

listo *adj*   ready, prepared (NB use *estar*):
¿Estás listo?   Are you ready?; *un traje
listo*   a ready-made suit
- also 'clever', 'sharp' (NB use *ser*): *¡Qué
listo eres!*   Aren't you clever!

litoral *nm*   coastline: *España tiene un
litoral muy largo*   Spain has a very long
coastline
- ie the coast<u>line</u>, as opposed to just
costa coast

llamar *vti*   to call, in various senses
- to shout: – *¿Dónde estás?* – *llamó*
'Where are you?', he called
- to wake: *¿Pueden llamarnos a las
ocho?*   Can you call us at 8?
- to name: *vamos a llamarle Jaime*

We're going to call him James
- to phone: *te llamaré mañana* I'll call/ phone/ring you tomorrow
- to knock: *llaman a la puerta* someone is knocking on the door
- **llamarse** *vr* to be called: *¿Cómo se llama tu hermano?* What's your brother's name?
- **llamada** *nf* call (in most senses: shout, knock, phone)
- **llamamiento** *nm* appeal, call (in that sense): *hacer un llamamiento (a alguien para que + subjunc)* to make an appeal/to call upon sb to ...); don't confuse these two nouns
- **llamativo** *adj* gaudy, showy

llano *adj* flat, even (eg surface, land)
- plain, simple, straightforward: *la verdad llana* the plain truth; see also *liso*
- **llanamente** *adv* plainly, simply, frankly

llave *nf* (in most senses, except to a problem: use *clave*)
- also: spanner

llegar *vi* -gue-, -gué to arrive (*a* at/in): *llegamos a Salamanca a las nueve* we arrived in Salamanca at 9
- *llegar a* to reach: *llegaron a un acuerdo* they reached an agreement; *nuestros fondos no llegan a mil euros* our funds don't reach 1,000 euros
- *llegar a + inf* to manage to, succeed in: *llegamos a convencerle* we managed to convince him (similar meaning to cf *conseguir, lograr*)
- *llegar a ser + n* one of the Sp phrases for 'to become' (usually after eg effort, qualifications etc): *llegó a ser jefa* she became the boss
- **llegada** *nf* arrival: *hora prevista de llegada* estimated time of arrival

lleno *adj* full (*de* of); normally used with *estar: el cubo estaba lleno de agua* the bucket was full of water
- *de lleno adv* fully, 'right': *el agua le*

cayó de lleno en la cabeza the water fell right on his head
- **llenar** *vt*/**llenarse** *vr* to fill, fill up (*de* with): *llenamos el cubo de agua* we filled the bucket with water; *el cubo se llenó de agua* the bucket filled up with water
- NB use cf *rellenar* for filling in forms, blanks and stuffing food

llevar *vt* to carry, take (somewhere): *¿Quién va a llevar las maletas?* Who's going to carry the cases?; *¿Adónde llevas ese paquete?* Where are you taking that package?; *¿Es para comer aquí o para llevar?* Is it to eat here or to take away?
- for other meanings of 'take', see *tomar, coger*
- also commonly means 'to wear', 'to have on' (talking of clothes, often used with *puesto*): *llevaba gafas* he was wearing glasses; *llevaba puesto un vestido nuevo* she was wearing a new dress, she had a new dress on
- also as *vti*: 'to lead' (*a* to): *esta carretera lleva a Alicante* this road leads to Alicante; *eso me lleva a pensar que...* that leads me to think that ...; *¡Qué vida llevas!* What a life you lead!
- useful idiom used to indicate periods of time spent: *llevamos tres años en Sevilla* we've been in Seville for three years; often with the gerund of a verb: *llevamos media hora esperando* we've been waiting for half an hour – NB tense of *llevar* – present for 'have been', imperfect for 'had been'; follow this up in a grammar book!
- this verb has many further idiomatic uses too many to list here: merits further research in a dictionary!
- **llevarse** *vr* to carry off, take away: *¡Se me llevó la cartera!* He went off with my wallet!; *se le llevaron a la cárcel* they took him off to jail
- *llevarse bien/mal con alguien* to get on well/badly with sb

llorar *vti* to weep, cry

- as *vt* weep over, mourn: *lloramos la muerte de X* we mourn the death of X
- corresponding *noun* is **llanto** weeping
- **llorón** *(llorona, llorones, lloronas) adj* weepy, tearful; as *nmf* cry-baby
- for 'cry' in sense of 'cry out', 'shout', use *gritar*

llover *vi* -ue- to rain

- NB *llueve* it rains (at certain intervals or now): *está/estaba lloviendo* is/it was raining (now/then)
- **lluvia** *nf* (the) rain
- don't confuse this noun with parts of *v llover* above!
- **lluvioso** *adj* rainy, wet: *un día lluvioso* a rainy/wet day (for getting and being wet of yourself and clothes etc see *mojarse/mojado*)

local *adj* local

- also used as *nm* place, premises
- **localidad** *nf* locality
- also used for: ticket (sport etc) (see also *entrada*)
- **localizar** vt -ce-, -cé to locate, place: similar meaning to cf *situar, ubicar*
- **localizarse** *vr* to be placed, situated

loco *adj* mad, crazy (tends to be used mainly with *estar*): *¡Tienes que estar loco!* You must be mad!; *estar loco por* to be mad/crazy over; *estaba loco por aquella chica* he was mad over that girl

- can also be used as a noun **loco/a** *nmf* (use *ser*): *es un loco* he's a madman
- **locura** *nf* madness, mad action: *es una locura* it's a crazy thing (to do/think etc)
- **locución** *nf pl locuciones* expression, phrase (cf *frase* means; 'sentence')

lodo *nm* mud, much the same as cf *barro*, not quite so foul as *fango*

lógico *adj* logical

- often used in phrase *es lógico* = of course, obviously
- **lógicamente** *adv* logically: also used in sense of: of course

lograr *vt* to (manage to), get, obtain (usually after some effort), achieve: *por fin logré un visado* I finally got (managed to get) a visa

- + *inf* to manage to (usually after some effort): *logramos verle* we managed to see him; + *que* + *subjunc*: *logramos que nos viese* we managed to get him to see us
- used much in the same way – and more regular than – cf *conseguir*

lucha *nf* fight, struggle (*por* for)

- NB *una/la lucha por* + *n* or *inf* a/the struggle for/to + *noun* or *inf*: *la lucha por la victoria* the struggle for victory; *la lucha por ganar la copa* the struggle/fight to win the cup
- also: wrestling
- **luchar** *vi* to fight, struggle
- NB *luchar por* + *n* or *inf* to struggle for + n or to + v: *lucharon por la copa* they fought for the cup; *lucharon por ganar la copa* they fought to win the cup
- also: to wrestle (both in the ring and figuratively eg *con los mandos* with the controls)

lucir *vti* -zc- to illuminate, light up

- to show off, 'sport': *lucía una corbata de seda* he was sporting a silk tie
- to shine, gleam: *la arena lucía a la luz del sol* the sand gleamed in the sunlight
- cf *alumbrar, brillar, relucir*, also further *syns iluminar, resplandecer*: Spain's sunny climate is reflected in the selection of verbs basically meaning 'to shine'!; but be careful, as they are not all used in the same way, nor do they represent the same intensity!
- **lucirse** *vr* to show off

☐ can also be used sarcastically, especially in the phrase *¡Te has lucido!* You've made a right mess of things/haven't you done brilliantly!

☐ **luciente** *adj* bright, shining

☐ **lucido** *adj* splendid, brilliant, successful

☐ can be used sarcastically, like 'brilliant!' in Eng, when something is anything but so: *¡Estamos lucidos!* That's a fine mess we're in!/Oh, that's brilliant!

☐ NB stress on *-i-*, don't confuse with **lúcido** *adj* lucid, clear

luego *adv* then, in the sense of 'next' in a time sequence: *¿Qué pasó luego?* What happened then/next?; *¿y luego?* and then?, and next?

☐ NB overlap in meaning with cf *entonces*: but not usually same as cf *pues*

☐ *hasta luego* see you soon; *desde luego* of course

☐ *conj: luego que* as soon as: NB + *indic* if action has/had happened: *luego que recibimos el dinero* as soon as we received the money; + *subjunc* if action has/had not yet happened: *luego que recibamos el dinero* as soon as we receive the money (we haven't yet); cf *así que, en cuanto, tan pronto como*

lugar *nm* place (in most general senses); *en primer/segundo lugar* in the first/second place; *en lugar de* in place of, instead of; *tener lugar* to take place; *yo en tu lugar* in your place, I …, if I were you …; *no hay lugar para* there's no place/cause for

☐ some overlap with cf *sitio*, especially in geographical context

☐ can mean 'place', in sense of village/town: *en un lugar de La Mancha* in a place in La Mancha

lujo *nm* luxury; *adj phrase de lujo* luxury, de luxe

☐ NB don't confuse with *lujuria*, which means 'lust', 'lechery'!

☐ **lujoso** *adj* luxurious: not *lujurioso* lustful, lecherous!

lumbre *nf* fire

☐ light (in sense of brightness or for a cigarette)

☐ much less used than cf *fuego* or *luz*

luto *nm* mourning: *estar de luto por* to be in mourning for

luz *nf pl luces* light (in most senses): *la luz del día* daylight; *a la luz de* in the light of (literally and figuratively); *a la luz de estas revelaciones* in the light of these revelations

☐ light, lamp (used much where Eng uses 'light/s'): *luces de freno* brakelights

☐ see also *lámpara, linterna, farol, farola* for specific types of lights

M

macho adj and nm just the normal Sp word for 'male': *una rana macha* a male frog

☐ also has the meaning imported into Eng: tough, 'butch', macho

☐ **machismo** *nm* masculinity, virility, but also 'male chauvinism' – or use this Sp word!

☐ **machista** *adj* and *nmf* sexist, chauvinist(ic)

M *(eme)* is pronounced much the same as in English. It never occurs as a double letter. In fact, words beginning 'imm' (eg immense) in English usually begin '*inm*' (*inmenso*) in Spanish

madera *nf* wood (timber)
- □ for wood in sense of group of trees, use *bosque*
- □ NB no *adj* – for 'wooden', use *de madera: una silla de madera* a wooden chair

madre *nf* mother: *madre soltera* single mother; *lengua madre* mother tongue

madrugada *nf* (very) early morning
- □ often used to refer to the time roughly from 1 to 7 am depending on context: *de madrugada* in the (very) early morning; *las dos de la madrugada* 2 am
- □ **madrugar** *vi* -gue-, -gué to get up early
- □ **madrugador/a** *adj* and *nmf pl* -ores, -oras early-rising, early riser

maduro *adj* ripe (eg fruit; use *estar*): *estos melones no están maduros* these melons aren't ripe
- □ also 'mature' (for person; use *ser*): *es muy maduro para su edad* he's very mature for his years
- □ for 'mature' (NB use of *ser* and *estar*) compare: *sus ideas son maduras* his ideas are mature (ie he has mature ideas, those of a mature person) with *su gran idea estaba madura* his great idea was mature (ie it had gone through a process and had now matured)
- □ **madurar** *vi* to ripen, mature; can also be used transitively: *hay que madurar la fruta* you have to ripen the fruit
- □ **madurez** *nf* ripeness, maturiry: *llegar a la madurez* to reach maturity

maestro/a *nmf* schoolteacher (usually in primary school)
- □ also as *n* or *adj* master/mistress; leader/leading (of eg a skill or craft): *es escultora maestra* she's a leading sculptress; *obra maestra* masterpiece; *interruptor maestro* master switch

magia *nf* magic: *como por magia* as if by magic
- □ **mágico** *adj* magic or magical; cf *encantado* in sense of 'enchanted'

magnífico *adj* magnificent, but also translates 'wonderful', marvellous', 'superb'; similar to *maravilloso, estupendo, excelente*

majo *adj* good-looking, attractive, pretty, esp *f*: *¡Qué maja estás!* You do look nice!

mal *adv* badly (opp of cf *bien*: well)
- □ NB this is an adverb and qualifies verbs and adjectives: *escribe muy mal* he writes very badly; *¡Qué mal terminado está!* How badly it's finished!; *oler/saber mal* to smell/taste bad/nasty
- □ often used when the action is not performed or performable properly: *veo/oigo muy mal* I don't see/hear very well; *entendí mal* I misunderstood
- □ useful expressions: *hacer mal en* + *inf* to be wrong in doing sth; *¡Menos mal!* That's a good job!, Thank goodness!; *menos mal que* + *indic* it's a good job that
- □ after *estar, sentirse* bad, poor, poorly: *estoy/me siento muy mal* I'm (feeling) very poorly
- □ as *nm* evil, wrong: *el bien y el mal* good and evil; also 'harm': *no te hará mal* it won't do you any harm; possibly less physical than cf *daño*
- □ **malo** *adj* bad (in most senses); this is the adjective, which is used with nouns: *una mala costumbre* a bad habit
- □ NB shortens to *mal* before *nmsing* only: *un mal olor* a bad smell, *malos olores* bad smells
- □ usually used before noun, but can come after to put greater emphasis on the adjective: *¡Es una situación muy mala!* It's a very bad situation!

□ mainly used with *ser*, but use *estar* for 'off': *el pescado está mal* the fish is 'off'

□ **maldad** *nf* (*n* from *malo*) badness, evil(ness), wickedness

□ there are many idioms involving both *mal* and *malo*: further dictionary research would be well rewarded!

❗ mal- *prefix* **❗**

□ indicates badness or unsuccessfulness of action, state, etc; here are some of the more common examples:

malcasarse *vr* to marry unhappily, unsuccessfully

□ *(estar)* **malcasado** *adj* (to be) unhappily married

maldecir *vti* to curse

□ has most parts like *decir* except *past part maldecido* when used as verb, but note form:

□ **maldito** *adj* cursed, or as mild expletive 'damned': *¡Este maldito coche!* This damned car!; *syn condenado*

□ **maldición** *nf pl maldiciones* curse

maleante *nmf* criminal, wrong-doer

malestar *nm* discomfort, uneasiness: opp of cf *bienestar*

malgastar *vt* to waste, squander (money, resources, etc) (ie to spend badly)

malhechor/a *nf* criminal, wrong-doer

malintencionado *adj* malicious, spiteful (eg words, article)

malnutrir *vt* to undernourish, underfeed

□ **malnutrido** *adj* undernourished, underfed

malograrse *vr* to fail, come to nothing: *el proyecto se malogró* the project failed; opp of cf *lograrse*; cf *fracasar, fallar*

□ **malogro** *nm* failure (in this sense); cf *fracaso, fallo*

---

maloliente *adj* evil-smelling, stinking

malparado *adj* in a bad way: *quedar/estar malparado* to be in a bad way

malquerer *vt* to dislike (person)

malsano *adj* unhealthy, insalubrious (eg place, climate, influence)

maltratar *vt* to ill-treat, mistreat

□ **maltrato** *adj* mistreatment, abuse (in that sense)

□ **maltrecho** *adj* injured, in a bad way: *le dejaron maltrecho en la calle* they left him in the street in a bad way; NB this is not the *past part* of *maltratar* when used in a compound tense – use *maltratado* as normal: *le habían maltratado* they had ill-treated him

---

mancha *nf* stain, spot (in that sense)

□ **manchar** *vt* to stain

□ **mancharse** *vr* (*la ropa*) to stain, get a stain on (one's clothes): *¡Cuidado que no te manches!* Mind you don't stain yourself/get a stain!; (*de* with): *está manchado de pintura* it's stained with a paint, got a paint stain

mandar *vt* to order, (in sense of) command

□ can be used + *inf* or + *que* + *subjunc*: *le mandé hacerlo* or *le mandé que lo hiciera* I ordered him to do it

□ used in certain formalities (eg in shop): *¿Qué manda Vd?* What can I do for you?; in Mexico *¿mande?* means 'sorry?', 'pardon?'

□ used intransitively 'to be in charge': *¿Quién manda?* Who's in charge?

□ also 'to send'; means exactly the same as cf *enviar*: *quiero mandar este paquete a Irlanda* I want to send this parcel to Ireland

□ **mando** *nm* command, control: *tener el mando* to be in command/control; *mando a distancia* remote control; *palanca de mando* joystick (in plane)

- **mandamiento** *nm* commandment: *los Diez Mandamientos* the 10 Commandments
- **mandón/-ona** *adj pl mandones/as* bossy

manejar *vt* to operate, manipulate, handle, use (in that sense)

- fairly wide application to eg machinery, tools, weapon, language, even this book: *¿Sabes manejar este libro?* Do you know how to use this book?; to manage/deal with a person: *yo sé manejar a ese joven* I know how to manage/deal with that youngster; in Sp Am also 'to drive'
- NOT to manage in sense of 'direct', (eg a business), use *dirigir*
- **manejarse** *vt* to behave; also to manage: *¿Te manejas?* Are you managing/coping?
- **manejo** *nm* operation, handling etc; noun for actions above; *conoce bien el manejo de esta máquina* he's well acquainted with the working of this machine
- **manejable** *adj* manageable (ie easy to use, manoeuvrable)

manera *nf* manner, way

- NB use of *de* before and after, ie for 'in' a certain manner: *de esta manera* in this way; *de una manera u otra* one way or another; *de cualquier manera/de todas maneras* anyway, in any case; *de ninguna manera* (in) no way; and way to/of: *no hay otra manera de hacerlo* there's no other way to do it
- NB *de manera que* + *subjunc* indicates purpose: *de manera que lo sepas* so that (ie with the purpose that) you know; + *indic* indicates result: *de manera que lo sabías* so that (ie with the result that) you knew (consult a grammar for more detailed explanation)
- NB in these expressions *manera* is

totally interchangeable with cf *forma* and *modo*

manga *nf* sleeve; hose (pipe)

- **manguero/a** *nmf* person who hoses down streets
- **mango** *nm* handle (of most things, but cf *asa*)

manía *nf* mania, but also often used in sense of 'fad', 'craze', 'obsession', 'funny way': *tiene manía de llevar zapatos* he's got a thing about wearing shoes; *la manía del yo-yo* the yo-yo craze; *todos tenemos nuestras manías* we've all got our funny little ways

- **maníaco/a** *nmf* or *adj* maniac(al)

manifestar *vt -ie-* to show, make evident: *manifiesta señales de fatiga* he's showing signs of fatigue; also 'to make public': *manifestó su aprobación* she expressed her approval

- **manifestarse** *vr* to become evident, show (in that sense): *la reacción se manifestó unos días después de la inyección* the reaction became evident a few days after the injection; also 'to demonstrate' (eg in street)
- **manifestación** *nf pl manifestaciones* demonstration (eg political); show (eg *de desengaño* of disappointment)
- **manifestante** *nmf* demonstrator
- **manifiesto** *adj* evident, manifest: *poner algo de manifiesto* to highlight, make sth clear

mano *nf* hand (NB it's *fem*!)

- common expressions: *hecho a mano* handmade; *en manos de* in the hands of; *a manos de* at the hands of; *echar una mano* to lend a hand; *estrecharle la mano a alguien* to shake hands with sb; *mano de obra* workforce
- as you might expect, there are many more: worth further research in the dictionary!
- **manosear** *vt* to handle, finger, 'paw'

manotada *nf* or **manotazo** *nm*
slap, smack

manual *adj* manual; also *nm*
handbook, textbook, manual

manso *adj* mild, meek (person), tame
(animal), gentle (eg breeze)

mansedumbre *nf* mildness,
gentleness, tameness

mantener *vt* has all the irregularities of
tener, + *tú* imperative: *mantén;* to
maintain (in most Eng senses)

to keep + *n* or *adj: mantener el
equilibrio* to keep one's balance;
mantener frías las bebidas to keep
the drinks cold

mantenerse *vr* to remain, stay, keep
(in that sense): *la estructura se
mantuvo en sitio* the structure
remained in place; *hay que mantenerse
en forma* you have to keep fit;
mantenerse vivo to stay alive

mantenimiento *nm* maintenance,
upkeep: *el mantenimiento del coche*
car maintenance; *mantenimiento de la
familia* upkeep of the family

manzana *nf* apple (fruit)

also: block (of houses or flats)

manzano *nm* apple tree

maña *nf* skill, knack: *tener maña para algo*
to have the knack of sth; *requerir más
maña que fuerza* to require more brains
than brawn; NB *mañas* can mean 'bad
habits', 'evil ways'; don't confuse with
manía above

mañoso *adj* clever, skilful

mañana *adv* tomorrow: *pasado mañana*
the day after tomorrow; *hasta mañana*
see you tomorrow

nf morning: *por la mañana* in the
morning; *mañana por la mañana*
tomorrow morning; but use *de* with
specific time: *las ocho de la mañana*
8 o'clock in the morning, 8 am

nm tomorrow (the future): *el
mañana no se ve claro* the future

cannot be clearly seen

mapa *nm* map (NB it's *masc*!)

maqueta *nf* model, mock-up: *avión
maqueta* model plane (ie a scaled down
replica that you build or play with); not
same as cf *modelo*

máquina *nf* machine (in most senses);
used also to mean 'locomotive'
(*locomotora*), 'camera'

máquina de afeitar razor; *máquina
de coser* sewing machine; *máquina
de escribir* typewriter; *máquina
tragaperras* fruit machine; and
others

hacer algo a máquina to do sth by
machine: *escribir a máquina* to type;
lavar a máquina to machine-wash

maquinista *nmf* machine operator;
engine driver

mar *n* (usually *masc* but see below) sea:
por mar by sea; *Mar Mediterráneo*
Mediterranean Sea

NB is *fem* in certain set phrases: *mar
gruesa* rough sea; *hacerse a la mar*
to put to sea

NB both *m* and *f* forms are used
colloquially to express a large
quantity: *un mar de ...* a lot of; *un
mar de dificultades* a host of
difficulties; *un mar de diferencia* a
world of difference; *tengo la mar de
cosas que hacer* I've got a load of
things to do

la mar de ... extremely, no end of;
está la mar de cabreado he's mighty
livid; *es la mar de guapa* she's very
good-looking

marea *nf* tide (use *subir* come in,
and *bajar* go out)

mareo *nm* seasickness, but also used
for any kind of nausea, sickness (in
that sense) and dizziness: *siento mareo*
I feel dizzy/sick

marear *vt* to make sick, dizzy: *el
movimiento me marea* the
movement makes me (feel) sick;

marearse *vr* to feel (sea)sick, dizzy: *me mareo en el coche* I get travelsick in the car; *si sube a una escala se marea* if he goes up a ladder he feels dizzy; *estar mareado* to feel sick, dizzy

☐ **marina** *nf* navy; **marino** *adj* marine, (to do with the) sea: *vida marina* marine life; **marinero/a** *nmf* sailor; **marítimo** *adj* maritime

☐ **marisco(s)** *nm* often *pl* seafood

maravilla *nf* marvel, wonder; *es una maravilla* it's wonderful/amazing/a marvel: *a maravilla/a las mil maravillas* wonderfully: *lo hizo a las mil maravillas* he did it wonderfully (well)

☐ **maravillar** *vt* to astonish, amaze: *me maravilla tu paciencia* your patience astonishes me

☐ **maravillarse** *vr* to wonder, be amazed (*de* at): *me maravillo de tu paciencia* I wonder at your patience

☐ these words express quite strong wonderment/astonishment: cf other words expressing 'surprise' of varying degree: *asombrar, admirar, extrañar, sorprender*

☐ **maravilloso** *adj* marvellous, wonderful (cf *magnífico* and further *syns estupendo, espléndido*)

marca *nf* mark (in general): *dejar su marca* to leave one's mark (cf *señal* or *huella* which are more specific)

☐ make (eg of car, computer etc); brand (of product): *de buena marca* of a good brand; *marca registrada* registered trade mark

☐ **marcar** *vt* -que-, -qué to mark (in most senses, but for 'to correct', use *corregir*); also common specialised uses: to show (eg instruments): *el velocímetro marcaba 150* the speedometer showed 150; to score (a goal, points etc); to dial (on phone)

☐ **marco** *nm* frame (in most senses), framework; goal, goalposts (the structure, not what you score, that's *gol*)

marcha *nf* march (in most senses); hike

☐ speed: *acelerar la marcha* to speed up; *a toda marcha* at full speed

☐ gear, speed (in that sense): *marcha atrás* reverse (gear)

☐ running, working: *poner en marcha* to start up, set in motion: *el tren se puso en marcha* the train set off

☐ progress, 'the trend', 'the latest' in that sense

☐ **marchoso** *adj* trendy (ie moving with *la marcha*)

☐ **marchar** *vi* to march, walk (in vigorous sense); to go, run, work (of machinery: but cf *andar, funcionar* are more usual)

☐ **marcharse** *vr* to go away, leave. be off: *bueno, me marcho* right I'm off (cf *irse*)

margen *nm pl márgenes* margin, edge; *escribir en el margen* to write in the margin; *al margen de la ciudad* on the edge of town; *margen de seguridad* safety margin

☐ sometimes used in *pl*: *dentro de estos márgenes* within these margins/limits

☐ NB is usually *fem* when meaning: bank, edge (of river)

☐ **marginar** *vt* to marginalise; **marginado/a** *adj* and *nmf* marginalised (use *estar* with *adj*); *los marginados* the deprived/underprivileged; **marginación** *nf* marginalisation, exclusion

marido *nm* husband; less formal than cf *esposo*

☐ NB likely fem '*marida*' does NOT exist: use cf *mujer, señora, esposa* depending on degree of formality

marrón *adj pl marrones* brown; no *fem* form in spite of -*ón* ending

mas *conj* but; formal literary alternative to *pero*; NB no accent

más *adv* and *adj* more

□ used to make comparatives with *que* than: *más café (que antes)* more coffee (than before); *más frecuente (que el tren)* more frequent (than the train); *más frecuentemente (que ayer)* more frequently (than yesterday)

□ and superlatives: *el río más largo de España* the longest river in Spain (note use of *de* for 'in' after superlative)

□ use *más de* before a number: *había más de cincuenta personas* there were more than 50 people; though *más que* may be used in negative in sense of 'only': *no había más que 50 personas* there were only 50 people

□ and use *de* before a clause: *recibí más de lo que esperaba* I got more than I expected: see a grammar for a full explanation of this use

□ there are many useful expressions, including: *cada vez más* more and more (see also under *cada*); *¿algo más?* anything else?; *nada más* nothing else; *¿quién más?* who else?; *más o menos* more or less; *como el que más* like anyone else; *nunca más* never again, not any more; consult a dictionary for more examples!

□ *cuanto más … más* the more … the more: *cuanto más pienso, más me confundo* the more I think the more confused I get

□ *por más que* + *subjunc* however much: *por más que trabajes* however much you work; similar to *por mucho que;* consult a grammar for more detail!

□ also means 'plus': *dos más dos* 2 + 2

masculino *adj* masculine, but also wider application – 'male': *instituto masculino* boys' school

matar *vt* to kill: *matar de un tiro* to shoot dead; *matar (a alguien) de hambre* to starve sb; *tengo un hambre que me mata* I'm starving

□ **matanza** *nf* slaughter, massacre

materia *nf* matter: *materia prima* raw material

□ **material** *nm* material(s) (equipment or the nescessary): *material de construcción* building materials; *material de enseñanza* teaching materials; also *adj* material (sense as Eng)

matrimonio *nm* marriage, matrimony (ie the institution, not wedding, see *boda*; cf also *casamiento*)

□ married couple: *un matrimonio anciano* an old couple; *cama de matrimonio* double bed

□ **matrimonial** *adj* matrimonial, marital

máximo *adj* and *nm* maximum; *doscientos como máximo* 200 at the most

mayor *adj* comparative and superlative of *grande*: bigger/biggest, larger/largest: (you can also use *más grande* in this sense): *estos edificios son mayores* these buildings are larger: *este pastel es el mayor* this cake is the biggest; *el mayor de todos* the biggest of all; *la mayor parte* the greater part, majority (usually of sth singular, cf *mayoría* below)

□ also 'older', 'elder': *eres mayor que yo* you're older than me; *mi hermana mayor* my elder/eldest sister

□ and 'adult', 'grown-up': *cuando seas mayor* when you're grown-up; *mayor de edad* of age

□ NB business term: *vender/comprar al por mayor* to sell/buy wholesale; in church: *altar mayor* high altar; *misa mayor* high mass; and *calle mayor* high/main street

□ don't confuse with *mejor* better, see below!

□ **mayoría** *nf* majority (usually of sth plural, cf *mayor parte* above): *la mayoría de los estudiantes* the majority of the students; *mayoría de mil votos* majority of 1,000 votes; *cumplir la mayoría* to come of age

mayúsculo *adj* or **mayúscula** *nf* capital (letter): *con M mayúscula* with a capital M; for other translations of 'capital' see *capital*

médico *nmf* (**médica** *nf* is sometimes used) doctor; more common as medical doctor than cf *doctor*
- **médico** *adj* medical: *reconocimiento médico* medical examination
- **medicina** *nf* medicine (ie the science); but use **medicamento** *nm* for what you take

medir *vti -i-* to measure: *medir una distancia* to measure a distance; to measure, be (ie a dimension): *¿Cuánto mides?* What do you measure?, What's your height?; *mido un metro 65* I'm/I measure 1 metre 65
- also 'to weigh up': *medir las soluciones* to weigh up the solutions
- **medida** *nf* measurement: *¿Qué medidas tiene la alfombra?* What are the measurements of the carpet?
- also 'measure': *hay que tomar las medidas necesarias* we must take the necessary measures; *una medida de azúcar para cada dos de harina* one measure of sugar for every two of flour; *en gran/cierta medida* to a great/certain extent
- **a medida que** *conj* as (indicates parallel progression): *a medida que se acercaba el invierno los árboles se iban poniendo más desnudos* as winter approached, the trees became more bare
- **medido** *adj* moderate: *soy muy medido en el comer* I'm a very moderate eater

medio *adj* half (NB in this sense precedes noun without indef art): *medio kilo* half a kilo; *media hora* half an hour; *media botella* half a bottle
- also 'average', 'mean' (in that sense), 'middle' (NB follows noun) *precipitación media* average/mean

rainfall; *clase media* middle class
- used also as *adv* therefore invariable: *la comida estaba medio terminada* the meal was half finished; *estaban medio dormidos* they were half asleep
- and as *nm el medio* the mean/average; *en medio* in the middle; *quitar algo/a alguien de en medio* to get sth/sb out of the way: *de por medio* in between, in the middle; *por medio de* by means of, through (in that sense): *lo supe por medio de la prensa* I found out through the press
- also 'means': *me faltan los medios para hacerlo* I don't have the means of doing it
- NB: *el medio ambiente* environment; as *nmpl los medios de comunicación/difusión* the media
- used in many useful phrases: worth further perusal in the dictionary!
- **mediodía** *nm* midday, noon; also 'the south'
- **medianoche** *nf* midnight
- **mediano** *adj* medium(-sized), average (in that sense): *de peso mediano* of medium weight
- **mediante** *prep* by means of, through, using (similar to cf *por medio de*) *mediante este proceso* by means of this process

mejor *adj* and *adv* better, best (comparative and superlative of *bueno* good, and *bien* well)
- *adj*: *una mejor ocasión* a better opportunity; *los mejores asientos* the best seats
- *adv*: *tú hablas español mejor que yo, pero Anita es la que lo habla mejor* you speak Spanish better than me; but Anita speaks it best
- useful phrases: *tanto mejor* so much the better; *cada vez mejor* better and better; *lo mejor* the best: *os deseamos todo lo mejor* we wish you all the best; *lo mejor es (que + subjunc)*

the best thing is (that)

- ☐ **a lo mejor** *adv* useful and common phrase meaning 'probably', 'possibly': *a lo mejor no sabe* he probably doesn't know; *a lo mejor no nos ven* with any luck/maybe they can't see us
- ☐ don't confuse with *mayor* bigger etc, above
- ☐ **mejorar** *vti* to improve, make/get better: *las condiciones han mejorado* conditions have improved; **mejorarse** *vr* to get better, recover (from illness): *¡Que te mejores pronto!* Get well soon!
- ☐ **mejora** *nf* or **mejoramiento** *nm* improvement; **mejorable** *adj* improvable, that can be improved

mellizo/a *nmf* or *adj* twin (not necessarily identical; cf *gemelo/a*, which strictly means identical twin)

memoria *nf* memory: *tengo mala memoria* I've got a bad memory; *de memoria* by memory, by heart; *en memoria de* in memory of; *se me ha ido de la memoria* it's slipped my mind
- ☐ NB used for faculty or action of remembering; for eg happy memories of sb and memory in sense of souvenir, see *recuerdo*

menester *nm* lit: need; used in *es menester* it is necessary: usually in fairly formal language: *es necesario*, *hay que* are in more common use
- ☐ **menesteroso** *adj* needy
- ☐ **menestra** *nf* mixed vegetables

menor *adj* smaller, smallest; lesser, least
- ☐ comparative and superlative of *pequeño*, though *más pequeño* is also common, esp for physical size; opp of and used similarly to cf *mayor* above
- ☐ *éste y otros problemas menores* this and other smaller problems; *éste es el menor de mis problemas* that's the least of my problems; *no tengo la menor idea* I haven't the slightest idea; *una cantidad menor* a smaller

quantity
- ☐ also 'younger/youngest', 'minor': *mi hermano menor* my younger/est brother; *eres menor que yo* you're younger than me; *eres todavía menor de edad* you're still a minor/under age; *prohibido a los menores de 15 años* forbidden to those under 15
- ☐ NB business phrase *(vender) al por menor* to (sell) retail
- ☐ **minoría** *nf* minority (NB spelling: min- not men-!)

menos *adv* less, fewer
- ☐ opp of cf *más* more; used in same way, but to make negative comparisons: *menos dinero* less money; *menos personas que ayer* fewer people than yesterday; *menos interesante* less interesting; *menos de diez* less than 10; *menos rápidamente de lo que esperaba* less quickly than I was expecting (for fuller notes on use of *que* and *de* after comparatives see under *más* or consult a grammar)
- ☐ useful expressions: *al menos, por lo menos* at least; *de menos* too little: *me dieron 100 libras de menos* they gave me £100 too little; *echar de menos* to miss (eg sb's company); *menos mal* a good job (see also under *mal*); *ni mucho menos* no way!; *nada menos que* nothing less than; *a menos que* + *subjunc* unless; and many more: have a browse in the dictionary!
- ☐ also 'except': *todos menos yo* everyone except me (cf *excepto*, *salvo*)
- ☐ and 'minus': *tres menos dos* 3 − 2

mente *nf* mind: *se me ha ido de la mente* it has slipped my mind
- ☐ some overlap in sense of physical 'brain' with cf *cerebro* and of abstract 'intellect' with cf *espíritu*

mentir *vi* -ie- -i- to lie, tell lies, *¡Miento!* Sorry, I'm lying!; *¡No mientas!*

Don't lie!

- □ **mentira** *nf* lie: *¡Parece mentira!* It doesn't seem possible!, It can't be!
- □ **mentirilla** *nf* fib, small lie, 'tease'
- □ **mentiroso/a** *adj* or *nmf* lying, liar: *¡Eres un mentiroso!* You're a liar!

menudo *adj* minute, (very) small: *en pedazos menudos* in(to) minute pieces; (used of person) slight: *es menuda de estatura* she's of slight build

- □ probably met most frequently in **a menudo** *adv* often (cf *con frecuencia, muchas veces*)
- □ NB ironic use – 'fine', 'great': *¡Menuda bronca has montado!* That's a fine row you caused!; *¡Menuda situación es ésta!* A fine situation, this!

merecer *vt* -*zc*- to deserve, merit

- □ + *inf* to deserve to: *merece ser castigado* he deserves to be punished; or + *que* + *subjunc* if there is a change of subject; *merece que le castiguen* he deserves to be punished; **merecerse** *vr* used in same way adds emphasis to the deserts: *se merece un premio* he deserves a prize; *se lo ha merecido* it serves him right (neg), he's earned it (pos)
- □ **merecido** *adj* well-deserved, merited: *llevarse su merecido* to get what one deserves/one's deserts; **merecidamante** *adv* deservedly
- □ **merecedor** *adj* -ora, -ores, -oras deserving, worthy (*de* of)
- □ **mérito** *nm* merit, worth; **meritorio** *adj* commendable, praiseworthy

merienda *nf* afternoon snack (ie between *el almuerzo* and *la cena*), roughly corresponds to 'tea', but one of those words which because of different Eng/Sp lifestyles does not have an exact translation; *merienda campestre* picnic

- □ **merendar** *vi* -ie- to have a

merienda; can also be used to say what you had for your *merienda*: *merendamos bocadillos de queso* we had cheese sandwiches for tea

- □ **merendero** *nm* snack bar; picnic area

mermelada *nf* NB general word for 'jam'; the Sp don't eat bitter Seville oranges of which marmalade is usually made

meta *nf* aim, objective, target, goal: *mi meta es terminar antes de agosto* my aim is to finish before August

- □ goal (football etc); and *nm* goalkeeper

metal *nm* metal

- □ NB cannot be used as *adj*: use *de metal* or *metálico*: *una escultura de metal/metálica* a metal sculpture
- □ **metálico** *adj* metallic, made of metal; *pagar en metálico* to pay cash

meter *vt* to put

- □ NB not a complete *syn* for cf *poner* or *colocar* as it usually conveys idea of 'insert', 'put into': *meter las manos en los bolsillos* to put one's hands into one's pockets; *meter la nariz en algo* to poke one's nose into sth; *meter la pata* to put one's foot in it; *meter a alguien en la cárcel* to put sb in prison
- □ used in a number of idioms: *meter ruido* to cause a fuss/stir; *le metí miedo* I gave him a fright, put the wind up him
- □ **meterse en** *vr* to go into (use with eg water, bed, shelter, etc): *se metió en el agua hasta la cintura* he went into the water up to his waist
- □ also 'to get involved in': *no te metas en esto* don't get involved in this
- □ worth further investigation in the dictionary
- □ **metido** *adj* in, within: *estaba metido en el agua hasta el cuello* he was in the water up to his neck; *estaba*

metido en el asunto he was involved in the matter; *metido en años* elderly

México *nm* Mexico; **mexicano** *adj* Mexican: can also be spelt **Méjico, mejicano**; in any case the *x* is usually pronounced as *j*

mezcla *nf* mixture
- **mezclar** *vt* to mix; **mezclarse** *vr* to mingle (*con* with); also 'to get mixed up', 'involved' (*en* in): *se mezcló en todo eso* he got involved with all that (cf *involucrarse, entrometerse*)

mezquino *adj* mean, stingy (ie person, same as *syn tacaño*); small-minded
- can also mean 'paltry' (eg amount, cf *escaso*)
- **mezquindad** nf meanness, small-mindedness, paltriness

mi *poss adj* my: *mi dinero* my money
- don't confuse with *disjunctive pron* **mí** me: *delante de mí* in front of me
- **mío** *poss pron* mine (used without *def art* after *ser*): *es mío* it's mine; (otherwise with *def art*): *tu hermana y la mía* your sister and mine
- consult a grammar for full explanation and practice

miedo *nm* fear
- NB *tener (mucho) miedo* to be (very) afraid/frightened; *dar/meter miedo a alguien* to frighten sb/give sb a fright (cf *asustar/dar un susto*)
- NB *tener miedo a + noun* to be afraid of sth/sb: *tener miedo a las arañas* to be afraid of spiders; *no me tienes miedo, ¿verdad?* you're not afraid of me, are you?; or *de + inf* to be afraid of doing sth: *tener miedo de encontrar una araña* to be afraid of meeting a spider; *por miedo a/de* 'for fear of' works similarly
- *de miedo* used as colloquial *adj* for 'tremendous', 'great': *fue una fiesta de miedo* it was a great party

- **miedoso** adj fearful, timid, shy; NOT frightened, afraid

mientras *conj* while; sometimes followed by optional *que: mientras (que) esperábamos* while we were waiting
- referring to future, means 'all the while', 'as long as it takes' + *subjunc: mientras sigas haciendo eso* all the while/as long as you carry on doing that
- also means 'whereas': *tú piensas así, mientras que ellos piensan de otra manera* you think like that, whereas they think differently; *que* tends to be retained here to help emphasise the contrast
- **mientras tanto** *adv* meanwhile

mil *nm* thousand
- NB for 1,000, use without *indef art*: *mil habitantes* 1,000 inhabitants
- in a number, does not change however many thousand: *tres mil* 3,000
- must be used as thousand unit: *mil trescientos* 1,300 (no equivalent of 'thirteen hundred'); this includes dates: *mil novecientos noventa y nueve* 1999
- NB can be used in *pl + de* as collective noun: *miles de personas*
- **millar** *nm* another collective noun for 'thousand' (+ *de* + *n/pron*): *un millar de soldados* (about) a thousand soldiers; *millares de ellos* thousands of them

milagro *nm* miracle
- NB spelling – order of letters; also in **milagroso** *adj* miraculous

millón *nm pl millones* million
- NB always + *de* + *noun: un millón/dos millones de habitantes* one/two million inhabitants

mínimo *adj* and *nm* minimum: *doscientos al mínimo* 200 at the least
- NB *(en lo) más mínimo* (in the) least/slightest: *no tengo la más mínima*

idea I haven't the slightest idea; *no me molesta en lo más mínimo* it doesn't worry me in the slightest

ministro/a *nmf* minister: *primer ministro/primera ministra* prime minister; don't confuse with:
  □ **ministerio** *nm* ministry

mirar *vti* to look (at), watch
  □ NB takes *dir obj: ¡Mira esto!* Look at this! but you nevertheless need a *personal a* before a definite person-object: *mira a tu hermano* look at your brother
  □ NB for 'look for', use *buscar*; for 'look' in sense of 'seem' (eg pleasant), use *parecer*
  □ **mirada** *nf* look, glance, gaze
  □ used in various 'look' expressions: *clavar la mirada en algo/alguien* to fix one's gaze on/stare at sth/sb; *mirada fija* stare; *echar una mirada a* to glance at
  □ **mirón** *adj mirona, -ones, -onas* inquisitive, nosey

misa *nf* (mass) in church)
  □ *ir a misa* equivalent of 'to go to church'; *oír misa* to hear/attend mass; *Misa de Gallo* Midnight Mass (24 Dec)

miseria *nf* poverty, destitution, squalor (for 'misery', use *sufrimiento, tristeza* depending on exact meaning: check in a good dictionary!); NB no accent/stress on *ia*!
  □ **mísero** or **miserable** *adj* wretched, paltry; also 'stingy', 'mean'; again not 'miserable' – nearest all-purpose equivalent is *triste*

mismo *adj* same (*que* as); *tiene el mismo nombre que yo* she has the same name as me
  □ NB neuter form used when not referring to a specific noun: **lo mismo** the same: *todos pensamos lo mismo* we all think the same; *lo mismo que* just like, just as; *lo mismo*

que todos los demás just like everybody else
  □ very, selfsame, noun + him/herself/themselves: *en aquel mismo sitio* in that very place; *la misma estrella de la pantalla* the screen star herself; *el mismo Cervantes escribió …* Cervantes himself wrote …
  □ sometimes the superlative **mismísimo** is used for extra emphasis: *en el mismísimo sitio* in the selfsame spot
  □ '-self/selves' – used with subject or disjunctive pron: *lo haré yo mismo* I'll do it myself; *vendrán ellas mismas* they will come themselves; *lo dijo para sí misma* she said it to herself
  □ *adv: aquí mismo* right here; *ahora mismo* right now
  □ NB Eng sometimes uses 'same' to mean 'similar' – use *parecido* or *semejante: llevaba un vestido semejante/idéntico al mío* she was wearing a similar/an identical dress to mine, or she was wearing the same dress as me: but *el mismo vestido* would mean you were both in the same dress – a bit tight!

mitad *nf* half (ie one of two definite halves): *sólo has comido la mitad de tu cena* you've only eaten half (of) your supper
  □ NB study carefully the difference between *mitad* and cf *medio*; meaning 'half', always used with *def art* NEVER *indef*!: compare *media botella* half a (ie any) bottle/a half-bottle, with <u>*la mitad de la*</u> *botella* half the bottle (ie the one in question)
  □ also 'middle', 'in half': *dividir por la mitad* to divide in half, split down the middle; *en mitad de la plaza* in the middle of the square; *en mitad de la lectura* halfway through the reading; *a mitad de precio* half-price

moda *nf* fashion: *estar de moda* to be in fashion; *estar pasado de moda* to be out of fashion/old-fashioned; *un vestido a la moda* a fashionable dress
- □ don't confuse with *modo* below

modelo *nm* model (example, pattern): *que sirva de modelo* let it serve as a model; *sigue según el modelo* continue according to the example/pattern; *el nuevo modelo del coche* the new model of the car
- □ also referring to person *nmf* model
- □ and can be used as *inv adj*: *alumna modelo* model pupil
- □ NOT same as cf *maqueta*, use for eg model railway, mock-up

modo *nm* way, manner: often interchangeable with cf *forma* and *manera*, including expressions such as *de todos modos, de cualquier modo, de modo que*; listed fully under *manera*
- □ can also mean same as **modales** *nmpl* manners: *buenos/malos modos/modales* good/bad manners

mojar *vt* to wet, make wet: *la lluvia ha mojado la hierba* the rain has made the grass wet
- □ general word, stronger than cf *humedecer* to dampen, moisten, but not necessarily so thorough as cf *calar*, *syn empapar*
- □ can also mean 'dip', 'dunk': *mojó el pan en la sopa* he dipped/dunked the bread in the soup
- □ **mojarse** *vr* to get wet, soaked etc: *nos mojamos bajo la lluvia* we got wet in the rain; *¡Cuidado que no te mojes!* Mind you don't get wet!; can also mean 'to wet oneself'
- □ **mojado** *adj* wet (use *estar*): *estábamos mojados hasta los huesos* we were soaked to the skin
- □ NB difference between *mojarse* to get wet and the resultant state *estar mojado* to be wet

moler *vt* -ue- to grind, mill: *café molido*

ground coffee
- □ **molino** *nm* mill: *molino de viento* windmill; use diminutive *molinillo* *nm* for coffee (or other domestic) mill/grinder
- □ **muela** *nf* tooth, strictly molar (ie 'grinder'); often used for teeth in general rather than cf *diente(s)*: *me duelen las muelas* I've got toothache

molestar *vti* to bother, disturb, be a nuisance, upset: *¿Le molesta si abro la ventana?* Do you mind/does it worry you if I open the window?; *me molesta el ruido de los aviones* the aeroplane noise upsets me/is a nuisance; *no quiero molestar* I don't want to be a nuisance/intrude
- □ **molestarse** *vr* to get upset, worried (*por* by/about): *¡No se molestará por eso!* She won't get upset over that!
- □ also 'to bother' (oneself) (*en* to): *¡No te molestes, lo haré yo!* Don't bother, I'll do it!; *ni siquiera se molestó en decírnoslo* he didn't even bother to tell us
- □ NB NOT 'molest' in Eng sense: possibly use *importunar* but consult dictionary with exact context
- □ **molestia** *nf* trouble, inconvenience, nuisance; *siento* or *perdone la molestia* sorry to bother you, sorry to be a nuisance; *¡Qué molestia!* What a nuisance!, What a hassle!; *darse/tomar la molestia de* to take the trouble to
- □ also 'discomfort': *tener molestia del estómago* to have an upset stomach
- □ **molesto** *adj* annoying, irritating: use *ser: tiene que ser muy molesto para Vd* it must be very irritating for you; *¡Qué niño tan molesto!* What a trying/troublesome child!
- □ also 'upset', 'annoyed' (use *estar*): *está muy molesta conmigo* she's very cross with me

moneda *nf* coin: *moneda de un euro* one-euro coin
- □ also 'currency': *pagar con moneda*

argentina to pay in Argentine currency

- □ for money, in general sense, use *dinero*
- □ **monedero** *nm* purse (ie where you carry coins!)

mono *adj* pretty, lovely (can refer to (female) person or things, esp clothes or furnishings): *¡Qué chica más mona!* What a pretty girl! *tiene la cara muy mona* she has a very lovely/pretty face; *¡qué cortinas más monas!* what lovely curtains!

- □ roughly on a par with cf *precioso, guapa*, not so strong as cf *bello, hermoso* in the beauty rating!

mono *nm* monkey, ape

- □ Collins Dictionary lists 13 meanings of the noun – look them up! Here are two more common ones:
- □ boiler suit, overalls, (child's) rompers
- □ 'cold turkey': *estar con el mono* to go cold turkey, have withdrawal symptoms (from drug)

montar *vti* to mount, ride: *montar a caballo/en bicicleta* to ride/mount/get on a horse/bicycle; *estar montado a caballo* to be on horseback

- □ also 'to set up', 'start up': *montar una exposición* to set up/mount an exhibition; *montar un negocio* to set up a business; *montar una bronca* to cause a row; *montar una tienda* to put up a tent
- □ and *montar sobre algo* to overlap sth
- □ **montarse a** *vr* to get on to: *montarse a un caballo* to get on to a horse (actual action); *montárselo* to be on to a good thing: *se lo monta bien* he's on to a good thing/got it going for him; *montarse un número* to make a scene
- □ NB for 'go up', in sense of Fr *monter*, use *subir*

monte *nm* mount, mountain (esp in titles): *Monte Blanco* Mont Blanc

- □ can also mean 'scrub' or 'woodland':

vivir en el monte to live in the country/sticks

- □ **montaña** *nf* mountain; often used *sing* to mean 'the mountains': *acampar en la montaña* to camp in the mountains
- □ **montón** *nm pl* montones pile, heap: used like Eng as expression for 'much/many': *tengo un montón de trabajo que terminar* I've got a pile of work to finish; *hay montones de cosas que hacer* there are heaps of things to do
- □ also colloquially as *adv* esp with *doler* and *gustar*: *duele un montón* it doesn't half hurt; *me gusta un montón* I like him/her/it a lot

moral *nf* or **moralidad** *nf* morality, ethics: *no tiene moral(idad)* he has no morals

- □ also: morale
- □ *adj* moral
- □ **moraleja** *nf* moral (eg of story)

moreno *adj* (applied to hair) dark, dark-haired

- □ (applied to complexion) dark-skinned, swarthy: *ponerse moreno* to get suntanned, brown

morir *vi -ue-, -u- past part:* muerto to die

- □ **morirse** *vr* to die
- □ as far as there is any difference, the reflexive form tends to be used for natural death, the intransitive for accidental, unexpected or formally reported death: *murió en un accidente de carretera* he died in a road accident; *se murió de una pulmonía* he died of pneumonia
- □ *morirse por algo* or + *inf* to be dying for sth/to: *se muere por ver jugar su equipo* he's dying to see his team play
- □ **muerte** *nf* death
- □ **muerto/muerta** *adj* dead: NB use *estar* in spite of 'dead' being a permanent state: *está muerta*

she's dead

□ also used as *nmf* dead man/woman

┌─────────────────────────────┐
│ □ DO NOT CONFUSE *muerte*
│   death, with *muerto/muerta* dead
│   man/woman!
└─────────────────────────────┘

mostrar *vt* -ue- to show; much the same
as cf *enseñar* used in this sense and
indicar when meaning is 'point out',
'indicate': *muéstrame tu trabajo* show
me your work; *¿Puede mostrarme por
dónde se va a Segovia?* Can you show
me how to get to Segovia?

□ **mostrarse** *vr + adj* to appear, seem
be: *se mostraba muy molesta* she
seemed very cross; *se mostró muy
amable con nosotros* she was very
kind to us

□ **mostrador** *nm* counter (in shop)

□ **muestra** *nf* sign, indication, show
(in that sense): *no dio ninguna muestra
de nervios* he gave no sign of nerves

□ also 'sample' (eg of product): *feria de
muestras* trade show/exhibition

motivo *nm* motive

□ NB has a wider meaning than in Eng,
and often translates 'reason' (*de*
to/for) and is often a better translation
than cf *razón*: *con este motivo* with
this reason; *no hubo ningún motivo de
hacer eso* there was no reason to do
that; *sin ningún motivo* without any
reason; *tendrá sus motivos* he'll have
his reasons; *con motivo del décimo
aniversario del hermanamiento* on
the occasion of the 10th anniversary
of the twinning

□ **motivar** *vt* to motivate;
motivación *nf* motivation;
motivador/a *adj pl* -ores, -oras
motivating

motor *nm* motor, engine (ie apparatus
which drives machinery)

□ can also be *adj* motor, motora,
motores, motoras: driving, motor:
fuerza motora driving force

□ **moto** *nf* NB *fem* short for
motocicleta *nf* motorbike

□ **motorista** *nmf* motorcyclist, NOT
motorist: use *automovilista* or
conductor

mover *vt* to move (in many senses except
move house – see *mudar*): *mover la
cabeza* to shake one's head; *mover la
cola* to wag the tail; *eso me movió a ir a
España* that moved me to go to Spain

□ **moverse** *vr* to move (intransitively):
¡No te muevas! Don't move!;
¡Muévete! Get moving!; *la máquina
se movió* the camera moved

□ **movida** *nf* 'scene': *la movida
madrileña* the Madrid 'scene'; *ahí
está la movida* that's where the
action is

□ **movimiento** *nm* movement (in
most senses)

□ **movedizo** *adj* movable (easily
moved): *tierra movediza* unstable
land

□ **móvil/movible** *adj* mobile; some
'mobile' services use *ambulante*: check
in dictionary!

muchacho *nm* boy; (colloquially) kid, guy
(masculine); **muchacha** *nf* girl

□ tends to refer to 'middle' years of
childhood and youth, but also esp
colloquially to a young person of
either sex up to about 20; cf *niño/a*
and *chico/a*

mucho *adj/adv/pron* much, many, a lot
(of), a great deal (of) as *adj* agrees with
noun: *muchas cosas*

□ NB used for 'very', with *tener/hacer*
expressions eg *tengo mucha sed*, as *sed*
etc are nouns

□ *adv*: *me gusta mucho* I like it a lot

□ *pron*: *hay muchos que están de acuerdo*
there are lots who agree

□ *ni mucho menos* no way, far from it
(usually to back up negative
statement): *no estoy de acuerdo, ¡ni
mucho menos!* I don't agree, no way!

□ *por mucho que* + *subjunc* however much: *por mucho que grites* however much you scream: cf *por más que* under **más**

□ **muchísimo** *adj/adv/pron* very much, very many, a great deal: *muchísimas gracias* thanks very much indeed

□ **muchedumbre** *nf* crowd, multitude (usually of people)

mudar *vti* to change (*en* into): *la bruja mudó a la princesa en rana* the witch changed the princess into a frog

□ to change for sth different, with *de*: *mudar de ropa* to change one's clothes

□ **mudarse** *vr* to change (*en* into): *la princesa se mudó en rana* the princess changed into a frog

□ *mudarse de casa* to move house

□ NB many of meanings are identical with cf *cambiar(se)* and some with cf *transformar(se)/convertir(se)*

□ **mudanza** *nf* change; also (house) 'removal': *camión de mudanzas* removal lorry

□ **muda** *nf* change of clothes (only); moult (of animals)

mueble *nm* piece of furniture (NB *sing* means just one piece, use *pl muebles* for furniture collectively)

□ **mobiliario** *nm* furniture, fittings; perhaps more of a trade/commercial/advertising term than *muebles*

□ **amueblar** *vt* to furnish: *cocina amueblada* fitted kitchen

□ for 'furnish' in sense of 'provide/supply', use *proveer, suministrar*

muela see **moler**

mugre *nm* dirt, grime (grimier than cf *suciedad*)

□ **mugriento** *adj* grimy, filthy (more limited than cf *sucio*, to describing physical state only: would not be used

of behaviour, thought, joke etc)

mujer *adj* woman; general term for adult human female: not same as cf *señora* lady

□ also 'wife', but not regarded as polite to refer to sb else's *mujer!* use *señora* or *esposa* in that case; you can say *¿Conoce Vd a mi mujer?* Have you met my wife?, but you should say *no conozco a su señora/esposa* I haven't met your wife

multi- *prefix* multi-, many-; there are a number of useful words beginning with this prefix:

□ **multicine** *nm* multiscreen cinema

□ **multilingüe** *adj* multilingual

□ **multiuso** *adj inv* multipurpose

mundo *nm* world (in most English senses); *todo el mundo* everybody (not 'all the world': use *el mundo entero*)

□ **mundial** *adj* (to do with the) world: *Segunda Guerra Mundial* 2nd World War; *Copa mundial* World Cup

□ **mundialmente** *adv* worldwide, universally: *está mundialmente conocida* she's known throughout the world/worldwide

□ **mundano** *adj* worldly, of the world: *placeres mundanos* worldly pleasures; for 'mundane' in sense of 'humdrum', use *trivial* or *rutinario*; can mean (to do with) high society, fashionable: *vida mundana* high society

muñeco *nm* or **muñeca** *nf* doll; *muñeco de nieve* snowman: *m* or *f* depending on what the doll represents!

□ also *nf* wrist

murmurar *vti* to murmur

□ also 'to mutter' (usually in sense of complain): – *la sopa está fría – murmuró* 'the soup's cold,' she muttered

□ and 'to gossip' (usually maliciously): *se murmura que no están casados* it's

rumoured they're not married

☐ and (to describe noise of eg water or insects): to murmur, hum

☐ **murmullo** *nm* murmur(ing), whisper(ing), hum(ming) etc

☐ **murmuración** *nf* (often used in *pl murmuraciones*) gossip, talk (in that sense): *según las murmuraciones* according to gossip; also: 'complaining'

muro *nm* wall: used for whole of structure

☐ not same as cf *pared*, which usually means interior wall, or surface on which you hang things

☐ **muralla** *nf* wall, (in sense of) battlement, eg town wall

música *nf* music

☐ **músico** *nm* **música** *nf* musician

muy *adv* very (used to qualify an adjective or adverb): *muy rápido* very quick; *muy rápidamente* very quickly

☐ NB not used with *tener/hacer + calor/frío* etc, which are nouns – use *mucho/a* in these cases

☐ NB can imply 'too': *estos zapatos son muy estrechos* these shoes are too tight

N (*ene*) is pronounced much the same in Spanish as in English, though some Spaniards may 'nasalise' it slightly, especially on the end of a word.

◆ It is one of only four Spanish consonants that can occur double. In these fairly rare cases, you pronounce both *ns*. There are a handful of words with the combination *inn*. They are either words beginning with *n-* made negative by the addition of the prefix *in-*, eg *innecesario, innegable*; or begin with the prefix *in-* meaning 'in' added to a base word beginning with *n-*, eg *innovación*. Another word with *-nn-* is *perenne* perennial

◆ For **Ñ** see section devoted to this letter.

nacer *vi* -zc- to be born

☐ NB this is an active verb in Sp, ie it's what the baby does, not what the mother does ('to give birth', 'bear' is *parir* or *dar luz*)

☐ **nacido** *adj/past part* born: *nacido en Toledo* born in Toledo; *recién nacido*

newborn; *mal nacido* rotten (applied to person); as *nmf* rotter, nasty piece of work

☐ **nacimiento** *nm* birth

☐ **natal** *adj* natal; but also 'native', 'home' (in that sense): *mi ciudad natal* my home town; **nativo** *adj* also has this meaning

☐ **natalidad** *nf* birth rate

nada *pron* nothing, not … anything

☐ NB as with all negative words, *no* is needed before verb when *nada* follows it: *no quiero nada* I don't want anything

☐ some useful expressions: *nada más* nothing else; *como si nada* as if nothing had happened; *antes de nada* before anything else, above all; *mejor que nada* better than anything/ nothing; *no servir para nada* to be of no use, not to be of any use; and many more: look in the dictionary!

☐ *adv* not at all: *el pronóstico no es nada bueno* the outlook is not at all good

☐ *nf la nada* nothing(ness), void: *salir de la nada* to come out of nowhere

nadar *vi* to swim

☐ NB this verb only describes the action of keeping yourself afloat and propelling yourself, it doesn't actually get you anywhere, you have to use **a nado** *adv* (by) swimming, so, 'to swim the river', (ie across the river) would be *cruzar el río a nado; cruzar/ir a Francia a nado* to swim to France; **nado** *nm* (swimming) stroke: *nado de pecho* breaststroke

- □ **natación** *nf* swimming: *mi interés principal es la natación* my main hobby is swimming; *natación de pecho* breaststroke (you can use either *nado* or *natación* for stroke)

nadie *pron* nobody, not … anybody; no-one, not … anyone
- □ NB as with all negative words, *no* is needed before verb when *nadie* follows it: *no viene nadie* no-one is coming
- □ when dir obj it is preceded by personal *a*: *no conozco a nadie* I don't know anyone

naipe *nm* Spanish-style playing card (they are different from international ones – use *cartas*), the four suits are *espadas, bastos, oros* and *copas; jugar a los naipes* to play cards

naranja *nf* orange
- □ NB used as *adj* it is invariable: *unas cortinas naranja* orange curtains
- □ **naranjo** *nm* orange tree (note gender); **naranjal** *nm* orange grove, orange 'orchard'; **naranjada** *nf* orangeade

narcótico *adj & n* narcotic; *narcóticos* drugs (in that sense)
- □ **narcotráfico** *nm* drug trafficking; **narcotraficante** *nmf* drug trafficker, dealer, colloquially sometimes abbreviated to **narco** *nmf*; **narcodependencia** *nf* drug dependency

nariz *nf* nose, nostril; often used in *pl narices* for 'nose'
- □ occurs in a wide variety of

expressions: *sonarse las narices* to blow one's nose; *darse de narices contra algo/con alguien* to bump into sth/sb (lit or fig); *dar de narices* to fall flat on one's face; *estar hasta las narices con algo/alguien* to be fed up to the back teeth with sth/sb; *meter las narices en* to poke one's nose into; *¡narices!* rubbish!; and more – look in the dictionary!
- □ there are various *adjs* for 'big-nosed': *narigudo, narizudo, narigón (-ona)*

natural *adj* natural (covers most Eng senses)
- □ also 'raw', 'uncooked': *legumbres naturales* raw vegetables
- □ *al natural* in natural state: *jugo de fruta al natural* fruit juice at room temperature
- □ *nmf* native, sb born in: *fue natural de Córdoba* s/he was a native of Córdoba
- □ *nm* character, nature (of person): *es de natural agradable* s/he has a pleasant nature
- □ **naturaleza** *nf* nature (in most senses); also in wider sense of 'wildlife': *me gusta observar la naturaleza* I like to watch the wildlife
- □ don't confuse with **naturalidad** *nf* naturalness: *con la mayor naturalidad (del mundo)* as if it were the most natural thing (in the world)

navaja *nf* penknife; also used for rather more vicious types of knife, razor ('cut-throat' type!); (not for eating meals, use *cuchillo*)

nave *nf* ship, vessel; definitely ship, not boat: see under *barco* for references to the various words for boat, vessel, etc
- □ also 'nave' (in church) and commonly in industrial context 'large shed', 'factory'
- □ **navegar** *vti* -gue-, -gué; to sail, navigate; also 'to surf' (the Internet)
- □ **navegación** *nf* navigation;

navegador/a or **navegante** *nmf*
navigator; **navegable** *adj* navigable

necesario *adj* necessary: + *inf* or + *que* +
subjunc: *es necesario ayudar* it's
necessary to help; *es necesario que
ayudemos* it's necessary that we help,
we must help
- □ **necesidad** *nf* necessity, need; *la
  necesidad de* + *n* / + *inf*: the need
  for/to; *no hay necesidad de* there's
  no need of/to
- □ **necesitado** *adj* *estar necesitado de*
  to be in need of; *nmpl los necesitados*
  those in need, the needy
- □ **necesitar** *vt* to need; *necesito una
  nueva falda* I need a new skirt; + *inf*
  to: *necesito comprar una nueva falda*
  I need to buy a new skirt; see also
  hacer falta (under *falta*) and cf *exigir,
  requerir*

negar *vti -ie-; -gue-, gué* to deny, refute:
niega haberlo hecho he denies having
done it; *negó que sus acciones causaran el
problema* he denied that his actions
caused the problem; *les negó ayuda* he
denied them help; *negar con la cabeza*
to shake one's head (ie meaning 'no')
- □ **negarse a** *vr* (+ *inf*) to refuse to: *se
  negó a ayudarles* he refused to help
  them
- □ **negación** *nf pl negaciones* negation;
  negativa *nf* negative; both can
  mean 'denial', 'refusal': *una negativa
  rotunda* a flat refusal
- □ **negativo** *adj* negative: *actitud
  negativa* negative attitude
- □ **negativamente** *adv* negatively:
  contestar negativamente to reply in
  the negative

negocio *nm* business (eg shop,
organisation), similar to cf *comercio: tiene
su propio negocio* he has his own
business; *montar un negocio* to set up a
business; also 'trade' *el negocio de la
confitería* the confectionery trade; and
'deal': *conseguir un buen negocio* to get

a good deal
- □ in *pl* business (ie the activity):
  hombre/mujer de negocios
  businessman/woman; *¿Cómo van los
  negocios?* How's business?
- □ **negociar** *vti* to negotiate, deal;
  negociación *nf pl negociaciones*
  negotiation; also 'deal', 'transaction'
- □ **negociante** *nmf* businessman/woman

nervio *nm* nerve
- □ occurs in a number of common
  expressions, eg: *eso me crispa los
  nervios* that gets on my nerves; *tengo
  los nervios destrozados* my nerves are
  in shreds; *tengo los nervios en punto*
  my nerves are on edge
- □ for 'nerve' in sense of 'cheek', use
  descaro, frescura
- □ **nervioso** *adj* nervous (to do with
  nerves): *crisis nerviosa* nervous
  breakdown; 'nervy' (ie by
  temperament): *es una persona muy
  nerviosa* she's a very nervy person;
  and 'nervous' (through circumstances):
  estar nervioso to be nervous; *¡Me
  pones nervioso!* You make me
  nervous!
- □ **nerviosidad** *nf* or **nerviosismo** *nm*
  nervousness, state of nerves

nevar *vi -ie-* to snow
- □ *nieva* it snows, it's snowing;
  está/estaba nevando it/is was
  snowing
- □ **nieve** *nf* snow: this is the noun,
  don't confuse it with the verb form
  nieva above!
- □ **nevada** *nf* snowfall, snowstorm
- □ **nevera** *nf* fridge, common
  alternative to *frigorífico* (nothing
  directly to do with snow, except it's
  cold!)

ni *conj* nor (negative of *o*, 'or'): *no lo tengo
ni lo quiero* I haven't got it nor do I
want it; *sin dinero ni comida* without
money (n)or food
- □ often occurs as **ni ... ni ...** neither

… nor, not … either … or: *no tiene ni hogar ni familia* he's got neither home nor family

□ NB like all negative words, *no* is needed before verb when *ni (… ni …)* follows it

□ also means 'not even': *no recibí ni una carta* I didn't even get a letter: *no dijeron ni adiós* they didn't even say goodbye; often used with cf *siquiera* in this sense: *ni siquiera vino a verme* he didn't even come to see me

□ *ni que* + *subjunc* not even if (used in expressions of emphatic rejection or annoyance): *¡Ni que me pagaran un dineral!* Not even if they paid me a mint of money!; *¡Ni que me lo dijera él mismo!* Not even if he told me so himself!; and without *que*: *¡Ni hablar!* or *¡Ni mucho menos!* No way!, Not on your life!

□ don't confuse with *tampoco*, 'neither' in sense of negative of *también*

niebla *nf* fog; *hay* (not *hace*) *niebla* it's foggy; *un día de niebla* a foggy day

□ usually thicker than cf *neblina* mist and cf *bruma* mist, haze: though it has to be said that the dividing line between these words is a bit

□ **nebuloso** *adj* nebulous, foggy, unclear (not used to describe weather): *definición nebulosa* vague definition

ninguno *adj* no, not any

□ NB shortens to *ningún* before *msing* noun: *ningún problema* no problem; but *ninguna respuesta* no reply

□ negative of cf *alguno*: *¿Hay alguna posibilidad? No, no hay ninguna posibilidad* Is there some possibility? No, there's no possibility (see also under *alguno* for more emphatic negative)

□ NB seldom used in *pl*

□ as *pron* ie without a noun: *¿Posibilidad? ¡No hay ninguna!*; in this case, *msing* does not shorten:

¿Cuál de estos pasteles quieres? No quiero ninguno Which of these cakes would you like? I don't want any/either (if two)

niño/a *nmf* boy/girl; child, baby: *los niños* the children

□ tends to refer to little ones, though difficult to put an age limit on it: to roughly age 8–9, where cf *chico/chica* tend to be used right up to 20+; cf *muchacho/a* are also used for the middle period

□ for children in sense of 'offspring', better to use cf *hijos*

□ some useful expressions: *desde niño/a* since (I/he/she) was a child, since childhood; *esperar/tener un niño* to be expecting/have a baby; *el Niño Jesús* Baby Jesus; *niño probeta* test-tube baby; *¡No seas niño/a!* Don't be such a baby!

□ **niñez** *nf* childhood: *en mi niñez* in my childhood

□ **niñero/a** *nmf* childminder; **niñería** *nf* childish act, trivial thing: *¡Déjate de niñerías!* Don't be so childish!, Stop acting like a child!

nivel *nm* level (in sense of) height: *nivel del mar* sea level *al nivel de* on the same level as, at/on the level of

□ also 'standard': *nivel de vida* standard of living; *hasta un alto nivel* up to a high standard

□ **nivelar** *vt* to level (out): *tendrán que nivelar el terreno* they will have to level the pitch; use **nivelarse** *vr* for intransitive form: *el desequilibrio se niveló* the imbalance levelled out

□ for *adj* 'level' (flat) use *llano, plano*; for 'horizontal', use *horizontal*

no *adv* other than meaning simply 'no', it means 'not' and is placed before the verb and any object pronouns to make the former negative: *¿No me quieres?* Don't you love me? *No, no te quiero* No, I don't love you it is needed before the verb when a negative word follows it: *no quiero nada* I don't want anything

when used in many phrases without a verb it tends to follow the word it makes negative: *ya no* no longer, not any more; *ahora no* not now; *todavía no* not yet; *yo no* not me; *eso no* not that; note also: *creo que no* I don't think so, I think not

also used like Eng *prefix* non- or un-, but not joined by hyphen: *no fumador* non-smoker; *países no cristianos* non-Christian countries; *embarazo no deseado* unwanted pregnancy

and often used in speech to convert a statement into a question in a similar but more colloquial way to *¿verdad?*: *¿Me quieres, ¿no?* You do love me, don't you?; *Es muy bonito, ¿no?* It's very pretty, isn't it?; *Tú harías lo mismo, ¿no?* You'd do the same, wouldn't you?

noche *nf* night

used also for late part of evening, from around 8 pm (before that it is cf *la tarde*); *buenas noches* used from about 8, possibly earlier if dark, to greet sb: *¡hola, buenas noches!* (hello) good evening; and to take leave: *¡adiós, buenas noches!* good night!

esta noche this evening, tonight; *anoche* last night; *de noche* at night; *por la noche* at night, in the night; *sábado por la noche* Saturday night; *a las once de la noche* eleven o'clock at night (ie use *de* when a time is expressed); *hasta muy entrada la noche* until very late (at night); *Nochebuena* Christmas Eve; *Nochevieja* New Year's Eve

also means 'dark' (in the sense of night having fallen): *está de noche* it's dark

see also *anochecer* *vi* to get dark

nombre *nm* name

NB in general sense eg of town, country, animal, company, organisation, etc; for person, specifically first/given/ Christian name: *nombre y apellidos* eg on form: first name and surname, full name; *nombre de pila* first name; you can, however say eg *mi nombre es Julia Domínguez Pelayo* when giving your full name (as alternative to *me llamo …*); *nombre de soltera* maiden name

en nombre de in the name of, for the sake of: *en nombre del sentido común* in the name of common sense; also *a nombre de alguien* in sb's name: *¿A nombre de quién? A nombre de Moreno* In what name? In the name of Moreno (eg when collecting mail)

also 'noun', though grammar books tend to prefer *sustantivo*

NB if you are learning French: *nombre* in Sp does NOT mean 'number'! (see *número, cantidad*)

nombrar *vt* to name; also 'to nominate' (esp in sense of 'appoint'): *fue nombrado director* he was appointed manager; **nombramiento** *nm* nomination, appointment

norma *nf* norm, but a commonly used word for 'rule', 'regulation': *hay que seguir las normas* we have to follow the rules; *normas de seguridad* safety regulations

normal *adj* normal, but with wider application of 'usual', 'common': *es normal* it's normal, usual; *pedí lo normal* I asked for the usual; *no es normal* it's unusual; **normalmente** *adv* normally, usually

normalidad *nf* normality, normal circumstance(s): *las calles han vuelto a la normalidad* the street are back to normal; *con (toda) normalidad* as normal

norte *nm & adj* north; *adj* is invariable: *regiones norte* northern regions

NB combinations: *nordeste* or *noreste*

north-east; *noroeste* north-west

☐ **Norteamérica, norteamericano**
see important note under *América*

nosotros/as *pron mf* we, us: subject and disjunctive (prepositional form); NB *f* form

☐ **nos** *pron* us, to us, (to) ourselves: indirect and direct object and reflexive form

☐ **nuestro** *adj & pron* our; ours

☐ consult a grammar book for full details and practice

nota *nf* note (in most Eng senses except banknote – use *billete*): *tomar notas* to take notes (same as cf *apuntes*); *de nota* of note, well-known

☐ also: bill (in eg restaurant, same as the more common *cuenta*)

☐ and: (school) mark: *sacar buenas notas* to get good marks

☐ **notar** *vt* to notice (much the same as cf *observar, reparar en,* and *syn percibir*): *se nota que …* you can tell that …; *le noté muy cansado* I found him very tired

☐ to note down (same as cf *apuntar*)

☐ **notable** *adj* notable, noteworthy, remarkable: *tiene una aptitud notable* s/he has a remarkable aptitude; also *nm* as school/university mark: 'good' (around 8/10!)

☐ **noticia** *nf* (item of) news: *no le gustó esta noticia* this piece of news didn't please him; *noticias* news (newspaper, TV, radio etc); *¿Tienes noticias de ella?* Have you any news of her? NOT: notice – use *aviso*

☐ **noticiario** *nm* newsreel, news programme (film/TV)

☐ **notorio** *adj* well-known; evident, obvious; notable: does not usually have the rather derogatory nuance of English 'notorious', eg for sth criminal, although the adv **notoriamente** can mean 'blatantly', 'glaringly': *una decisión notoriamente equivocada* a glaringly wrong decision

notario/a *nmf* notary (about the closest equivalent to 'solicitor', but Sp and Eng legal roles and activities do not correspond exactly); cf *abogado/a*

novecientos *adj* nine hundred

☐ NB it's not *nueve-* but *NOVEcientos*, and it agrees with its noun: *novecientas viviendas* 900 dwellings

novia *nf* (steady) girlfriend, fiancée, bride

☐ yes, all three stages: usage dates from the time when a steady girlfriend would inevitably become the boy's wife; still used in all these senses, though the sequence may not necessarily be taken for granted!

☐ *prometida* is also often used for fiancée, *recién casada* for newly-wed

☐ **novio** *nm* male equivalent of all the above!; *los novios* the engaged couple, the bride and groom; *viaje de novios* honeymoon

☐ **noviazgo** *nm* engagement

nube *nf* cloud: *los precios se han puesto por las nubes* prices have gone sky-high, rocketed; *siempre anda por las nubes* he's always got his head in the clouds

☐ also: swarm (of insects, people)

☐ **nublado** *adj* cloudy, overcast: *ayer estaba muy nublado* it was very overcast yesterday; also *nm* storm cloud

☐ **nublar** *vt* to cloud, obscure, darken

☐ **nuboso** *adj* cloudy: *cielos nubosos en Castilla* cloudy skies in Castilla; **nubosidad** *nf* cloudiness, (abundance of) clouds: *se dispersará la nubosidad en Castilla* clouds in Castile will disperse

☐ **nubarrón** *nm pl nubarrones* storm, cloud, big black cloud

nudo *nm* knot; *un nudo en la garganta* a lump in one's throat

☐ NOT 'nude' – that's *desnudo*

☐ **anudar** *vt* to knot

☐ **nudoso** *adj* knotty

nuevo *adj* new (most senses as in Eng, but note difference of meaning depending on position)

- □ after noun (brand) new: *tenemos un coche nuevo* we've got a (brand) new car
- □ before noun fresh, different: *tenemos un nuevo coche* we've got a new (ie a different) car; or 'further': *¿has tenido algunas nuevas ideas?* have you had any further/fresh ideas?
- □ useful phrases: *de nuevo* again; *algo nuevo* anything/something new; *nada nuevo* nothing new; *¿qué hay de nuevo?* what's new?
- □ **novedad** *nf* novelty, innovation; *últimas novedades* latest fashions or models (in shop); *sin novedad* without problem: *todo transcurrió sin novedad* everything went off with no problem
- □ **novedoso** *adj* novel, original: *ha tenido unas ideas novedosas* he's had some novel ideas

número *nm* number (in most Eng senses – number of house, room, phone, magazine, etc); numeral

- □ figure: see also *cifra*
- □ quantity: *un gran número de* a large number of (see also *cantidad*)
- □ size (esp of shoe): *¿Qué número?* What size?
- □ act, turn (in theatre etc)

nunca *adv* never, not … ever

- □ NB as with all negative words, *no* is needed before verb when *nunca* follows it: *no vamos nunca* we never go
- □ useful phrases: *casi nunca* hardly ever; *más que nunca* more than ever; *nunca más* never again, never any more
- □ much the same as but perhaps not so strong as cf *jamás*

Ñ

Ñ (*eñe*) is pronounced like the '-ni-' in 'onion' or the '-ny-' in 'canyon'. It is regarded as a separate letter from N and comes after it in the alphabet.

- ◆ There are few words that begin with it, most of them very colloquial eg *¡ñam-ñam!* yum-yum!
- ◆ It is mainly found in the middle of a word; *año, señor, madrileño,* etc.

O

O is one of the five Spanish vowels, and always has the same sound, wherever it occurs in a word: *hombre, ojo, ocho, orden.*

♦ It forms a diphthong after -*i*- (*Dios, camión*) and before -*i*/-*y* (*oigo, hoy*), but is pronounced separately from *a* and *e* (*cacao, creo, roa, roe*)

♦ A word ending in o is usually masculine, with just a few exceptions.

o *conj* or
- becomes *u* before *o/ho: siete u ocho, mujeres u hombres; ... o ... o ...* either ... or ...: *o me lo das o te lo quito* either you give it to me or I take it away from you

obedecer *vti* -*zc*- to obey
- *obedecer al hecho de que ...* to be due to the fact that ...

objeto *nm* object
- most senses as Eng, ie thing, purpose, grammatical: *objectos perdidos* lost property

obligar *vt* -*gue*-, -*gué* to oblige, force, compel
- + *a* + *inf: obligar a alguien a hacer algo* to oblige/force/compel sb to do sth; *estar obligado a hacer algo* to be obliged/forced/compelled to do sth
- *estar obligado a alguien* to be obliged/indebted to sb
- **obligatorio** *adj* obligatory, usual Sp for 'compulsory'

obra *nf* work
- work of art, music, etc: *obra de teatro* play (often simply *obra: ¿Te gustó la obra?* Did you like the play?)
- work, eg of charity: *una obra de caridad*

- roadworks *obras de carretera*
- repair work: *cerrado por obras* closed for repairs; *acceso prohibido a toda persona ajena a la obra* access forbidden to anyone not involved in the work
- matter, question: *es obra de unos días* it's a matter of a few days (eg to get something done)
- NB has these specific uses and not the same as cf *trabajo, labor*
- **obrar** *vti* to work, in following senses:
- to work eg wood or other material
- more frequently used as to work in sense of 'act', 'proceed', 'operate': *obra con cuidado* he works/proceeds/operates with care cf *operar; este tratamiento obra bien* this treatment works well; there is some overlap with cf *funcionar*, which refers to rather more mechanical processes
- not same as cf *trabajar* which has more to do with labour/toil
- **obrero/a** *nmf* workman (*m* only), worker, labourer: *obrero autónomo* self-employed worker
- *adj* working, as in *clase obrera* working class (not 'working' as in 'working model': use *que funciona*)

obsequio *nm* present, gift (slightly more formal word for *regalo*)
- **obsequioso** *adj* obliging, helpful
- not 'obsequious', use *servil*

observar *vt* to observe (in most Eng senses) ie watch, respect, remark/comment
- **observación** *nf pl* observaciones observation, in most Eng senses
- also translates 'watching': *observación de pájaros* birdwatching
- and 'remark', 'comment': *hizo la observación siguiente* he made the following remark/comment

obsesionar *vt* to obsess
- **obsesionarse** *vr* to be obsessed (*con/por* with); you can also say *estar obsesionado/a*

obstante occurs as **no obstante** *adv*
however, nevertheless; also *prep* in spite
of, notwithstanding (more formal than cf
a pesar de)

obstinado *adj* obstinate, stubborn
- **obstinarse** *(en)* *vi* to persist
  (obstinately) (in), insist (on) + noun
  or inf: *se obstina en fumar* he persists
  in smoking
- stronger than *persistir/insistir en*

obstruir *vt* *pi: obstruyo, -uyes, -uye, -uyen;
ps: obstruya; ger: obstruyendo; pret:
obstruyó/obstruyeron; imp subj:
obstruyera/obstruyese* to obstruct
- **obstrucción** *nf pl obstrucciones*
  obstruction

obtener *vt* (NB has all irregularities of *tener*,
+ *tú imperative: obtén*) to obtain, get (in
that sense); you can also often use cf
conseguir

ocasión *nf pl ocasiones* occasion
- time: *en esta ocasión* on this
  occasion
- chance, opportunity: *tener la ocasión de*
  to have the chance/opportunity to
- cause, motive: *no hay ocasión para
  preocuparse* there's no cause for
  concern
- *de ocasión* second-hand: *coches de
  ocasión* second-hand cars
- **ocasional** *adj* (most common use)
  chance, incidental: *fue un encuentro
  ocasional* it was a chance meeting
- for Eng 'occasional', meaning 'from
  time to time', use *poco frecuente,
  intermitente, que pasa de vez en
  cuando* (whichever fits the context)
- **ocasionalmente** *adv* by chance,
  accidentally
- not 'occasionally', see *ocasional* above

occidental *adj* western
- used with countries, eg the former
  Alemania Occidental West Germany;
  los poderes occidentales the western
  powers; more formal than cf *oeste*

ocio *nm* leisure, free time (in that sense)
- **ocioso** *adj* idle, not doing anything;
  implies idleness or even pointlessness:
  fue una observación ociosa it was a
  useless/pointless observation
- for 'leisurely', use *pausado/con calma*

ocultar *vt* to hide, conceal (*a/de* from);
ocultarse *vr* to hide/conceal (oneself)
- same as more common *esconder(se)*
- **oculto** *adj* hidden, concealed (use
  with *estar/quedar*)
- also 'secret', 'occult', as in Eng

ocupar *vt* to occupy (in most senses)
- **ocuparse** *vr* has a variety of
  meanings:
- to concern oneself (*de* with): *no se
  ocupa de nosotros* he is not
  concerned with us
- busy oneself (*de* with): *se ocupa del
  cuidado de su jardín* he busies
  himself with looking after his garden
- take care of, attend to: *nosotros nos
  ocuparemos de esto* we'll take care of
  this; *ocuparse de lo suyo* to mind
  one's own business
- **ocupado** *adj* occupied
- taken, 'engaged': *¿Está ocupado aquel
  asiento?* Is that seat taken?; *el baño
  está ocupado* the bathroom is
  engaged
- see also *comunicar* when phone line is
  engaged
- occupied, busy (of a person): *¿Estás
  ocupado?* Are you busy?

ocurrir *vi* to occur
- used much more than Eng equivalent:
  'to happen', 'to be going on',
  especially for events in progress: *¿Qué
  ocurre aquí?* What's going on here?;
  lo que ocurre es que ... the thing is
  that ...
- **ocurrirse** *vr* used in phrases such as
  se me ocurre que ... it occurs to me
  that ...; *no se le ocurrió que* or + inf:
  it didn't occur to him/her that .../to
  ..., s/he didn't think that .../to ...

□ **ocurrencia** *nf* event, happening, occurrence

□ NB one *c* and two *rrs*!

odiar *vt* to hate (stronger than *detestar*)

□ **odio** *nm* hate, hatred

oeste *adj/nm* west; as *adj* is invariable: *la costa oeste* the west coast; cf *occidental*

ofender *vt* to offend

□ **ofenderse** *vr* to take offence, be offended: *no te ofendes, ¿verdad?* you're not offended, are you?/don't take offence, do you?

oferta/ofertar see **ofrecer**

oficio *nm* job, occupation, profession, office (in this sense only)

□ emphasis is on nature of the work: *aprender un oficio* to learn a trade; *es un oficio prestigioso* it's a prestigious job/profession; not same as *trabajo*, some overlap with cf *puesto*

□ also: (religious) service

□ **oficina** *nf* office (as place of work, but cf *despacho*)

□ **oficial** *adj* official (sense as Eng); *nmf* officer, official

□ NB **oficioso** *adj* (be careful!) semi-offical, unofficial; kind, helpful: only occasionally Eng sense of 'officious', 'meddlesome'

ofrecer *vt* -zc- to offer (most senses. though cf *ofertar*)

□ + *inf* to offer to: *ofrecieron ayudarnos* they offered to help up

□ **ofrecerse** *vr a* + *inf* to offer oneself, volunteer to

□ to present itself, arise, eg opportunity: *se ofreció la oportunidad de ir a México* the opportunity arose to go to Mexico

□ **ofrecimiento** *nm* offer (in general sense, cf *oferta, ofrenda*)

□ **oferta** *nf* offer (in most senses, but esp commercial)

□ **ofertar** *vt* usually rather limited commercial meaning of 'to tender' or

'sell on offer': NOT same as cf *ofrecer*

□ **ofrenda** *nf* (usually religious) offering

oír *vti* pi: *oigo, oyes, oye, oímos, oyen*; ps: *oiga*; ger: *oyendo*; pret: *oí … oyó… oyeron*; imp subj: *oyera/oyese* to hear

□ often used where Eng uses 'listen': *oír la radio, música*, etc to listen to the radio, music, etc; *¡oye!/¡oiga!* listen!, hark!; also used to attract attention: I say!', 'oi!' NB overlap with cf *escuchar*

□ *oír hablar de algo/alguien* to hear of sth/sb; *oír decir que …* to hear that …

□ **oído** *nm*; (inner) ear, ie the hearing organ

□ not the same as cf *oreja; taparse los oídos* to cover/block one's ears; *hablarle al oído a alguien* to talk into someone's ear

□ sense of hearing: *tengo el oído malo* I don't hear very well

□ **oyente** *nmf* (eg radio) listener

ojalá an expression derived from Arabic meaning 'would to Allah!'

□ when used by itself as *interj*: if only!, I hope so! (also ironically 'some hope!'); *– ¡A ver si nos toca la lotería! – Ojalá!* – I wonder if we've won the lottery! – I wish we could!/Some hope/That'll be the day!'

□ *conj ojalá (que)* + *pres* or *imp subj*: *ojalá nos toque la lotería* I wish we could win the lottery! (*imp subj* suggests the likelihood is more remote)

ojo *nm* eye; occurs in a number of idioms, eg:

□ *clavar los ojos en* to stare at

□ *el ojo de la llave* keyhole

□ *¡ojo!* watch out!, beware!; *ojo con ése!* be careful with that one!

ola *nf* wave

□ of sea, heat, fashion, etc, but not radio (see *onda*) or hair (use *ondulación*)

oler *vti ue* to smell
- NB stem change always preceded by h-: *huelo, hueles; huela, etc*
- both transitive (to smell something) and intransitive (to smell of something)
- *oler a* to smell of: *huele a aceite de oliva* it smells of olive oil
- **olor** *nm* smell (*a* of)

oliva *nf* olive
- used mainly in phrase *aceite de oliva* olive oil; *aceituna* is more commonly used for the fruit
- **olivo** *nm* olive tree

olvidar *vt* to forget
- + *inf: olvidé comprar mi billete* I forgot to buy my ticket
- can imply 'to leave behind': *olvidé mi billete* I forgot (left behind) my ticket
- **olvidarse (de)** *vr* to forget, but often used 'back to front' with an 'object': *se me olvidó el billete* I forgot my ticket; or with a verb: *se me olvidó comprar mi billete* I forgot to buy my ticket; this reflexive use tends to emphasise the accidental nature of the forgetting
- **olvido** *nm* forgetfulness; oversight: *por olvido* through an oversight
- also: oblivion

omitir *vt* to omit, leave out; + *inf* to omit to (do)

onda *nf* wave (radio): *onda corta/larga* short/long wave
- not same as cf *ola*
- has slang meaning of 'fashion': *estar en la onda* to be with it, 'hip'

operar *vti* to operate, used largely as in Eng but NB:
- *operaron al paciente de una hernia* they operated on the patient for a hernia
- **operarse** *vr* to have an operation: *el mes pasado me operé de una hernia*

last month I had a hernia operation
- overlap with cf *obrar* in sense of 'work'

opinar *vti* to think, be of the opinion: *¿Qué opinas tú?* What do you think about it?; *muchos no opinaron* many didn't have an opinion

oponer *vt* (has all the irregularities of *poner*, + *tú* imperative: *opón*) to set against
- used more commonly as **oponerse** *vr* to be opposed, to object (*a* to): *me opongo a estas ideas* I object/am opposed to these ideas; *nos oponemos a hacerlo* we object to doing it
- **oposición** *nf* opposition
- NB *pl oposiciones* public competition for a post/job; many public service jobs, eg teachers, are allocated on this basis in Spain: *hacer oposiciones para profesor* to apply/be a candidate for a teaching post
- **opuesto** *adj* opposite, in sense of 'opposing': *la opinión opuesta* the opposite opinion; *en el sentido opuesto* in the opposite sense/direction; similar to cf *contrario*

oportunidad *nf* opportunity, chance (in that sense) (*de* to/of); *¡oportunidades!* bargains! (in shop window)

oprimir *vt* to squeeze, press (button, handle, etc)
- also: to oppress

optar *vi* to opt (*por* + *noun* for); opt, choose (*por* + *inf* to + verb)
- **optativo** *adj* optional (commoner than *opcional*)

optimista *nmf/adj invariable in sing* optimist, optimistic

opuesto see **oponer**

oración *nf* *pl oraciones* oration, but NB commoner meanings of:
- prayer
- as a linguistic term – 'sentence',

'clause': *oración directa/indirecta*
direct/indirect speech

orden *nm* or *nf pl* **órdenes**   order

- □ can be *m* or *f*, with different meanings:
- □ *nm* 'arrangement' or 'organisation': *por orden cronológico*   in chronological order; *el orden público*   public order; *poner en orden*   to put in(to) order
- □ *nf* order, in sense of 'command': *dar la orden de* + *inf*   to give the order to + verb; *¡a sus órdenes!*   at your command/service!; also military or religious order: *la Orden de Calatrava* the Order of Calatrava; and *orden bancaria*   banker's order
- □ **ordenar** *vt*   to put in order, arrange; to order (command)
- □ **ordenado** *adj*   orderly, tidy; **ordenadamente** *adv*   tidily, in an orderly manner
- □ **ordenador** *nm*   computer

ordinario *adj*   ordinary; cf *corriente*

- □ can be used derogatorily – 'common', 'vulgar': *¡qué gente tan ordinaria!* what common people!

oreja *nf*   ear

- □ the outside, visible attachment to the head, not same as cf *oído; aguzar las orejas*   to prick up one's ears

organismo *nm*   organism

- □ NB often used for 'organisation' in the sense of 'institution'
- □ **organización** *nf pl* *organizaciones* organisation
- □ act of organising or institution, but cf also *organismo* for latter meaning above
- □ **organizar** *-ce-, -cé vt*   to organise

orgullo *nm*   pride

- □ can also have derogatory meaning of arrogance, haughtiness
- □ **orgulloso** *adj*   proud (*de* of); haughty
- □ NB difference with s*er/estar: estar orgulloso de*   to be proud of; *ser muy*

orgulloso   to be very haughty, arrogant

Oriente *nm*   east: *el Cercano/Medio/ Lejano Oriente*   the Near/Middle/Far East

- □ **oriental** *adj*   oriental, but often used meaning simply 'eastern', more formal alternative to *este*; opp of cf *occidental*

origen *nm pl* **orígenes**   origin

- □ *dar origen a algo*   to give rise to, cause sth

orilla *nf*   edge, border, and, more especially, bank, shore (of water): *a orillas del mar*   at the seaside; *a orillas del río*   on the riverbank

oro *nm*   gold

- □ NB no *adj*: use *de oro*   (of) gold, golden

orquesta *nf*   orchestra (NB spelling and pronunciation)

osar *vi*   to dare (+ *inf*   to); much the same as cf *atreverse a*

oscilar *vi*   to oscillate

- □ also commonly used meaning to fluctuate, vary: *el precio oscila entre 1.000 y 2.000 pesetas*   the price varies between 1,000 and 2,000 pesetas; cf *fluctuar, variar* are also used in this sense

oscuro *adj*   obscure

- □ also, more frequently 'dark': *a oscuras* in the dark; *verde oscuro*   dark green
- □ **oscuridad** *nf*   obscurity
- □ more frequently 'darkness'; much the same as cf *tinieblas* in this sense

ostentar *vt*   to show (off)

- □ often used derogatorily – 'flaunt', 'show off': *ostentaba sus músculos* he was flaunting his muscles
- □ used also for 'to hold' eg title: *ostenta el título olímpico*   she holds the Olympic title

otorgar *vti* *-gue-, -gué*   basically 'to grant'; a surprisingly common verb with somewhat elusive meanings:

□ to grant (eg *privilegio*), confer (eg *poderes*), devote (*tiempo, esfuerzo*)

□ *a + inf* to agree, consent to

otro *adj/pron* (an)other

□ never used with *un(a): otro día* another day

□ *otros/as* others; *los/las otros/as* the others

□ NB optional order with *muchos: y otras muchas cosas* and lots of other things

□ *lo otro* the rest (cf *lo demás*)

□ *a/en otra parte* somewhere else; *otra persona/cosa* someone/thing else

□ worth further study in a grammar or detailed dictionary

oveja *nf* sheep, ewe

□ not used for meat (for 'mutton', use *cordero*)

oyente see **oír**

P

> **P** (*pe*) is pronounced almost as in English, except that the lips are more tensed and you do not emit a puff of air. A good way to practise is to hold a lighted match as close to your mouth as you can (without singeing your nose!), and try English 'papa' or 'poppy' – you will blow the flame out; then try Spanish *papa* or *papá* – you must not blow the flame out!

padecer *vti -zc-* to suffer, undergo: *padecer hambre* to suffer hunger

□ used more often as *vi* with *de* from to 'suffer': *padece mucho* s/he suffers a great deal; *padece de bronquitis* s/he suffers from bronchitis

□ **padecimiento** *nm* suffering

□ much the same as cf *sufrir/sufrimiento* in this sense

padre *nm* father (in both parental and clerical senses); NB *los padres* parents; cf *papás* below

pagar *vti -gue-, gué* to pay

□ NB what you pay <u>for</u> is the direct object: *pagué los zapatos* I paid for the shoes UNLESS the amount of

payment is expressed, in which case use *por: pagué cuarenta euros <u>por</u> los zapatos* I paid 40 euros for the shoes

□ **pago** *nm* payment: *en pago de* in payment for

país *nm* country (as political unit): see also cf *patria;* for country as opposed to town use *campo*

□ **paisaje** *nm* landscape, countryside, scenery: the emphasis is on the visual impact

pálido *adj* pale

□ NB useful verb **palidecer** *vi -zc-* to turn/go pale

panorama *nm* panorama, view: NB it's *masc*!

pantalla *nf* screen (cinema, TV, computer)

□ also: lamp/lightshade

pantalones *nmpl* trousers; usually *pl*, but can occur in *sing: pantalón; pantalones cortos* shorts

paño *nm* cloth, material; *paño de cocina* dishcloth; *paño de secar* tea towel

□ **pañería** *nf* drapery (ie shop that sells *paño*): don't confuse with *panadería* bakery (ie the shop that sells *pan!*)

□ **pañal** *nm* nappy

□ **pañuelo** *nm* handkerchief; also scarf (for neck or head)

Papa *nm* Pope

papa *nf* potato (in Sp Am)

papá *nm* dad, daddy (NB stress on 2nd syllable); *mis papás* my mum and dad (cf *padres*)

> note differences in stress and meaning of 3 similar words!

papel *nm* paper; NB *un papel* a piece of paper (see also *hoja* in this sense)
- □ also role, part (eg in play): *jugar/ desempeñar un papel* to play a role
- □ **papelera** *nm* wastepaper/litter basket/bin
- □ **papelería** *nf* stationery shop: NB NOT newsagent (newspapers tend to be sold in a *quiosco)*; for 'newspaper' use *periódico*
- □ **papeleo** *nm* paperwork: *hay tanto papeleo* there's so much red tape
- □ note also **empapelar** *vt* to paper (walls); **empapelado** *nm* wallpaper (when in position on wall, otherwise eg in shop *papel pintado*)

par *nm* pair: *un par de guantes* a pair of gloves; also use for 'a couple of: *un par de horas* a couple of hours; suggests rather looser relationship than cf *pareja* below
- □ *nm* par: *al par de* on a par with: *un equipo al par del Barcelona* a team on a par with Barcelona; *abrir de par en par* to open wide (eg door); is sometimes *f: a la par* at par
- □ *adj* even: *número par* even number; opp *impar* odd

para *prep* for: *esto es para ti* this is for you
- □ used frequently before *inf* meaning (in order) to: *para abrir cortar aquí* (in order) to open, cut here; it answers the question *¿para qué?* for what purpose?, what for? (compare with *¿por qué?*)
- □ NB *para* expresses destination or intention: it is not possible to give a large number of examples here; the use of *para* and the possible areas of confusion with cf *por* are dealt with fully in most grammars
- □ **para que** *conj+subjunc* in order that, so that: *para que lo sepas* so that you know

parar *vti* to stop (can be both transitive and intransitive): *paré el coche* I stopped the car; *el coche paró* the car stopped; in this sense it is much the same as *detener vt* and *detenerse vr*
- □ can also mean 'cease': *la lluvia no paró en todo el día* the rain didn't stop all day; same as cf *cesar* in this sense; *parar de hacer algo* to stop doing sth: *paró de gritar* s/he stopped shouting
- □ also 'to stay' (esp in eg place, hotel while on journey): *paramos dos noches allí* we stayed there 2 nights
- □ **pararse** *vr* to stop (gives intransitive meaning, cf *detenerse*): *el coche se paró delante del hotel* the car stopped in front of the hotel
- □ **parada** *nf* stop (place or action): *parada de autobús/taxis* bus stop/taxi stand; *hacen una parada de dos horas* they make a 2-hour stop
- □ **paro** *nm* unemployment; also 'stoppage' (of work, machinery, heart)
- □ **parado/a** *adj* or *nmf* unemployed (person); same as cf *desempleado*
- □ **paradero** *nm* whereabouts: *su paradero actual* his present whereabouts
- □ **parador** *nm* state-run hotel in Spain, usually in historic building
- □ **para-** *prefix* usually has the meaning of stopping sth; it forms a compound noun which is always *m* and if it ends with *-s* is invariable, ie it doesn't add a further *-s* in the *pl*; some examples: **paraguas** umbrella (stops water); **parabrisas** windscreen (stops the wind); **paracaídas** parachute (stops your

fall); **parachoques** (car) bumper (stops bumps); **pararrayos** lightning conductor (stops lightning); **parasol** sunshade (stops the sun)

parcela *nf* plot of land
- for 'parcel', use *paquete*

parecer *vi -zc-* to seem, look, appear (in that sense): *pareces cansado* you seem/look/appear tired; *según parece/al parecer* as it appears, by all appearances; *¿qué te parece?* what do you think? how does it seem to you? *me parece que …* I think that …
- NB this verb indicates one's impressions about sth/sb, ie how things seem or appear; for 'to appear' in sense of come into sight, use *aparecer*
- **parecer** *nm* opinion: *a mi parecer* in my opinion; *somos del mismo parecer* we're of the same opinion
- **parecerse a** *vr* to resemble, look like: *¡Cómo te pareces a tu madre!* Aren't you like your mother!
- **parecido** *adj* similar: *los dos niños son muy parecidos* the 2 children are very alike; *¡Nunca he visto cosa parecida!* I've never seen anything like it!; much the same as cf *semejante, similar*
- *nm* resemblance: *esto niños tienen un gran parecido* these children are very like each other; much the same as cf *semejanza*

pared *nf* wall (used for inner walls of building and their vertical surface): *pintar las paredes de blanco* to paint the walls white; not the same as cf *muro* (complete wall) and *muralla* (battlement, town wall)

pareja *nf* couple, pair; implies a unit of two and a closer relationship than cf *par* above: *una joven pareja* a young couple; *la pareja de la Guardia Civil* the pair of Civil Guards
- also in *sing* – 'the other one of a pair': *¿Dónde está la pareja de este calcetín?*

where's the other sock (ie of this pair)?
- **parejo** *adj* equal, similar; less used than cf *semejante, parecido, similar*

pariente *nmf* relative; NB for 'parent', see *padre*; cf also *familiar* for 'relative'

parque *nm* park (for leisure, pleasure); *parque natural* country park; *parque zoológico* zoo; NOT car park: use *aparcamiento*

parte *nf* part (in many senses as Eng):
- portion, section: *la tercera parte* third part, third; *la mayor parte* the greater part, most (of) NB usually + singular noun: *la mayor parte del dinero* the greater part/most of the money
- area, region, situation: *¿En qué parte del país vives?* Which part of the country do you live in? *por todas partes* everywhere; *a/en alguna parte* somewhere; *a/en ninguna parte* nowhere; *a/en cualquier parte* anywhere; *a/en otra parte* somewhere else; cf this use of *sitio*
- also *tomar parte en* to take part in; *¿De parte de quién?* Who's calling? (on phone); *de parte de mi hermano* on behalf of my brother; and many more common expressions: worth a browse in the dictionary!
- NB for part in play etc use *papel*; for part of machinery etc use *pieza*

parte *nm* report (giving information); less common than cf *informe, boletín*

particular *nm* private: *una casa particular* a private house; in this sense same as cf *privado*
- also used similarly to Eng – 'particular', (specific): *en este caso particular* in this particular case; or 'peculiar', 'individual': *lo hace de su manera particular* he does it in his own particular way; *nada de particular* nothing (in) particular

partir *vt* to cut, split; *partir algo en dos* to cut sth in two; *partir por la mitad* to split/cut down the middle; *partirle la cara a alguien* to smash sb's face in

☐ *vi* to leave, set off: rather more formal and less frequent than cf *salir, ponerse en camino, irse, marcharse*

☐ **a partir de** *prep* as from: *a partir de mañana* as from tomorrow; *a partir de la cuarta farola* from the fourth street lamp onwards: perhaps a shade more emphatic than cf *desde*

☐ **partida** *nf* departure: more formal and less used than cf *salida*; also 'game': *una partida de cartas* a game of cards; tends to be used for indoor games

☐ **partido** *nm* match (football and outdoor games); also (political) party: *Partido Popular* Popular Party (Sp Conservative party); and *sacar partido de algo* to benefit/profit from sth

☐ **partidario/a** *adj* in favour, keen (in that sense) (*de* + *n* or *inf* of/on): *soy muy partidario de esta solución/de solucionar el problema así* I'm very keen on this solution/on solving the problem in this way; also as *nmf* supporter (of policy, party, etc)

☐ *partir* and all the words based on it are worth further research in the dictionary

pasar *vi* to pass, pass by/through, go past: wider use than Eng equivalent: *¡Dejen pasar!* Let people through!; *¡Pase Vd!* Come in!; *¡Pasen!* Cross! (on green light on some pedestrian crossings); *¿A qué hora pasa el autobús?* When does the bus come?; *¿Por qué no pasas por casa?* Why don't you pop in to see us?; *pasar de* to go beyond: *ha pasado de lo aceptable* he's gone beyond the acceptable

☐ also 'to happen': *¿Qué pasa?* What's going on?; *¿Qué te pasa?* What's the matter/what's up with you?; *¿Qué te ha pasado?* What's

happened to you?; *esto pasó hace siglos* that happened centuries ago; except in the various colloquialisms, cf *suceder* and *ocurrir* can often be substituted

☐ *pasar por* to pass as, be taken for: *pasa por un español* he passes for/as a Spaniard

☐ *vt* to pass: *¿Quieres pasarme el azúcar?* Please pass me the sugar; *pasar el líquido por un colador* pass the liquid through a filter

☐ also 'to pass/spend time': *pasamos las vacaciones en Mallorca* we spent our holidays in Mallorca; *pasó un mal rato* he had a bad time of it; *pasarlo bien/mal* to have a good/bad time; *pasarlo bomba/fatal* to have a super/rotten time

☐ **pasado** *nm* past: *en el pasado* in the past; *un fantasma del pasado* a ghost from the past

☐ *adj* 'last' when referring to days/dates: *el viernes pasado* last Friday; *el año pasado* last year; NOT last in series – use *último*; also *pasado de moda* old-fashioned, out of date

☐ **pasada** *nf* wipe, rub; *dar una pasada con un trapo* to give a wipe with a rag

☐ **pasajero/a** *nmf* passenger

☐ **pasillo** *nm* passage, corridor

☐ **paso** *nm* (foot)step: *está a dos pasos* it's no distance away; *oí pasos* I heard steps

☐ (act of) passing, going over or through: *el paso de invierno a primavera* the passing from winter to spring; *prohibido el paso* no entry; *paso de peatones* pedestrian crossing

☐ pace: *apretar/aflojar el paso* to quicken/slacken one's pace

☐ dictionaries devote more than a page to *pasar* and *paso*: worth further research!

☐ **pasota** *nmf* or *adj* drop-out, hippy

□ **pasotismo** *nm* drop-out lifestyle
or mentality

Pascua *nf* Easter: more exactly *Pascua
Florida* or *de Resurrección* Easter
Sunday; for the period loosely called
Easter in Eng, esp school holidays, use
Semana Santa (strictly) Holy Week:
las vacaciones de Semana Santa Easter
holidays; *Pascuas* is also used in *pl* for
other religious festivals esp Christmas:
¡Felices Pascuas! Happy Christmas

paseo *nm* walk, ride, trip
□ important to remember that this can
be done in a vehicle, not just on
foot, that it is for pleasure, and the
verb is *dar: dar un paseo por el
parque* to go for a walk in the
park; *paseo en coche* car ride; *paseo
en barco* boat trip
□ also: avenue, promenade (ie road with
wide pavements to accommodate
people walking); refers also to the
traditional evening 'promenade' in
most parts of Spain
□ **pasear** *vi* or **pasearse** *vr* to go for
a *paseo* ie walk or ride; can also be *vt*
eg *pasear el perro* to walk the dog;
not the same as cf *andar/andando*
which indicates walking as the means
of propulsion
□ don't confuse with *pasar* above

pasmar *vt* to amaze, stun; **pasmarse** *vr*
to be amazed, stunned: stronger than cf
asombrar(se)

pasta *nf* pasta (spaghetti etc)
□ also: pastry
□ and 'paste': *pasta de tomates* tomato
paste/puree; *pasta dentífrica*
toothpaste
□ **pastel** *nm* cake: *pastel de boda*
wedding cake; use cf *torta* for a more
elaborate gâteau, especially with fruit,
cream etc on top
□ **pastelería** *nf* cakeshop (NB does
not usually sell bread unless also
designated *panadería,* but may well

sell confectionery: cf *confitería*)

pastilla *nf* pill, tablet, pastille; used as
general term for most solid medicines
you suck or swallow; more specific are
comprimido tablet, *píldora* pill

pata *nf* leg, foot, paw (NB of animal or
furniture); use *pierna* for human being
□ except in certain ironic or humorous
expressions: *meter la pata* to put
one's foot in it; *estirar la pata* to
kick the bucket; *patas arriba* upside
down
□ **patada** *nf* kick, stamp (of foot); *dar
una patada* to kick/stamp (once)
dar patadas to kick/stamp
(repeatedly)

patio *nm* courtyard, yard
□ NB a good example of a word
changing its meaning when
incorporated into another language:
this is a word of Sp origin referring
usually to an enclosed courtyard as in
many old Andalusian houses, or an
enclosed yard or playground eg of a
school; for 'patio' in the Eng sense of
a paved area for sitting out, better to
use *terraza*

patria *nf* (one's home) country,
'fatherland', 'motherland'; *luchar por la
patria* to fight for one's country; *patria
chica* one's hometown; not the same,
therefore, as cf *país*

patrimonio *nm* patrimony (in similar
legal etc sense to Eng)
□ but also often used in sense of
'heritage': *patrimonio nacional*
national heritage

pausa *nf* pause
□ **pausado** *adj* slow and deliberate;
pausadamente *adv* slowly and
deliberately

paz *nf pl* **paces** peace; *hacerse las paces*
to make peace, make it up; *dejar a
alguien en paz* to leave sb in

peace/alone; *que en paz descanse* (may s/he) rest in peace

□ *v* is *apaciguar -güe-, -güé* to pacify

pecho *nm* chest, breast; *dar pecho a* to breastfeed; *nadar (estilo) pecho* to do the breaststroke

□ also 'heart' (in emotional sense): *tomarse algo a pecho* to take sth to heart

□ **pechuga** *nf* breast (of animal to eat): *pechuga de pollo* chicken breast

pedazo *nm* piece, bit (in that sense): *pedazo de carne* piece of meat; *hacer pedazos de algo* to break sth into pieces, smash sth up; *hacerse pedazos* to break (ie itself) into pieces, smash

□ also used untranslatably in exclamations eg of fondness: *¡pedazo de mi corazon!* my darling!; or insults: *¡pedazo de animal!* You brute!

pedir *vt -i-* to ask for, request: *pidió un billete* s/he asked for a ticket; *pedir algo a alguien* to ask sb for sth: *pidió un billete al taquillero* s/he asked the clerk for a ticket; can also mean 'order' (eg in café): *pidió una limonada* s/he ordered a lemonade; *pedía mucho dinero por su coche* s/he was asking a lot of money for her/his car;

□ *pedir a alguien que haga algo* to ask sb to do sth; NB this construction <u>must</u> take subjunc, not infinitive: *me pidió que cerrase la ventana* he asked me to close the window

□ NB NOT used to ask a question – use *preguntar*; cf more formal *rogar* in sense of 'ask/request sb to do sth'

pegar *vt -gue-, -gué* to stick, glue (*a* to)

□ 'to hit': *no me pegues* don't hit me (similar to cf *golpear*)

□ and *vi* 'to match', 'go together': *estos colores no pegan* these colours don't go together

□ NB use with various expressions,

loosely 'to give': *pegarle a alguien una patada/bofetada* to give sb a kick/slap; *pegarle un tiro a alguien* to shoot sb; *¡Qué susto me pegaste!* What a fright you gave me! *¡Qué catarro me has pegado!* That's a right cold you've given me!

□ used in a variety of other expressions: worth further research in the dictionary

□ **pegajoso** or **pegadizo** *adj* sticky

□ **pegamento** *nf* glue

□ **pegatina** *nf* sticker

peinar *vt* to comb; **peinarse** *vr* to do one's hair (including with brush!)

□ **peine** *nm* comb

□ **peinado** *nm* hairstyle, hairdo

pelea *nf* quarrel, fight (can be verbal or physical)

□ **pelear** *vi* to quarrel, fight (ie to disagree verbally – cf *reñir* – or with blows)

□ can also mean to struggle, fight ie to achieve sth (*por algo*): *pelearon por su libertad* they fought for their freedom (cf *luchar* in this sense)

□ **pelearse** *vr* to quarrel, fight (ie with each other): *se peleaban en el bar* they were fighting in the bar

película *nf* film, movie; it's also what you put in your camera, though you would ask for *un carrete* or *un rollo*; can also be used for film (eg of dust), though *capa* would be more common; cf *film, filme*

pelo *nm* hair (ie a single hair), or one's hair (complete): *cortarse el pelo* to get one's hair cut; more used than cf *cabello(s)*

□ worth a look in the dictionary at the many expressions using this word

pelota *nf* ball (small eg golf, tennis, hockey, squash, etc); use cf *balón* for large inflated one (football, rugby, basketball, etc)

pena *nf* sadness, sorrow, grief: *me da pena* it grieves me; *¡Qué pena!* What a pity/shame!; *no vale la pena (hacerlo)* it's not worthwhile (doing it)
- ☐ some but not total overlap in meaning with cf *tristeza, dolor, lástima*
- ☐ used in *pl penas* to mean 'sorrow', 'woes', 'hardships': *pasar muchas penas* to undergo many hardships
- ☐ also 'penalty', 'punishment': *pena de muerte* death penalty; *bajo* or *so pena de* under the penalty of, on pain of
- ☐ **penoso** *adj* painful, distressing: *es una tarea penosa* it's a distressing task; also 'laborious', 'difficult': *fue un viaje penoso* it was a difficult journey

pendiente *adj* lit hanging
- ☐ commonly used with *estar pendiente de* to be dependent on, to be waiting for: *estamos pendientes de su decisión* we await your decision, we are dependent on your decision; *todo está pendiente del resultado* everything is dependent on the result; *estamos pendientes de lo que hacen* we're watching to see what they do

penetrar *vti* to penetrate
- ☐ NB used more widely than Eng equivalent, to describe entry involving infiltration: *la luz penetraba detrás de las cortinas* the light was coming in from behind the curtains; *el aire penetraba por debajo de la puerta* a draught was coming under the door; *los ladrones penetraron por la ventana del servicio* the thieves got in through the loo window
- ☐ **penetración** *nf pl penetraciones* penetration, entry (in above senses)
- ☐ **penetrante** *adj* penetrating; sharp (eg intellect)

península *nf* peninsula
- ☐ NB *la Península* is often used to

mean 'mainland Spain', ie not including Balearic and Canary islands
- ☐ **peninsular** *adj* peninsular
- ☐ NB respective spelling of *n* and *adj* in both languages!!

pensar *vti -ie-* to think (in most senses): *déjame pensar* let me think
- ☐ NB to think of, in sense of have an opinion about – *pensar de*: *¿Qué piensas de esto?* What do you think of/about this?; to think of, in sense of directing your thoughts towards, use *pensar en*: *estaremos pensando en ti* we'll be thinking of you; *piensa en un número* think of a number; to think about sth in sense of 'think it over' takes dir obj: *vamos a pensarlo* we're going to think it over
- ☐ *pensar que* to think that: used much the same as cf *creer que; pienso que es maravilloso* I think it's wonderful; *pienso que sí/no* I think/don't think so; NB need for subjunc after *pensar que* used in negative or interrogative when denial or doubt is implied: *no pienso que vaya a ocurrir* I don't think (ie I doubt) it's going to happen; *y tú, ¿piensas que vaya a ocurrir?* and do you (ie really) think it's going to happen?;
- ☐ NB *pensar + inf* to intend to: *¿Qué piensan Vds hacer?* What do you intend to do?
- ☐ **pensamiento** *nm* thought (in all senses)
- ☐ **pensativo** *adj* pensive, thoughtful

pensión *nf pl pensiones* pension
- ☐ also 'guesthouse'
- ☐ and *pensión completa* full board; *media pensión* half board
- ☐ **pensionista** *nmf* pensioner; also: guest, lodger (in guesthouse)

peor *adj/adv comparative/superlative* of *malo/mal* worse, worst: *cada vez peor* worse and worse; *ella canta peor que yo* she sings worse than me; *pensar lo peor* to think the worst

- *más malo* is sometimes possible, particularly when the 'badness' or 'evilness' needs to be emphasised: *en la novela Cristina es más mala que su madre*   in the novel, Cristina is more bad/evil than her mother
- cf also use of opp *mejor*

pequeño/a *adj*   small, little; *nmf*   little one, small child

- tends come before noun unless smallness needs to be emphasised: *un pequeño pueblo de Castilla*   a small village in Castile; *es un pueblo muy pequeño*   it's a very small village
- note diminutives *pequeñito, pequeñín/-ina*   tiny, teeny–weeny
- **pequeñez** *nf pl* **pequeñeces** smallness; also 'trifle': *tales pequeñeces* such trifles

perder *vti -ie-*   to lose (in most senses); *he perdido mi reloj*   I've lost my watch; *muchos perdieron la vida*   many lost their lives; *el Sevilla perdió 2 a 0*   Seville lost 2-0

- also 'to miss' (bus/train/opportunity etc): *vamos a perder el tren*   we're going to miss the train; *perdiste la ocasión de hablarle*   you missed the opportunity to speak to him; and 'waste' (time): *no pierdas tiempo*   don't waste time
- **perderse** *vr*   to get lost: *nos perdimos en las calles estrechas*   we got lost in the narrow streets
- **perdido** *adj/past part*   lost: *estar perdido*   to be lost, but can also mean 'to have had it', 'to be done for': *estoy perdida si mi mamá me ve* I've had it if my mum sees me; or 'to be confused': *estoy totalmente perdido* I'm totally confused/lost
- **pérdida** *nf*   loss (in most senses); note 1st syllable stress

perdón *interj*   sorry, I beg your pardon, excuse me

- NB: this is an interjection that you utter when you have caused sb an inconvenience or discomfort, wish to interrupt them, or have not understood what they said; for a more formal or emphatic 'I'm sorry' use *lo siento*; see **sentir**
- *nm*   pardon, forgiveness: *le pedí perdón*   I begged/sought his pardon, asked for his forgiveness (depending on context)
- **perdonar** *vti*   to forgive, pardon: *le perdonamos sus faltas*   we forgave him (for) his faults; *perdóname* forgive me
- also means 'excuse': *perdone Vd* excuse me; *perdone la molestia*   sorry to trouble you; *perdone mi voz* excuse my voice

perecer *vi -zc-*   to die, perish (in that sense); quite common alternative for cf *morir/fallecer* in journalistic style for violent or accidental death: *perecieron carbonizados*   they were burnt to death

- for 'perish' (eg rubber) use *deteriorarse*, for food use *estropearse*

perenne *adj*   perennial: NB 2 x *n*, and both are heard

permanecer *vi -zc-*   to remain, stay; much the same as this meaning of the more common *quedar(se)*: *permaneció inmóvil* s/he stayed/stood still; *permanecieron en contacto*   they remained in contact/touch

- **permanente** *adj* permanent; *nf* perm
- **permanencia** *nf*   permanence, but also 'continuity': *mantener la permanencia*   to keep up continuity

permitir *vt*   to permit, allow; *no se permite* it's not allowed; *¿Se permite?*   Is it allowed?; *¿Me permite?*   May I?

- NB + *inf* or + *que* + *subjunc*: *no le permitieron entrar/no permitieron que entrara*   they didn't allow him to come in

□ **permitirse algo** *vr* to allow oneself sth, afford sth: *no puedo permitirme ese lujo* I can't afford that luxury

□ **permiso** *nm* permission: *pedir permiso de hacer algo* to ask for permission to do sth; *con permiso (de Vds)…* with your permission, may I?… (when asking others if you may do sth); also 'leave', 'time off': *dos días de permiso* two days' leave; and 'licence', (eg driving)

perseguir *vt -i-, -g- persigo, persigues; persiga* to pursue, chase (more common than Eng 'pursue'); used to get over idea of chasing after, with more intent or urgency involved than with basic *seguir*: *le persiguieron por las calles* they pursued/chased him through the streets

□ also: to persecute

□ **persecución** *nf pl persecuciones* pursuit, chase; or persecution

persistir *vi* to persist: *en algo* in sth or *en hacer algo* in doing sth; cf also *porfiar*

persona *nf* person

□ NB always *fem*, regardless of sex of person: *Jorge es una persona muy simpática* George is a very pleasant person

□ NB: *pl* can mean either 'persons' or 'people', and you <u>must</u> use it (rather than *gente*) after numerals: *había tres personas en la habitación* there were three people in the room; *capacidad ocho personas* capacity 8 people (eg lift); cf *gente*, which means 'people' collectively or in general: either is possible in the following examples, though *personas* may tend to put more emphasis on the individuality of each person: *había mucha gente/muchas personas* there were a lot of people; *hay gente que dice …/personas que dicen …* there are people who say …

□ **personaje** *nm* character (in play, film etc); also important figure, personality (in that sense): *es un personaje deportivo* s/he's a sporting personality; NB always *masc* regardless of sex of person!

□ **personal** *adj* personal; *nm* staff, personnel

□ **personalidad** *nf* personality (ie one's character); can also be used in sense of eg sporting personality, like *personaje*, above

perspectiva *nf* perspective

□ also 'prospect', 'outlook': *las perspectivas no son nada buenas* the outlook isn't at all good

□ and 'view': *desde allí hay una maravillosa perspectiva* from there there's a suberb view

persuadir *vt* to persuade: *a alguien a + inf* or *para/de que + subjunc*: *le persuadieron a volver* or *le persuadieron para/de que volviera* they persuaded him to go back

□ NB: *persuadir a alguien de + noun* to persuade sb of + noun: *le persuadieron de la necesidad de volver* they persuaded him of the need to go back

□ **persuasión** *nf pl persuasiones* persuasion (all senses); **persuasivo** *adj* persuasive

pertenenecer *vi -zc-* to belong (*a* to)

□ **perteneciente** *adj* belonging (*a* to)

pertinente *adj* relevant, appropriate: *explicó los puntos pertinentes* he explained the relevant points; *en lo pertinente a su pedido* with regard to your order; NOT *relevante*, which means notable, outstanding

□ **pertinencia** *nf* relevance: *no tiene ninguna pertinencia* it has no relevance

pescar *vti -que-, -qué* to fish, catch (fish)

□ also 'to catch' (eg cold): *pesqué un catarro* I caught a cold; and 'catch sb doing sth': *le pesqué con las manos en la masa* I caught him red-handed (*lit* with his hands in the dough)

□ **pesca** *nf* fishing: *ir a la pesca* to go fishing; *prohibida la pesca* fishing forbidden

□ **pescado** *nm* fish (ie 'fished' fish): in the fishmonger's or on your plate

□ **pez** *nm pl peces* fish (ie alive and in the water)

□ NB distinguish between **pescador(a)** *nmf* fisherman/woman, angler (catches the fish) and **pescadero/a** *nmf* fishmonger (sells it); **pescadería** *nf* fish shop

pesimista *nmf* pessimist, or *adj* pessimistic: *sing* always *-ista*

peso *nm* weight; *ganar/perder peso* to put on/lose weight

□ currency unit of Argentina, Chile, Mexico, Uruguay and some other Sp Am countries

□ **pesa** *nf* weight that you put on scales or lift: *levantamiento de pesas* weightlifting

□ **pesar** *vti* to weigh: *este paquete pesa tres kilos* this parcel weighs 3 kilos: NB a useful way to say that sth is heavy is to use this verb: *¡pesa mucho!* it's very heavy!

□ also 'to cause sorrow or distress': *me pesa mucho su situación* I feel very sorry about her situation (cf *nm pesar* below, and also *pena*)

□ **pesar** *nm* sorrow, regret: *me da mucho pesar* it gives me much sorrow/regret (cf *pena*)

□ **pesadumbre** *nf* grief, sorrow (more emphatic than *pesar*)

□ **pésame** *nm* condolence(s), sympathy (in that sense); **dar el pésame** to offer one's condolences (on a bereavement)

□ **a pesar de** *prep* in spite of; **pese a**

prep means the same, but is rather more formal

□ **pesado** *adj* heavy (in most senses, though see also *fuerte* for rain and other circumstances where force is implied): *maquinaria pesada* heavy machinery, *comida pesada* heavy food; also 'heavy-going', 'tiresome', 'tedious': *le encuentro muy pesado como escritor* I find him heavy-going as a writer

□ **pesadez** *nf* boringness, tedium: *¡Qué pesadez!* What a bore!, How tedious!

petróleo *nm* oil (in crude state); you put *aceite* in your car or cooking; and remember that 'petrol' is *gasolina*

□ **petrolero** *adj* (to do with) oil: *industria petrolera* oil industry; also *nm* oil tanker

pico *nm* beak (eg of bird)

□ also (mountain) peak

□ *y pico* and a bit: *dos y pico* 2 and a bit

□ **picar** *vt -que-, -qué* to sting, bite (insects)

□ also: to chop, mince (food eg parsley, meat)

□ *vi* to itch, and (of food) to be hot, spicy (as eg curry)

□ **picadura** *nf* sting, (insect) bite; **picor** *nm* itch, itching

□ **picante** *adj* hot (spicy, eg curry): for hot in sense of high temperature, use *caliente*

pie *nm* foot

□ NB expressions: *ir a pie* to go on foot, walk (as opposed eg to ride); *ponerse de pie* to stand up; *estar de pie* to be standing (up); *en pie* (used of objects) standing, upright: *quedarse en pie* to remain upright; *al pie de* at the foot/bottom of

piel *nf* skin

□ also 'leather': *bolso de piel* leather handbag; and 'fur': *abrigo de piel* fur coat

- **peletería** *nf* in store: leather goods department; also 'furrier's shop'

pieza *nf* piece (part, component (ie of a whole)): *prenda de dos piezas* a two-piece garment; NOT a detached piece of sth: use *pedazo*; part (of apparatus): *pieza de recambio* spare part
- also 'coin', 'piece' (in that sense): *una pieza de un euro* a one-euro piece
- and 'room', though much less used than cf *cuarto, habitación*

pijama *nm* pyjama(s) (NB *masc*, spelt with -i-, and used in *sing*): *camisa/pantalón de pijama* pyjama top/trousers

pila *nf* battery (more common than cf *batería*)
- also 'pile', 'heap', cf the more usual *montón: tengo una pila de cosas que hacer* I've got a pile of things to do
- also 'sink', 'basin', 'trough'; and 'font', hence: *nombre de pila* Christian name, first name

píldora *nf* pill: *píldora anticonceptiva* contraceptive pill; see also *pastilla*

pillar *vt* to catch (rather colloquial): *¡Que no te pillen!* Mind they don't catch you/you don't get caught!; *¡Te pillé!* Got you!; *me pilló la niebla* I got caught in the fog; cf *atrapar, coger*

piloto *nmf* pilot; also *nm* pilot light; and side/rear light (on vehicle)

pinchar *vt* to prick, puncture
- **pincharse** *vr* to burst (eg of tyre); also 'to shoot up', 'inject oneself' (with drug)
- **pinchazo** *nm* puncture; also 'fix' (of drug)
- **pincho** *nm* another word for cf *tapa*, portion of food served at bar esp in N Sp

pintar *vti* to paint
- **pintarse** *vr* to put on make-up, make oneself up: *maquillarse* is more

common

- **pintoresco** *adj* picturesque: watch the spelling!
- **pintura** *nf* painting (action of or resultant picture); also 'paint' (ie the material): *atención a la pintura* wet paint
- **pintor** *nm* **pintora** *nf* painter
- **pinta** *nf* spot, dot: *vestido con pintas* spotted dress; *tener pinta de* to look, ie have the appearance of; *no tiene pinta de mejicano* he doesn't look Mexican; *tener buena pinta* to look good
- there are several more interesting uses of these words: look in the dictionary!

pisar *vti* to tread, step (on): *¡Has pisado mis flores!* You've trodden/trampled on my flowers!; *¡No pisar el césped!* Keep off the grass!; *tenemos que pisar con cuidado* we've got to tread carefully
- in spite of its appearance and sound, this verb has nothing to do with urination: use *orinar, mear*!
- **pisada** *nf* footstep or footprint
- **piso** *nm* floor (storey (of building)): *tercer piso* 3rd floor; also 'flat', 'apartment'

pista *nf* track, trail: *estar sobre la pista de algo/alguien* to be on the track/trail of sth/sb
- a surface laid out for a wide range of particular purposes: *pista de tenis* tennis court; *pista de atletismo* athletics race track; *pista de esquí* ski run, piste; *pista de aterrizaje* (aircraft) runway; *pista de patinaje* skating rink
- and clue: *no encontramos ni una pista* we didn't find a single clue
- cf also *despistado* confused

placer *nm* pleasure, enjoyment: perhaps more modest enjoyment than cf *disfrute, gozo; tengo placer en + inf* I have pleasure in -ing

- **placer** *vi ps: plazca* to please (rather formal, only used in 3rd pers sing): *como le plazca* as you please; *como le guste* would be more common

plan *nm* plan (project or programme): *plan de estudio* syllabus; means much the same as cf *proyecto*

- NB **planear** *vt* is corresponding verb, 'to plan', similar to cf *proyectar*; also means 'to glide'; **planeador** *nm* glider: don't confuse this series of words with:
- **plano** *nm* plan (eg of town): *plano de la ciudad;* also: plane, (in sense of level): *en el primer plano* in the foreground
- *adj* flat (eg surface)
- NB corresponding verb **planificar** *vt -que-, -qué* to plan
- **planificación** *nf* planning: *planificación familiar* family planning

planeta *nm* planet (NB *masc*!)

planta *nf* plant

- also 'floor' (storey); always use *planta baja* for 'ground floor'; for other floors, interchangeable with cf *piso*
- **plantar** *vt* to plant (ie put plants into ground)
- also 'to ditch', 'dump', 'jilt', 'leave in the lurch': *le plantó* or *dejó plantado* she jilted him
- **plantilla** *nf* staff, personnel (similar to cf *personal*)
- **plantear** *vt* to pose, raise, create (usually used with problem, difficulty): *esto plantea varias dificultades* that creates several difficulties
- **plantearse** *vr* (problem etc) to arise: *varios problemas se plantean* several problems arise

plata *nf* silver (NB no *adj,* use *de plata*): *una copa de plata* a silver cup

- also in Sp Am: money

plato *nm* plate (for food): *lavar/fregar los platos* to wash the dishes

- also 'course' (of meal): *primer/segundo plato* first/second course
- and 'dish' (recipe): *platos regionales* regional dishes

plaza *nf* square (in town) (ie open space where various streets meet, often with seats)

- also: *plaza de toros* bullring
- and 'place', 'position' (in limited contexts): *un asiento de dos plazas* a seat with two places; *es mi plaza* that's my place (ie seat)
- **plazoleta, plazuela** *nf* are common diminutive forms: small square

plazo *nm* period of time: *a corto/largo plazo* in the short/long term

- also 'instalment': *pago a plazos* payment by instalments

plegar *vt -ie-, -gue-, -gué* to fold (some overlap with cf *doblar*, esp eg paper)

- **plegarse** *vr* to fold (up), bend, crease
- **plegable** or **plegadizo** *adj* folding: *silla plegable* folding chair
- **pliegue** *nm* fold, crease

pleno *adj* full, (in sense of) total, complete: *en pleno verano* in full summer; *en plena cara* right in the face; *plenos poderes* full powers

- NB for 'full up', see *lleno, completo*

población *nf pl* *poblaciones* population

- also: town (usually but not necessarily small)
- **poblar** *vt -ue-* to populate (*de* with)
- **poblado** *adj/past part* populated: *una región poco poblada* an underpopulated area; also 'filled' (*de* with/by): *está poblado de animales e insectos* it's filled with animals and insects
- **pueblo** *nm* village (usually larger than cf *aldea*); also 'people' (nation,

community): *el pueblo mejicano* the Mexican people; and the 'common people': *'el pueblo unido jamás será vencido'* 'the people united will never be defeated'

- NB for people in general, see *gente*, for 'person/s', see *persona*

pobre *adj* poor
- NB position – for 'having no money' place after noun: *una mujer pobre* a poor woman; for 'wretched', 'hapless', place before noun: *¡la pobre mujer!* the poor woman!
- also, as Eng 'weak': *su trabajo es muy pobre* his work is very poor/weak
- *nmf* poor person: *los pobres* the poor
- **pobrecito/a** *dim adj* or *nmf* used in sense of eg (you) poor thing
- **pobreza** *nf* poverty; can be used as English in eg *pobreza de ideas* poverty of ideas; *pobreza de espíritu* mean-mindedness

poco *adj* little (in sense of, and often equivalent to 'not much'): *tengo poco dinero* I've little money/I've not got much money; *nos queda poco tiempo* we've not got much time left; in *pl* 'few': *tiene pocas ideas* he has few ideas/hasn't got many ideas; can also be *adv*: *te gusta poco, ¿no?* you don't like it very much, do you? *vamos muy poco al cine* we go very little to the cinema/ we don't go to the cinema very much
- **un poco (de)** *sing* a little: *añade un poco de sal* add a little salt; **unos pocos** *pl*: a few: *añade unas pocas aceitunas* add a few olives
- NB difference between *poco(s)*, which has a negative emphasis *and un poco de/unos pocos,* whose emphasis is positive: *cobro poco dinero* I earn little (ie not much) money; *he cobrado un poco de dinero* I've earned a bit of money (ie maybe not much but something at least!); *tiene*

pocas ideas he has few ideas (ie he's pretty unimaginative); *me ha dado unas pocas ideas* he's given me a few ideas (not that many, not as many as cf *algunas*, but some at least)
- to sum up, where Eng has 'a little', 'a few', Sp also has un poco/unos pocos
- also used to make an adj negative: *poco interesante* uninteresting; *poco deseable* undesirable
- some useful phrases: *hace poco* not long ago; *cada poco* every so often; *poca cosa* not much; *poco a poco* little by little; *tener algo/a alguien en poco* not to think much of sth/sb; *poco más o menos* more or less
- **poquito** *dim* is used quite often: *dame un poquito* give me a tiny bit; *estoy un poquito cansado* I'm just a tiny bit tired
- **poquísimo** *superlative adj/adv* very little, very few: *había poquísima agua en el río, y poquísimos peces* there was very little water in the river, and very few fishes
- **poquedad** *nf* scarcity, lack (*de* of): can be used when there isn't much/aren't many of sth: *había una poquedad de casas por ahí* there was a lack of houses around there; cf the more frequent *falta, escasez*

poder *vi pi:* puedo, puedes, puede, pueden; *ps:* pueda, puedas, pueda, puedan; *ger:* pudiendo; *fut/condit:* podré/podría; *pret:* pude, pudiste, pudo, pudimos, pudisteis, pudieron; *imp subj:* pudiera/pudiese to be able to, can/could
- + *inf*: *no puedo andar* I can't walk
- means 'to be able to', depending on circumstances: *no podemos nadar aquí, el agua está contaminada* we can't swim here, the water's polluted; *¿A qué hora puedes estar aquí?* What time can you be here?
- you use it to ask permission: *¿Puedo utilizar tu ordenador?* Can/may I use your computer? *¿Se puede?*

May I?, May one?

- □ you don't use it when 'be able/can' involves an acquired skill, (ie to know how to), use *saber* + *inf: sabes utilizar esta máquina?* can you (do you know how to) use this machine?
- □ you don't normally use it with verbs of the senses: *¿Ves/Oyes aquel pájaro?* Can you see/hear that bird?
- □ be careful rendering 'could' into Sp: a good dodge is to convert it into 'be able to', and that will give you the tense if you are not sure; it might be *conditional: yo no podría hacerlo* I couldn't (wouldn't be able to) do it; or past (*impf* or *pret*): *no podía/pude hacerlo* I couldn't (wasn't able to) do it
- □ 'could have done sth' is normally *condit* or *impf* of *poder* + *haber* + *past part: podías/podrías haber llegado antes* you could have arrived earlier
- □ phrases: *no puedo más* I can't go on, I can't take any more; *a más no poder* to one's limits, till one can't take any more: *se rio a más no poder* he laughed until he could laugh no longer
- □ *puede (ser) que* + *subjunc* it's possible that, maybe; *puede que lo sepa* maybe he knows, he may know
- □ consult a grammar for a fuller explanation of these points
- □ **poder** *nm* power (in most senses); *poder adquisitivo* purchasing power; not same as cf *potencia*
- □ **poderoso** *adj* powerful

policía *nf* police (ie the force)
- □ also: *nmf* policeman/woman
- □ similar in both uses to cf *guardia*

política *nf* politics (NB it's *sing*)
- □ also 'policy': *la política del gobierno* government policy; for 'insurance policy', use *póliza*
- □ **político** *adj* political; also *familia política* in-laws

polivalente *adj* multi-purpose (a

surprisingly useful word): *sala polivalente* multi-purpose hall

pollo *nm* (when alive) chick, young chicken; on menu/table: chicken; not same as cf *gallina* hen

polución *nf* pollution
- □ **polucionar** *vt* to pollute
- □ NB purists prefer to use cf *contaminación/contaminar,* though most up-to-date dictionaries list it without comment

polvo *nm* dust
- □ NB 'to dust', (ie remove dust) is: *quitar el polvo (a algo); espolvorear* given by some dictionaries is 'to dust sth (eg powder) on to sth'
- □ *hacer algo polvo* to smash sth; *hacer polvo a alguien* to shatter sb; *estar hecho polvo*: to be all in, to be a wreck
- □ also (often *pl*): powder (in most senses except gunpowder, *pólvora*)
- □ **polvoriento** *adj* dusty

poner *vt pi: pongo, pones; ps: ponga; tú imperative: pon; fut/condit: pondré/pondría; past part: puesto; pret: puse, pusiste, puso, pusimos, pusisteis, pusieron; imp subj: pusiera/pusiese* to put
- □ translates 'put' in most senses; contrast with the more limited *colocar* and *meter*
- □ can also have wider meaning of 'give', 'supply': *póngame un kilo de patatas* give me a kilo of potatoes; *le pusieron una inyección* they gave him an injection; *me puso mucho miedo* it made me very frightened; *¿Qué ponen en el cine?* What's on at the cinema?
- □ and 'put on', 'switch on': *voy a poner la calefacción/radio* I'm going to put the heating/radio on
- □ other common uses: *poner la mesa* to lay the table; *poner en marcha* to start up (eg engine); *pongamos que …*

let's suppose that …; *póngame con el Sr Pérez* (on phone): put me through to Mr Pérez; *poner huevos* to lay eggs

- **ponerse** *vr* to put on (clothes): *me puse el impermeable* I put on my raincoat; also: to get into a position, situation or state: *ponerse de rodillas* to get (down) on one's knees; *ponerse de pie* to stand up; *ponerse de acuerdo* to agree; *el sol se estaba poniendo* the sun was setting
- NB this is often the best way to translate 'to become' + *adj*: *ponerse triste* to become sad; *ponerse rojo* to become/turn red
- also *ponerse a + inf* to begin to, set about –ing; usually implies more suddenness or vigour than simply cf *empezar/comenzar: la pianista se puso a tocar* the pianist started to play; *se puso a llover* it started to rain
- this verb is used in a wide number of expressions and is well worth further investigation in the dictionary!
- **puesta** *nf* (action of) putting, setting: *la puesta en marcha* setting in motion, starting up; *la puesta en práctica* putting into practice; *puesta en libertad* setting free; *la puesta del sol* sunset
- **puesto** *nm* place, position, post: *puesto de trabajo* job, position (in that sense); also 'stall' (in market)
- *adj/past part* on (of clothes): *¿Qué llevaba puesto?* What did s/he have on?
- **puesto que** *conj* since (in sense of 'as'): *puesto que ya has decidido* since you've already decided

por *prep* by, through, because of
- NB the uses of this preposition are too wide to list in full here; they are dealt with in detail in most grammar books, and you should study carefully what they say
- take great care not to confuse it with

para, the usual word for 'for'
- *por* only means 'for' in very specific circumstances, eg 'in exchange for'; *di 20 euros por el jersey* I gave 20 euros for the sweater; or 'for sb's sake or on their behalf': *lo hice por ti* I did it for you (ie your benefit)
- it occurs in many self-contained expressions eg *por si acaso* just in case; *por ahora* for now: many of these are listed in this book under the second element of the phrase

porfiar *vi -í-* to insist, persist (*en algo* or + *inf* on/in + *n* or *v*): *¿Por qué porfías en hacerlo?* Why do you insist on/persist in doing it? cf *persistir, insistir*

porque *conj* because (don't confuse with the question):
- **¿por qué?** why? (NB two words, and accent); also NB there is a difference between *¿por qué?* ie for what reason? and *¿para qué?* for what purpose?, what for?, which in theory at least is demanding a reply *para + inf* in order to (see also *para*)

porvenir *nm* future: *en el porvenir* in the future; *sin porvenir* with no future; as *n*, more or less interchangeable with *futuro*; for *adj* you must use *futuro*

poseer *vt ger: poseyendo; past part: poseído; pet: poseyó, poseyeron; imp subj: poseyera/poseyese* to possess, own
- **posesión** *nf pl posesiones* possession (meaning as in English)

posible *adj* possible
- **posibilidad** *nf* possibility
- NB phrases containing these words followed by *que* require *subjunc: es posible/hay la posibilidad de que tengas razón* it's possible/there's the possibility (that) you're right
- **posibilitar** *vt* to make possible: *su entrenador posibilitó su éxito* his trainer made his success possible

posterior *adj*   later, subsequent, following: *en una ocasión posterior*   on a later/subsequent occasion; *eso fue posterior a la guerra*   that was subsequent to the war
- also 'rear', 'back' (as *adj*): *los asientos posteriores*   the rear seats
- not used as a noun
- **posterioridad** *nf*   *con posterioridad* subsequently, later: *eso ocurrió con posterioridad*   that happened later; don't confuse with **posteridad** *nf* posterity
- **posteriormente** *adv*   later, subsequently: *eso ocurrió posteriormente*   that happened later
- cf opps *anterior, anterioridad, anteriormente*

potente *adj*   powerful, potent
- **potencia** *nf*   power, potency
- **potencial** *adj* and *nm*   potential
- **potenciar** *vt*   to boost, promote, ie increase power or potential
- not exactly the same as cf *poder* and related words: some overlap, but these words describe potency and tend to be applied to machinery, things technical, sexual prowess; whereas *poder* etc describes power in the sense of 'might', or eg political power

práctica *nf*   practice (in most Eng senses): *en la práctica*   in practice; *poner algo en práctica*   to put sth into practice
- **practicar** *vt* -que-, -qué   to practise (in most senses); also used for play, take part in: *practicar los deportes*   to take part in sports
- **práctico** *adj*   practical, but often has wider meaning of 'useful', 'convenient': *un aparato práctico*   a handy gadget; *un piso muy práctico*   a very convenient flat
- **prácticamente** *adv*   practically (ie in a practical way); also used as Eng to mean 'nearly': *la botella estaba prácticamente llena*   the bottle was practically/nearly full

practicable *adj*   practicable, workable

prado *nm*   meadow, field (of grass); see *campo* for general word for field
- NB many Sp words for 'field' denote their crop: *maizal, trigal*, etc
- **pradera** *nf*   grassland, prairie

precio *nm*   price
- **precioso** *adj*   lovely, gorgeous, really nice: used more with objects than people, and probably higher than *bonito* in the prettiness/loveliness scale, but not as high as cf *hermoso/bello*; can also mean 'precious', 'valuable'
- **preciosidad** *nf*   a lovely thing: a more emphatic way of saying sth is *precioso: esta pintura es una preciosidad*   this painting is really lovely; *¡Qué preciosidad de cuarto!* What a lovely room!

precipitar *vt*   to precipitate, hasten (sth): *esto precipitó su dimisión*   this precipitated/hastened his resignation
- **precipitarse** *vr*   to rush *no hay que precipitarse*   there's no rush; *todos se precipitaron hacia la escena*   they all rushed to(wards) the scene; + *a* + *inf* to + verb: *todos se precipitaron a ayudar*   they all rushed to help
- also 'to plunge': *el avión se precipitó al agua*   the plane plunged/hurtled into the water
- **precipitación** *nf pl precipitaciones* precipitation (eg of rain); also 'haste': *hacer algo con precipitación*   to do sth in haste/a hurry; *¿Por qué tanta precipitación?*   Why such a hurry?
- **precipitado** *adj*   hurried, hasty: *una decisión precipitada*   a hasty decision
- **precipitadamente** *adv*   hastily, hurriedly, in a hurry: *se fue precipitadamente*   he left in a hurry
- all these words denote haste or speed: cf *prisa, apresurarse* which are similar but usually do not imply such precipitousness!

preciso *adj*   precise, exact
- □ also, quite frequently, 'necessary': *fue preciso arrestarle*   it was necessary to arrest him
- □ **precisión** *nf*   precision: *hacer algo con precisión*   to do sth with precision, precisely; also 'need', 'necessity': *tener precisión de algo/de hacer algo*   to need, require sth/to do sth
- □ **precisar** *vt*   to fix exactly, specify: *tenemos que precisar la fecha y hora* we have to fix/specify the date and time; also 'to need', 'require': *esto precisa buenos nervios*   this requires good nerves; cf *necesitar, requerir, exigir*
- □ note dual meaning of above words denoting either exactness or necessity
- □ **precisamente** *adv*   precisely, exactly: *era precisamente lo que me hacía falta*   it was precisely/exactly/just what I needed

predilecto *adj*   favourite: a slightly less used alternative for cf *preferido, favorito*
- □ **predilección** *nf* pl *predilecciones* preference, predilection

preferir *vt* -ie-, -i-   to prefer; + *inf*   to + verb: *preferimos quedarnos aquí*   we prefer to stay here; *preferimos comer dentro*   we prefer eating indoors; when you prefer sb else to do sth + *que* + *subjunc*: *prefieren que comamos dentro* they prefer us to eat indoors; cf *gustar más*   like better, ie prefer
- □ **preferencia** *nf*   preference; *de preferencia*   preferably
- □ **preferido/a** *adj* or *nmf*   favourite: cf *predilecto, favorito*
- □ **preferente** *adj* special, ie for person(s) in question: *servicio preferente*   special service
- □ **preferible** *adj*   preferable (*a* + *noun/pron* or *inf*): *éste es preferible a aquél*   this one is preferable to that one; NB compare: *es preferible a comer fuera*   it's preferable to eating

outside to: *es preferible comer fuera* it's preferable to eat outside

preguntar *vti*   to ask (enquire): *–¿Cómo estás? – preguntó*   'How are you?' he asked; *me preguntaron cuánto dinero llevaba*   they asked me how much money I was carrying
- □ NB NOT ask in sense of 'ask for': use *pedir*; nor 'request', 'ask to (do sth)': use *pedir* or *rogar*
- □ **pregunta** *nf*   question: *hacer una pregunta a alguien*   to ask sb a question; *contestar (a) una pregunta* to answer a question (purists would argue that the *a* is necessary, though it seems to be omitted quite frequently nowadays)
- □ **preguntón, -ona** *pl preguntones, -onas adj*   nosy; *nmf* nosy parker, busybody

prender *vti*   to catch, arrest (a person)
- □ also 'to fasten', 'pin'; *tenía la etiqueta prendida en su chaqueta*   the label was pinned on his jacket; **prendedor** *nm*   brooch
- □ to catch fire/alight: *el fuego no prende* the fire won't catch; *prender fuego a algo*   to set fire to sth
- □ NB not usually 'to take': don't confuse with Fr *prendre*!
- □ **preso/a** *adj*   captured, imprisoned; *nmf*   prisoner

prensa *nf*   press, often used to mean 'the papers': *¿Qué dice la prensa?*   What do the papers say?
- □ also 'press' in most other senses eg for wine, printing, etc

preocupar *vt*   to worry, concern: *¿No te preocupa esto?*   Doesn't this worry you?
- □ **preocuparse** *vr*   to be worried (*por* about): *me preocupo por su seguridad* I'm worried about his safety; *¡No se preocupe!*   Don't worry!; also *preocuparse de algo*   to concern oneself with/see to sth: *Jorge se*

preocupa de la comida Jorge is seeing to the food (cf *ocuparse de* in this sense)

- **preocupado** *adj* worried, concerned (*por* about): *estoy preocupado por ello* I'm worried about it; *esto me tiene muy preocupado* this has got me very worried
- **preocupante** *adj* worrying
- **preocupación** *nf pl preocupaciones* worry, concern
- in sense of 'worry/worried', much the same as cf *inquietar(se)/inquieto*

preparar *vt* to prepare, get (sth) ready (*para* for/to)

- **prepararse** *vr* to get ready, prepare oneself (*para* for/to)
- **preparación** *nf pl preparaciones* preparation (in most senses); also (state of) 'preparedness'; and is sometimes used to mean 'education' (cf *educación*), 'training' (cf *formación*)
- **preparativos** *nmpl* preparations (*para* for): *los preparativos para el viaje* preparations for the journey: *pl* tends to be preferred to *preparaciones*
- **preparado** *adj/past part* ready, prepared; use *estar*: (*para algo/para hacer algo* for sth/for doing sth; *a + inf* to + verb): *no estaba preparada para esto* I wasn't prepared for this; contrast *no estaba preparada para jugar el tenis* I wasn't ready to play tennis, with *no estaba preparada a jugar* I wasn't prepared to play (ie I didn't want to)
- for 'ready', see also: *dispuesto, listo*

prescindir *vi de algo/alguien* to do/get by without sth/sb; also to get rid of, give up sth/sb: *hemos prescindido del televisor* we've got rid of the television

- **prescindible** *adj* dispensable, ie 'do-withoutable'; cf opp *imprescindible*

presentar *vt* present (in most Eng senses)

- also 'to introduce' (*alguien a alguien* sb to sb): *quiero presentarle a mi primo* I'd like to introduce you to my cousin
- **presentarse** *vr* to present onself, turn up; crop up (eg problem, cf *surgir*); also 'introduce oneself'
- **presentación** *nf pl presentaciones* presentation; also 'introduction' (of person)
- **presentador(a)** *nmf* presenter (TV etc)
- **presente** *adj* present (ie in a place, in sth), use *estar*: *la contaminación siempre está presente* pollution is always present; NB to be present at: *asistir a* or *presenciar* (see below)
- in a time context, in formal expressions eg *el presente mes* inst/the current month, but otherwise cf *actual* is preferred: *el presidente actual* the present president; *nm* the present (time or tense)
- **presencia** *nf* presence (meanings much as Eng)
- **presenciar** *vt* to witness, be present at: *presencié el estreno* I was present at/witnessed the first performance; similar to cf *asistir a*

prestar *vt* to lend; NB *prestar ayuda/apoyo* to give help/support, and: *prestar atención* to pay attention

- NB also *dar algo prestado* to lend sth; *pedir/tomar algo prestado* to borrow sth: however, 'May I borrow your bike?' is often best rendered by *¿Me quieres prestar tu bici?*, ie 'Will you lend me your bike?'
- **préstamo** *nm* loan, borrowing (eg from bank)

presumir *vt* to presume, but used rather less than cf *suponer*: *es de presumir que* one must presume that, presumably …

- *vi* to show off, swank: *le gusta*

presumir he likes to show off; *presume de progre* he likes to think he's trendy/with it;

- **presunción** *nf pl presunciones*: presumption (supposition); also 'presumptuousness', 'conceit', 'arrogance'
- **presuntuoso** *adj* presumptuous, conceited; don't confuse with:
- **presunto** *adj* presumed, suspected, alleged: *el presunto ladrón* the alleged thief

pretender *vt* to try (+ *inf* to): *¿Qué pretendes hacer?* What are you trying to do?

- NB not entirely the same as other words for 'try' (*intentar, procurar, tratar de*) in that there is usually an implication that the action will not succeed or will only do so with some difficulty
- also 'to claim,' 'allege': *pretende tener la solución* he claims to have the solution
- and (+ *subjunc*) to expect sb to do sth: *¿Pretendes que lo haga yo?* Do you expect me to do it?
- NB for 'pretend' in sense of 'feign', use *fingir(se)*
- **pretensión** *nf pl pretensiones* claim, aim, object; also pretension: *tiene pretensiones de ser rico* he claims to be rich (and isn't)

pretexto *nm* pretext; can also be used to mean 'excuse': *y ¿cuál es tu pretexto?* and what's your excuse? (ie reason for (not) doing sth)

prevenir *vt* (has all the irregularities of *venir* + *tú* imperative *prevén*) to prevent, (NB less wide meaning than Eng: *es mejor prevenir los accidentes* it's better to prevent accidents; for 'prevent sb/sth from doing sth', use cf *impedir que*)

- also 'to warn': *le previnimos del problema* we warned him about the

problem (similar to cf *advertir*)

- **prevenirse** *vr* to prepare for: *prevenirse para el invierno* to prepare for winter; also 'to provide oneself' (*de* with): *se previnieron de lo necesario* they provided themselves with the necessary; *prevenirse contra* to take precautions against; *se previnieron contra el frío* they took precautions against the cold
- **prevenido** *adj/past part* (well-) prepared; *estaban prevenidos* they were well-prepared; also forewarned
- **preventivo** *adj* preventive; *medicina preventiva* preventive medicine
- **prevención** *nf* prevention; also *pl prevenciones* precautionary measures

prever *vt* has all irregularities of its root verb *ver*, plus accent in parts of *pi*: *prevés, prevé, prevén*, *tú imperative*: *prevé* and *pret*: *previó* to foresee, anticipate: *preveo problemas* I foresee problems; also 'to envisage': *¿Qué remedio prevés?* What solution to you envisage?; *hora prevista de llegada* estimated time of arrival

- **previsión** *nf pl previsiones* forecast, prediction: *previsiones meteorológicas* weather outlook; also 'precaution': *en previsión de* as a precaution against
- **previsible** *adj* foreseeable

primero *adj* first (NB shortens before *masc sing noun* only): *primer piso* first floor; don't confuse with:

- **primario** *adj* primary

primordial *adj* primordial, but often used to mean 'fundamental', 'paramount': *una razón primordial* a fundamental reason; *de una importancia primordial* paramount importance

principio *nm* beginning (much the same as cf *comienzo*); *al principio* at first; *a principios de* at the beginning of (month, season or other time-span): *a* *principios de mayo* in early May

- ☐ also 'principle' (in most senses)
- ☐ **principiar** *vti* to commence, begin (formal and less common than cf *empezar, comenzar*)
- ☐ **principiante** *nmf* beginner
- ☐ **principal** *adj* principal, main

prisa *nf* haste, rush, hurry: *tener prisa* to be in a hurry; *ir de prisa* to be in a hurry, or go fast; *darse prisa* to hurry up: *¡Date prisa!* Hurry up!; *¿Corre prisa?* Is it urgent?/Is there any hurry?; *no hay/corre prisa* no hurry; *de prisa* or *deprisa* quickly

- ☐ NB for 'hurry' see also *precipitarse*, 'hurry up' see *apresurarse*; for 'quick(ly)', 'fast' see also *rápido, veloz/velocidad*

privado *adj* private: much the same as cf *particular*

probable *adj* probable; **probabilidad** *nf* probability

- ☐ NB all expressions involving these words + *que* need *subjunc*: *es probable/hay la probabilidad de que nos vean* it's probably/there's the probability (that) they'll see us

probar *vt* -ue- to prove (cf *demostrar, comprobar*)

- ☐ also, often, 'to try (out)': *¿Has probado la sopa?* Have you tried the soup?; *voy a probar mi nuevo ordenador* I'm going to try out my new computer
- ☐ and *probar a + inf* to try to: *voy a probar a abrirlo* I'm going to try to open it (may have an element of tentativeness about it: not so frequent or all-purpose as cf *tratar de, intentar, procurar*)
- ☐ **probarse** *vr* to try on: *¿Me puedo probar esta chaqueta?* May I try on this jacket?
- ☐ **prueba** *nf* proof; also 'test': *ahora viene la prueba* now comes the test; *poner algo a prueba* to put sth to

the test; *a prueba de* -proof; a *a prueba de agua* waterproof

- ☐ **probeta** *nf* test tube: *niño/a probeta* test-tube baby

problema *nm* problem (NB it's *masc*!); use *plantear un problema* to pose a problem, and *resolver* or *solucionar* to solve it

proceso *nm* process; also trial (in court)

procurar *vt* to try (+ *inf* to + verb); much the same as cf *intentar, tratar de*

- ☐ can also mean 'procure', 'obtain', but is more formal than eg *conseguir, obtener*

producir *vt* pi: produzco, produces; ps: produzca; pret: produje, produjiste, produjo, produjimos, produjisteis, produjeron; imp subj: produjera/produjese to produce (in most senses)

- ☐ also 'to cause': *le produjo una decepción profunda* it caused her deep disappointment
- ☐ **producirse** *vr* to happen, occur: *se produjo una explosión enorme* there was an enormous explosion
- ☐ **producción** *nf* pl producciones production (most senses)
- ☐ **producto** *nm* product; **productor(a)** *nmf* producer and *adj* producing: *una región productora de carbón* a coal-producing area

profesor(a) *nmf* teacher, lecturer; for 'professor', use *catedrático/a*

- ☐ **profesión** *nf* pl profesiones profession, but with wider meaning than in English to encompass 'trade', 'occupation'; *es fontanero de profesión* he's a plumber by trade
- ☐ **profesional** *adj* professional, but with similar wider meaning: *formación profesional* professional/vocational training
- ☐ **profesar** *vt* to profess

profundo *adj* deep, profound; cf *hondo*

- ☐ to say how deep use: **profundidad**

adj depth: *la piscina tiene dos metros de profundidad* the pool is 2 metres deep; *en profundidad* in depth

☐ **profundizar** *vi -ce-, -cé* to go into sth in depth: *hay que profundizar más* we must go into it more deeply

programa *nm* program(me) (of most kinds); NB it's *masc*!

progreso *nm* progress; often used in *pl* with *hacer: hemos hecho muchos progresos* we've made a lot of progress

☐ **progresar** *vi* to progress, make progress

☐ **progresivo** *adj* progressive (in sense of) advancing, continuous

☐ **progresista** *adj* or *nmf* progressive (person), ie one who has progressive thoughts; **progresismo** *nm* progressiveness, the process of having progressive thoughts! **progre** *nmf* trendy (person)

prohibir *vt pi:* prohíbo, prohíbes, prohíbe, prohíben; *ps:* prohíba, prohíbas, prohíba, prohíban; to prohibit, forbid: (*algo a alguien* sb sth): *el gobierno ha prohibido a los médicos el uso de esta droga* the government has prohibited doctors the use of this drug; *prohibir a alguien hacer algo,* or *prohibir a alguien que haga algo* to forbid sb to do sth: *te prohíbo hablarme así,* or *te prohíbo que me hables así* I forbid you to talk to me like that

☐ **prohibirse** *vr* to be prohibited/forbidden: *se prohíbe fumar* smoking prohibited

☐ **prohibido** *adj/past part* prohibited, forbidden: (*está*) *terminantemente prohibido hablar con el conductor* (it is) strictly forbidden to talk to the driver

☐ **prohibición** *nf pl* prohibiciones prohibition, ban

promesa *nf* promise; *cumplir (con)/faltar a una promesa* to keep/go back on a promise

☐ **prometer** *vt* to promise (+ *inf* to

+ verb): *prometiste comprarme una cerveza* you promised you'd buy me a beer; also 'to augur': *su respuesta no promete nada bueno* his reply doesn't augur at all well

☐ **prometerse** *vr* to get engaged; NB also *prometérselas muy felices* to have high hopes

☐ **prometido/a** *adj* engaged; or *nmf* fiancé(e)

☐ **prometedor/a** *adj* promising: *un rendimiento prometedor* a promising performance

promover *vt -ue-* and **promocionar** *vt* to promote (interchangeable in senses of 'push' eg a product, or 'move up' a rank/scale etc)

☐ **promoción** *nf pl* promociones promotion (both senses)

pronto *adv* soon; also 'right now': *hazlo – ¡pronto!* do it! this minute!; *lo más pronto posible* as soon as possible; *tan pronto como* as soon as (+ *subjunc* if referring to future: *tan pronto como lo recibas* as soon as you receive it; same as cf *en cuanto, así que*): *de pronto* suddenly

☐ also used as *adj*: prompt (fairly formal): *le agradezco su pronta respuesta* thank you for your prompt reply

☐ **prontitud** *nf* promptness; *hacer algo con prontitud* to do sth speedily, quickly

propaganda *nf* propaganda; but also 'advertising' (much same as cf *publicidad*)

propina *nf* tip (ie of money); also 'pocket money': *¿Cuánto te dan de propina?* How much pocket money do you get?

propio *adj* (of) one's own, own: *¡Qué bien tener un piso propio!* How nice to have a flat of one's own! NB follows noun when used emphatically like this, but precedes it in phrases such as: *lo hice* *con mis propias manos* I made it with my own hands, where it is an integral part of the phrase

- □ also 'typical', 'characteristic', 'fitting': *es un mueble propio de la época* it's a piece of furniture typical of the period; *una comida propia para un rey* a meal fit for a king
- □ and 'proper', 'correct' 'appropriate': *su actitud fue poco propia de la ocasión* his attitude was not very proper for the occasion
- □ and 'him/herself', (the) 'very': *hablé con el propio Rey* I spoke to the King himself; cf *mismo*
- □ **propiedad** *nf* property: *propiedad ajena* other people's property; sometimes used to express 'belong to': *es la propiedad del Estado* it belongs to the State; also 'properness': *hacer algo con propiedad* to do sth correctly, properly
- □ **propietario/a** *nmf* proprietor/ -tress, owner; NB spelling *proPIEtario* – no -r-; similar to *syn dueño/a*

proponer *vt* has all irregularities of its root verb *poner*, plus *tú imperative: propón* to propose (most senses)

- □ also 'suggest': *¿Qué propones?* What do you suggest? (+ *que* + *subjunc* propose/suggest that): *¿Qué propones que hagamos?* What do you suggest we do? (similar to cf *sugerir* in this sense)
- □ **proponerse** *vr* to plan, make up one's mind, intend (*hacer algo* to do sth): *me he propuesto dimitir* I've made up my mind/intend to resign
- □ **proposición** *nf pl proposiciones* proposal, suggestion; also 'proposition'
- □ **propuesta** *nf* proposal, suggestion (interchangeable with *proposición* in this sense); also 'offer': *una propuesta de trabajo* an offer of work
- □ **propósito** *nm* intention, aim, purpose: *no era mi propósito ofenderte*

it wasn't my intention to offend you

- □ **a propósito** *adv* by the way: *A propósito, ¿qué haces esta tarde?* by the way, what are you doing this evening?; and 'on purpose', 'deliberately': *lo las hecho a propósito* you did it deliberately
- □ **a propósito de** *prep* on the subject of, talking about: *a propósito del tiempo, ya está lloviendo* talking about the weather, it's now raining

proporción *nf* proportion: *en proporción a* in proportion to; can be used in *pl proporciones* as Eng meaning 'dimensions': *de grandes proporciones* with/of big dimensions

- □ **proporcionar** *vt* to provide, supply (in that sense) (*algo a alguien* sb with sth): *su trabajo no le proporciona suficiente dinero* his job doesn't provide him with sufficient money
- □ also 'to cause', 'give rise to': *su llegada les proporcionó a todos una gran sorpresa* his arrival gave everyone a great surprise
- □ therefore has wider and slightly more abstract meaning than cf *suministrar*, and *proveer*
- □ **proporcionado** *adj* proportionate, in proportion (*a* to): *proporcionado a su salario* in proportion to his salary
- □ **proporcional** *adj representación proporcional* proportional representation

protagonista *nmf* protagonist, leading role (in play, film, novel etc)

- □ **protagonizar** *vt* -ce-, -cé to play the leading role in: *protagoniza la película Javier Bardem* Javier Bardem plays the leading role in the film; *una película protagonizada por Javier Bardem* a film with Javier Bardem in the leading role; also, by extension, 'to be responsible for', 'lead': *la huelga fue protagonizada por*

Comisiones Obreras   the strike was set up/initiated by Comisiones Obreras

proteger *vt* -jo, -ja-   to protect, defend, shelter: *los árboles nos protegen del viento*   the trees protect us from the wind
- **protección** *nf*   protection
- **protector(a)** *nmf*   protector and *adj*   protective: *capa protectora*   protective layer/film

protestar *vi*   to protest (*contra*   about)
- also 'to complain' (*por/de*   about): *protestaban por la falta de agua*   they were complaining about the water shortage; similar to cf *quejarse* in this sense, perhaps a shade stronger
- **protesta** *nf*   protest; complaint (as described above); where 'protest' means 'demonstration', better to use *manifestación*; 'protester' would be *manifestante*

provecho see **aprovechar**

proveer *vt*   irreg in *ger*: *proveyendo past part*: *provisto pret*: *proveí, proveíste, proveyó, proveímos, proveísteis, proveyeron*; *imp subj*: *proveyera/proveyese*   to provide, supply (*a alguien de algo*   sb with sth): *me proveyó de toda la información*   he provided me with all the information; similar to cf *suministrar*, lacks wider 'give rise to' meaning of *proporcionar*
- **provisto** *adj/past part*   provided (*de* with)
- **provisión** *nf*   provision (in all senses); *pl provisiones*   food (supplies)
- **provisional** *adj*   provisional; **provisionalidad** *nf* provisional/temporary character: *debido a la provisionalidad del arreglo* owing to the provisional nature of the arrangement

provocar *vt* -que-, -qué   to provoke
- also 'to bring about', 'cause': *su comportamiento provocó un escándalo* his behaviour caused a scandal
- and, in Mexico 'to like', 'fancy': *¿Te provoca una cerveza?*   Do you fancy a beer?

próximo *adj*   next: *el próximo sábado* (the) next Saturday; *la próxima parada* the next stop; can be *pron*: *hasta la próxima (vez)*   till the next (time)
- also 'near', 'close' (*a*   to + *n* or *inf*): *su casa está próxima a la nuestra* their house is close to ours; *estaba próxima a las lágrimas/a llorar*   she was close to tears
- **proximidad** *nf*   proximity, closeness; *en las proximidades de*   in the vicinity of

proyecto *nm*   project
- **proyectar** *vt*   to plan (similar to cf *planear*): *proyectamos reunirnos mañana* we're planning to meet tomorrow
- also 'project' (show film, slides etc)
- for 'stick out', use *sobresalir*
- **proyector** *nm*   projector; *retroproyector*   overhead projector

prudente *adj*   prudent, sensible, careful: *es un inversor prudente de dinero*   he's a careful investor of money; *invirtió una cantidad prudente*   he invested a sensible amount
- **prudencia** *nf*   prudence, ie care: *obra con prudencia*   he works/operates carefully
- NB these words have a wider range of meaning than their Eng counterparts

público *adj*   public; also *nm*   public: ie (theatre) audience, (sports) spectators, (newspaper) readership; *'para todo público'*   'U' film; *en público*   in public
- **publicidad** *nf*   publicity; also 'advertising'; *hacer publicidad de algo* to advertise sth; (cf *propaganda*)
- **publicitario** *adj*   advertising; *agencia publicitaria*   advertising agency

□ **publicar** *vt* -que-, -qué to publish; also 'to make public', 'divulge'; don't confuse with **publicitar** *vt* to publicise

□ **publicación** *nf pl* publicaciones publication (act of publishing, or book/magazine etc)

pueblo see **población**

puente *nm* bridge (most senses, including violin, spectacles, dental), except card game: *bridge*

□ *hacer puente* to take day(s) off to link a public holiday and a weekend

puerta *nf* door; also 'gate' (usually wooden, and in airport); (NB an iron gate is: *verja*; if the gate is more of a barrier, eg level crossing, use *barrera*)

□ **portal** *nm* doorway, entrance; cf *entrada*

□ **portero/a** *nmf* doorkeeper, caretaker, concierge (in block of flats), (hotel)porter: for porter eg on station, use *mozo*

□ **portería** *nf* portero/a's office

□ **puerto** *nm* port, harbour; also 'mountain pass': *Puerto de Somosierra* Somosierra Pass

pues *adv* well (this is the word that Spaniards often use while they are thinking what to say next: they extend it as Eng extend 'well' to we-e-e-e-e-ll *pu-e-e-e-e-s*): *pues ..., ¿qué sé yo?* well ..., how should I know?; *pues, vamos a ver, sí, puede ser ...* well, let's see, yes, maybe ...

□ also 'so' (therefore, then): *¿No quieres irte? Pues, ¿por qué te vas?* You don't want to go? Then/So why are you going?; *¿Qué vas a hacer, pues?*

What are you going to do, then?; NB in this sense used similarly to cf *entonces* and *conque*

□ NB does NOT mean 'then' in sense of 'next': use *luego* or *entonces*

□ worth a look in the dictionary for further phrases

puesta, puesto see **poner**

punta *nf* point tip: usually refers to sth/somewhere sharp or pointed

□ **punto** *nm* point (in most other senses): *hasta cierto punto* to a certain point/extent; *explicó estos puntos* he explained these points; *punto por punto* point by point; *ganas tres puntos* you win 3 points; *punto de ebullición* boiling point; *punto de partida* starting point

□ also 'dot', 'full stop': *punto y aparte* full stop, new paragraph; *punto y coma* semi-colon; *punto de interrogación* question mark

□ also 'stitch' (in sewing/knitting): *hacer punto* to knit

□ **puntería** *nf* aim (when eg shooting sth)

□ **puntiagudo** *adj* sharp, pointed

□ **de puntillas** *adv* on tiptoe

puño *nm* fist

□ also 'cuff' (of sleeve)

□ **puñetazo** *nm* punch: *le dio/pegó un puñetazo* he punched him

puro *adj* pure (in most senses): *agua pura* pure water

□ also, as Eng 'pure', 'sheer': *de pura alegría* out of sheer joy

□ *nm* cigar

□ **pureza** *nf* purity

□ **purificar** *vt* -que-, -qué to purify

Q

que this is one of the most frequently occuring words in Sp! It has various functions, which are explained at length in most grammar books, which you should consult for further details. However, its uses are dealt with below under general headings, such as 'relative pronouns', 'the subjunctive', etc rather than simply under '*que*', so look it up in a grammar under the underlined headings below.

relative pron   who, which, that
- *el libro que estoy leyendo*   the book (which/that) I'm reading (NB can't be omitted as in Eng)
- *lo que*   what (that which): *lo que no me gusta*   what I don't like

conj
- 'that' – in indirect speech used after a verb to introduce a clause: *dijo que no vale*   he said (that) it's no good; (NB can't be omitted in Sp)
- in clauses of result after *tan* or *tanto*: *hacía tanto calor y estábamos tan cansados, que no podíamos seguir*   it was so hot and we were so tired that we couldn't continue
- after comparatives, meaning 'than': *bebo más/menos café que té*   I drink more/less coffee than tea
- after *tener* and *hay*, linking with an infinitive, even if there is an object: *tenemos/hay mucho trabajo que terminar*   we've/there's a lot of work to finish; *tenemos/hay que volver* we've got to/it's necessary to go back

- many subjunctive clauses are introduced by *que*, where it may replace a different Eng word: *dudo que valga*   I doubt whether it's any good; *que te diviertas*   may you have a good time, ie 'enjoy yourself'
- in various compound conjunctions: *de modo que, para que, ya que, desde que, cuandoquiera que*, etc
- in various idiomatic phrases: *yo que tú*   if I were you; *¡Que sí! ¡Que no!* Oh yes (it is)! Oh no (it isn't)!

¿qué? *interrogative pron/adj*
- NB this is the interrog form, (ie the one that asks a question). It always has an accent, because it is always stressed in the sentence.
- Although Eng may use the same or similar words to the *relative pronoun* above, in both languages these words are used in a different way as interrogatives. Again, refer to a grammar book for a full and detailed explanation under the underlined headings!

interrogative pron   what?
- stands by itself, as subject, object or after a preposition: *¿qué?*   what?; *¿qué quieres?*   what do you want?; *¿qué es?*   what is it?; *¿para qué sirve?*   what's it (used) for?; *¿de qué está hecho?*   what's it made of?

interrogative adj   what?, which?
- always + *noun*: *¿qué hora es?*   what time is it?; *¿qué vestido prefieres?* which dress do you prefer?

adj also occurs in exclamations ...
- with a *noun* meaning 'what a ...!', 'what ...!': *¡qué problema!*   what a problem!, *¡qué problemas!*   what problems!
- with an *adj* meaning 'how ...!': *¡qué simpática (es)*   how nice (she is)!
- with a *noun* + *adj*, note need for *tan* or *más*: *¡qué libro tan/más interesante!*   what an interesting

book! NB *tan/más* not needed if *adj* precedes nouns: *¡qué buena idea!* what a good idea!

quebrantar *vt*   to break

- □ to some extent the same as *romper* and *quebrar* (below), but often has a fairly strong meaning, rather like 'shatter' or 'force'; used with breaking, shattering eg *promesa* (break promise), *ley* (break law), *cerradura* (force lock), *caja fuerte* (force safe, strongbox)
- □ also 'to weaken': *resistencia, cimientos* (foundations), etc
- □ **quebrantarse** *vr*   to be shattered, broken, especially health

quebrar *vt -ie-*   to break, smash

- □ much overlap with cf *romper* and *quebrantar*
- □ to interrupt, in sense of *carrera* (career), *formación* (training) etc
- □ **quebrarse** *vr*   to get broken, smashed

quedar *vi*   to stay, remain (in various senses):

- □ to stay (in general, but NB notes below and under *quedarse*): *vamos a quedar dos semanas*   we're going to stay for two weeks
- □ used with states, where it can sometimes simply mean 'to be': *quedamos atónitos*   we were astonished; *quedó inmóvil* he stood still/motionless; or 'to become', 'go' in that sense: *quedar sordo*   to become/ go deaf; *quedar embarazada*   to get pregnant
- □ *quedar bien/mal con alguien*   to be on good/bad terms with sb
- □ to be situated, to lie: *el pueblo queda a unos pocos kilómetros de allí*   the village is (situated) a few kilometres from there
- □ NB idiomatic use 'to be left', 'to have left' – this works 'back to front' compared to Eng structure: *me*

quedan diez botellas   I've got ten bottles left; this structure is also used in the sense 'still to go': *quedan tres días para las vacaciones*   there are three days to go to the holidays

- □ to agree to, come to an agreement about: *entonces, ¿quedamos en el sábado a las tres?*   so, we agree to Saturday at three? *quedar en + inf* to agree to (do sth)
- □ *quedar por* – used to indicate what remains/is still to be done: *quedan seis camisas por planchar*   there are still six shirts to iron/be ironed
- □ **quedarse** *vr* the reflexive form occurs very frequently:
- □ there is a large overlap with the basic form *quedar* (above), especially in the basic sense of 'to stay', 'remain', as in the first two bullet points: *todos se quedaron atrás*   everybody stayed behind
- □ use this form for 'to stay' in some form of accommodation: *esta vez nos quedamos en un hotel*   this time we stayed in a hotel
- □ use it also when a supply of something has come to an end or run out, especially with *sin*: *me quedé sin dinero*   I ran out of money; *me quedé sin trabajo*   I lost my job
- □ also 'to keep', 'hold on to sth': *quédese con la vuelta*   keep the change; *me lo quedo*   I'll keep it (when chosing sth eg in shop); *se quedó con mi monedero*   he walked off with my purse
- □ can also be used with *ger.* to continue doing sth, especially if sense suggests to remain and continue doing sth: *nos quedamos hablando de la política* we (stayed and) continued talking politics
- □ both basic and reflexive forms of the verb merit further study in a large dictionary or good grammar book!

quehacer *nm* job, task, chore
- usually domestic or everyday, rather like cf *faena*; *tarea* is more general in application

queja *nf* complaint, grumble (in that sense)
- for a formal complaint, eg, to a hotel, you would make *una reclamación* in the *libro de reclamaciones*
- can also mean 'moan', 'groan' (ie the noise)
- the verb is **quejarse** *(de) vi* to complain, grumble (about); also to moan, groan (noise); the noun in this sense is **quejido** *nm*
- *quejarse de que …* to complain that …

quemar *vt* to burn
- NB this is the transitive verb, ie when you burn something
- *ayer quemé todos mis papeles* yesterday I burnt all my papers
- can be used as *vi* when something burns, eg the mouth, the skin: *esta salsa quema* this sauce burns (ie stings); cf *picar*
- also 'to scald'
- if you burn (a part of) yourself, you must use the reflexive form **quemarse** *vr*: *me quemé el dedo* I burnt/scalded my finger
- the reflexive form is also used when something burns, in the sense of being consumed by flames and smoke or at least scorched: *el coche se quemó por completo* the car burnt out completely; *se quemaron los pasteles* the cakes were burnt/scorched
- for the process of burning ie being alight, see also *arder*
- see also *incendiar* for burn down, 'torch'
- **quemadura** *nf* burn

querer *vt pi*: quiero, quieres, quiere, queremos, queréis, quieren; *ps*: quiera *etc*; *fut/cond*: querré/querría, *pret*: quise, quisiste, quiso, quisimos, quisisteis, quisieron; *imp subj*: quisiera/quisiese has a variety of meanings:
- to want sth or to want/wish to + *inf*: *Merche quiere un nuevo bolso* Merche wants a new handbag; *no queremos salir hoy* we don't want to go out today; in this sense means the same as, but is rather more used than, *desear*
- NB to want sb or sth to do sth, use *querer que* + *subjunc*: *no queremos que ellos salgan hoy* we don't want them to go out today; consult a grammar for more details
- 'will' in the sense of wishing to do sth:*¿Quieres venir aquí? ¡No, no quiero!* Will you come here? No, I won't!
- also means 'to love': *¡te quiero!* I love you; *ya no me quiere* he/she doesn't love me any more; cf also *amar*, which is perhaps a little more formal
- can be used as *nm* meaning 'love', 'affection': *con todo mi querer* with all my affection
- **querido** *adj* dear: at beginning of letter: *querida Ana* dear Ana; dear, beloved: *sus queridas flores* her beloved flowers; as *nmf* darling, dear, 'love': *¿dónde estás, querido/a?* where are you, darling?

quien *relative pron* who, whom
- has plural form *quienes*, when its antecedent is plural
- used mainly after preposition, but also in certain circumstances as subject or object of clause: consult a grammar for the full treatment of this important word, especially its use vis-à-vis *que* (above)
- also used meaning 'he who', 'anyone who': *quien cree eso …* anyone who believes that … (*quienes creen …* if the implication or emphasis is on more than one person believing it)

¿quién? *interrogative pron* who? whom?
- □ NB accent on interrog word
- □ has plural form *quiénes* if the question is being asked about more than one person: *¿Quiénes han hecho esto?* Who has done this?
- □ used as subject, object and after prepositions
- □ NB *¿De quién(es) es …?* Whose is …?; *De quién es este coche?* Whose is that car?

quienquiera *pron* whoever
- □ followed by *que* + *subjunc*: *quienquiera que sea* whoever it may be

quieto *adj* still, motionless (rather than 'quiet', although meaning does perhaps contain an element of silence!)
- □ with this meaning, use with *estar*
- □ occurs in a number of useful expression: *quedarse quieto* to remain still; *¡estáte quieto!* or just *¡quieto!* stand still!
- □ also 'calm', placid' (applied to a person); use with *ser*

quinientos *num, adj* five hundred
- □ NB the special form, not *cinco …*
- □ don't forget all hundreds from 200 to 900 are *adjs* and agree with their noun: *quinientas veces* five hundred times
- □ **quinto** *num, adj* fifth: no set pattern

of forming ordinal numbers!

quitar *vt* to remove, take away
- □ NB takes *a* + person: *los aduaneros le quitaron el pasaporte al viajero* the customs officers took the passenger's passport away
- □ there are a number of idiomatic uses: *quitar la mesa* to clear the table; *quitar tiempo* to take up time; *quitar el sueño a alguien* to stop sb sleeping
- □ **quitarse** *vr* to take off (clothes): *me quité la chaqueta* I took off my jacket
- □ NB don't confuse with Fr *quitter* – in most senses it does not mean 'to leave': see *dejar, salir*
- □ merits research in a dictionary for the various further idiomatic uses of both transitive and reflexive forms
- □ **quita-** *prefix* several words with meaning 'taking away' begin with it: **quitamanchas** *nm inv* stain remover; **quitanieves** *nm inv* snowplough **quitasol** *nm* sunshade

quizá/quizás *adj* perhaps, maybe
- □ either form is correct, with no particular trend one way or the other
- □ tends to take subjunc, depending somewhat on the degree of doubt introduced: consult a grammar for further examples!
- □ see also *acaso, tal vez, puede ser*

R

R (*ere*) is pronounced in all Spanish-speaking countries by rolling the end of the tongue. Scottish students should have no problem with this, though speakers from other parts of Britain and the English-speaking world may need to practise it rather more, paying particular attention to words ending in -*r* (which includes all infinitives!): *rabo, retiro, reír, rico, rosa, ruso, treinta y tres; hablar, ver, ser, ir.*

◆ It is one of the few Spanish consonants which can occur double, and double -*rr*- is rolled even more strongly: *ferrocarril, barro, guerra, porra, burro.* To practise the difference between -*r*- and -*rr*-, try *pero/perro, caro/carro, oro/horror.*

rabia *nf* rage, fury: *dar rabia a alguien* to infuriate sb; *¡Me da rabia ese chico!* That boy infuriates me!
- □ also 'rabies'
- □ **rabioso** *adj* furious; also 'raging': *tengo un rabioso dolor de muelas* I've got a raging toothache; also 'rabid'
- □ **rabiar** *vi* to rage, be furious; NB *rabiar por algo* to be dying for sth; *rabiar por hacer algo* to be dying to do sth
- □ other 'anger' words: *syns furia, ira;* cf *enfadar(se), enfurecer(se), enojar(se)*

rabo *nm* tail: more or less interchangeable with cf *cola* in this sense, but not in other senses of *cola; de cabo a rabo* from beginning to end

ración *nf pl raciones* portion (of food, more frequent than *porción*) bigger than

cf *pincho*, share (of sth); also 'ration(s)'

radio *nf* radio; NB it's *fem* (in Spain, but often *masc* in Sp Am)
- □ also *nm* radius
- □ **radioyente** *nmf* radio listener
- □ **radiografía** *nf* X-ray
- □ **radiografiar** *vt* to X-ray; **radiografiarse** *vr* to have an X-ray

raíz *nf pl raíces* root (in most senses); *echar raíces* to take root
- □ **a raíz de** *prep* as a result of: *a raíz de las acciones del gobierno* as a result of the government action

rama *nf* branch (of plant/tree etc); for branch of company, use *sucursal*; for railway etc, use *ramal*
- □ **ramo** *nm* bunch, bouquet (of flowers); NB don't confuse *rama/ramo!*
- □ **ramificación** *nf pl ramificaciones* ramification; also 'branch' (in computing)
- □ **ramificarse** *vr -que-, -qué* to branch (most senses)

rápido *adj* quick, fast; can also be used as exhortation: *¡Rápido!* Quick!, Hurry up! (overlap with cf *prisa* in this sense)
- □ *nm* fast train, express
- □ **rápidamente** *adv* quickly: NB retains accent -*á*-; some overlap with *de prisa*, which, however, implies haste rather than just speed
- □ **rapidez** *nf* speed: *hacer algo con rapidez* to do sth quickly/speedily

raro *adj* rare (in most senses but for meat use *poco hecho*); *rara vez* seldom, not often
- □ also, often 'strange', 'funny', 'odd', 'curious' (in that sense): *¡qué raro!* how funny!; *tiene el sentido del humor muy raro* he's got a very odd sense of humour
- □ **raramente** *adv* rarely, seldom
- □ **rareza** nf rarity; also 'oddity',

'peculiarity' (in that sense):' *tener sus rarezas* to have one's funny little ways (cf *manía*)

rascar *vt* -que-, -qué to scratch, scrape;
    rascarse *vr* to scratch oneself
- **rascacielos** *nm inv* skyscraper
- NB don't confuse with *rasgar* group below

rasgar *vt* -gue-, -gué to tear (ie sth): *rasgué el paño* I tore the cloth
- **rasgarse** *vr* to tear: *el paño se rasgó* the cloth tore
- NB don't confuse with *rascar* above

rasgo *nm* feature, trait, characteristic cf *característica; los rasgos* (facial) features: same as cf *facciones* in this sense

rata *nf* rat: *fem* regardless of sex of rat!
- **ratón** *nm pl ratones* mouse: unusual for 'augmentative' in -*ón* to mean something smaller than its root word!

rato *nm* while, short time: *esperé un rato* I waited a while; *hace un rato* a while ago; *pasar un mal rato* to have a bad/hard time of it;
- used in various useful phrases: *al poco rato* soon after (ie looking back in time); *dentro de un rato* soon, shortly (ie looking forward); *a ratos (perdidos)* every so often; *largo rato/un buen rato* a long time
- compare use with *tiempo, temporada,* and partial *syn período*
- **ratito** *nm dim* short while, little while: *¡un ratito!* half a moment!

raya *nf* line, stripe: *traje a rayas* striped suit
- also, a variety of meanings: parting (in hair); crease (in trousers); boundary: *la raya con Portugal* the Portuguese border; *pasar de la raya* to overstep the mark; *tener a raya* to hold back/at bay
- **rayar** *vti* to border (*con* on): *eso raya con lo imposible* that borders on the impossible; *Cantabria raya con*

Asturias Cantabria borders on/ is next to Asturias; also 'to draw lines/ 'stripes'; *chaqueta rayada* striped jacket
- NB don't confuse with *rayo* group below

rayo *nm* ray, beam: *los rayos del sol* the sun's rays: *rayo láser* laser beam
- (flash of) lightning; thunderbolt: *le mató un rayo* he was killed by lightning

raza *nf* race (ie ethnic origin or make-up)
- breed (of animal): *de raza pura* pedigree, thoroughbred
- **racial** *adj* racial; **racismo** *nm* racism

razón *nf pl razones* reason, in senses of:
- faculty: *ha perdido la razón* he's lost his reason, or he's gone out of his mind; *le metí en razón* I made him see sense
- motive: *por esta razón* for this reason; *tengo mis razones* I have my reasons; cf *motivo* which is often preferable in this sense
- rightness, correctness: *tener razón* to be right; *no tener razón* to be wrong; *te doy la razón* I admit you're right; *y con razón* and rightly (so), with reason
- information: *se vende piso, razón teléf: 12345* flat for sale, for information, tel 123456
- **en razón de** *prep* with regard to, because of
- 'the reason for' is a bit of a minefield! It often helps to use another word: if 'reason' means 'cause' use *causa: la causa de su actitud* the reason for his attitude; if it means 'motive', use *motivo: el motivo de sus acciones* the reason for his actions
- **razonar** *vti* to reason, argue (in this sense); **razonamiento** *nm* reasoning
- **razonable** *adj* reasonable: *a precios razonables* at reasonable prices; *es*

una persona razonable   she's a reasonable person

re- *prefix* has two main functions: (1) often used to intensify a word (almost any part of speech): *¡rebueno!*   jolly good!; *¡digo que sí, resí!*   I say yes, yes, yes!

(2) also used as in Eng and Fr meaning re-, ie 'again', or 'back' (eg repay, pay back) but NB this use often tends to be a result of Eng or Fr influence, and is not so widely practised in Spain, so you can't automatically assume you can use it in this way

re- (1)

a sample of words which use the prefix **re-** to intensify their meaning; they will all behave like their root word, which is given

rebuscar	*buscar*	to search thoroughly, rummage
recalentar*	*calentar*	to overheat
rellenar*	*llenar*	to stuff, fill in
relleno*	*lleno*	stuffed
remojar	*mojar*	to soak
retorcer	*torcer*	twist, tangle
retorcido	*torcido*	twisted, tangled

* see also entry in main text

re- (2)

a sample of verbs where **re-** means 're-' as in English, ie to do the action again; NB they all behave exactly like their root verb, which is given

reabrir	*abrir*	to reopen
reafirmar	*afirmar*	to restate/reaffirm
rearmar	*armar*	to rearm
recargar	*cargar*	to recharge
reciclar	*ciclar*	to recycle
reconquistar	*conquistar*	to reconquer
reemplazar	*emplazar*	to replace
regenerar	*generar*	to regenerate
rehabilitar	*habilitar*	to rehabilitate
rehacer	*hacer*	to redo, remake
reintegrar	*integrar*	to reintegrate, reinstate
remodelar	*modelar*	to remodel, redesign
renacer	*nacer*	to be reborn
reorganizar	*organizar*	to reorganise
reponer	*poner*	to replace, put back
restablecer	*establecer*	to reestablish, restore
reunificar(se)	*unificar(se)*	to reunify, reunite
revender	*vender*	to resell
revitalizar	*vitalizar*	to revitalise

real *adj* royal: *Familia Real* Royal Family
also 'real': less common in this sense than
cf *verdadero*

□ **realeza** *nf* royalty

□ **realidad** *nf* reality: *en realidad* in
reality, in fact, actually; *en realidad, es
una broma* actually, it's a joke

□ **realizar** *vt -ce-, -cé* to carry out
(objective, task etc), fulfil (dreams etc):
realizó su sueño she fulfilled her
dream

□ also 'to realise', 'sell' (assets etc): *realizó
sus acciones* she sold her shares

□ NB therefore has meaning of 'to
make real' in the senses described
above; NOT realise in Eng sense of
'become aware (that)': use *darse
cuenta de (que);* for 'understand', use
comprender

□ **realización** *nf* realisation
(fulfilment, sale, as for above)

□ **realizable** *adj* achievable, attainable:
es una ambición realizable it's an
attainable ambition

reanudar *vt* **reanudarse** *vr* to resume,
start again: *reanudó su historia* he
resumed his story; *la saga se reanudó*
the saga resumed; (has lost its connection
with *nudo* knot)

rebajar *vt* to lower (eg prices, level)

□ **rebajarse** *vr* to lower/humble
oneself

□ **rebaja** *nf* reduction, sale: *las rebajas
de enero* the January sales; also,
discount; same as cf *descuento* in
this sense

□ more specific in application than root
words *baja/bajar*

rebelde *nmf* rebel; or *adj* rebellious

□ also 'unmanageable': *niño rebelde* unruly
child; *tos rebelde* persistent cough

□ **rebeldía** *nf* rebelliousness, defiance
(ie characteristic)

□ **rebelión** *nf pl* **rebeliones** rebellion
(ie act of)

□ **rebelarse** *vr* to rebel (*contra* against)

recado *nm* message; same as *mensaje* in
this sense

□ also 'errand': *hacer recados* to run
errands

recalentar *vt -ie-* **recalentarse** *vr* to
overheat; also 'to warm up', 'rewarm';
'heat up', 'reheat' (usually food)

□ **recalentamiento** *nm* overheating:
el recalentamiento global global
warming

recambio *nm* spare part, refill (in this
sense, eg pen); *rueda de recambio* spare
wheel

recelar *vt* to suspect (*que + subjunc* that)

□ **recelar** *vi* or **recelarse** *vr* (*de algo/
alguien*) to suspect, distrust (sb/sth):
me recelo de sus promesas I distrust
his promises

□ **recelo** *nm* suspicion; fear; distrust: *le
miró con recelo* she looked at him
suspiciously/distrustfully

□ **receloso** *adj* suspicious (ie
suspecting) distrustful

□ NB this group basically indicates a
combination of suspicion, fear and
mistrust: not as strong as cf *miedo* and
maybe not as positive a feeling as cf
sospecha/sospechar, in fact a mixture
of these and cf *desconfianza*!

receta *nf* recipe (in cooking)

□ also 'prescription' (medical)

□ **recetar** *vt* to prescribe: *me recetó
aspirinas* he prescribed me aspirins

rechazar *vt -ce-, -cé* to reject, turn down
(eg idea, offer, suggestion, etc):
rechazaron mi propuesta they turned
down my proposal; *su cuerpo rechazó el
trasplante* his body rejected the
transplant; also 'repel', 'push back' (eg
enemy, attack)

□ **rechazo** *nm* rejection

□ a useful group indicating 'refusal to
accept'

recibir *vt* to receive (in most senses)

□ also 'to welcome': *nos recibieron*

cordialmente they welcomed us cordially (rather matter–of fact: see also *bienvenida, acoger/acogida*)

☐ **recibo** *nm* receipt

☐ **recepción** *nf pl recepciones* reception (in most senses, but use *banquete, cena* at a wedding)

☐ **recepcionista** *nmf* receptionist

reciente *adj* recent

☐ **recientemente** *adv* recently: *¿Qué has hecho recientemente?* What have you been doing recently? (cf also *últimamente* in this sense)

☐ **recién** *adv*: NB abbreviated form of *recientemente* used before a number of past participles to indicate 'recently'/'newly': *recién casados* newly weds; *recién nacido* new-born; *recién llegados* newcomers; *casa recién construida* newly-built house; *película recién estrenada* newly released film; and others

recinto *nm* quite widely used word to denote enclosed space/place: could be shopping precinct, university precinct or campus, (eg castle) grounds, leisure area (it has defined boundaries, whatever the purpose): *prohibido fotografiar dentro del recinto* no photographs within the grounds/precinct

reclamar *vt* to claim, (in sense of) demand (rights, share etc): *reclamó su porción* he claimed his portion; some overlap with cf *exigir* and *reivindicar*

☐ also 'to complain', (lodge a complaint); more formal and specific than cf *quejarse, protestar*

☐ for 'to claim that ...' use *mantener que*

☐ **reclamación** *nf* claim (in sense of) demand; complaint: *libro de reclamaciones* complaints book

recobrar *vt* to recover, get back: *recobró la salud* she regained her health; *no recobró su dinero* he didn't get his money back

☐ **recobrarse** *vr* to recover, get better

(from illness): *está completamente recobrada* she's completely recovered; cf *recuperar(se)*, which can also be used in all above senses, and *reponerse* for recover from illness

☐ **recobro** *nm* recovery (in same way)

recoger *vt* -jo, -ja-: *recojo, recoges; recoja* to pick up: *recogió sus gafas de la mesa* he picked up his glasses from the table; *te recojo en tu casa a las seis* I'll pick you up at your house at 6; *voy a Correos a recoger el paquete* I'm going to the post office to pick up the parcel; *recogió la leche derramada* he mopped up the spilt milk

☐ also 'to pick', 'collect in': *están recogiendo uvas* they are picking grapes

☐ **recogerse** *vr* to withdraw, retire; also: *recogerse el pelo* to tie up one's hair

☐ NB nouns: there is an overlap of meaning between three of them: **recogida** *nf* harvest(ing); also (postal) collection; **recogimiento** *nm* harvesting; also withdrawal, retirement (in that sense); and **recolección** *nf* harvesting (it does NOT mean 'recollection' in Eng sense – use *recuerdo*)

☐ **recogido** *adj* quiet, secluded: *una vida recogida* a quiet life; *en una casa recogida* in a secluded house

reconocer *vt* -zc- to recognise, acknowledge (admit); also 'to examine' (medically)

☐ **reconocimiento** *nm* recognition, acknowledgement: *en reconocimiento a* in recognition/acknowledgement of; also (medical) examination

☐ **reconocido** *adj* obliged, grateful: *les estoy muy reconocido* I am very obliged/grateful to you (rather more formal than cf *agradecido*)

recordar *vti* -ue- to remember, recall: *no recuerdo* I don't remember; NB takes direct object: *¿Recordaste el cumpleaños de Lola?* Did you remember Lola's birthday?; in this sense much the same as cf *acordarse (de)*

- also 'to remind' (*algo a alguien* sb of sth): *recuerda mi cumpleaños a Juan* remind John of my birthday; *¿No te recuerda Benidorm?* Doesn't it remind you of Benidorm?; *recordar a alguien que + subjunc* to remind sb to do sth: *¡Recuerda a Juan que me compre un regalo!* Remind John to buy me a present!

- **recuerdo** *nm* memory (ie something you remember – for faculty see *memoria*); also 'souvenir': *recuerdo de Benidorm* souvenir of Benidorm; *tengo recuerdos felices de Benidorm* I have happy memories of Benidorm; *recuerdos a Juan* best wishes/remember me to Juan

- **recordatorio** *nm* reminder

recorrer *vt* to travel all over; *recorrer Europa* to travel around/all over Europe; you can also do it with the eye: to look all over, scan, scour: *recorrió la tienda* she looked all round the shop; *recorrió el periódico* he scanned the newspaper

- **recorrido** *nm* trip, journey: *trenes de largo recorrido* long-distance trains; also 'round' (of golf); (ski) 'run'

- one of those words which has a surprising number of common idiomatic uses and no direct Eng equivalent!

recto *adj* straight: *en línea recta* in a straight line; *siga toda recto* go straight on (cf *derecho* in this sense)

- also 'honest', 'upright' (person)

recuperar *vt* to recover, get back, recuperate (health, strength, losses, etc)

- **recuperarse** *vr* to recover, get better (from illness)

- **recuperación** *nf* recovery, recuperation (in above senses)

- interchangeable with cf *recobrar* in these senses

recurrir *vi* to resort, have recourse (*a* to): *tuvimos que recurrir a otros medios* we had to resort to other means

- **recurso** *nm* recourse, report: *como último recurso* as a last resort

- also, in *pl* resources: *recursos naturales* natural resources

red *nf* net (of most kinds, including *la Red* the Net (ie Internet))

- also 'network', 'supply' (gas/electric). 'mains (water), 'chain' (of businesses): *he aquí la red del metro* here's the Metro network; *conectarse con la red* to be connected to the supply/mains; *otro hotel de la red* another hotel in the chain

- and 'luggage rack' (in eg train)

- the group **enredar(se)** *vr* to (get) tangle(d), and **enredo** tangle is based on *red*

reducir *vt pi:* reduzco, reduces; *ps:* reduzca; *pret;* reduje, redujiste, redujo, redujimos, redujisteis, redujeron; *imp subj:* redujera/redujese to reduce (most senses)

- **reducirse** *vr* to diminish, be reduced; *todo se reduce a esto* it all comes down to this

- **reducción** *nf pl* reducciones (most senses)

- considerable overlap with cf *disminuir(se)/disminución*

- **reducido** *adj/past part* reduced; but often just means 'small', 'limited'; *espacio reducido* limited space; *cantidades reducidas* small/limited quantities

referir *vt -ie-, -i-* to tell, report: *refirió lo que había pasado* he reported/recounted what had happened (similar to cf *contar* in this sense)

- also 'refer' (*alguien a alguien/algo* sb to sb/sth): *a veces referimos nuestros lectores al diccionario* sometimes we refer our readers to the dictionary

□ **referirse** *vr* to refer (ie oneself) (to *a*): *el libro no se refiere a la guerra* the book doesn't refer to the war; *¡me refiero a ti!* I'm referring to you!

□ **referencia** *nf* reference: *con referencia a* with reference to

reflejar *vt* to reflect (light)

□ **reflejo** *nm* reflection (of light); also 'reflex'

□ NB DON'T CONFUSE WITH:

□ **reflexionar** *vi* to reflect: *en/sobre* on/about; *¿Quieres reflexionar?* Would you like to think about it?

□ **reflexión** *nf pl* *reflexiones* reflection (thought)

□ THEY ARE NOT INTERCHANGEABLE

□ **reflexivo** *adj* reflexive: *verbos reflexivos* reflexive verbs, though NB many dictionaries and grammars are now calling them *verbos pronominales*; also 'reflective' (thoughtful)

reformar *vt* to reform

□ also NB 'to alter', 'change', 'improve' (buildings, roads etc)

□ **reforma** *nf* reform; also 'alterations', 'improvements', (as above)

refrán *nm pl refranes* saying, proverb; for 'refrain', use *estribillo*

refrescar *vt* -que-, -qué to refresh, cool down; *refrescar la memoria* to refresh one's memory

□ **refresco** *nm* soft (ie non-alcoholic) drink

refugiar *vt* to give refuge, shelter

□ **refugiarse** *vr* to take refuge (*de algo* from sth)

□ **refugio** *nm* refuge, shelter (in this sense); also 'traffic island'

□ some overlap with *abrigo/abrigar(se)*, *cobijo/cobijar(se)*, esp against elements

□ **refugiado/a** *nmf* refugee

regalar *vt* to give as a present: *regalar algo a alguien: voy a regalar un CD a mi hermano* I'm going to give my brother a CD

□ **regalo** *nm* gift, present

regar *vt* -ie-; -gue-, -gué to water, hose: *regar las plantas* to water the plants; *regar la tierra* to irrigate the land; *regar las calles* to hose the streets

□ also 'to bathe' (eg wound): *regar la herida en agua salada* bathe the wound in salt water

□ and 'spill': *regó cerveza por todas partes* he spilt beer everywhere

□ **riego** *nm* watering, hosing; irrigation: *sistema de riego* irrigation system

régimen *nm* (NB change of stress accent in pl: *regímenes*) diet: *estar/ponerse a régimen* to be/go on a diet; much the same as cf *dieta* in this sense

□ also 'regime': *bajo el régimen de Franco* under Franco's regime

□ **regir** *vti* -i-, -jo, -ja-, *pi rijo, riges; ps: rija* to govern, rule: *Franco rigió durante casi cuarenta años* Franco ruled for nearly 40 years; also 'to be in force': *estos precios ya no rigen* these prices no longer apply (*syn estar en vigor*)

registrar *vt* to register (births, deaths, etc: otherwise not exact equivalent: consult a dictionary for correct word according to context)

□ also 'to search': *los aduaneros le registraron el equipaje* the customs officers searched his baggage

□ and 'to record' (eg temperature, sound, although *grabar* is more common for tape/video-record)

□ for register(ed) mail, use: *certificar/ado*

□ **registrarse** *vr* to be recorded: *ayer se registraron temperaturas de 35 grados* yesterday temperatures of 35 degrees were recorded; also 'to register', 'sign in' (at eg hotel)

□ **registro** *nm* register, list (eg births and deaths); (act of) recording,

registration; also 'search', 'recording' (as for verbs above); and (musical or language) 'register'
- □ for 'take the register' in school, use *pasar lista*
- □ this is a word with numerous specialised meanings: worth a further look in the dictionary

regla *nf* ruler (ie to draw lines with)
- □ also 'rule': *reglas del juego* rules of the game; *por regla general* as a general rule; some overlap in this sense with cf *norma*; *hacer algo con regla* to do sth in moderation
- □ and (menstrual) period
- □ **reglamento** *nm* regulations, rules (ie as a whole): *reglamento profesional* professional code of conduct; *reglamento de tráfico* traffic regulations, rules of the road
- □ **reglamentario** *adj* set, statutory: *horas reglamentarias de trabajo* statutory working hours
- □ **reglar** vt to rule (line etc); for 'rule country', see *regir*

regocijar *vt* to gladden, cheer (up)
- □ **regocijarse** *vr* to rejoice, be glad (*de/por algo* about sth)
- □ **regocijo** *nm* joy, rejoicing, happiness
- □ **regocijado** *adj* joyous, joyful (eg mood); jolly (eg person)
- □ similar, but perhaps conveys a stronger emotion than cf *alegrar(se)/alegría/ alegre*

regresar *vi* to return, come/go back
- □ **regreso** *nm* return, (act of) coming/ going back: *a su regreso* on his return, when he got back; *viaje de regreso* journey back/home
- □ more or less interchangeable with: *volver/ vuelta* in this sense; not the same as:
- □ **regresión** *nf pl regresiones* regression, backwards move; also used in sense of 'decline', 'recession':

regresión económica economic recession
- □ **regresivo** *adj* regressive, backward (in that sense): *política regresiva* regressive policy
- □ these last two words indicate the opp of *progreso/ivo*

regular *adj* regular (in most senses): *compás regular* regular beat; *verbos regulares* regular verbs
- □ also 'so-so', 'not very good': *la comida es regular* the food is so-so/not up to much; *-¿Cómo te sientes?- -Pues, regular-* How do you feel? – All right, I suppose
- □ and 'average' (eg size): *de tamaño regular* middle-sized
- □ **regular** *vt* to regulate, adjust (eg apparatus): *para regular la temperatura* to adjust the temperature
- □ **regulación** *nf* regulation, (in sense of) adjustment, control; NB in sense of rules, better to use cf *reglamento, reglas, normas*
- □ **regularidad** *nf* regularity; *con regularidad* frequently used for 'regularly'

rehacer *vt* (has all the irregularities of *hacer*) to redo, remake
- □ **rehacerse** *vr* to get over, recover (*de* from), (eg illness); cf *reponerse, recobrarse, recuperarse*

rehusar *vt* to refuse, decline (sth); cf *rechazar*; + inf to refuse to: *rehusó hacerlo* he refused to do it
- □ NB there is no such verb as '*refusar*', though *recusar* also exists with a similar meaning to this; the other (more common) verb for 'refuse to + verb' is cf *negarse a + inf*

reinar *vi* to reign; NB as in Eng, silence, confusion, terror, weather etc can reign as well as royalty: *sigue reinando la presión alta* high pressure still prevails
- □ **reinado** *nm* reign: *bajo el reinado de Felipe II* under/in the reign of Philip

II; be careful not to confuse with:

- **reino** *nm* kingdom, realm: if you remember *Reino Unido* as United Kingdom, it will help you to differentiate these two words!
- **rey** *nm* king; NB *los reyes* the king and queen; *los Reyes Magos* the three Wise Men (of the Nativity); *(día de) Reyes* Twelfth Night, 6th January (when Sp give presents)
- **reina** *nf* queen
- see also **real**

reír *vi* basically -i- type stem change, but NB need for accent when -í-: is stressed: *pi: río, ríes, ríe, reímos, reís, ríen; ps: ría, rías, ría, riamos, riáis, rían; ger: riendo; pret: reí, reíste, rio, reímos, reísteis, rieron; imp subj: riera/riese* to laugh: *echarse a reír* to burst out laughing; *es para reír* it's laughable

- **reírse** *vr* to laugh (*de algo/alguien* at sth/sb): *no me río de ti* I'm not laughing at you; *¡cómo se rieron!* how they laughed!
- NB the reflexive form tends to be more common; if there are any differences between the two forms, use *reír* when it means 'laugh' in general without specific reference to any person – or if there is already an object pronoun: *me haces reír* you make me laugh; conversely, use *reírse* to indicate a personal reaction: *me reí a carcajadas* I laughed my head off; use *reírse de* if you are laughing at sth/sb: *todos se rieron de mi sombrero* they all laughed at my hat
- **hazmerreír** *nm* laughing stock
- **risa** *nf* laughter; *¡Qué risa!* How funny! What a laugh!; *estar muerto de risa* to be dying with laughter

reivindicar *vt* -que-, -qué to demand, claim (in that sense); commonly used concerning labour demands, political disputes, etc; cf *reclamar* used in this sense; also 'to vindicate'

- **reivindicación** *nf pl reivindicaciones*

demand, claim; cf *reclamación*

relación *nf pl relaciones* relation(ship) (*con* with) also (useful) 'contacts', 'connections': *tener relaciones* to have contacts

- and 'account', 'story': *hacer una relación de algo* to give an account of sth
- **relacionar** *vt* to relate, connect: *relacionando A con B llegamos a C* linking A and B we arrive at C
- **relacionarse** *vr* to be connected/related (*con algo* with sth): *esto debe relacionarse con su enfermedad* this must be connected to/with his illness; also 'to make contacts'; for 'to be related by family', use *ser pariente (de)*
- **relato** *nm* story, account
- **relatar** *vt* to relate, (tell, report)
- **relativo** *adj* relative (*a* to); NB not noun: for 'relative'/'relation' as member of family, use *pariente*; **relativamente** *adv* relative(ly) (*con* with/to): *relativamente con su peso corre bien* relative to his weight he runs well

relajar *vt* to relax: *relajó su atención* he relaxed his attention

- **relajarse** *vr* to relax, 'unwind'; also 'to decline', 'become lax' (eg morals)
- **relajación** *nf* relaxation (action or state); also 'slackening' (eg of rules, vigilance): *hubo una relajación de las normas* there was a slackening of the rules
- **relajado** *adj/past part* relaxed; **relajante** *adj* relaxing

relevar *vt* to replace, take the place of: *relevó al delantero* he replaced/took the place of the forward

- also, in a fairly formal sense 'to relieve' (*a alguien de algo* sb of sth), ie to take away sth from sb (usually job, function, etc): *le relevó de sus responsabilidades* he relieved him of his responsibilities; for 'take away' in a more everyday sense, see *quitar*

- □ for 'relieve' in sense of 'alleviate', use *aliviar*
- □ **relevante** *adj* outstanding: *tiene unas cualidades relevantes* she has some outstanding qualities; NB for 'relevant', use *pertinente*
- □ **relieve** *nm* relief (in geographical or dimensional sense); *en relieve* in relief; also 'importance', 'prominence': *alguien de relieve* sb important; for relief eg of pain, use *alivio*

rellenar *vt* to stuff (eg turkey, cushion) (*de/con* with); this is an example of *re* used as an intensifier, ie going further than simple *llenar* to fill
- □ also 'to fill in/up/out' (*formulario* form) and 'to refill'
- □ **relleno** *adj* stuffed; also 'plump', 'chubby' (often using *dim rellenito*)

reloj *nm* both 'clock' and 'watch'; context usually distinguishes, but you can be more exact: *reloj de pulsera/bolsillo* wrist/pocket watch; *contra reloj* against the clock; *en el sentido de las agujas del reloj* clockwise; *en dirección contraria a las agujas del reloj* anticlockwise

relucir *vi* pi: *reluzco, reluces*; ps: *reluzca* to shine, glitter; *todo lo que reluce no es de oro* all that glitters isn't gold; similar to *brillar*, not same as base word *lucir*
- □ **reluciente** *adj* shining, glittering, gleaming; *toda la casa estaba limpia y reluciente* the whole house was clean and shining
- □ this group is based on cf *luz*

relumbrar *vi* to shine brightly
- □ **relumbrante** *adj* brilliant, dazzling, glaring: *la luz estaba relumbrante* the light was very bright/dazzling
- □ NB stronger than *relucir* (above) and *brillar*; based on cf *lumbre*
- □ you can also use *deslumbrar/ante* in sense of 'dazzle'/'dazzling'

rematar *vti* to finish off, conclude, end, put finishing touches to; not usually anything to do with *matar*!: *remató la carta con su firma* he finished off the letter with his signature; *la carretera remata en un bosque* the road ends up in a forest
- □ a surprisingly common word which often eludes an easy Eng equivalent
- □ also: (in tennis) 'to smash'; (football) 'to shoot'
- □ **remate** *nm* finishing off/touch, conclusion: *para remate* to crown it all; *poner remate a algo* to put the finishing touches to sth
- □ 'smash', 'shot' (sport)
- □ **rematado** *adj* complete, utter, out-and-out: *es un loco rematado* he's a complete madman

remedio *nm* remedy, cure, solution
- □ occurs in a number of common phrases: *no hay/tiene remedio* there's nothing we can do; *no hay otro/más remedio* there's nothing for it, there's no other way; *no hay más remedio que + inf* there's no other way but to: *no hay más remedio que pagar* there's nothing for it but to pay up
- □ **remediar** *vt* to remedy, cure (*syn curar*), put right (*syn rectificar*): *¿Cómo vamos a remediar el problema?* How are we going to solve/cure the problem?; also 'to avoid': *no podrás remediarlo* you won't be able to help/avoid it

remitir *vt* to send, (rather formal, like 'remit')
- □ also 'to postpone' (same as cf *aplazar, posponer*)
- □ **remitente** *nmf* sender (often abbreviated on back of envelope to *rte*)
- □ **remisión** *nf pl remisiones* act of remitting/sending; also 'postponement' (same as *aplazamiento*); 'remission' (senses as in Eng)

remover *vt -ue-* to stir (up): *remover el líquido* stir the liquid
- □ NOT usually 'remove', use *quitar* in most senses, and possibly cf *relevar*

rendir *vti -i-* to produce, yield: *la tierra rinde poco* the land produces little
- □ also 'to defeat', 'overcome': *rendimos al enemigo* we overcame the enemy; *me rindió el sueño* I was overcome by sleep
- □ and 'perform': *los empleados rinden bien* the employees perform/work well; (NOT in sense of perform eg music): use *tocar* or verb relevant to the activity
- □ NB this verb has a number of idiomatic meanings (more in the dictionary!), but seldom means exactly 'render'!
- □ **rendirse** *vr* to surrender, give up/in (in that sense): *me rendí al sueño* I gave in to sleep
- □ **rendido** *adj/past part* exhausted, all in: use *estar* (similar to cf *agotado*)
- □ **rendimiento** *nm* performance (in sense of the way people/things work/function/achieve): *el rendimiento de los empleados es sobresaliente* the performance of the employees is outstanding also 'yield' (eg of land)
- □ **rendición** nf surrender; NOT 'rendition' (eg of music): use *interpretación*

renta *nf* income; for 'rent', use *alquiler*
- □ **rentable** *adj* profitable; **rentabilidad** *nf* profitability

renunciar *vi* to renounce, give up (*a algo* sth): *renunciar al tabaco* to give up smoking; also 'to resign' (same as cf *dimitir*)
- □ **renuncia** *nf* renunciation, action of giving up (*a* of): *renuncia a la presidencia* renunciation of/resignation from the presidency

reñir *vi -i- ger: riñendo pret: riñó, riñeron imp subj: riñera/riñese* to argue, quarrel,

fall out (*con alguien* with sb)
- □ also *vt* 'to tell off', 'scold': *su padre la riñó por volver tarde a casa* her father told her off for coming home late
- □ **reñido** *adj* hard-fought, tough (in that sense): *un partido reñido* a hard-fought match; also 'on bad terms with': *está reñido con sus compañeros* he's fallen out with his mates

reparar *vt* to repair, fix (you can usually also use cf *arreglar* for machinery)
- □ also 'put right', 'make up for': *he reparado lo del anillo* I've made up for the matter of the ring
- □ **reparar en** *vi* to notice: *¿Has reparado en mi nuevo vestido?* Have you noticed my new dress?; *no había reparado en los cambios* he hadn't noticed the changes; overlap here, depending on exact meaning, with: cf *darse cuenta de* to realise, *observar, notar* to notice, observe, *hacer caso a* to take (any) notice of
- □ **reparación** *nf pl reparaciones* repair; also 'reparation'
- □ **reparo** *nm* reservation, objection: *puso reparos a todo lo que dije* he raised objections to/found fault with everything I said

repartir *vt* to distribute, give out, share out: *repartió los caramelos entre todos* she shared out the sweets amongst everybody (not same as cf *compartir* to share, ie have a share in eg room or use of sth)
- □ also 'to deliver' (eg newspaper), ie to distribute them amongst customers; cf also *entregar* in this sense
- □ no connection with *partir*
- □ **reparto** *nm* distribution: *reparto de premios* distribution of prizes; *reparto a domicilio* home delivery
- □ **repartición** *nf pl reparticiones* share-out: *la repartición de las ganancias* the share-out of profits (overlap with *reparto* in sense of act of sharing out, but not in sense of delivery)

□ **repartidor/a** *nmf* delivery person

repasar *vt* to revise, look over: *repasar los verbos españoles* to revise Spanish verbs; *¿Has repasado tus respuestas?* Have you checked over your answers?
  □ **repaso** *nm* revision, checking

repente occurs as **de repente** *adv* suddenly (same as cf *de pronto*)
  □ **repentino** *adj* sudden (ie happens quickly) (same as cf *súbito* also *inesperado* for unexpected)
  □ **repentinamente** *adv* suddenly

repetir *vt -i-* to repeat (in most senses)
  □ **repetirse** *vr* to repeat oneself; also 'to recur', 'happen again': *la historia se repite* history repeats itself
  □ **repetición** *nf pl repeticiones* repetition
  □ **repetido** *adj/past part* repeated; *repetidas veces* time and time again, over and over again; *tengo este CD repetido* I've got 2 copies of this CD

replicar *vt -que-, -qué* to retort, reply (with some force, much stronger than cf *responder, contestar*)
  □ **réplica** nf retort, reply (force as for verb); also 'replica', 'copy' (in that sense)

reponer *vt* (has all irregularities of *poner*, + *tú imperative: repón*) to put back, replace
  □ also 'to perform action of *poner* again', eg *reponer una película* to rerun/reshow a film (see *poner* for full list of possible phrases)
  □ **reponerse** *vr* to get better, recover; *estar repuesto* to be better, recovered
  □ **reposición** *nf pl reposiciones* (act of) replacement, putting back; also 'rerun', 'repeat' (film, series, etc)
  □ **repuesto** *nm* spare (part): *rueda de repuesto* spare wheel (much the same as cf *recambio*)

reportar *vt* bring (about), produce, yield (in limited sense of): *el sistema reporta*

beneficios/pérdidas the system brings benefits/losses; for 'report', see *informar, denunciar*; suprisingly NOT stem-changing!
  □ **reportaje** *nm* report, article, feature (for media); for 'report' (in education, business etc), use *boletín*
  □ **reportero/a** *nmf* reporter

representar *vt* to represent (in most senses)
  □ also 'to perform', 'put on' eg play: *en el colegio representaron 'La casa de Bernarda Alba'* at school they put on 'La casa de Bernarda Alba'; or 'to play (role of)': *la directora representó a Bernarda* the headmistress played Bernarda
  □ also 'to look' (appear): *no representa 70 años* he doesn't look 70
  □ **representarse** *vr* to imagine, envisage: *tienes que representarte la escena* you must picture/imagine the scene
  □ **representación** *nf pl representaciones* representation; also performance, production (of play etc)
  □ **representante** *nmf* representative: *representante de compañía* company representative
  □ **representativo** *adj* representative, (in sense of) typical: *su obra es representativa de la época* his work is representative of the period
  □ NB take care to distinguish the *noun* from the *adj*

reprimir *vt* to repress
  □ also 'suppress', 'stifle': *reprimió sus lágrimas/su ira/sorpresa* she held back her tears/stifled her anger/surprise
  □ **reprimido/a** *adj* repressed: *un pueblo reprimido* a repressed people; *nmf* repressed person
  □ **represión** *nf pl represiones* repression; also suppression
  □ **represivo** repressive: *régimen represivo* repressive regime

reproducir *vt* (has all irregularities of *producir*) to reproduce (in most senses): *están tratando de reproducir el gene* they are trying to reproduce the gene; *no pudieron reproducir el triunfo del año pasado* they couldn't reproduce/repeat last year's triumph

- **reproducirse** *vr* to reproduce, breed: *se reproducen como unos conejos* they're reproducing/breeding like rabbits; also 'to recur', 'happen again': *para que un desastre de este tipo no se reproduzca* so that a disaster of this kind doesn't happen again
- **reproducción** *nf pl reproducciones* reproduction (all senses)
- **reproductor(a)** *adj* reproductive; *órganos reproductores* reproductive organs; NB NOT *reproductivo*

repugnancia *nf* revulsion, repugnance: *sentir repugnancia por algo* to be revolted by sth, be unable to stand sth, feel disgust for sth; cf *asco*

- **repugnar** *vt* to revolt, disgust: *me repugna su actitud* I find his attitude loathsome; *le repugnan los ratones* he loathes/can't stand mice; NB 'back-to-front' construction (what you loathe 'revolts you'); similar to cf *dar asco*
- **repugnante** *adj* disgusting, revolting: *¡Qué olor tan repugnante!* What a disgusting smell!; cf *asqueroso*

requerir *vt* -ie-, -i- to require: *esta tarea requiere paciencia* this task requires patience; *se requiere repartidor/a de periódicos* newspaper boy/girl required; *requerir que alguien haga algo* to require sb to do sth: *requieren que nos presentemos en persona* they require us to present ourselves in person; overlap with cf *necesitar* need (in this sense), cf *querer* (in sense of 'want', but stronger), but usually not so strong as cf *exigir* (demand)

requerimiento *nm* or more commonly **requisito** *nm* requirement: *hemos cumplido con todos los requisitos* we have fulfilled all the requirements; not used as *adj* – for 'requisite', use *necesario, requerido*, or possibly *adecuado, apto*

resbalar *vi* or **resbalarse** *vr* to slip (up): *(me) resbalé sobre el hielo* I slipped on the ice

- also 'slide'; but usually tends to have more accidental 'feel' than cf *deslizar(se)*
- **resbaladizo** *adj* slippery

reseña *nf* review (of film, book, etc); NOT *revista* which is a magazine

- **reseñar** *vt* to review

reservar *vt* to reserve (in most senses)

- **reserva** *nf* reservation, booking: *quisiera hacer una reserva* I'd like to make a reservation/booking
- also 'reserve': *reservas de energía* reserves of energy; *reserva natural* nature reserve
- *reservas pl* reservations (doubts): *tengo mis reservas* I've got my reservations
- **reservación** *nf pl reservaciones* reservation (frowned upon in Spain, used mainly in Sp Am for 'reservation' meaning 'booking' or 'doubt')

resfriar *vt* -í- resfrío, resfría; resfríe to cool (down), chill: *voy a resfriar las bebidas* I'm going to chill the drinks

- **resfriarse** *vr* to catch a cold/chill
- **resfriado** *nm* chill, cold (in that sense); *coger/pescar un resfriado* to catch a cold; one of several expressions describing the common cold: cf also *catarro, (estar) constipado*

resignarse *vr* to resign oneself (*a + algo* or *inf* to sth or to doing sth)

- **resignado** *adj/past part* estar *resignado a* to be resigned to (as above)

□ **resignación** *nf* resignation: *hacer algo con resignación* to do sth with resignation, resignedly

□ for 'resign/ation' (eg from office), use *dimitir/dimisión*

resistir *vti* to resist (eg temptation, attack, proposal): *la ciudad resistió el ataque* the town resisted/withstood the attack; *no tienen armas para resistir* they don't have the weapons to resist

□ also 'to stand up to', 'tolerate', 'bear': *no resisto el calor de verano* I can't bear/stand the summer heat; same as cf *aguantar* in this sense

□ **resistirse** *vr* to resist (*a algo/alguien* sb/sth): *no me resisto al chocolate* I can't resist chocolate

□ also 'to be reluctant to', 'refuse to': (*a + inf* do sth) *se resiste a firmar* he refuses/is reluctant to sign

□ can also be used in sense of 'cause difficulties': *se me resiste el francés* I can't get on with French; *se le resistía el tornillo* the screw wouldn't give/he couldn't undo the screw

□ **resistencia** *nf* resistance (in most senses); also 'stamina', 'endurance': *prueba de resistencia* test of stamina/endurance

□ **resistente** *adj* resistant (*a* to): *resistente al agua* water-resistant

□ NB Sp -*encia/-ente*, Eng –*ance/-ant*

resolver *vt* -*ue*-; *past part: resuelto* to solve (puzzle, crime, problem etc)

□ also: to resolve, decide (+ *inf* to): *resolvieron marcharse* they decided to leave; much the same as cf *decidir, determinar* in this sense

□ **resuelto** *adj/past part* resolved, decided, determined (*a + inf* to) (use *estar*): *estoy resuelto a hacerlo* I'm resolved/determined to do it; (of person) decisive (use *ser*): *es muy resuelta* she's very decisive

□ **resolución** *nf pl resoluciones* resolution (in most senses); also: decision: *tomar una resolución* to take a decision; and: determination: *hacer algo con resolución* to do sth with determination; also solution (act of solving): *la resolución del problema* the solution of the problem

□ **resoluto** *adj* resolute, determined

respecto *nm* used as *prep: respecto a* with regard to, as regards: *respecto a su pedido* as regards your order; and as *adv al respecto* in this respect, as regards the matter;

□ **respectar** *vt* to concern (only used in sense of eg *en lo que respecta a este asunto* as regards this matter)

□ NB take great care not to confuse the words with -*c*-, above, all meaning 'concern/ing' with those without, below, which involve the feeling of 'respect'

□ **respeto** *nm* respect: *con respeto* with respect; *tener respeto a algo/alguien* to have respect for sth/sb

□ **respetar** *vt* to respect; also used in sense of 'observe', 'obey': *hay que respetar las normas* we have to observe the rules

□ **respetable** *adj* respectable; used also meaning 'considerable', as English: *una cantidad respetable de dinero* a respectable sum of money

□ **respetuoso** *adj* respectful

responder *vi* to answer, reply (*a* to): *no respondieron a mi carta* they didn't reply to my letter; in this sense more or less interchangeable with cf *contestar*

□ also 'respond': *está respondiendo al tratamiento* s/he's responding to the treatment

□ in certain contexts 'to correspond' (*a* to/with): *responder a una descripción* to correspond to a description; *esto no responde a lo que nos dijeron* this doesn't correspond with what we were told

□ **respuesta** *nf* reply, answer (much the same as cf *contestación*); also 'response'

□ **responsable** *adj* responsible (*de* for) (in most senses): *es muy responsable* he's very responsible; *es responsable del bienestar de todos* he's responsible for everyone's wellbeing; *fue responsable del incendio* he was responsible for the fire

□ **responsable** *nmf* person responsible/ in charge: *¿Quién es el responsable?* Who's in charge?

□ **responsabilizar** *vt* -ce-, -cé to hold sb responsible (*de* for)

□ **responsabilizarse** *vr* to be responsible ie admit responsibility (*de* for): *se responsabilizaron del incendio* they were responsible for the fire; also 'to take responsibility for': *se responsabilizaron del cuidado del niño* they took responsibility for the care of the child

□ **responsabilidad** *nf* responsibility (*de* for)

□ NB respons*able* in Sp, responsib*le* in Eng!

resto *nm* rest, remainder, (ie, what's left): much the same as cf *lo/los demás*: *el resto es para ti* the rest is for you

□ **restos** *nmpl* remains: *restos mortales* mortal remains

□ **restar** *vt* to take away (in maths): *restar tres de cinco* to take away three from five

□ sometimes used like cf *faltar/quedar*: *restan dos semanas para la Navidad* only 2 weeks to Christmas

□ **restante** *adj* remaining: *los títulos restantes* the remaining titles

□ NB NEVER means 'rest' in sense of 'repose': see *descansar*

restringir *vt* -jo, -ja- to restrict;
restringirse *vr* to restrict oneself, be restricted (*a* to)

□ **restringido** *adj/past part* restricted, limited

□ **restricción** *nf pl restricciones* restriction

resultar *vi* to result, turn/work out:

siempre resulta así it always works out like that; *resultó que …* it turned out that …; *resultó más difícil de lo que pensábamos* it turned out more difficult than we expected

□ sometimes more or less equivalent of simply *ser* + *adj*: *resultó imposible* it was imposssible; *resultó mejor no hacer nada* it was best to do nothing

□ **resultado** *nm* result; *el resultado fue sorprendente* the result was surprising; NB ending -ado

□ **resultante** *adj* resulting/resultant (used before noun): *el problema resultante* the resultant problem

resumir *vt* to summarise; *en resumidas cuentas* in short, to cut a long story short; NOT 'to resume' (eg an activity), use *reanudar*

□ **resumen** *nm pl* *resúmenes* summary, résumé; *en resumen* in short, to sum up

retener *vt* (has all the irregularities of *tener*, + *tú imperative*: *retén*: NB accent) to retain (in most senses), keep/hold back: *retener información* to hold back information; *retener las llaves* to hold on to the keys

□ also 'to detain' (in most senses); NB cf *detener* means 'stop'

□ **retenerse** *vr* to restrain oneself

□ **retención** *nf* (act of) retention, holding back; also: (act of) detaining, detention

retirar *vt* to move (sth) away: *retiró la mano del volante* he removed his hand from/off the steering wheel; *retiró el papel de la impresora* she removed the paper from the printer: in this sense, some overlap with cf *quitar*, though there may be sometimes a movement back implied

□ also 'withdraw': *el director retiró a dos miembros de la selección* the manager withdrew two members from the team

□ **retirarse** *vr* to move back, withdraw (ie oneself) (*de* from)

□ also 'to retire' (as pensioner), though cf *jubilarse* is more usual

□ **retirada** *nf* withdrawal (most senses); retreat (eg of army)

□ **retiro** *nm* (describes actions of above verbs depending on context) withdrawal, removal: *el retiro de dos miembros del equipo* the withdrawal of two members of the team; also 'retirement': *está en retiro* he's in retirement; *vive en el retiro* he lives in seclusion

retraso *nm* delay (see also *demora*): *un retraso de media hora* half an hour's delay; *el tren lleva media hora de retraso* the train is half an hour late

□ **retrasar** *vt* to delay, make (sb/sth) late: *me retrasó la nieve* I was held up by the snow

□ **retrasarse** *vr* to be late: *se retrasaron dos meses en escribirme* they delayed two months/were two months late in writing to me; also 'to be slow (clock): *tu reloj se retrasa 10 minutos* your clock is 10 minutes slow; NB *¡llegas tarde!* you're late!

□ **retrasado** *adj* backward, retarded (person); *estar retrasado* to be behind (eg in a subject); also (of clock) 'to be slow': *tienes el reloj diez minutos retrasado* your clock is 10 minutes slow

□ cf **atraso/atrasar**

retro- *prefix* has meaning of 'back(wards)', eg: **retrovisor** *nm* driving mirror; **retroproyector** *nm* overhead projector

retroceder *vi* to move back, step back; implies a (maybe involuntary) retreat or recoil rather than a return; so not the same as *volver/regresar*: *retrocedió dos pasos* he moved back two paces

□ **retroceso** *nm* movement backwards; also (economic) recession

reunir *vt pi: reúno, reúnes, reúne, reúnen; ps: reúna* to gather (together), assemble (in that sense): *reunió todos sus argumentos* he assembled all his arguments; *consiguió reunir el dinero necesario* she managed to get together the necessary money; *reunieron a todos sus amigos* they got all their friends together

□ **reunirse** *vr* to gather together, join together, meet (together): *todos se reunieron en el Hotel Asturias* they all met at the Asturias Hotel; *se reúnen así cada año* they meet/gather together like that every year

□ cf *juntar(se)*

□ **reunión** *nf pl reuniones* meeting, gathering: *reunión de usuarios de los trenes* meeting of train users; also: reunion: *reunión de ancianos soldados* old soldiers' reunion

revelar *vt* to reveal

□ also, usefully: to develop (film)

□ **revelación** *nf pl revelaciones* revelation; but **revelado** *nm* development (of film)

□ **revelador** (*reveladora, reveladores, reveladoras*) *adj* revealing

revés *nm* other side/way from point of reference: *al revés* vice versa, the other way round; *al revés del documento* on the back of the document; *al revés de lo que se esperaba* contrary to what was expected; *ponlo al revés* put it the other way round

□ wrong side/way: *llevas el jersey al revés* you've got your pullover on inside out; *llevas los guantes al revés* you've got your gloves the wrong way round/on the wrong hand; *la foto está al revés* the photo is upside down (or the wrong way round – depending on context!); *todo le sale al revés* everything goes wrong/nothing goes right for him

revisar *vt* to check through, look over (eg document): for 'revise', use *repasar* (for eg schoolwork); *cambiar, modificar* for 'alter'/'change'

- □ **revisión** *nf pl revisiones*   check, checking (as above); use *repaso* for school revision, *cambio, modificación* for alteration
- □ also 'check' (inspection): *revisión mecánica*   mechanical inspection, service (of vehicle); *revisión dental* dental inspection/check–up
- □ **revisor/a** *nmf*   inspector, conductor (eg on train)

revolver *vti -ue-, past part: revuelto* basic meaning is 'to move things around', more particularly:

- □ to stir (up): *revolver mientras cuece* stir while it's cooking;
- □ also 'to turn over', 'rummage': *revolvieron todos mis papeles*   they rummaged amongst all my papers; *ese hombre me revuelve las tripas*   that man turns my stomach/makes me sick
- □ NB for 'revolve', use *girar*
- □ **revolverse** *vr*   to squirm, fidget, toss and turn; also 'to turn round' (same as cf *volverse*)
- □ **revuelto** *adj/past part*   in disorder, in a mess: *toda la habitación estaba revuelta*   the whole room was in a mess/turned upside down; *huevos revueltos*   scrambled eggs; there are many further applications, eg rough (sea), restless (character)
- □ **revuelta** *nf*   bend, turn (in road); also 'commotion', 'riot': *revueltas raciales*   race riots
- □ **revoltoso** *adj*   naughty, mischievous (child); can mean 'rebellious'; see also *rebelde* in both these senses
- □ **revolución** *nf pl   revoluciones* revolution (all senses)
- □ **revolucionar** *vt*   to revolutionise
- □ **revólver** *nm*   revolver (NB stress on -ó-!)
- □ there are many more applications of the words in this group: well worth further research in the dictionary!

rey see **reinar**

rezar *vi -ce-, -cé*   to pray (por *algo/alguien* for sth/sb)

- □ also: to read, go: *la descripción reza así* the description reads like this

rico *adj*   rich (often used to compliment food): *¡Qué rica está la sopa!*   this soup is beautiful!

- □ NB use and spelling of superlative: *¡El postre está riquísimo!*   The dessert is very nice!
- □ **riqueza** *nf*   wealth, richness (applies to all senses of *adj*), riches

riesgo *nm*   risk: *correr un riesgo de + inf* to run a risk of –ing; *a/con riesgo de*   at the risk of

- □ see also *arriesgar*   to risk; *arriesgado* risky

rincón *nm pl rincones*   (inside) corner: *estaba sentada en el rincón*   she was sitting in the corner; also used in sense of 'nook', 'niche', 'spot'; *es un rincón precioso*   it's a lovely spot

- □ NB don't confuse with cf *esquina* (outside) corner

rival *adj or nmf*   rival

- □ **rivalidad** *nf*   rivalry; often useful translation of 'competition' (in this sense): *la rivalidad entre los equipos de la liga*   competition between the league teams cf *competencia*
- □ **rivalizar** *vi -ce-, -cé*   to rival, compete (*con* with); *los equipos rivalizan con afán*   the teams complete keenly with each other cf *competir*

robar *vti*   to steal, rob; *robar algo a alguien* steal sth from sb/rob sb of sth: *robaron la cartera al anciano*   they stole the old man's wallet; *robaron el banco*   they robbed the bank

- □ **robo** *nm*   theft, robbery
- □ for 'robber', 'thief', use *ladrón*

rodar *vti -ue-*   to roll, turn (eg wheel); *tráfico rodado*   wheeled traffic; also used figuratively: *rodar por la escalera*   to tumble down the stairs; *ir rodando*   to drift (ie from place to place)

□ also 'to shoot/make a (film)': *la película se rodó en la Sierra Morena* the film was shot in the Sierra Morena

□ **rodaje** *nm* shooting (of film); running in (of motor etc)

□ **rueda** *nf* wheel; *rueda de prensa* press conference

rodilla *nf* knee (related in fact to above group)

□ NB phrases: *(estar) de rodillas* to be kneeling, on one's knees; *ponerse de rodillas* to kneel down; also see: *v arrodillarse*

□ **rodillazo** *nm* blow with the knee; *dar un rodillazo a alguien* to knee sb

rogar *vt -ue-; -gue-, -gué* to beg, request, ask (in that sense): *se ruega* you are requested; + *inf* commonly used on notices: *se ruega no pisar el césped* you are requested not to walk on the grass: also takes *que + subjunc: les rogué que me devolviesen el dinero* I begged them to return my money; *que* is sometimes omitted, especially in formal requests: *les rogamos contesten lo antes posible* we beg you to answer as soon as possible; some overlap with cf *pedir*, but tends to be stronger or more formal

rol *nm* role, part (in that sense): *juego de roles* role-play; purists might argue that cf *papel* is preferable, but *rol* seems to be in quite common use in this sense

rollo *nm* roll (of paper, film, etc)

□ also has a number of meanings in popular speech: *¡Qué rollo!* What a bore/drag!; *sus clases son un rollo* his lessons are a right bore

□ and 'thing', 'business', 'affair': *¿De qué va el rollo?* What's it all about?; *ese rollo de la nueva autopista* that business about the new motorway

□ has further colloquial meanings, especially among the younger generation; worth a further look in the dictionary, but as colloquialisms

can change quite frequently, best to consult an under-25 Sp speaker to check the latest uses!

□ *v is enrollar/arrollar* roll up

□ **rollizo** *adj* chubby, plump

romper *vt past part: roto* to break, smash: *rompí el vaso* I broke the glass

□ *vi* to break (*con alguien* with sb): *ha roto con su novio* she's broken with her boyfriend

□ **romperse** *vr* to break (ie to become broken): *el vaso se rompió* the glass broke; or to break a part of the body: *me he roto el dedo* I've broken my finger

□ also 'to tear (up)': *rompió el papel* he tore up the paper; *me he roto la camisa* I've torn my shirt; *la camisa se rompió* the shirt tore/got torn

□ **roto** *adj/past part* broken (down); torn: *el vaso está roto* the glass is broken; *la camisa está roto* the shirt is torn; *la máquina está rota* the machine is broken down

□ **rompecabezas** *nm inv* puzzle, teaser; **rompeolas** *nm inv* breakwater

□ NB the corresponding noun is **ruptura** *nf* (act of) breaking (off): *ruptura de relaciones* breaking off of relations

□ some overlap with cf the more limited *quebrar(se)* in sense of break physically

ropa *nf* clothes: *ropa interior* underclothes; NB it's *sing* and doesn't mean 'rope'! (for 'rope' use *cuerda, soga*)

rosa *nf* rose; *adj inv* pink: NB doesn't agree with noun: *calcetines (de color) rosa* pink socks, though you can use **rosado** *adj* which does: *pantalones rosados* pink trousers

ruptura see **romper**

ruta *nf* route: *¿Qué ruta tomaron?* Which route did they take?; similar to cf *itinerario* in sense of 'planned route', 'itinerary'; for 'road', use *carretera*

S

S (*ese*) is pronounced similarly to its English equivalent (in 'sausage'), though some speakers in Spain pronounce it from the palate, thus giving it a very faint trace of *sh*.

◆ Before *-b, -d, -m,* and *-n,* it is pronounced like the '-s-' in 'is': *atisbar, desde, mismo, cisne.*

◆ It only occurs double in words of foreign origin, eg *cassette,* and even then the 'native' Castilian adaptation *casete* is often preferred. Some Catalan place names will also have *-ss-: Tossa de Mar.*

saber *vti pi: sé, sabes; ps: sepa, etc; fut/cond: sabré/sabría etc; pret: supe, supiste, supo, supimos, supisteis, supieron; imp subj: supiera/supiese* to know
- used in the sense of 'to be aware of':
- a fact: *¿Sabes la hora?* Do you know the time?
- when, whether, where, that, etc in indirect questions and statements: *no sé cuándo terminaré* I don't know when I'll finish; *no sé si van a llamar* I don't know whether/if they are going to phone; *¿Sabes dónde están mis zapatos?* Do you know where my shoes are?; *sé que no están aquí* I know they are not here
- know how to + verb: often equivalent of Eng 'can' in this sense: *¿Sabes montar a caballo?* Can you (ie do you know how to) ride a horse?
- NB: for to know in the sense of 'be acquainted with' use cf *conocer*
- in preterite often has sense of 'learn', 'find out': *sólo supe ayer que van a casarse* I only learnt/found out yesterday that they are going to get married

- occurs in a number of idioms and colloquial expressions: worth a browse in the dictionary!
- **saber** *nm* or **sabiduría** *nf* knowledge, learning, widom
- **sabio** *adj* learned, wise
- **a sabiendas** *adv* knowingly, wittingly

saber *vi* same irregularities as *saber* to know (above); to taste (*a* of): *sabe a ajo* it tastes of garlic; *sabe mal* it tastes bad
- **sabor** *nm* taste (*a* of): *tenía un sabor a ajo* it had a taste of garlic
- NB for the transitive verb to taste sth (ie try it), use *probar/prueba*; for 'good/bad taste' etc use *gusto*
- **saborear** *vt* to savour; **sabroso** *adj* tasty, delicious

sacar *vt -que-, -qué* to take out, pull out (sth from somewhere)
- used in a variety of common expressions: *sacar entradas* to get tickets; *sacar fotos* to take photos; *sacar la lengua* to stick out one's tongue; *sacar una idea de algún sitio* to get an idea from somewhere; *sacar copias* to make copies; and many more: consult your dictionary!
- **saca-** *prefix* making up compound nouns involved in taking things out: *sacacorchos* corkscrew; *sacamanchas* stain remover; *sacapuntas* pencil-sharpener: all *nm inv*

saco *nm* bag (usually fairly big – see also *bolsa/bolso* shopping, handbag etc); *saco de dormir* sleeping bag; *saco de viaje* travelling bag; also means 'jacket' in Sp Am

sacudir *vt* to shake
- usually fairly vigorously or violently; in sense of 'astonish' use *asombrar, pasmar, dejar atónito*
- **sacudida** *nf* shake, jerk

sal *nf* salt: it's *fem*!
- also 'wit'; **salado** *adj* witty

sala *nf* room, hall
- ◻ ie a big, usually public, room or hall: domestically only used in *sala de estar* living room, lounge; *sala de fiestas* dance hall; *sala de espera* waiting room
- ◻ not usually the same as cf *cuarto, habitación*

salchicha *nf* (individual) sausage; **salchichón** *nm* *pl salchichones* salami-type sausage you slice

salir *vi pi:* salgo, sales, *etc; ps* salga; *tú imperative:* sal; *fut/cond:* saldré/saldría to go/come out, leave (*de* from): *¿A qué hora sales de casa?* At what time do you leave home?
- ◻ *salir a + inf* to go/come out and/to + *verb*: *salió a vernos* he came out to see us/came out and saw us
- ◻ to turn out: *todo salió bien* everything turned out well; *salir caro* to work out expensive
- ◻ to leave (transport): *el tren sale a las dos* the train leaves at two
- ◻ used reflexively, the going out or leaving is intensified: *el avión se salió de la pista* the plane left/ran off the runway; *salirse con la suya* to get one's own way: *¡Siempre te sales con la tuya!* You always get your own way!
- ◻ many more idiomatic uses: consult your dictionary!
- ◻ **salida** *nf* exit, way out (ie the door you go through, but can also be used figuratively): *no hay otra salida* there's no other solution/way out
- ◻ also 'departure': *llegadas y salidas* arrivals and departures
- ◻ **saliente** *adj* salient, sticking out

salón *nm* *pl salones* lounge (but *sala/cuarto de estar* seems to be preferred nowadays); *salón de actos* (school) assembly hall
- ◻ also 'parlour': *salón de belleza* beauty parlour; *juego de salón* parlour game

salsa *nf* sauce; *salsa de tomate* tomato sauce; also used for 'gravy'

saltar *vti* to jump, leap (over): *saltó la valla* he jumped (over) the fence
- ◻ use *sobresaltar* for when sth makes you 'jump' with surprise
- ◻ **salto** *nm* jump, leap: *de un salto* with one jump or 'in a jiffy'; *dar un salto* to jump (with surprise)
- ◻ also, (in sport), 'jump', 'dive': *salto de largo* long jump; *salto de palanca* high dive

salud *nf* health: *estar bien/mal de salud* to be in good/bad health, to be well/unwell; *¡salud!* cheers! often: *¡Salud y pesetas!* Here's to health and wealth!
- ◻ **saludable** *adj* healthy
- ◻ **saludar** *vt* to greet, say hello; at end of formal letters: *le/la saluda atentamente* yours faithfully
- ◻ **saludo** *nm* greeting; often used in letters: *saludos* best wishes; *un saludo cordial* yours sincerely

salvaje *adj* wild: has sense of both 'savage' and 'undomesticated', 'untamed': *animales salvajes* wild animals
- ◻ NB for wild plants use *silvestre: flores silvestres* wild flowers

salvar *vt* to save, rescue (cf *rescatar*)
- ◻ a number of idiomatic uses: *salvar apariencias* to keep up appearances; also 'to clear', 'cross' where there is a challenge or danger: *salvar el río* to cross the river; *salvar los rápidos* to shoot the rapids
- ◻ NB for save money, time, use *ahorrar*
- ◻ **salvación** *nf* salvation (all senses including rescue, cf *rescate*); some overlap with **salvamento** *nm* rescue, but also means 'salvage', 'salvaging'
- ◻ **salva-** *prefix* denotes saving/rescuing in some way: **salvaguarda** *nm* **salvaguardar** *vt* safeguard; **bote salvavidas** *nm* lifeboat; **chaleco**

salvavidas *nm* lifejacket

☐ **salvo** *adj* safe (out of harm's way): *sano y salvo* safe and sound (ie more limited use than cf *seguro*); **a salvo** *adv* safe: *ponerse a salvo* to get out of danger, get somewhere safe

☐ **salvo** *prep* except, save (in that sense): *todos salvo yo* everyone except me; cf *excepto, menos*

☐ **salvo que** *conj* except that (+ *indic*): *vale, salvo que no entiendo* OK, except that I don't understand; unless (+ *subjunc*): *entraré, salvo que me detengan* I'll go in, unless they stop me

sangre *nf* blood: NB it's *fem*!

☐ **sangriento** *adj* bloody: *una guerra sangrienta* a bloody war

☐ **sangrante** *adj* bleeding: *una herida sangrante* a bleeding wound

☐ **sangrar** *vti* to bleed is mainly used transitively, (ie extract blood from a patient), or metaphorically, (to bleed an organisation of money etc); if a wound etc is bleeding, use *echar sangre* or with person as ind obj: *me sangra el dedo* my finger is bleeding

☐ the nearest to the Eng swear word 'bloody' is probably *puñetero*: *¡No me gusta este puñetero libro!* I don't like this bloody book!

sano *adj* healthy, fit, sound (of objects): *ese árbol no parece muy sano* that tree doesn't look very healthy; *esta naranja no está sana* this orange isn't good

☐ **sanidad** *nf* health: tends to be used in 'officialese': *Sanidad Pública* Public Health; for personal health, use *salud*

☐ **sanitario** *adj* sanitary; to do with health

santo *nm* **santa** *nf* saint

☐ NB as a title the *m* abbreviates before singular name to **San**: *San Sebastián, San Pedro* St Sebastian, St Peter; not, however *Santo Domingo* St Dominic

and *Santo Tomás* St Thomas (because of the *Do-/To-*; *San Tomás* would sound like *Santo Más* St More!)

☐ also 'Saint's Day', ie day commemorating the saint whose name you have as your first name: *Juan* would have his Saint's Day on 24 June, *día de San Juan*

☐ *adj* holy: *Semana Santa* Holy Week (often used loosely to refer to what we call Easter, meaning the Easter holiday period); *Viernes Santo* Good Friday

☐ sometimes used colloquially preceding noun, rather like 'blessed' in Eng: *y todo el santo negocio* and the whole blessed business

☐ **santidad** *nf* sanctity, holiness

☐ **santiguarse** *vr* -güe-, -güé- to cross oneself

satélite *nm* satellite

☐ NB stress, and also *televisión vía/por satélite* satellite television; satellite dish is *antena parabólica*

satisfacer *vt* (NB has all the irregularities of cf *hacer*, on which it is based: *pi*: *satisfago, satisfaces*; *ps*: *satisfaga*; *tú imperative*: *satisfaz*; *fut/cond*: *satisfaré/satisfaría*; *past part*: *satisfecho*; *pret*: *satisfice, satisficiste, satisfizo, satisficimos, satisficisteis, satisficieron*; *imp subj*: *satisficiera/satisficiese* to satisfy

☐ **satisfacerse** *vr* to satisfy oneself

☐ **satisfecho** *adj* satisfied; *¿Estás satisfecho?* Are you satisfied?

☐ **satisfacción** *nf* satisfaction; **satisfactorio** *adj* satisfactory

secar *vt* -que-, -qué to dry (sth): *sequé la ropa en el balcón* I dried the clothes on the balcony; **secarse** *vr* to dry, ie become dry: *la ropa se secaba en el balcón* the clothes were drying on the balcony

☐ also: to wipe, where this action involves drying: *se secó los ojos* she wiped/dried her eyes; see also less used *enjugar*, where 'wipe' means 'clean', use *limpiar(se)*

- □ **seco** *adj* dry; mainly used with *estar*: *la ropa está seca* the clothes are dry, unless describing eg personal characteristic with meaning of 'disagreeable': *¡qué seco es!* how disagreeable he is; *en seco* sharply, abruptly: *parar en seco* to stop suddenly

- □ **secamente** *adj* drily; but also 'abruptly', 'curtly'

- □ NB **secador** *nm* drier: *secador de pelo* hair dryer: **secadora** *nf* clothes drier

- □ **secante** *nm* blotting paper

- □ **sequedad** *nf* dryness

- □ **sequía** *nf* drought

sed *nf* thirst

- □ NB *tener mucha sed* to be very thirsty (*mucha* because *sed* is a noun)

- □ **sediento** *adj* thirsty: don't use it in everyday language; mainly literary: *el desierto sediento* the thirsty desert; *sediento de conocimientos* thirsty for knowledge

seducir *vt pi: seduzco seduces; ps: seduzca; pret: seduje, sedujiste, sedujo, sedujimos, sedujisteis, sedujeron; imp subj: sedujera/sedujese* to seduce, but has a wider sense than the amorous: 'to charm', 'captivate', (eg an audience); *sedujo al público* she captivated the audience

seguir *vti -i-: -go, -ga-: pi sigo, sigues; ps siga, sigas; ger siguiendo; pret siguió, siguieron; imp sub siguiera/siguiese* to follow

- □ can be used transitively, in sense of 'pursue': *seguimos el coche* we followed the car; and intransitively, in sense of 'comes next': *lea lo que sigue* read what follows

- □ also 'to continue', 'carry on' (alternative to cf *continuar*), followed

by *ger*, not *inf*: *siguieron hablando* they continued/carried on talking

- □ and 'to be still', 'continue to be' (in condition or circumstance): *si sigues así la semana que viene* if you are still like this next week; often used with *sin + noun* or *inf* meaning 'to still be without', 'still not have': *sigo sin dinero; sigo sin recibir dinero* I still haven't (received) any money; *seguimos sin saber lo que va a pasar* we still don't know what's going to happen

- □ *sigue* (in book, paper, etc) continued, (on page) PTO; *seguir adelante* to go on, continue (ie progress, journey)

- □ 'to follow by' is usually *seguir de: sopa, seguida de pescado* soup, followed by fish

- □ **en seguida** *adv* at once, immediately; cf *al instante*, *inmediatamente*

- □ **siguiente** *adj* following, next (in that sense): *al día siguiente* on the next day; cf *próximo*; *y luego escribió lo siguiente* and then he wrote the following

según *prep* according to: *según mi profesor* according to my teacher

- □ can also be used as *conj* in sense of 'depending on', 'according to how/ whether/what': *según te lo expliquen* according to how they explain it to you; *según reaccione* depending on how s/he reacts; *según me dijeron* according to what they told me; NB *+ subjunc* if action has not yet taken place, otherwise *indic*

- □ and as *adv* to mean 'it depends' (in response to a choice of options): *¿Estás a favor? – ¡Según!* – Are you in favour? – It all depends!

segundo *adj* and *nm* second

- □ NB **secundario** *adj* secondary

seguro *adj* safe, secure (use *estar*): *estamos*

seguros aquí we're safe here; *un sitio seguro* a safe/secure place

- also 'sure', 'certain'; (much the same as cf *cierto*) (use *estar*): *¿Estás seguro?* Are you sure?; *estoy seguro de que no lo sabe* I'm sure he doesn't know

- also 'sure' in sense of 'firm', 'trustworthy' (use *ser*): *un amigo seguro* a firm friend; *una superficie segura* a firm/steady surface; *es seguro* he's reliable

- as *nm* insurance: *seguro de viaje* travel insurance

- **seguridad** *nf* safety, security: *cinturón de seguridad* safety belt; also 'certainty', 'sureness' (cf *certeza*): *en la seguridad de que …* in the certainty that …

- **seguramente** *adv* surely (used much same as Eng) *seguramente nos lo van a decir* they're surely going to tell us

- 'safely' is often better rendered by eg *con seguridad, sin peligro,* depending on exact context

seiscientos *adj* six hundred

- remember! it's all one word and agrees with noun: *seiscientas flores* 600 flowers

selección *nf pl selecciones* selection, choice

- can also mean in sporting parlance: team, side: *la selección italiana* the Italian team

- **seleccionar** *vt* to select, choose (similar to cf *escoger, elegir*)

- **selectivad** *nf* university entrance exam; (besides 'selectivity', of course)

selva *nf* forest, wood

- implication is usually larger and maybe wilder than cf *bosque*; *selva tropical* rainforest

- also: jungle; cf *jungla*

semáforo *nm* traffic light (only for traffic): for other types of light see *luz, lumbre, lámpara, farol, farola*

semana *nf* week; *entre semana* midweek, during the week

- **semanal** *adj* weekly; **semanario** *adj* or *nm* weekly (paper or magazine)

semejante *adj* similar (a to), alike: *su casa es semejante a la nuestra* their house is similar to ours; *nuestras casas son muy semejantes* our houses are very similar/very much alike; cf *parecido, similar*

- such (a): *en mi vida he visto cosa semejante* never in my life have I seen such a thing; cf *tal*

- **semejanza** *nf* similarity, resemblance (*con* to/with): *tiene cierta semejanza con mi hermana* she has a certain resemblance to my sister

- **semejarse a** *vr* to resemble, be like: *se asemeja a mi hermana* she's like my sister

sencillo *adj* simple

- plain/uncomplicated, or easy: *un diseño sencillo* a simple (plain) design; *un problema sencillo* a simple (easy) problem

- single (as opposed to double or multiple); *una flor sencilla* a single flower

- NB not exactly the same as cf *simple*

- **sencillez** *nf* simplicity (ie plainness or straightforwardness)

sendos *adj pl* one each

- the following examples will help to explain how this very idiomatic – and quite useful – word works (NB it agrees with the object that sb or sth has one each of): *les envió sendas cartas* he sent them a letter each; *llegaron en sendas bicicletas* each one arrived on a bicycle; *había tres casas con sendos jardines* there were three houses, each with a garden

sentar *vti -ie-* to sit/seat (sb/sth somewhere)

- also 'to suit', 'agree with' (in that

sense): *ese vestido no te sienta bien* that dress doesn't suit you; *los mejillones no me sientan bien* mussels don't agree with me

- **sentarse** *vr* to sit down: *¡siéntese!* sit down
- NB difference between the reflexive verb *sentarse*, which means 'sit <u>down</u>', (ie getting into a sitting position), and *estar sentado/a*, which means 'to be sitting', (ie already in a sitting position).
- NB also use of *past part*, which agrees with the sitter(s): *estábamos sentados en el sofá* we were sitting on the settee
- NB 'to sit <u>up</u>' is *incorporarse!*

Senses and feelings

NB pay particular attention to these sense and feeling words which are all based on *sentir*, can have rather unexpected meanings and don't necessarily coincide with their apparent Eng equivalents!

sentir *vt* to feel; its basic meanings is 'to sense'

- 'feel' (used for feeling through the human senses, although *tocar, palpar* are often used for 'feel' by touch); *sentir el calor* to feel the heat; *sentir los perfumes del crepúsculo* to feel/smell the twilight scents; *sentir el ruido del trueno* to hear the noise of thunder
- 'to be sorry for': *siento las dificultades que he causado* I'm sorry for the difficulties I've caused; *sentimos no habérselo dicho* we're sorry we didn't tell you; when you don't state what you are sorry for, use *lo siento* I'm sorry (more strongly felt than cf *¡perdón!*)
- **sentirse** *vr* to feel + *adj* or *adv*: *no me siento bien* I don't feel well; *me siento indefensa* I feel defenceless
- **sentido** *nm* sense
- bodily senses: *el sentido de la visión* sense of vision; *sentido del humor*

sense of humour; *sentido de la dirección* sense of direction; *perder el sentido* to lose consciousness

- judgement: *sentido común* common sense
- meaning: *en el sentido de* in the sense of
- direction: *sentido único* one-way street; *en el sentido opuesto* in the opposite direction
- **sentimiento** *nm* sentiment, feeling, esp emotional: *sentimiento del deber* feeling of duty
- regret: in this sense it is the noun for the 'sorry' meaning of *sentir*: *lo hacemos con un profundo sentimiento* we are doing it with deep regret

sensación *nf pl sensaciones* sensation

- in most senses, ie, 'feeling', 'feel': *una sensación de miedo* a feeling/ sensation of fear, and also 'success', 'big impression': *¡Serás una sensación!* You'll be a sensation!
- **sensacional** *adj* sensational; **sensacionalismo** *nm* sensationalism
- **sensato** *adj* sensible (ie showing good sense); **sensatez** *nf* sense (ie good sense)
- **sensible** *adj* sensitive (*a* to): *es muy sensible a la crítica* s/he's very sensitive to criticism; also noticeable, (ie which can be felt): *una subida sensible de precios* a noticeable rise in prices
- NB NOT 'sensible'/having good sense: see *sensato* immediately above
- **sensiblemente** *adv* perceptibly, appreciable; **sensibilidad** *nf* sensitivity
- **sensual** *adj* sensual, sensuous

Warning: 'feeling' can therefore be *sensación, sentido,* or *sentimiento* – read these definitions before you decide which is the best Sp word!

seña *nf* mark, sign, indication: often used in *pl*: *señas* address (same as cf *dirección*); *señas personales* personal description

- **señal** *nf* sign, signal: *hacer una señal con la mano* to wave, signal with the hand
- also 'mark', 'trace': *desaparecer sin dejar señal* to leave without leaving a trace
- and 'traffic sign': *¡atención a las señales!* watch out for the signs!
- there is some overlap between *seña* and *señal*, though you use *señal* for a sign that is actively made, whereas *seña* is a mark or sign that occurs more naturally, is just 'there'
- **señalar** *vt* to mark, denote: *eso señala un cambio de dirección* this denotes a change in direction
- to point to/out, indicate: *el guía señaló las ruinas* the guide pointed to/out the ruins (cf *indicar*)
- **señalado** *adj* notable, special: *fue un éxito señalado* it was a notable success; **señaladamente** *adj* especially, clearly, plainly

señor *nm* gentleman (more formal and polite than cf *hombre*): *este señor quisiera hablarle* this gentleman would like to talk to you

- can mean 'owner', 'master': *el señor de la propiedad* the owner of the property
- Lord: *nuestro Señor Jesucristo* our Lord Jesus Christ
- Mr: *el señor González* Mr González; NB use of article except when speaking directly to the person; also used for politeness with other titles: *(el) señor médico* the doctor; *(el) señor Presidente* Mr President
- sir: *buenos días, señor* good morning, sir; *Muy señor mío* Dear Sir (in letter)
- **señora** *nf* lady (more formal and polite than cf *mujer*): *la señora de la casa* the lady of the house
- also 'wife', (esp of other people's wives): *no conozco a su señora* I

don't know your wife

- Mrs: *la señora (de) González* Mrs González (the *de* is rather old-fashioned); *señora Presidenta* Madam President (when addressing her)
- madam: *buenas tardes, señora* good afternoon, madam; *Muy señora mía* Dear Madam (in letter)
- **señorita** *nf* young lady (up to about mid-twenties)
- 'Miss', but does not refer directly to unmarried status, and not used for mature women: safer to use *señora!*; because of this the modern blurring of the Miss/Mrs distinction by using Ms is not necessary; increased informality in Sp has in any case meant a decrease in recent years in the use of these titles
- **señorito** *nm* young gentleman, (but careful, it is not the direct equivalent of the *f señorita*, as it tends to have a derogatory meaning of 'rich kid')

septiembre *nm* September

- can be spelt *setiembre*; in any case, the *p* is silent

serio *adj* serious, grave (as English)

- also 'proper', 'dignified', 'formal': *un traje serio* a formal suit; *poco serio* unreliable, undignified; *en serio* seriously, in earnest: *ahora trabajamos en serio* now we're working in earnest; cf *grave*, which is preferable when the meaning is 'grave'
- **seriamente** *adv* seriously (all above senses)
- **seriedad** *nf* seriousness (all senses: gravity, formality, earnestness, reliability)

servir *vti -i-* to serve (in most Eng senses)

- to be of use: *¿Para qué sirve esto?* What's the use of this? What's this used for?; *esto no sirve (para nada)* this is no good (for anything)
- **servirse** *vr* to serve/help oneself: *¡Sírvase!* Help yourself! *¡Sírvanse*

Vds! Help yourselves!

- □ *servirse de algo* to use/make use of sth: *suelo servirme de esta máquina* I often make use of this machine; (similar to cf *aprovecharse*)
- □ *+ inf:* be kind enough to: *sírvase contestar cuanto antes* please/be kind enough to reply as soon as possible
- □ **servicio** *nm* service (in most Eng senses); also 'toilet', 'loo'

sesión *nf pl sesiones* session

- □ but also (in theatre, cinema) 'performance', 'showing': *sesión de noche* late-night performance

seso *nm* brain; (in cookery) *sesos* brains; common but less formal or clinical alternative to *cerebro*

- □ **sesudo** *adj* brainy, intelligent, wise

setecientos *adj* seven hundred

- □ NB *sete-* (not *siete-*), and it agrees with its noun: *setecientas casas*

si *conj* if (NB no accent)

sí *adv* yes (NB with accent)

- □ can also be used to give affirmative emphasis: *ellos no quieren pero nosotros sí* they don't want to but we *do; creo/pienso que sí* I think so; *eso sí que no* no way!, certainly not! certainly not! *¡Que sí! ¡Que no!* Oh yes (it is)! Oh no (it isn't); *¡Yo sí que voy!* I certainly am going!
- □ *dar el sí* to say yes, consent
- □ worth some dictionary research into further expressions

sí *pers pron* (NB also with accent) oneself; himself; herself; yourself (*Vd*); themselves; yourselves (*Vds*); this is the reflexive form of the disjunctive pronoun; see a grammar for full explanation

siempre *adv* always: *como siempre* as usual; *para siempre* for ever

- □ **siempre que** *conj* (+ *indic*)

whenever (in sense of 'always when'): *siempre que te llamo te estás duchando* whenever I phone you you're having a shower

- □ (+ *subjunc*) provided that: *siempre que sepas lo que estás haciendo* provided you know what you are doing

significar *vt* -que-, -qué to mean, signify: *¿Qué significa esto?* What does this mean?; *significa que no tenemos dinero* it means we haven't got any money (same meaning as cf *querer decir*)

- □ **significado** *nm* meaning, significance (much preferred to less common *significación*)
- □ **significativo** *adj* significant, meaningful: *un gesto significativo* a meaningful gesture

signo *nm* sign, symbol (eg mathematical): *signo de menos* minus sign

- □ not same as cf *seña*, some overlap with cf *señal: el signo/la señal de la cruz* the sign of the cross

silbar *vti* to whistle, hiss; to boo (in theatre etc)

- □ **silbido** or **silbo** *nm* whistle, whistling (ie sound)
- □ **silbato** *nm* whistle (ie instrument)

silencio *nm* silence

- □ **silencioso** *adj* silent (NOT *silente!*); **silenciar** *vt* to silence; **silenciador** *nm* silencer

sillón *nm pl sillones* armchair; largely the same as cf *butaca*

similar *adj* similar; cf also *parecido, semejante*

- □ NB *n* is **similitud** similarity

simpatía *nf* not really 'sympathy' …

- □ liking, affection: NB *tener simpatía por/hacia* to have a liking/affection for: *tiene una gran simpatía por su hijo* she has a great affection for her son: but *tener mucha simpatía* to be likeable; and *tener simpatías*   to be liked: *no tengo muchas simpatías por aquí*   I'm not much liked around here

- charm, attractiveness, warmth: *es una persona con mucha simpatía*   she's a warm-hearted person

- support, solidarity: *por simpatía mutua*   by mutual solidarity

- in sense of 'pity' use *compasión*; and for conveying sympathy (after bereavement etc) use *dar el pésame*

- **simpático** *adj*   NOT sympathetic, but expresses the various qualities of *simpatía*, above; nice, pleasant, congenial (especially of people): *¡Qué profesora tan simpática!*   What a nice teacher!

- **simpatizar** *vi -ce-, -cé*   to get on well (*con alguien*   with sb)

- for 'sympathise with' use *compadecerse con*

- **simpatizante** *nmf*   sympathiser (*de* with)

simple *adj*   simple, uncomplicated, plain (cf *sencillo*)

- also 'sheer', 'mere', 'pure' (in that sense): *por simple codicia*   through sheer/pure greed; cf *puro*

- and 'just an ordinary': *soy un simple profesor*   I'm just an ordinary teacher; cf *corriente*

- and 'simple-minded', 'gullible'

- not, therefore a straight *syn* of cf *sencillo*

- **simpleza** *nf* simple-mindedness; also 'trifle', 'little thing': *se inquieta por cualquier simpleza*   he gets worried over any little thing; NOT simplicity, which is **simplicidad** *nf* from this root, or better cf *sencillez* above

- **simplificar** *vt -que-, -qué*   to simplify; **simplificación** *nf pl simplificaciones*   simplification

sin *prep*   without

- normally occurs without indef art: *sin sombrero*   without a hat; if indef

art is used, it is usually with *solo* and means 'without one single …': *sin una sola peseta*   without a single peseta

- used + *inf* to mean 'without …ing': *sin esperar*   without waiting; this can often be used for Eng 'un- + past part', sometimes after *estar* or *quedar*: *película sin revelar* undeveloped film; *el problema quedó sin resolver*   the problem remained unresolved

- *sin que* + *subjunc*   without (sb/sth) …ing: *sin que me viesen*   without them seeing me (see a grammar for full explanation)

siniestro *adj*   sinister, ominous

- but also as *nm* disaster, catastrofe: *siniestro aéreo*   air disaster

sino *conj*   but

- NB used when contradicting a negative statement: *no habrá coches sino peatones*   there won't be cars but pedestrians; *no unos pocos sino miles*   not a few but thousands

- use *sino que* with following clause: *no hay remedio sino que lo hagamos nosotros*   there's no other way but to do it ourselves

- also means 'except', 'bar' (in that sense): *nadie sino yo*   no-one except/bar me

síntoma *nm*   symptom: NB spelling and it's *masc* !

sinvergüenza *nmf*   rogue, rotter, shameless person (either gender)

siquiera *adv*   at least: *déjame invitarte siquiera*   at least let me treat you

- more often used negatively: **ni siquiera, ni … siquiera**   not even: *ni siquiera me hablaron* or *ni me hablaron siquiera*   they didn't even speak to me

- whether … or … (+ *subjunc*): *siquiera me quiera, siquiera no me quiera* whether he loves me or whether he doesn't love me

sistema *nm* system, method; NB it's *masc*!

sitio *nm* place
- NB its use as equivalent of Eng '... -where' words: *a/en algún sitio* somewhere; *a/en cualquier sitio* anywhere; *a/en ningún sitio* nowhere (cf same use of *parte*)
- also 'space', 'room' (in that sense): *no hay sitio para eso* there's no room for that
- and 'job', 'post' (in that sense): *por fin encontré un sitio (de trabajo)* at last I found a job: cf *puesto*
- and 'siege'
- **situación** *nf pl situaciones* situation, position: *la situación de la mujer* the position of women
- **situar** *vt* -ú-: *sitúo, sitúas; sitúe* to situate, place: *situaron el nuevo edifico en las afueras* they situated the new building in the suburbs; similar to cf *ubicar, localizar*
- **situarse** *vr* to be situated; sometimes used for **estar situado**: *se sitúa/está situado en las afueras* it's situated in the suburbs; cf *ubicarse, localizarse*
- can also mean 'to get a good position' (eg in work)

soberbio *adj* proud, haughty, arrogant
- **soberbia** *nf* pride, haughtiness, arrogance
- perhaps emphasises haughtiness more than cf *orgullo, orgulloso*

sobra *nf* this noun and its associated words carry the idea of excess, surplus:
- mainly used in **de sobra** spare, over (in that sense): *tenemos dos botellas de sobra* we've got two bottles over/to spare; *hay comida de sobra* there's plenty of food/food to spare; *estamos de sobra* we're superfluous; *las sobras* the leftovers (of meal)
- **sobrar** *vi* to be in excess, to be left over, to be spare (it works like *gustar,*

ie the indirect object is the person or thing that has the excess, and what is in excess is the subject): *le sobra dinero* he's got too much/heaps of money; *le sobra energía* he's got spare energy/energy to spare; *nos sobran diez botellas* we've got 10 bottles left over/too many
- **sobrado** *adj* more than enough, superfluous: *tenemos comida sobrada* we've got more than enough/ample food; *estamos sobrados de ayuda* we've plenty of help
- **sobradamente** *adv* amply, too (much, well): *saber sobradamente* to know only too well
- **sobrante** *adj* over, to spare (similar to *sobrado* above): *comida sobrante* leftovers; also 'redundant': *plantilla sobrante* redundant staff; and *nm* redundant worker

sobre *prep* on, over, on top of: *sobre el agua* on/over the water; *sobre la mesa* on/over the table; *sobre todo esto* on top of all this; for 'on' cf *en*; for 'over' cf *encima de*
- also 'about' (approximately) *sobre las ocho* at about 8 o'clock
- and 'about', 'on' (concerning): *un libro sobre España* a book on/about Spain
- and 'out of' (in eg exam or as proportion): *ocho sobre diez* 8 out of 10
- *nm* envelope

sobre- *prefix* equivalent to 'over-', 'sur-', 'super-': *sobrecargar* to overload or to surcharge; *sobreabundancia* superabundance

sobresalir *vi* *sobresalgo, sobresales; sobresalga; tú imperative: sobresal; sobresaldré/ía* to stand out, project
- **sobresaliente** *adj* outstanding, excellent; projecting; *nm* outstanding mark (in school/university): *sacar un sobresaliente* to get top marks

sobrevivir *vi* to survive

- □ always + *a algo/alguien: sobrevivió a su hermano* he survived his brother: *sobrevivió al desastre* he survived the disaster
- □ **sobreviviente** or **superviviente** *nmf* survivor; *adj* surviving

sociedad *nf* society

- □ also (commercial) 'company'; *Sociedad Anónima* (abb *SA*) limited (Ltd)
- □ **socio** *nmf* member (of club, society etc)

socorro *nm* help

- □ suggests greater necessity and commitment than the general *ayuda*; used when the person helped is in difficulties or distress: *¡Socorro!* Help!
- □ **socorrer** *vt* to help (when eg in distress, more specific than *ayudar*)
- □ **socorrido** *adj* helpful, obliging (person)
- □ NB also: **socorrismo** *nm* lifesaving; **socorrista** *nmf* lifeguard

sofá *nm* sofa, settee: NB it's *masc*!

sol *nm* sun: *hacer (mucho) sol* to be (very) sunny (*mucho* because *sol* is a noun); *tomar el sol* to sunbathe

- □ **soleado** *adj* sunny: *una terraza soleada* a sunny terrace

soler *vi* -ue- to be accustomed to, to usually do

- □ use mainly confined to *pres* and *imperf indic* and *subjunc*
- □ used + *inf* to express habitual actions in the present or past, giving the habitualness a shade more emphasis than the pure present or imperfect: *suelo oír la radio por la mañana* I usually listen to the radio in the morning; *no suelo beber alcohol* I don't usually drink/I'm not in the habit of drinking alcohol; *solíamos ir a verla los domingos* we used to go and see her on Sundays

solicitar *vt* to ask for, request

- □ NB *solicitar un puesto (de trabajo)* to apply for a job
- □ **solicitud** *nf* care, concern, solicitude: *hacer algo con solicitud* to do sth with care, concern; also (job) application
- □ **solícito** *adj* careful, solicitous, concerned (*por* for): *estaba muy solícita por mi salud* she was very concerned about my health
- □ **solicitante** *nmf* applicant (for job); for 'solicitor' use *abogado, notario*

solo *adj* alone, by oneself: *¿estamos solos?* Are we alone?; *lo terminó sola* she finished it by herself; *estar a solas* to be by oneself

- □ also 'lonely', 'alone' (in that sense): *me sentí muy solo* I felt very lonely
- □ and 'single', 'sole': *no tiene ni una sola idea en la cabeza* he hasn't a single idea in his head; *queda un solo problema* one single problem remains
- □ as *nm* solo (in eg music)
- □ **sólo** (NB with accent) or **solamente** *adv* only: *sólo/solamente tenemos diez minutos* we only have ten minutes; *sólo/solamente tienes que preguntar* you only have to ask; at end of phrase for emphasis use *solamente: hay diez solamente* there are only ten, there are ten only (cf *(no) más que/de* under *más*)

> So take care: **solo** is an *adj* and **sólo** is an *adv*!

- □ **soledad** *nf* solitud, loneliness
- □ **solitario** *adj* solitary, lonely: *una casa solitaria* a solitary/lonely house; *nos sentíamos muy solitarios* we were feeling very lonely

soltar *vt* -ue- to let go of, loose, loosen, undo, unfasten

- □ quite a range of uses, involving undoing, loosening or slackening

things that are done up or tight: *soltar un nudo, una hebilla, el freno, una cuerda, etc:* to loosen/slacken a knot, a buckle, the brake, a rope, etc; in this sense it is often the opp of cf *apretar*
- also 'to release', 'let loose', 'let out': *soltaron a los presos* they let the prisoners go; *soltaron los animales que habían cogido* they let go the animals they had caught; *¡suéltame!* let me go!, let go of me!
- and 'to let out' (often an expression of emotion, eg a laugh): *soltó una carcajada* he let out a laugh; *soltó un taco* he uttered a swear word
- **soltarse** *vr* to come undone, untied, etc, break/work loose, ie intransitive version of most of the above meanings: *los cordones se soltaron* the laces worked loose, came undone
- **suelto** *adj* free, loose, unattached, detached (the adjective describing the state achieved by the above actions, best illustrated by some examples): *un tornillo suelto* a loose screw; *páginas sueltas* loose pages, or separate pages (ie detached from whole book); *un vestido suelto* a loose(-fitting) dress; *andar suelto* to be on the loose; *caramelos sueltos* loose sweets (ie not in packet); *suelto de lengua* cheeky, tending to answer back; also 'free', 'fluent': *estar suelto en español* to be fluent in Spanish
- **soltura** *nf* looseness, slackness, *con soltura* fluently
- all these words are worth further research in the dictionary!

soltero/a *nmf & adj* single man/woman, single
- *apellido de soltera* maiden name; *madre soltera* single mother; *padre soltero* single father, single parent, although *madre soltera* would be used if the parent were known to be female

- normally used with *ser: soy soltero* I'm single, I'm a bachelor; but if the singleness of the person's situation or the result of an event is emphasised, use *estar: como estoy soltera* since I'm single
- related to *soltar/suelto* above, ie someone 'unattached'

solución *nf pl soluciones* solution (in all senses)
- **solucionar** *vt* to solve (useful regular alternative to cf *resolver!*)

sombra *nf* shade; shadow
- **sombrear** *vt* to shade, give shade; **sombreado** *adj* shady: *un sitio sombreado* a shady spot; not same as **sombrío** *adj* sombre, dismal, gloomy (place or person)
- also origin of **sombrero** *nm* hat (in Sp situation your head needs protection from the sun rather than the cold and rain!)

someter *vt* to conquer (eg a country); to submit (to present report etc)
- **someterse** *vr* to give in, surrender; also 'to undergo': *someterse a un tratamiento* to undergo a treatment
- **sometimiento** *nm* also has both meanings of submission, ie giving in, or presentation (eg of article, speech)

son *nm* sound (in general, of any kind)
- **sonido** *nm* sound, sounding; ringing (quite a lot of overlap, but not always same as *son* above, often the result of *v sonar* below: *el sonido de la alarma* the sound of the alarm; *el sonido del agua contra el rompeolas* the sound of the water against the breakwater; *el sonido de la trompeta* the sounding (ie actual playing) of the trumpet (cf *me gusta el son de la trompeta* I like the sound of the trumpet – ie the habitual noise it makes)
- **sonar** *vti -ue-* to sound; to ring,

212

strike (clock): *¿Ha sonado el timbre?* Has the bell rung/gone?; *si suena el teléfono …* if the phone rings …; *estaban sonando las doce* it was striking 12

- also 'sound familiar': *me suena* it sounds familiar; and 'sound right': *me suena bien* it sounds all right to me
- *sonarse las narices* to blow one's nose
- **sonoro** *adj* sonorous, loud, but also (to do with) sound: *banda sonora* soundtrack

sonreír *vi* to smile

- like *reír*, it's a group 3 stem change, though it looks more complicated: *sonrío, etc; sonría, etc; sonriendo; sonrió, sonrieron; sonriera/sonriese*
- *sonreír a alguien* to smile at (ie directly at) sb; *sonreír de algo* to smile at (ie about) sth
- **sonriente** *adj* smiling
- **sonrisa** *nf* smile

soñar *vti* -ue- to dream

- NB *soñar con alguien/algo* or + *inf* to dream of sb/sth/-ing: *siempre sueño contigo/con un coche deportivo/con ir a Sudamérica* I'm always dreaming of you/of (having) a sports car/of going to South America
- **soñoliento** *adj* sleepy, drowsy; but for 'to feel sleepy' see *sueño* below
- **soñado** *adj* dreamed-of: *ya tiene su soñado coche deportivo* he's now got his much dreamed-of sports car
- **sueño** *nm* sleep: *le hace falta mucho sueño* he needs a lot of sleep; *(no) conciliar el sueño* (not) to get to sleep
- also 'sleepiness': *tener sueño* to feel/be sleepy
- and 'dream': *es mi sueño + inf* it's my dream to + *verb*; *¡ni en sueños!* no way!, not on your life!

soplar *vti* to blow

- has slang meaning of 'to charge',

'sting': *me soplaron un montón de dinero* they stung me for a mound of money; also 'to nick': *le soplaron el monedero* they nicked her purse

soportar *vt* to bear, endure, tolerate (in that sense); cf *aguantar: no lo soporto más* I'm not putting up with it/I can't stand it any more

- can mean support in sense of 'physically hold up', but in sense of 'lend support to' better to use *apoyar*
- **soportable** *adj* bearable, tolerable; NB frequently used neg *insoportable* (see frame p.110) unbearable, intolerable

sordo *adj* deaf

- but NB also used to describe a noise as it might sound to a person with impaired hearing: 'muffled', 'dull': *un ruido sordo* a muffled/dull noise; NOT a deafening one, use *ensordecedor;* also describes pain: *un dolor sordo* a dull pain (as opposed to eg *agudo* sharp)
- **ensordecer** *vt* -zc- to deafen; **ensordecerse** *vr* to go deaf; **ensordecedor/a** *adj pl* -edores, -edoras deafening (see also frame on p.81)

sorprender *vt* to surprise: *no me sorprende* it doesn't surprise me (much overlap with cf *extrañar;* perhaps not quite as strong as cf *asombrar*)

- also 'take by surprise', 'catch' (in that sense): *me sorpendiste planchando* you caught me ironing
- **sorprenderse** *vr* to be surprised (*de* at): *no me sorprendo de eso* I'm not surprised at that
- **sorprendiente** *adj* surprising
- **sorpresa** *nf* surprise

sosegar *vt* **sosegarse** *vr* -ie-; -gue-, -gué to calm (down); much same as cf *calmar; sosegar temores* to calm/allay fears

- **sosiego** *nm* calm(ness); cf *calma*

soso *adj* insipid, dull (applied to food, places, people)

sospechar *vti* to suspect
- **sospecha** *nf* suspicion: *tengo mis sospechas* I've got my suspicions
- **sospechoso** *adj* suspicious, suspect (NB used in sense of 'causing suspicion'): *es muy sospechoso* he's very suspect/suspicious
- in sense of 'to feel suspicion/ suspicious about' use *v sospechar de, recelarse de,* or *tener sospechas acerca de* and *adj receloso*
- **sospechoso/a** *nmf* suspect: *han arrestado a los sospechosos* they have arrested the suspects

sostener *vt* (has all the irregularities of *tener* + *tú imperative: sostén*) to support, sustain
- support, hold up: *estas columnas sostienen el edificio* these pillars support the building; some overlap with cf *soportar*
- sustain, keep sb going: *tu presencia me sostiene* your presence keeps me going; *estos bocadillos nos sostendrán hasta la cena* these sandwiches will keep us going until supper
- NB fills a number of the roles of Eng 'maintain', 'keep up': *sostuvo su promesa* he kept his promise; *hay que sostener la presión* you've got to keep up/maintain the pressure; *el testigo sostenía que tenía razón* the witness maintained that he was right; cf *mantener*
- **sostenerse** *vr* to support oneself, earn one's living: *¿Cómo te vas a sostener?* How are you going to support yourself?'; also, to remain + *adj*: *el tiempo se sostendrá soleado* the weather will remain sunny
- **sostén** *nm pl sostenes* support; also bra(ssière); **sostenimiento** *nm* support, sustenance, maintenance (in the above senses)
- **sostenido** *adj* sustained, steady,

continuous: *una campaña sostenida* a steady campaign; **sostenidamente** *adv* steadily, continuously: *hay que obrar sostenidamente* we have to act in a sustained manner

standing *nm* an Eng word (usually pronounced *estandin*) which has been adopted by modern Sp with sense of 'rank', 'quality': *de alto standing* top-quality, high-class: *apartamentos de alto standing* top-quality apartments

suave *adj* indicating soft, gentle, etc, often as opp of *duro*
- has a variety of Eng equivalents: smooth (surface, liquid, etc); gentle, mild (movement, colour, climate); soft (music); meek, sweet (person); some overlap with cf *blando*
- never 'suave' in Eng sense, use *elegante*
- **suavidad** *nf* softness, gentleness, (relevant *n* from the qualities described above)
- **suavizar** *vt* -ce-, -cé; to smooth, soften, tone down; ie to render (more) *suave* in any of its meanings; **suavizarse** *vr* to become *suave*

subir *vi* to go/come up, rise, ascend: *subimos al castillo* we went up to the castle; *¡Cómo han subido los precios!* How prices have gone up!
- can be used as *vt*: *subimos la cuesta/la escalera* we went up the slope/stairs; also in sense of bring/take up(stairs): *¿Quieres subir las maletas?* Will you bring the cases up(stairs)?
- **subida** *nf* (act of) going up, ascent: *la subida de la montaña* the ascent of the mountain; also 'rise': *la subida de los precios* the rise in prices; and 'slope', 'hill': *es una subida empinada* it's a steep slope (cf *cuesta*)

súbito *adj* sudden: *un ruido súbito* a sudden noise (as *adj* cf *repentino*)
- **de súbito** or **súbitamente** *adv*

suddenly (much the same as cf *de repente*)

subrayar *vt*   to underline
  □ also 'to emphasise', 'stress' (in that sense): *hay que subrayar que ...*   it must be emphasised/stressed that ...

suceder *vi* to happen (same as *pasar* in that sense, and the less common *acontecer, acaecer*)
  □ also 'to suceed' (+ *a*) (NB ONLY in sense of 'come after'): *el Príncipe Felipe sucederá a su padre Juan Carlos* Prince Felipe will succeed his father Juan Carlos; for 'succeed' in sense of 'be succcesful', see under *éxito* and also *conseguir, lograr*
  □ **suceso** nm   event, happening; for 'success', see *éxito*
  □ **sucesión** *nf*   succession; **sucesor/a** *nmf*   successor, heir

sucio adj   dirty: covers range of Eng: filthy, grubby, foul, vile, obscene (can be applied to language, sporting tactics, act, etc)
  □ occurs most frequently with *estar*: *esta taza está sucia*   this cup is dirty; however, if 'dirty' is the basic characteristic of the subject, use *ser*: *sus métodos son muy sucios*   his methods are very dirty
  □ **suciedad** *nf*   dirt(iness), filth(iness) also: dirty act, filthy remark

Sudamérica or **América del Sur** *nf* South America (use either form; *Sudamérica* tends to be more common in modern Sp)
  □ **sudamericano** *adj*   South American (but see note under *América*)

sudeste, sudoeste *adj* & *nm*   south-east, south-west; alternative form **sureste/ suroeste**: both forms are used indiscriminately
  □ as *adjs* invariable: *la costa sureste* the south-east coast

□ see also under *sur*

Suecia *nf*   Sweden; **sueco** *adj*   Swedish; **sueco/a** *nmf* Swede; *nm* Swedish (ie the language)
  □ don't confuse with *Suiza/suizo* below!

suelo *nm*   ground, floor
  □ some overlap with cf *tierra*, but with some differences: *caer al suelo*   to fall to the ground (eg off a table); *caer a tierra*   to fall to earth (usually from a greater height, eg the sky); for 'soil', ie what crops grow in, *tierra* is more usual: *la tierra es muy fértil*   the land/soil is very fertile; *suelo* is used for 'floor': *el suelo era de baldosas* the floor was paved

suelto see **soltar**

suerte *nf*   luck, fortune (cf *fortuna*): *buena/mala suerte*   good/bad luck
  □ NB *tener (mucha) suerte*   to be (very) lucky; *¡suerte!* often used by itself, meaning 'good luck!'; *por suerte* luckily, as luck would have it
  □ also 'fate', 'destiny': *dejar a alguien a su suerte*   to abandon sb to their fate; *tentar a la suerte*   to tempt fate
  □ *echar suertes*   to draw lots

suficiente *adj*   enough, sufficient, adequate (means same as cf *bastante*)
  □ also 'competent', 'capable' (person): *es muy suficiente*   she's very capable
  □ and (in school marks) 'satisfactory'
  □ **suficientemente** *adv*   sufficiently, adequately, enough
  □ **suficiencia** *nf*   (the noun for the above qualities) sufficiency, adequacy; competence

sufrir *vt*   to suffer
  □ NB wide range of meaning: *sufrir una crisis nerviosa*   to have/suffer a nervous breakdown; *sufrir un revés*   to undergo a setback; *sufrir cambios profundos*   to undergo sweeping changes

also 'to tolerate', 'put up with' (cf *soportar*): *esto no lo sufro* I'm not putting up with this; *no sufro a esta gente* I can't stand these people

□ **sufrir de** *vi* to suffer from/with: *sufre del corazón* he suffers from/with his heart

□ **sufrimiento** *nm* suffering; patience, tolerance

□ much the same meaning as cf *padecer/padecimiento* with exception of 'tolerate'

□ **sufrido** *adj* long-suffering, tolerant (person); hard-wearing (eg material)

ℹ Suggestion, autosuggestion and influence ❗

Study these groups carefully, and note particularly the meanings of *sugestión* and *sugestionar*: not 'suggestion' and 'suggest'!

sugerir *vt -ie-, -i-* to suggest

□ **sugerencia** *nf* suggestion

□ if 'suggest/suggestion' means 'propose/proposal' cf *proponer/propuesta* are alternatives

□ **sugerente** *adj* full of suggestions, rich in ideas; NOT suggestive, as in 'suggestive remark', use *indecente*

□ don't confuse this group of words with those under *sugestionar* below

□ **sugestionar** *vt* to influence (sb's will), talk sb into: *te sugestionó para que lo hicieras* he influenced you to do it, he talked you into doing it

□ **sugestionarse** *vr* to talk oneself into, allow oneself to be influenced to: *te sugestionaste* you talked yourself into it

□ **sugestionable** *adj* impressionable, readily influenced: *es muy sugestionable* he's very impressionable/easily led

□ **sugestión** *nf* hint, prompting; also power to influence others, influence (in that sense); NOT 'suggestion', use *sugerencia*

---

suicidio *nm* suicide (ie act of killing oneself)

□ **suicida** *nmf* suicide (ie person who has committed suicide) or *adj* suicidal; *sing* always ends in *-a*

□ **suicidarse** *vr* to commit suicide

Suiza *nf* Switzerland; **suizo** *adj* Swiss; **suizo/a** Swiss (person)

□ don't confuse with *Suecia/sueco* Sweden/Swede/Swedish above

□ *un suizo* is also a type of bun (not a Swiss roll!)

sujeto *adj* fastened, firm: *tenía las manos sujetas* he had his hands tied

□ *sujeto a* subject to, liable to: *esta zona está sujeta a vientos fuertes* this area is subject to strong winds

□ *nm* (grammatical) subject: *el sujeto de la frase* the subject of the sentence: also 'chap', 'guy': *es un sujeto simpático* he's a nice guy

□ NOT school subject – use *asignatura*; nor a subject you talk about – use *tema, asunto*; and not eg a king's subject – use *súbdito*

□ **sujetar** *vt* to hold tight, hold down, fasten: *los guardias le sujetaron* the police held him down; *le sujetaron las manos* they fastened his hands; *no puedo sujetarme el pelo* I can't keep my hair in place

suma *nf* (act of) adding up, addition; also 'sum' (total)

□ **sumar** *vti* to add up (not same as cf *añadir* to add (to))

suministrar *vt* to supply, provide (used in a practical, often commercial context); cf closest *syns facilitar, proveer*, also *proporcionar*, which tends to be more abstract

□ **suministro** *nm* supply, provision (in that sense); **suministrador/a** *nmf* supplier

sumo *adj* great, extreme: *con suma diligencia* with the greatest of care; *con*

sumo entusiasmo extremely
enthusiastically
- **sumamente** *adv* to the greatest
extent: *estaban sumamente contentos*
they were very, very pleased (often
equivalent of superlative in *-ísimo*);
estábamos sumamente agradecidos
we were extremely thankful

superficie *nf* surface; also area, space, (eg
for playing field, supermarket etc, esp
when giving dimensions): *una superficie
muy grande* a very large area; *una
superficie de 1.000 metros cuadrados* a
space of 1,000 square metres
- **superficial** *adj* superficial (a
reminder that the superficial does not
go below the surface!)
- **superficialidad** *nf* superficiality,
shallowness

superior *adj* superior, better: *prefiero una
calidad superior* I prefer better/higher
quality
- but also, 'often 'higher', 'upper': *en la
planta superior* on the upper (top)
floor; *piensa en un número superior a
diez* think of a number higher than
10
- NB this is one of the comparative
adjs in *-erior* which don't change in
fem: cf its opp *inferior*

suplemento *nm* supplement (in most
senses); also extra/excess fare (on train,
plane etc): *con suplemento de 1.000
pesetas* 1,000 pesetas extra (to pay)
- **suplementario** *adj* supplementary,
often translates 'extra': *ponen vuelos
suplementarios* they're putting on
extra flights

suponer *vt* (has all irregularities of *poner* +
tú imperative: supón) to suppose, assume
- *supongo que ...* I suppose that ...;
es de suponer que ... it's to be
expected that ...; *supongamos que ...*
let's suppose/assume that ...
- also 'to mean', 'imply', 'involve': *eso
supone una gran cantidad de dinero*

that implies/involves a large sum of
money; *supone la voluntad de su
parte* it implies the will on his part
- and 'to credit with', 'attribute': *le
suponemos unos 30 años* we think
he's about 30
- **supuesto** *adj* supposed, apparent,
alleged: *el supuesto ladrón* the
alleged thief; can mean self-styled: *el
supuesto director* the self-styled
manager; *dar algo por supuesto* to
take sth for granted
- **suposición** *nf pl* suposiciones
supposition, assumption

suprimir *vt* to suppress
- but has wider use: *suprimir un sollozo*
to stifle a sob; *suprimir una ley* to
abolish a law; *suprimir un servicio de
ferrocarril* to cut a rail service; *suprimir
un obstáculo* to remove an obstacle;
suprimir un libro to ban a book
- **supresión** *nf pl* supresiones
suppression; also noun for above
actions

sur *nm* & *adj* south
- *adj* is invariable; *sud* sometimes
occurs, but is less common; see
compounds under *sudeste*

surgir *vi* -jo, -ja-: *surjo, surges; surja:* to
arise, crop up, emerge
- another 'happen' verb, usually when
something, often a problem, happens
or 'arises/crops up' unexpectedly: *si
surge algún problema médico* if
some medical problem arises
- also 'gush' (forth/out): *el agua surge
del manantial* the water gushes
from the spring

susceptible *adj* capable, liable (*de*
of/to): *carretera susceptible de
inundación* road liable to flood; *está
susceptible de cambios repentinos de
humor* he's subject/liable to sudden
changes of mood
- also 'sensitive', 'touchy': *es una
persona muy susceptible* she's a very

sensitive person (similar to cf *sensible*)

- □ can mean 'susceptible to (*a*)' if it touches on these qualities, otherwise use *propenso a*
- □ **susceptibilidad** *nf* liability, sensitivity, susceptibility (*a* to)

suscribir *vt past part: suscrito* to sign, ratify (agreement, promise etc)

- □ NB no *-b-*
- □ **suscribirse** *vr* to subscribe (*a* to): *me suscribo a Cambio 16* I subscribe to *Cambio 16*
- □ **suscripción** *nf pl suscripcones* subscription

suspender *vt* to suspend (most senses), hang up

- □ NB as *vt* or *vi* to fail (in exams etc) *me suspendieron* they failed me; *suspendí* I failed; *suspendí matemáticas* I failed maths
- □ **suspenso** *adj* suspended, hanging; also 'astonished', 'taken aback': *quedamos suspensos de la noticia* we were taken aback by the news
- □ *nm* suspense: *estar en suspenso* to be in suspense
- □ **suspenso/a** *nmf* student who has failed exam

sustancia *nf* substance; *sin sustancia* hollow, shallow, lacking in substance

- □ **sustancial** *adj* fundamental, vital: *hay un problema sustancial* there's a fundamental problem; not same as **sustancioso** *adj* substantial, solid, ie having a lot of substance: *una comida sustanciosa* a solid/heavy meal

□ NB no *-b-*!

sustentar *vt* to hold up, support: similar to cf *sostener*

- □ **sustentarse** *vr* to live, subsist (*con* on/off)
- □ **sustento** *nm* support; sustenance (ie food)

sustituir *vt –y– pi: sustituyo, -uyes, -uye, -uyen; sustituya; sustituyendo; sustituyó, sustituyeron; sustituyera/sustituyese* to substitute, replace: *sustituir a un futbolista por otro* to replace one footballer with another

- □ *vi* to replace, be in place of: *estas monedas pequeñas sustituyen a las grandes* these small coins are replacing the big ones
- □ **sustitución** *nf pl sustituciones* substitution, replacement (*por* for, by, with)
- □ NB no *-b-*

susto *nm* fright, scare: *¡Me diste tal susto!* You gave me such a fright!; *¡Qué susto!* What a fright!

- □ see also *asustar(se)*

sutil *adj* one of those words with multiple applications, and by no means always the obvious one of 'subtle'

- □ thin, delicate, (thread, slice), light (material, breeze etc); sharp, observant (person)
- □ only means 'subtle' when applied eg to remark: *fue una observación sutil* it was a subtle remark
- □ **sutileza** *nf* the noun for the qualities described above
- □ NB no *b*!

T *(te)* in Spanish is pronounced with the tongue against the back of your top teeth, thus making a rather crisper sound than its English equivalent. In fact, it's useful to say 'top teeth' in this way to highlight the difference! Otherwise, except that in common with most Spanish consonants it nevers occurs double, it is a very straightforward letter.

♦ Note also that words mainly of Greek origin which have 'th' in English, simple have *t* in Spanish: *teología* theology.

tabaco *nm* tobacco (note spelling)
- □ also wider meaning of 'smoking': *renunciar al tabaco* to give up smoking; and 'cigarette': *¿Quieres tabaco?* Would you like a cigarette?
- □ **tabaquismo** *nm* addiction to smoking

tabla *nf* plank, board (of most kinds): *tabla a vela* surfboard; *tabla de planchar* ironing board

taco *nm* pad (of paper), book (of eg metro) tickets
- □ also 'swear word': *soltar un taco* to let out a swear word
- □ one of those Sp words with a wide variety of meanings: look it up in a dictionary!

tacón *nm* pl *tacones* heel (of shoe)
- □ **taconeo** *nm* word for stamping of heel in flamenco dancing; also **taconear** *vi* to stamp with heel
- □ for heel of foot use *talón*

táctica *nf* tactic, tactics: NB use in *sing* in Sp; *adj* tactical

tacto *nm* touch (ie sense of touch); *al tacto* to the touch
- □ can mean 'tact': *tener tacto* to be tactful, but might be safer to use *discreción: hacer algo con/sin discreción* to do sth with/without tact or tactfully/tactlessly

tal *adj & pron* such (a)
- □ NB indef art not used with it: *tal situación* such a situation; *tal persona* such a person; *tales cosas* such things; cf *semejante*
- □ *tal como* such as: *una casa tal como la mía* a house such as mine; also 'just as': *está tal como me lo imaginé* it's just as I imagined
- □ also in some common phrases: *¿Qué tal (estás)?* How are you?; *¿Qué tal está la paella?* How do you find the paella?, What's the paella like?
- □ **con tal que** *conj + subjunc* provided that, on condition that: *con tal que me llames por teléfono* on condition that you phone me; cf *a condición de que* (under *condición*)

talante *nm* mood, disposition: *de buen/mal talante* in a good/bad mood
- □ also 'appearance', 'look' (in that sense): *tiene el talante antipático* he looks unpleasant; cf *aspecto*
- □ not to be confused with *talento* talent

taller *nm* workshop (for most kinds of craft, manufacture or repair); *taller mecánico* car repairs, 'garage' in sense of where you take your car to be repaired

talón *nm pl talones* heel (of foot)
- □ for heel of shoe, use *tacón*
- □ also 'cheque' (used at least as much as *cheque*); **talonario** chequebook

talud *nm* bank (of earth, grass)
- □ NB it's *masc* in spite of ending in -*d*

tamaño *nm* size
- □ in sense of degree of

bigness/smallness: for size of garment, see and use *talla, número*

- ☐ *¿De qué tamaño es?* What size is it?, How big is it?; *de tamaño corriente* normal size

---

 Don't confuse … ❗

talla *nf* height, stature (of person): *de poca talla* short, not very tall

- ☐ also, talking of clothes 'size': *¿Qué talla gasta Vd?* What size do you take? (but use *número* for shoes!)

talle *nm* waist

- ☐ also 'figure', 'build': *tener buen talle* to have a good figure; *de talle fuerte* of strong build

tallo *nm* stem (of plant)

Támesis *nm* (river) Thames

- ☐ one of the few hispanicised names of British places, rivers etc: the only others are *Londres* London; *Edimburgo* Edinburgh

tampoco *adj* neither, not … either

- ☐ it's the negative of *también*: compare – *yo tomo pescado* – – *yo también* – 'I'm having fish' – 'And me as well'; and – *yo no tomo pescado* – – *ni yo tampoco* – 'I'm not having fish' – 'Neither am I'
- ☐ in common with all negative words, when it follows the verb it requires *no* before it: *yo no tomo pescado tampoco* I'm not having fish either
- ☐ don't confuse with *ni … ni …* neither … nor …

tan *adj* so, as (+ *adj* or *adv*): *tan inteligente(mente)* so intelligent(ly)

- ☐ *(no) tan* + *adj/adv* + *como* (not) as/so + *adj/adv* as: *mi dormitorio (no) es tan bonito como el tuyo* my bedroom is (not) as/so nice as yours
- ☐ *tan* + *adj/adv* + *que* … so + *adj/adv* that …: *hablaba tan de prisa que no*

entendí ni una palabra he was talking so quickly that I didn't understand a word

- ☐ *tan sólo* just (a shade more emphatic than *sólo* by itself): *había tan sólo tú y yo* there were just you and me

tanto *adj* so much (*sing*), so many (*pl*), such a lot of

- ☐ used before noun as *tan* above is used before adj: *¡Tengo tantos primos!* I've got so many cousins!; *no tienes tantos primos como yo* you don't have as/so many cousins as I do; *tengo tantos primos que no les conozco a todos* I have such a lot of cousins (that) I don't know them all
- ☐ *adv* so much, such a lot: *¡no hables tanto!* don't talk so much!; + *adv* + *como/que* so/as much as/that: *no hablo tanto como tú* I don't talk as much as you; *hablas tanto que nadie te hace caso* you talk so much that no-one takes any notice of you; *tanto … como …* both … and … *tanto mi hermano como mi hermana saben* both my brother and my sister know
- ☐ used in many useful phrases, eg: *estar/ponerse al tanto de* to be fully abreast/informed about; *mientras tanto* meanwhile; *tanto mejor* so much the better; *no es para tanto* no need to make such a fuss; *tanto más porque …* the more so because …; *un tanto* or often *un tantito* a little bit, a shade: *estaba un tant(it)o enfadado* he was a little bit miffed
- ☐ worth some further investigation in the dictionary

tapa *nf* lid, cover, cap (of most kinds of containers)

- ☐ also 'tapa', (ie the snacks you get in Spanish bars to go with your drinks: because they act as a cover or lid for the alcohol in the drinks!)
- ☐ **tapar** *vt* to cover (up) (*de* with): *tapar una botella* to put the top

on/cork in a bottle; *taparse los oídos* to cover one's ears; *taparse la cara* to hide/cover one's face

- □ occurs in some compound words indicating cover: eg **taparrabo(s)** *nm inv* swimming trunks (ie tailcover!)
- □ **tapón** *nm* stopper, bung, cap; alternative to *tapa*, mainly for bottles; also 'plug' for sink/bath, 'valve cap' (on tyre)

tapia *nf* (garden) wall (usually of stone or mud)

- □ one of the several 'wall' words you may come across: cf *muro, muralla, pared,* which all have different meanings!

taquilla *nf* ticket or box office; window (in that sense, eg in bank)

- □ **taquillero/a** *nmf* person who works in a *taquilla*, clerk; also used as *adj* box-office success: *una película taquillera* a film which has been a big success; *una actriz taquillera* an actress who is a big draw

tarde *adv* late

- □ used to express lateness in relation to a specific point in time: *es muy tarde* it's very late; *más tarde* later (on); can mean 'too late': *llegamos tarde* we arrived too late
- □ for delay to trains, planes etc, use *llevar retraso* to be late: see under *retraso*
- □ *nf* afternoon, early evening (ie the time between lunch and about 8 pm or dusk); NB *pl*: *buenas tardes* good afternoon/evening
- □ **tardío** *adj* late, overdue; this is an adj, which must have a noun to refer to: *un verano tardío* a late/an overdue summer (ie slow to arrive)
- □ **tardar** *vti* to take time; has several idiomatic uses …
- □ to take/be a long time (*en* + inf to/in verb): *tardó mucho en contestar* he took a long time to reply, he was a long time replying

- □ (in neg) not to be long in: *no tardó en contestar* he wasn't long/slow in answering; *¡no tardes!* don't be long!
- □ to take (a certain) time doing sth (+ *en* + *inf*): *tardé dos horas en escribir esta carta* I took two hours to write this letter
- □ **tardanza** *nf* tardiness, slowness, delay (in time taken to do sth)
- □ **atardecer** *vi* -zc- to get dark

tarea *nf* task; more general use than cf *faena, quehaceres*

- □ **atareado** *adj* busy, having a lot to do

tarifa *nf* price, tariff (used more often than Eng equivalent, esp on notices, eg list of prices, rather than cf *precio(s)*)

tarjeta *nf* card (of most kinds): *tarjeta postal* postcard; *tarjeta de identidad* identity card; *tarjeta roja* red card; *tarjeta de visita* visiting card; *tarjeta de Navidad* Christmas card, though cf *chrismas* is often used; compare use with *carta* which usually means 'letter'

tasa *nf* rate (referring to finance): *tasa de cambio* exchange rate; *tasa* or *tipo de interés* interest rate; for 'tax', use *impuesto*

taza *nf* cup; NB *taza de té* cup of tea; *taza para té* teacup

- □ **tazón** *nm pl tazones* large cup, (nearest equivalent to) mug

techo *nm* means both 'roof' and 'ceiling'; *bajo techo* indoors

- □ for 'roof' see also *tejado* below

tecla *nf* key (of musical instrument or typewriter/computer)

- □ **teclado** *nm* keyboard (for above)

teja *nf* (roof) tile

- □ for ceramic wall tile, use *azulejo*; for floor tile, use *baldosa*
- □ **tejado** *nm* (esp tiled) roof
- □ **tejar** *vt* to tile (roof)

tejanos *nmpl* jeans: less common alternative to *syn vaqueros*; lit 'Texans', because Texas was originally named *Tejas* (then spelt *Texas*) by the Sp colonisers!

tela *nf* cloth, fabric, material (in that sense); *poner en tela de juicio* to (call into) question, query (in that sense)
- □ **telón** *nm pl telones* curtain (in theatre/cinema)

teléfono *nm* (tele)phone; *-f-* not *-ph-*!
- □ **telefonear** *vt* (*a alguien/algún sitio*): *voy a telefonear a la oficina* I'm going to phone the office; NB *te-le-fo-ne-ar* NOT 'telefonar' or 'telephonear': *llamar (por teléfono)* is a common alternative and less of a mouthful!
- □ **telefonazo** *nm* (phone) call: *dame un telefonazo* give me a call
- □ **telefónico** *adj* (to do with) telephone; **telefónicamente** *adv* by phone

televisión *nf* television (ie the medium); *televisión por satélite/cable* satellite/cable television; **tele** *nf* (*colloquial*) TV, telly; *¿qué hay/ponen en la tele?* what's on TV?
- □ **televisor** *nm* television (ie the set, apparatus)
- □ **televisivo/a** *adj* (to do with) television, televised: *deporte televisivo* televised sport, sport on TV; as *nmf* TV personality
- □ **telespectador/a** or **televidente** *nmf* TV viewer
- □ **telenovela** *nf* soap opera

tema *nm* NB *masc*! theme, topic, subject (in these sense): *es un tema interesante* it's an interesting subject
- □ **temario** *nm* (in general) programme or collection of topics; (in school) curriculum, syllabus
- □ **temática** *nf* range of topics, collection of subjects

temblar *vi -ie-* to tremble, shake; *temblar de frío* to shiver; *temblar de miedo* to

shake with fear; NB for shake in sense of tremble/ shiver cf *estremecer(se)*: *sacudir(se)* is more violent
- □ NB no *-r-* after the *t-*!
- □ **temblor** *nm* trembling, shaking
- □ **tembloroso** *adj* trembling, shaking (voice etc)

temer *vti* to fear, be afraid (of): *no hay nada que temer* there's nothing to fear/be afraid of
- □ also 'to be afraid that': used as Eng to tone down eg an unpalatable fact: *temo que has suspendido* I'm afraid you've failed; + *subjunc* when expressing fear re future event: *temo que vayas a suspender* I'm afraid you might fail
- □ **temor** *nm* fear (*a* of + *n*): *temor a las arañas* fear of spiders; (*de* + *inf*): *sin temor de ser descubierto* without fear of being discovered; similar to cf *miedo*
- □ **temeroso** *adj* timid, frightened
- □ **temible** *adj* fearsome, frightful
- □ **temeridad** *nf* rashness, recklessness: *tiene mucha temeridad* he's very reckless; *fue una temeridad* it was a rash thing to do; means 'temerity' in that sense, but for 'to have the temerity to', use *atreverse a*
- □ **temerario** *adj* rash, reckless

temperatura *nf* temperature
- □ much as Eng, but NB *tener fiebre* is often used for 'to have/run a temperature'

tempestad *nf* storm, tempest (mostly used in figurative sense): *una tempestad de indignación* a storm of indignation
- □ for 'thunderstorm' use *tormenta*

templar *vt* to temper, moderate: *templar el clima* to moderate, the climate; *templar sus opiniones* to moderate/tone down one's opinions; *templar un instrumento* to tune (up) an instrument
- □ **templarse** *vt* to be(come) moderate, restrained: *se templa en el*

beber   he drinks moderately

□ **templado** *adj*   moderate, restrained;
(of temperature) *clima templado*
temperate climate; *agua templada*
lukewarm water; (of instrument) *bien
templado*   well-tuned

temporada, temporal, temporáneo see tiempo

temprano *adv*   early; implication is
sometimes 'too early': *has venido
temprano*   you've come (too) early; cf
similar use of *tarde*   (too) late

□ also used as *adj* applied to writer,
painter, etc: *es una de sus obras
tempranas*   it's one of his early works

tender *vt*   -ie-   to stretch (out), spread; it's
the same word as when you are asked to
'tender exact fare' on the bus!

□ *tendió la mano*   he stretched out his
hand; *tendimos el mapa sobre la mesa*
we spread the map out on the table

□ also 'to hang out' (washing, etc): *tendí
la ropa a secar*   I hung out the
clothes to dry

□ *vi*   to tend (*a*   to + *inf* or towards +
n): *las cosas tienden a hacerse de un
modo diferente*   things tend to be
done in a different way; *tiende al
parecer opuesto*   he tends towards the
opposite opinion

□ **tenderse** *vr*   to lie down, stretch
out: *se tendió en el suelo*   he stretched
out on the ground

□ *(estar)* **tendido** *adj*   to be lying,
stretched out (cf *tumbado, echado*)

□ **tendencia** *nf*   tendency, trend; *tener
la tendencia a* + *inf*   to have a
tendency to, tend to

□ **tienda** see under separate entry

tener *vt*   *pi:* tengo, tienes, tiene, tenemos,
tenéis, tienen; *ps:* tenga *etc;* tú *imperative:*
ten; *fut/cond:* tendré/tendría; *pret:* tuve,
tuviste, tuvo, tuvimos, tuvisteis, tuvieron;
imp subj: tuviera/ tuviese   to have (in
sense of possess, hold; not used as
auxiliary verb, see *haber*)

□ NB used in variety of expressions
where Eng uses 'be' or verb other
than 'have': *tener … x años, hambre,
sed, calor, frío, razón, suerte, miedo,
cuidado, ganas, celos;* and for
dimensions (for further information
look under these words)

□ **tener que** + *inf*   to have (got) to:
tengo que irme   I've got to go; still
links with *que* when there is a direct
object: *tengo muchas cosas que hacer*
I've got a lot of things to do

□ NB can be used with *past part*, which
agrees with object: *tengo escrita la
carta;* this is more emphatic than the
straightforward *perfect: he escrito la
carta*   I've written the letter; it means
'I have the letter written', ie it's here,
written, in front of me; *¿Qué te tengo
dicho?*   What have I just told you?

□ **tenerse** *vr*   to consider oneself: *se
tienen por muy valientes*   they
consider themselves very brave; *se
tiene en mucho*   he thinks a lot of
himself

□ this verb has a wide range of
idiomatic uses and meanings and
would repay further research in both
dictionary and grammar

tentar *vt* -ie-   to touch, feel: *íbamos
tentando por el pasillo oscuro*   we
groped our way along the dark passage;
tienta esta tela   feel this cloth

□ also 'to try' (same uses as cf *probar*) in
sense of 'try out': *¿Has tentado este
coche?*   Have you tried out this car?;
and 'to try to' (+ *inf*): *¿Has tentado
conducir este coche?*   Have you tried
to drive this car?

□ and 'to tempt' + *a* + *inf: me tentó a
conducir su coche*   he tempted me to
drive his car; *tentar a alguien con algo*
to tempt sb with sth

□ **a tientas** *adv*   gropingly, feeling
one's way: *ir a tientas*   to feel one's
way

□ **tiento** *nm*   feel, touch (in that

sense); also 'tact', 'wariness': *ir con tiento*   to go carefully

- **tentación** *nf pl tentaciones* temptation; *la tentación de + inf*   the temptation to + *verb*
- **tentador** *adj -adora, -adores, -adoras*   tempting; as *nmf* tempter/temptress
- **tentativa** *nf*   attempt (*de*   to/at); **tentativo** *adj*   tentative

teñir *vt pi:* tiño, tiñes, tiñe, tiñen; *ps* tiña; etc; *ger.* tiñendo; *pret:* tiñó, tiñeron; *imp subj:* tiñera/tiñese   to dye, tinge

tercero *adj*   third (in order)

- NB *tercer* before *msing* noun: *tercer mundo*   third world
- **tercermundista** *adj inv*   belonging to/of the third world
- **tercio** *nm*   third (part), ie fraction; *dos tercios*   two thirds; but you often use *la tercera parte* third for specific third of sth: *la tercera parte del dinero se despilfarró*   a third of the money was squandered (cf similar use of *la mitad*   half)

terminar *vti*   to finish, end, conclude

- used both transitively and intransitively: *quiero terminar mi trabajo*   I want to finish my work; *las clases terminan a las seis*   classes end at six o'clock
- *+ de + inf*   to finish doing sth: *por fin terminó de hablar*   at last she stopped talking
- *+ por + inf* or *ger*   to finish by doing sth: *terminó por agradecerles a todos/agradeciéndoles a todos*   she finished (up) by thanking everyone
- cf *acabar*, though remember that *acabar de + pres* or *impf* means have/ had just
- **terminarse** *vr*   to end, draw to a close (rather more emphatic intransitive use): *se terminaban las vacaciones*   the holidays were coming to an end

- **terminación** *nf pl terminaciones* ending, conclusion, termination
- **terminal** *adj*   terminal; NB *nf* (eg electrical) terminal; *nm*   (air/rail/etc) terminal, terminus
- **término** *nm*   end, finish (cf *fin*)
- also 'term', in most Eng senses other than school (use *trimestre*): *en términos generales*   in general terms; *por término medio*   on the average; has a range of idiomatic or specialised meanings: worth a look in the dictionary!
- **terminante** *adj* **terminantemente** *adv*   decisive(ly), categorical(ly): *está terminantemente prohibido*   it is categorically/strictly forbidden

terraza *nf*   terrace, but note:

- used in sense of balcony, pavement café, and where Eng misuses the Sp word *patio*, which in Spain is an enclosed courtyard!; also a series of stepped garden or agricultural plots eg in a vineyard
- a terrace of (joined-up) houses would be *una hilera de casas*

terreno *nm*   terrain, land (in that sense)

- also 'plot' or 'piece of land', 'ground' (in that sense): *terreno de fútbol* football ground
- and (eg scientific) 'field': *en el terreno de la biología*   in the field of biology

terso *adj*   smooth; suggest also glossiness, more so than cf *liso*

- **tersura** *nf*   smoothness, glossiness

tertulia *nf*   originally: informal social gathering

- NB on TV/radio: chat show, phone-in

tesoro *nm*   treasure: NB not *tr-*!

ti see **tú**

tía see **tío**

tibio *adj*   lukewarm, tepid; usually applied to liquids, but can refer to person meaning unenthusiastic, cool (*con towards sb/sth*)

- **tibieza** *nf* lukewarmness; coolness (relating to above explanation)

tiempo *nm* time (ie the concept or duration of it): *¿Cuánto tiempo?* (For) how long?; *mucho tiempo* a long time; *a tiempo* in/on time; *al mismo tiempo* at the same time
- period of time, often in *pl*: *en los tiempos de Colón* in Columbus's time
- (in game) half: *segundo tiempo* second half
- (in grammar) tense: *tiempo pretérito* preterite tense
- NOT a time or number of times in sense of occasion(s), see *vez/veces*; nor time of day, see *hora*; nor have a good time, use *divertirse, pasarlo bien*
- NB its other main meaning – 'weather' *¿Qué tiempo hace?* What's the weather like?; *hace buen/mal tempo* the weather's good/bad
- **temporada** *nf* season (esp sporting, tourist, festive etc): *temporada de fútbol* football season; *temporada alta/baja* high/low season; for the four seasons of the year, better to use *estación*
- **temporal** *adj* temporary; **temporáneo** *adj* is also possible; NB not *temporario*, although this is sometimes used in Sp Am

tienda *nf* shop
- NB its other meaning – 'tent'; strictly *tienda de campaña*, but in a camping context, *tienda* is sufficient!

tierno *adj* tender, soft
- **ternura** *nf* tenderness, softness
- see also **enternecer** *vt* **enternecerse** *vr* in frame on p. 81: to make/become tender, to soften: *se le enternecían los ojos* his/her eyes were watering (ie with tears)

tierra *nf* earth, land in the following variety of senses …
- planet: *el planeta Tierra* Planet Earth

- soil: *la tierra es buena por aquí* the land/soil is good around here; *lo cubrieron de tierra* they covered it with earth/soil
- land (for eg farming or building): *tienen mucha tierra* they have a lot of land
- (as opposed to sea): *por fin vieron tierra* at last they saw land
- country (much the same as cf *país*): *España es una tierra bastante grande* Spain is quite a big country
- not same as cf *suelo*

tieso *adj* stiff, rigid (can be used of objects and also of character or sb's demeanour)
- **tiesura** *nf* stiffness, rigidity (as applied to above)

timbre *nm* bell (electric or mechanical, with repeating, usually external clapper); not same as cf *campana, campanilla*
- also printed stamp or seal, but not usually postage stamp: use *sello* (different words may be used in different parts of Sp Am)

tímido *adj* timid, but also 'shy', 'nervous'
- **timidez** *nf* timidity, shyness

tinieblas *nfpl* darkness (quite common alternative to cf *oscuridad*)

tinta *nf* ink; has a number of connected words, some with rather different connotations …
- **tintero** *nm* ink pot, ink bottle, inkwell
- **tinto** *adj* red (wine only!); otherwise means 'stained', 'tinted'
- **tinte** *nm* dye, tinge (of colour)
- **tintorería** *nf* strictly dyer's shop, often used for 'dry cleaner's'
- **tintorero/a** *nmf* dry cleaner
- **tintura** *nf* dyeing, dye

tío/tía *nmf* uncle/aunt
- NB collective *pl*: *mis tíos* my uncle(s) and aunt(s); *tío* is sometimes used colloquially to mean 'guy', 'bloke': cf also *tipo*; *tía* can mean woman, but

tends rather to be a slang word for girl, eg 'bird', 'chick': not very politically correct, and perhaps best avoided!

tipo *nm* type (kind sort): *un tipo de coche* a type of car (cf this similar use of *clase*); *¿Qué tipo de café te gusta?* What sort of coffee do you like?

□ also 'guy', 'chap', 'bloke' (cf similar use of *tío*): *no conozco a ese tipo* I don't know that guy/bloke

□ and 'rate' (interest, etc): *el tipo de interés/cambio* the interest/exchange rate

□ **típico** *adv* typical; **típicamente** *adv* typically (used much as in Eng)

tirar *vti* has a variety of common meanings …

□ 'to throw' (cf *lanzar, echar,* not necessaily as vigorous as *arrojar*); more specifically 'throw away' (cf *echar*): *prohibido tirar basura* do not throw rubbish here; *tirar bombas* to drop bombs

□ 'to knock over': *he tirado el café* I've knocked over the coffee

□ as *vi* to shoot, fire: *¡tira!* fire!; NB intransitive use only; for 'fire a gun', use *disparar*; 'to shoot a person', use *fusilar* or *matar a tiros*

□ *tirar <u>de</u> algo*: 'to pull sth' *¡tira de la cuerda!* pull the string!

□ 'to get by', usually in form *ir tirando*: *vamos tirando* we're managing

□ **tiro** *nm* throw

□ also 'shot', 'shooting': *pegarle un tiro a alguien* to shoot sb; *oír un tiro* to hear a shot; *tiro al pichón* clay pigeon shooting; *tiro libre* free kick

□ you will find a whole list of further idiomatic and colloquial uses in the dictionary!

□ **tirón** *nm pl tirones* pull, tug: *dar un tirón a algo* to give sth a tug; *de un tirón* with a tug/jerk

□ **tirita** *nf* sticking plaster

título *nm* title

□ also 'degree', (qualifying) 'certificate': *título universitario* university degree

□ **titular** *vt* to entitle: *un libro titulado ¡Dime más!* a book entitled *¡Dime más!*; **titularse** *vr* to be called, entitled; also 'to graduate', 'take one's degree' (*en* in)

□ **titular** *nm* headline, main story; often *pl: los titulares* headlines, main stories

tocar *vti -que-, -qué* to touch (in most senses): *¡no toques!* don't touch!; *su solicitud me tocó el corazón* his caring touched my heart

□ has various other meanings …

□ play an instrument or apparatus: *tocar el clarinete* to play the clarinet; *tocar un CD* to play a CD

□ to concern: *¡eso no te toca a ti!* that's no concern/business of yours!, mind your own business!

□ to fall to sb's lot, be up to sb: *ahora me toca a mí* now it's my turn; *te tocará a ti arreglar todo esto* it will be your concern/up to you to sort all this out

□ further research in the dictionary recommended!

□ **toque** *nm* touch (in most senses); also used for noise made by specific apparatus being played, eg: *toque de campanas* peal of bells; *toque de trompeta* trumpet call

□ **tocante a** *prep* with regard to, concerning: *no encontramos nada tocante a su vida* we didn't find anything concerning his life

□ **tocador** *nm* dressing table

todavía *adv* still, yet: *todavía más inteligente* still more intelligent; *todavía no tenemos entradas* we still don't have tickets; *no les hemos visto todavía* we haven't seen them yet/ we still haven't seen them: much the same as cf *aún*

todo *adj* all, whole: *toda la ciudad* all the town, the whole town; *todo el tiempo* all the time, the whole time; *todos los alumnos* all the pupils; can be used *sing* to mean 'every'/'each' (cf *cada*): *toda persona* each/ every person

- *pron sing* all, everything: *se acordó de todo* he remembered everything/ remembered it all; *todo está en orden* everything is in order; NB *todo lo que* all that/everything which: *todo lo que dice* everything (that) he says
- *pron pl* everybody: *¡hola, todos!* hallo, everyone!; *todos estaban contentos* everybody was pleased
- **todo el mundo** also means 'everybody', but NB takes *sing* verb: *todo el mundo estaba contento; NB todos los que/las que* all those who/ everybody who
- *adv* all, completely: *estoy todo nervioso* I'm all nervous
- other useful expressions: *con todo* all the same, even so; *a pesar de todo* in spite of everything, all the same; *del todo* (with negative) completely: *no estoy del todo loco* I'm not completely mad; *después de todo* after all; and many other expressions which you will find listed in a dictionary

tolerar *vt* to tolerate (bear, endure) same as *aguantar, soportar;* 'allow' (same as *permitir*)

- **tolerancia** *nf* toleration, tolerance; **(in)tolerable** *adj* (in)tolerable much the same as cf *(in)aguantable, (in)soportable*

tomar *vt* to take (in a very wide sense): eg in one's hand, bath, shower, decision, measure, sun, bus, train, air, class, etc

- NB used with food where Eng uses 'have': *¿qué vas a tomar?* what are you going to have?
- better to use *sacar* for 'take photos', and *coger* (NOT in some parts of Sp Am) for 'take hold of'

- NB *tomar a alguien por algo/alguien* to take sb for sth/sb: *¿Por quién me tomas a mí?* Who do you take me for?
- *vi* to take (root): *todas mis plantas tomaron* all of my plants took
- *toma por la izquierda* turn left
- **tomarse** *vr* used reflexively in certain more emphatic expressions: *tomarse la molestia de* to take the trouble to; *tomárselo a mal* to take it badly
- **toma** *nf* (action of) taking; capture, seizure: *la toma se Granada* the taking of Granada; also 'take' (in filming); and *toma eléctrica* electric plug/socket

tonto/a *adj* stupid, silly, foolish; *nmf* fool, silly person

- **tontería** *nf* silliness, foolishness; but also esp in *pl* 'nonsense', 'rubbish': *siempre va diciendo tonterías* he's always talking rubbish; *vender algo por una tontería* to sell sth for a pittance

topar *vt* or *vi* + *con* to run into, bump into sb: *le topé* or *topé con él en el mercado* I bumped into him in the market; *topar contra algo* to bump into sth

tópico *adj* topical; used as *nm* 'topic' in Sp Am, but in Spain *tema* or *asunto* is preferable

torcer *vt* -ue-; -zo, -za to twist, bend

- *vi* to turn: *tuerza a la izquierda* turn left
- **torcerse** *vr* to twist, sprain (a part of body): *me torcí la muñeca* I sprained my wrist

tormenta *nf* storm; don't confuse with ...

- **tormento** *nm* torment, torture
- **tormentoso** *adj* stormy
- NB verb is **atormentar** to torment, torture

tornar *vt* give back, return: *devolver* is more common; *vi* to return, go back: *volver* and *regresar* are more common

- mainly used in *tornar a + inf* to do

sth again: same as *volver a: tornó a leer la carta* he read the letter again

- **en torno a** *prep* around: much the same as but less common than *alrededor de*

torpe *adj* clumsy, awkward; or dim, slow-witted (person)

- **torpeza** *nf* clumsiness, awkwardness; dimness, slow-wittedness

tostar *vr* to toast

- **tostarse** *vt* to tan, get brown (in sun); **tostado** *adj* tanned, sunburnt
- **tostada** *nf* piece of toast

total *adj* total, whole, complete, utter: *fue un éxito total* it was a complete/utter success

- *nm* total: *en total* all in all; *total que* the upshot is/was that …; *total que tuvo que dimitir* the upshot was that he had to resign
- **totalmente** *adv* totally, wholly, completely
- **totalidad** *nf* totality: *en su totalidad* as a whole, in full

trabajar *vi* to work (ie in order to earn living, to complete a task, etc) *trabajar de enfermero/a* to work as a nurse; *trabajar en un proyecto* to work on a project

- NB *trabajar mucho/más* to work hard/harder; *trabajar por + inf* to strive to
- can be used in sense of 'function', but better to use cf *funcionar, andar*
- can be used as *vt trabajar una sustancia* to work a substance
- **trabajo** *nm* work (in general), job (in particular): *no le gusta el trabajo* he doesn't like work; *le gusta este trabajo* he likes this work/job
- *trabajo a tiempo parcial* part-time job; *quedarse sin trabajo* to lose one's job; *estar sin trabajo* to be unemployed
- **trabajador/a** *nmf* worker, labourer; or *adj* hard-working

- **trabajoso** *adj* laborious, painful: *una tarea trabajosa* a laborious/painful task; **trabajosamente** *adv* laboriously, painfully
- be careful with contexts where *trabajar* and its derivatives are not used: see *obra* for work of art, roadworks, etc, *obrero/a* for 'worker'; *funcionar, andar, obrar* for 'function/operate'

traducir *vt -zc-: pi: traduzco, traduces; ps: traduzca, etc;* and *-j-: pret: traduje, -ujiste, -ujo, -jimos, -jisteis, -jeron; imp subj: tradujera/tradujese* to translate

- **traductor/a** *nmf* translator; **traducción** *nf pl traducciones* translation

traer *vt pi: traigo, traes, etc; ps: traiga etc; ger: trayendo; pret: traje, trajiste, trajo, trajimos, trajisteis, trajeron; imp subj: trajera/trajese* to bring

- can mean to wear (cf *llevar*): *traía camisa amarilla* s/he was wearing a yellow shirt
- also 'to have', 'keep', in following sense: *todo esto me trae muy preocupado* all this has/keeps me very worried
- and 'to carry' (eg newspaper): *¿Qué traen los periódicos del asunto?* What have the papers got to say about the matter?
- **traerse** *vr* to be up to; *estos niños siempre se traen algo* these children are always up to something

tráfico *nm* traffic (both vehicular and in eg drugs, cf *narcotráfico*)

- **traficante** *nmf* trader, dealer (*en* in); cf *narcotraficante*

tragar *vt -gue-, -gué* to swallow; *no poder tragar algo/a alguien* not to be able to stomach sth/sb

- **tragarse** *vr* reflexive form gives more impact — 'to swallow down', 'swallow up': *se tragó la botella entera* s/he knocked back the whole bottle; cf similar use of *comerse, beberse*

□ also 'to swallow' (a story), 'accept' (a fact etc)

□ **trago** *nm* drink, (act of) swallow(ing), gulp, swig: *de un trago* in one gulp, with one swig: *echarse un trago* to have a drink

traje *nm* (in general) dress, costume, suit: *traje de baño* bathing costume; *traje de luces* bullfighter's costume; *traje típico* typical costume

□ also, more specifically (man's) suit; and can be used for 'a dress' in sense of woman's frock, but *vestido* is often preferred

□ **trajeado** *adj* well-dressed, smart: *estar/ir bien trajeado* to be smartly dressed

trama *nf* plot (of book, play, etc)

□ **tramar** *vt* to plot, scheme: *¿Qué están tramando?* What are they hatching up?

tramo *nm* section, stretch (eg of road): *un largo tramo de la carretera está en obras* there are roadworks on a long stretch of the road

trampa *nf* trap, snare: *caer en la trampa* to fall into the trap

□ also 'trick', 'swindle': *hacer trampas* to cheat, fiddle

□ **tramposo/a** *adj* cheating; or *nmf* cheat: *¡eres (un) tramposo!* you're a cheat!

trance *nm* moment, juncture (usually a difficult one): *salir de un trance* to come out of a difficult time; *estar en trance de* to be on the point of (usually sth unpleasant!); *esta especie se encuentra en trance de extinguirse* this species is on the point of extinction

□ also 'trance'

tranquilo *adj* still, calm, quiet, peaceful (wider meaning than just 'tranquil'): *¡(Estáte) tranquilo!* Stay still!, Keep

quiet!, Relax!

□ often has meaning of 'unpreoccupied', 'unconcerned': *ahora estamos más tranquilos ahora que lo sabemos* we're more relaxed now we know

□ **tranquilidad** *nf* quiet, calm, peace (in that sense)

□ **tranquilizar** *vt -ce-, -cé* to calm (down); tranquilise; **tranquilizarse** *vr* to calm down, relax, stop worrying: *¡Tranquilízate!* Calm down!, Relax!

□ **tranquilizador/a** *adj* *pl -adores, -adoras;* soothing, calming; *música tranquilizadora* soothing music

□ **tranquilizante** *nm* tranquiliser (ie drug); can also be *adj* calming

transcurrir *vi* to pass (by); elapse (used of time, years, etc); useful alternative to *pasar* in this sense

□ **transcurso** *nm* passage, course (of time): *en el transcurso del año 2001* in the course of the year 2001

transformar *vt* and **transformarse** *vr* lit: to transform, but a useful alternative to *cambiar(se)* change (in that series): *han transformado por completo el centro de la ciudad* they have completely changed the town centre; *la princesa se transformó en rana* the princess changed into a frog; cf also *convertir(se), trocar(se), mudar(se)*

□ **transformación** *pl transformaciones nf* transformation, change

tránsito *nm* transit

□ but also 'traffic': *una carretera de mucho tránsito* a very busy road

transporte *nm* transport; sometimes used in *pl*: *transportes públicos* public transport

tras *prep* behind (much same as cf *detrás de*): *tras él venía toda su familia* behind him came all his family

□ also 'after': *año tras año* year after year; *uno tras otro* one after the other; *correr tras algo/alguien* to run after sth/sb; + *inf* after doing: *tras pensar mucho* after thinking a great deal maybe emphasises time taken more than cf *después de*

- also 'beyond': *tras las montaños* beyond/over the mountains
- **trasero** *adj* back, rear: *las ventanas traseras* the back/rear windows; also *nm* bottom, backside (colloquial but not rude, *syn culo*)

trascendencia *adj* importance, significance (in fact stronger than *importancia*, 'far-reaching implications': *un asunto de mucha trascendencia* a matter with many implications

- **trascendente/trascendental** *adj* important, significant, momentous: *una decisión trascendente* a momentous decision, a decision with far-reaching implications; useful alternative to *muy importante, importantísimo* when this is the sense

trasladar *vt* to transfer, move (in that sense): *tenemos que trasladar todo esto a la nueva aula* we've got to move/transfer all this to the new classroom

- **trasladarse** *vr* to move: *nos venimos trasladando de un sitio a otro* we keep moving from one plce to another
- **traslado** *nm* transfer, move, removal (in that sense): *el traslado de prisioneros* the transfer of prisoners

trasto *nm* piece of furniture or household junk

- **trastero** *adj* (to do with) junk: *cuarto trastero* spare room, junk room

trastorno *nm* upset, disorder: *trastorno del estómago* stomach upset; *trastorno económico* economic upset/upheaval

- **trastornar** *vt* to upset, knock over (same as cf *volcar* in this sense); disturb: *la trastornó lo que vio* she was upset/disturbed by what she saw;

la chica le trastornaba the girl was driving him mad/crazy

- **trastornarse** *vr* to get upset/disturbed: *se le trastornaron las ideas* his ideas went haywire; *se trastornó el proyecto* the project fell through

tratar *vti* to treat: *hay que tratarle con cuidado* you have to treat him with care; *le tratan con una nueva droga* they are treating him with a new drug

- *tratar a* or *con alguien* to have dealings, relations with sb: *no le trato nunca/no trato nunca con él* I never have anything to do with him
- *tratar de algo/alguien* to be about, to deal with sth/sb (in that sense): *¿De qué trata la película?* What's the film about?
- *tratar de + inf* to try to: *trato de llamar por teléfono* I'm trying to make a phone call
- *se trata de + n* or *inf* it's about: *se trata del nuevo estudiante* it's about the new student; it's a question/matter of: *se trata de cobrar dinero* it's a question of earning money
- *tratarse de tú/Vd* to call each other tú/Vd
- **trato** *nm* dealing(s), deal: *¡trato hecho!* it's a deal!, done!
- also 'treatment', ie way sb is dealt with: *le dieron mal trato* they treated him badly (not quite same as cf *tratamiento* below)
- and 'manner', 'behaviour': *tiene el trato agradable* he's got a pleasant manner, he's easy to get on with
- **tratamiento** *nm* treatment: eg medical, or in sense of processing or handling: *tratamiento de textos* word processing, *tratamiento de datos* data processing, ie more specific than *trato* above

través occurs as **a través de** *prep* (physically) across: *pusieron una barrera a través de la calle* they put a barrier across the street

- also 'through' (physically or by means of): *a través de la niebla* through the fog; *a través de mis contactos en España* through my contacts in Spain
- **travesía** *nf* (act of) crossing: *tuvimos una buena travesía* we had a good crossing; not pedestrian crossing or crossroads, see *cruce* and *paso*
- NB verb is **atravesar** *vti -ie-* to cross; much the same as this use of cf *cruzar*

travieso *adj* naughty, mischievous

- **travesura** *nf* naughtiness, mischief
- don't confuse with 'crossing' words above!

trecho *nm* stretch (of road, cf *tramo*), distance (in that sense)

- used in some handy phrases: *a trechos* here and there, in parts; *de trecho en trecho* every so often; *hemos cumplido un buen trecho* we've covered a good distance

tremendo *adj* tremendous (in most Eng senses), but also wider meaning: *tengo un hambre tremenda* I'm ravenously hungry

- also terrible, frightening: *fue una situación tremenda* it was a terrible/ frightening situation
- look in the dictionary for more colloquial uses

trepar *vti* to climb (usually + *a* + *n*): *trepar a un árbol* to climb a tree; tends to involve physically climbing: more specific effort in this sense than cf *subir* which simply means 'go up'

- **trepador** *adj* climbing (eg plant); **trepadora** *nf* climber (plant, not person: use *alpinista*!)

trepidar *vi* to shake, tremble, vibrate (not necessarily with fear): *la tierra trepidó* the ground shook; cf *temblar*

- **trepidación** *nf* *pl* trepidaciones

vibration, shaking (Eng 'trepidation' would be better rendered by *turbación, agitación*)

tribuna *nf* platform (for speaker)

- also 'grandstand' (football etc)
- and 'dock' (in court, see *tribunal* below)
- **tribunal** *nm* court (of justice); *comparecer ante el tribunal* to appear in court
- also 'tribunal'

trimestre *nm* school/university term

- three month period, quarter (in that sense): *pago por trimestre* quarterly payment

tripa *nf* gut, 'innards': often *pl*: *este tipo me revuelve las tripas* that character turns my stomach; *me duelen las tripas* I've tummy ache; *hacer de tripas corazón* to pluck up courage

- NB the politeness rating of this word in sense of stomach/belly/tummy is on a par with 'tummy' in Eng: not vulgar, but somewhat colloquial; less vulgar than *barriga*, less clinical than *vientre* or *abdomen*!

triste *adj* sad …

- NB has a wider meaning … miserable, gloomy, mournful, sorrowful: *¿Por qué me siento tan triste?* Why am I feeling so miserable?; *es un sitio tan triste* it's such a gloomy/dismal place; *¡Qué día más triste!* What a miserable/ gloomy/dismal day!
- **tristeza** *nf* noun for all the states described above: sadness, sorrow, gloom(iness), dismalness: *una sensación de tristeza* a feeling of sadness/ gloom/etc

triunfo *nm* triumph

- also used in sense of 'victory', 'win' (in sport); and 'success', 'hit': *otro triunfo para el conjunto* another success for the group

□ **triunfar** *vi* to triumph (*sobre* over)

□ also 'win', 'succeed': *España triunfó en la Copa* Spain won the Cup; *esta chica va a triunfar en la vida* the girl will succeed in life

□ NB spelling: *-nf-* not *–mph–*!

trocar *vt -ue-; -que-, -qué* to change, exchange (*por* for)

□ partial *syn* of *cambiar* in sense of 'exchange (for)': *trocó su vida cómoda por las aventuras* he exchanged his comfortable life for adventure

□ also 'change sth into sth': *troqué mis pesetas en euros* I changed my pesetas into euros

□ and 'to change (ie move) around': *has trocado los muebles* you've changed the furniture around

□ **trocarse** *vr* to change (*en* into): *la princesa se trocó en rana* the princess changed into a frog; cf *convertirse, transformarse*

□ **trueque** *nm* exchange, change (in the above senses): *a trueque de* in exchange for

tronar *vti -ue-* to thunder

□ can be used of voice: – ¡*ven aquí!* – *tronó* 'Come here!' he thundered

□ **trueno** *nm* thunder

tropezar *vi -ie-; -ce-, cé* to trip, stumble; *tropezar con alguien* to bump into sb, meet sb by chance (cf *topar con*)

□ **tropiezo** *nm* slip, blunder (ie mistake); also 'hitch', 'setback'

trozo *nm* piece, slice; similar to cf *pedazo*

□ also 'passage', 'piece' (of book, poem, music, etc)

truco *nm* trick, dodge: *nuestro profe tiene varios trucos para hacer más fácil el español* our teacher has various dodges to make Spanish easier; ¿*Coges el truco?* Do you get the knack?

□ NB does not have French *truc* meaning of 'gadget', 'thingummy'; use *chisme*

tú *subj pron* you (familiar or informal form); NB disjunctive or prepositional form is **ti**: *delante de ti* in front of you

□ NB don't confuse *tú* ('you', with accent) with **tu** *poss adj* ('your', no accent)

□ **tuyo** *poss pron* yours

□ refer to a grammar book for full explanation and practice of these words

□ **tutear** *vt* to address sb as *tú*: *puedes tutearme si quieres* you can call me *tú* if you like

tubo *nm* tube, but also 'pipe': *tubo de escape* exhaust pipe

□ **tubería** *nf* collective word for pipes, plumbing (in that sense)

tumbar *vt* knock down, knock over: *un olor que tumba* a smell that knocks you back; more often occurs as …

□ **tumbarse** *vr* to lie down; and (*estar*) **tumbado** *adj/past part* to be lying down; NB in common with most bodily positions, agreeing *past part*: *Elena estaba tumbada en el sofá* Elena was lying in the settee; cf *echarse/estar echado*

□ **tumbo** *nm* fall, tumble: *dar un tumbo* to tumble, lurch; *dar tumbos* to stagger

□ don't confuse with **tumba** *nf* tomb

turbar *vt* to disturb (ie upset, inconvenience)

□ more commonly 'to worry', 'alarm', 'upset' (in that sense): *su condición la turbó bastante* his condition worried her quite a lot

□ and can mean 'embarrass': *sus atenciones la turbaban* his attentions embarrassed her

□ **turbarse** *vr* to get worried, alarmed, upset, embarrassed (in senses described above): *se turbó al ver su condición* she became worried/alarmed when she saw his condition; **turbado** *adj* worried, alarmed, etc

□ **turbación** *nf* disturbance, worry, alarm, embarrassment, etc

turismo *nm* tourism

□ **turista** *nmf* tourist (ie the person)

□ **turístico** *adj* tourist, to do with tourism: *la industria turística* the tourist industry; *una ciudad turística* a tourist/holiday town; NB this is an adjective, not a noun, you can't and

mustn't talk about *muchos turísticos* (a common error made by A level students!)

turno *nm* turn (go, opportunity); for most other translations of 'turn', see *volver/vuelta*

□ also 'shift': *turno de noche* night shift

□ don't confuse with *torno*: see above

---

ubicar *vt* -que-, -qué to place, locate, situate

□ *past part* frequently used with *estar: la fábrica está ubicada en Italia* the factory is situated in Italy

□ **ubicarse** *vr* to be situated: *el pueblo se ubica en un valle fértil* the village is situated in a fertile valley

□ **ubicación** *nf* situation, position

Ud(s) see **usted(es)**

ulterior *adj* later, subsequent

□ used mainly in a time context: *en una ocasión ulterior* on a later/subsequent occasion

□ not usually 'ulterior' in Eng sense: 'ulterior motive' might be *motivo oculto*

□ comparative with no *f* form

último *adj* has a variety of meanings …

□ 'last' (in time or a series): *en el último momento* at the last minute; *llegué el último/la última* I came last; *por*

última vez for the last time; *el último tren del día* the last train of the day

□ NB not same as cf *pasado (lunes pasado* last Monday etc)

□ 'latest', ie most recent: *la última edición* the latest edition; *la última película de Almodóvar* Almodóvar's last/latest film (meaning could be ambiguous: the last he ever produced or his most recent, but this is usually clear from context)

□ 'furthest away (in various senses): *la última fila* the back row; *el último rincón del mundo* the furthest corner of the globe

□ **últimamente** *adv* lastly, finally

□ also often 'lately', recently': *últimamente he estado algo enfermo* I've been rather ill lately

□ **ultimar** *vt* to finish, complete, conclude

□ perhaps gives more emphasis on 'finishing off' than other 'ending' verbs cf *acabar, concluir, terminar*

ultramarinos: tienda de ultramarinos *nf* grocery shop

□ a little old-fashioned in these days of supermarkets, but still used for small 'corner' type grocery shops

umbral *nm* threshold

□ *estar en los umbrales de …* to be on the threshold/verge of … (in the sense of 'to be almost there')

un(o) *m* **una** *f num* one

□ NB *un* before *m* and *una* before *f* noun, even when on end of higher number and the noun is plural: *treinta y un bolígrafos* thirty-one biros, *cincuenta y una flores* fifty-one flowers

□ **uno** *pron* one

□ as *subject pron*, always *m*: *uno no sabe lo que va a pasar* one doesn't know what is going to happen

□ has to be used where verb is already reflexive and 'one' cannot be conveyed by *se*; compare: *se lavan los tomates* one washes the tomatoes/the tomatoes are washed, with: *uno se lava en el cuarto de baño* one washes in the bathroom (*se lava* would mean 'he/she washes him/herself …)

□ *pron mf – uno mismo* oneself: *si lo hace uno mismo* if one does it oneself

□ *uno(s) a otro(s)* (to) each other, (to) one another (used with reflexive verb): *se escriben uno a otro* they write to each other; *uno tras otro* one after the other: *las jirafas salieron una tras otra* the giraffes came out one after the other

□ **unos/as** *adj* some, a few; sometimes occurs as *unos pocos*: *tengo unas pocas ideas* I've got a few ideas

□ *pron unos … otros …* some … others …; *unos hacen esto, otros hacen aquello* some do this, others do that

□ see also *algunos*, which tends to be more emphatic or distinguishing

único *adj* only

□ NB not same as *solo*: must be used in the sense 'one and only': *ésta es la única camisa que tengo* this is the only shirt I've got; *soy hija única* I'm an only daughter; *dirección única* one direction only, one-way (street)

□ also 'unique'

□ **únicamente** only

□ rather more emphatic than cf *sólo/ solamente*

unir *vt* to join, unite, bind (in that sense)

□ **unirse** *vr* to join together, be joined together/united; some overlap with cf *juntar(se)*

□ **unidad** *nf* unity, oneness

□ also 'unit' (in most senses)

□ **unido** *adj* united

□ also 'joined' (*por* by): *las dos ciudades están unidas por el ferrocarril* the two towns are joined by the railway

□ **unión** *nf pl uniones* union

□ in most senses, though not 'trade union': use *sindicato*

universidad *nf* university

□ **universitario/a** *adj la vida universitaria* university life; and *nmf* university student

urbanización *nf pl urbanizaciones* urbanisation

□ also often 'housing estate', 'residential development'

urgencia *nf* urgency; *con urgencia* urgently

□ also 'emergency': *salida de urgencia* emergency exit

□ *Urgencias* Casualty Department

urna *nf* urn

□ more frequently 'ballot box': *acudir a las urnas* to go to the poll

uso *nm* use: *hacer (buen) uso de algo* to make good use of sth; *estar en/fuera de uso* to be in/out of use

□ wear (and tear): *sin valor por el uso* valueless through wear and tear

□ usage, custom: *al uso del siglo 18* according to 18th century usage/custom

□ **usar** *vti* to use: *¿Cómo se usa?* How do you use it?: similar in meaning to cf *utilizar, emplear* in this sense

□ also 'to wear', 'wear out'; *past part* **usado** as *adj* worn out: *estos zapatos están usados* these shoes are worn out (cf *gastar/gastado*)

□ **usar** + *inf*   to be accustomed to (less common than cf *soler*): *usan veranear en la costa*   they usually go on holiday to the coast

□ **usarse** *vr*   to be used, to be worn: *esta ropa sólo se usa en las fiestas* these clothes are only worn at festivals

□ **usual** *adj*   usual; but cf *normal, corriente* which are also in common use with similar meaning

□ **usuario/a** *nmf*   user

usted/ustedes *prons*   you (polite form, *sing* and *pl*): often abbreviated to *Vd/Vds* or (less often) *Ud/Uds* or *U/Us*.

□ used as subject and disjunctive (prepositional) form of this pronoun: *como usted/es sabe/n*   as you know; *con usted/es*   with you

□ in much of Sp Am, it is used as the only plural form of 'you'

□ for dir and indir obj use 3rd person prons *le(s)*, *la(s)*; refer to a grammar for full explanation

□ its derivation is <u>*Vuestra merced/ Vuestras merced<u>es</u>*</u>   'your grace/your graces', hence the abbreviation, and also the reason why it takes the 3rd person pronouns and possessives: *¿Va Vuestra merced con su señora?*   <u>Is</u> your grace going with his lady? ie 'Are you going with your wife?'

utensilio *nm*   tool, implement, utensil; lighter than cf *herramienta*

útil *adj*   useful

□ NB stress on *ú*: that's what the accent is for!

□ **utilizar** *vt* -ce-, -cé   to use

□ little difference from *usar*; see also *emplear*

V (*uve*) has the same two sounds as *b*, ie a 'b' sound at the beginning of a word, as in *vamos*, and a much lighter sound between vowels, where your lips just come together and part again, as in *uva*. Normally it does not have the 'fricative' sound (rubbing your top teeth against your bottom lip) that it has in English, French and some other languages.

vacaciones *nfpl*   holiday(s), vacations

□ NB always use in the plural

□ means a main holiday, not a day off (see *fiesta, feria, festivo, permiso*)

□ *marcharse/irse de vacaciones* to go off on holiday; *las vacaciones escolares*   the school holidays

vacío *adj*   empty, vacant (job etc)

□ *nm*   emptiness, void

□ **vaciar** *vt* -í-: *vacío, vacías*; *vacíe* to empty (out), pour (when this means emptying the container)

□ **vaciarse** *vr*   to empty, become empty: *la sala se vació*   the room emptied

vacilar *vi*   to hesitate

□ similar to cf *dudar* used in this sense

vacuna *nf*   vaccine; **vacunación** *nf* vaccination; **vacunar** *vt*   to vaccinate

□ NB form and spelling!

vago/a *adj*   vague

□ also: lazy, idle, slack

□ and *nmf*   idle person, slacker

vagón *nm pl* *vagones*   coach, carriage, wagon (of train); *vagón-restaurante* restaurant car

vajilla *nf*   crockery, china, (ie cups, saucers, etc, not the material, use *loza/porcelana*): *lavar la vajilla*   to wash up

valer *vti pi: valgo, vales; ps: valga; fut/condit: valdré/valdría* to be worth, cost: *¿Cuánto vale este reloj?* How much is this watch?, How much is this watch worth?; *no vale nada* it's not worth anything; used same as cf *costar* in this sense
- also 'to be of use': *¿Vale o no?* It is any use or not?; *¡Vale!* Good!, OK! (in Sp only); *esta vez sus armas no le valieron* this time his weapons were of no avail/use to him
- **valerse de** *vr* to make use of, avail oneself of (cf *aprovecharse*): *me valí de los descuentos que dan* I availed myself/ made use of the reductions they give
- **vale** *nm* coupon, token
- **valor** *nm* value: *objetos de valor* objects of value, valuable objects
- also: bravery, courage
- **valorar** *vt* to value, ie put a value on; also 'value' (appreciate): *valoro tu amistad* I value/appreciate your friendship
- NB take care over meaning of various associated words: **validez** *nf* validity; **válido** *adj* valid; **valiente** *adj* brave, valiant (cf but not same as *bravo*, rough, rugged); **valioso** *adj* valuable

vano *adj* vain (most senses); *en vano adv* in vain

vapor *nm* vapour
- steam: *locomotora a vapor* steam locomotive

varios *adj pl* several, a number of: *hay varios tipos* there are several sorts/kinds
- for 'various', use *diversos*
- **variar** *vti -í- varío, varías; varíe*, etc to vary, change, alter: *el precio varía cada día* the price varies every day; *para variar* for a change
- **variados** *adj* varied, assorted

varón *nm* and *adj pl varones* male
- cf use of *hembra* for 'female', and cf

macho, masculino
- *hijo varón* male child
- **varonil** *adj* virile, manly

vaso *nm* tumbler, glass (in that sense)
- *un vaso de vino* glass of wine; *un vaso para vino* wineglass
- not same as cf *copa*

Vd/Vds see **usted(es)**

vecino/a *nmf* neighbour
- *nmpl vecinos* inhabitants, residents: *un barrio de 1.000 vecinos* a district of 1,000 inhabitants
- *adj* neighbouring, next (in that sense): *el pueblo vecino* the neighbouring/next village
- **vecindad** *nf* neighbourhood, district (of town); similar to cf *barrio* in this sense
- 'vicinity' in Eng often implies wider area: if so, use *región*

vela *nf* sail; sailing; *hacer (la) vela* to go sailing, *hacerse a la vela* to set sail
- also 'candle'
- and 'vigil', 'sleeplessness': *pasar la noche en vela* to have a sleepless night
- **velo** *nm* veil
- **velar** *vt* to watch (keep watch over); also 'to stay awake', 'not get to sleep'
- and 'to veil', 'conceal'

veloz *adj pl veloces* fast, swift; cf *rápido*, which is more commonly used
- **velocidad** *nf* speed, velocity: *¿A qué velocidad viajábamos?* At what speed/how fast were we travelling?
- also 'gear': *la caja de velocidades* gearbox; *cambiar de velocidad* to change gear

vencer *vti -zo, -za-: venzo, vences; venza, venzas* to defeat, beat (in that sense)
- also 'overcome' (obstacles etc)
- 'to win' (through), 'succeed'
- **vencedor/a** *nmf* winner; and *adj*

winning: *el equipo vencedor* the winning team
- **vencido** *adj/past part* defeated, beaten; **darse por vencido** to give up, acknowledge defeat

vendar *vt* to bandage
- NB don't confuse its parts with *vend<u>e</u>r* to sell!

vender *vt* to sell
- also often used reflexively: *se vende* for sale
- don't confuse parts with *vend<u>a</u>r* to bandage!
- **vendedor/a** *nmf* seller, vendor
- *f* also used meaning 'salesgirl/woman' in shop (cf *dependienta*)

vengar *vt -gue-, -gué* to avenge
- **vengarse de** *vr* to avenge oneself, to take revenge (*de algo/alguien* for sth/on sb): *me vengué de su crueldad* I took my revenge for his cruelty; *me vengué de él* I took revenge on him
- don't confuse its parts with *venir* to come!
- **venganza** *nf* revenge, vengeance (*de* for): *como venganza de la derrota del año pasado* as revenge for last year's defeat

venir *vi pi: vengo, vienes, viene, venimos, venís, vienen; ps: venga; tú imperative: ven; ger: viniendo; fut/cond: vendré/vendría; pret: vine, viniste, vino, vinimos, vinisteis, vinieron; imp subj: viniera/viniese* to come (in most senses)
- NB many idiomatic expressions:
- the imperative is used meaning: *¡ven!/¡venga!* 'come on!'
- *venir a + inf* to come and/to be coming to + verb: *¿Cuándo vienes a vernos?* When will you come and see us/When are you coming to see us?
- with days, months, years: *… que viene* next; *el sábado que viene* next Saturday; *el año que viene* next year
- to suit: *ese vestido te viene bien* that dress suits you

- with *ger* to make a continuous tense, especially if the logic is leading towards a particular point in time or place in which the speaker is situated: *hace años que venimos diciendo esto* we've been saying that for years; *venían corriendo por la calle* they were running along the street (ie in the direction of the speaker); cf and contrast similar use of *ir*
- NB 'I'm coming!' in answer to call is *¡ya voy!*, (from *ir*) because you can only 'come' to where you are already: in this case you are *going* towards the caller …
- **venirse** *vr* the reflexive form is also used in some useful idioms: *venirse para abajo* to come tumbling down; *venirse encima de alguien* to come down/be upon sb: *este año se nos ha venido encima un montón de problemas* we've had a pile of problems land on us this year

venta *nf* sale, (method or act of) selling
- occurs in a number of useful phrases: *venta de liquidación* clearance sale; *venta al detalle* retail sale; *venta al por mayor* wholesale
- use *rebajas* for 'sales' in shops

ventaja *nf* advantage
- a number of useful phrases: *llevar la ventaja a* to have an/the advantage over; *sacar ventaja de* to profit from, to use to one's (own) advantage (usually with more emphasis on one's own selfish purpose, ie not quite same as cf *aprovecharse de*)
- see also opps *desventaja, inconveniente.*
- **ventajoso** *adj* advantageous, profitable (usually in a personal sense): *este negocio le salió muy ventajoso* this business turned out to be very profitable for him; not same as cf *rentable*, ie 'profitable' in cash sense

ventana *nf* window; NB use of *dim* …

□ **ventanilla** *nf* 'small window', but often used of window in ticket offices (cf *taquilla*) and banks, etc; also used for window in a vehicle

ventilador *nm* ventilator
□ but also (electric) fan (not same as cf *abanico*!)

ventura *nf* happiness
□ also 'luck', (usually implies good fortune): *la mala ventura* bad luck; *a la ventura* at random; *por ventura* fortunately
□ see also other 'luck'/'fortune' words for comparison: *azar, dicha, fortuna, desgracia*
□ **venturoso** *adj* happy; lucky, fortunate

ver *vt pi: veo, ves; ps: vea; ger: viendo; impf: veía; past part: visto; pret: vi, viste, vio, vimos, visteis, vieron; imp subj: viera/viese* to see
□ you don't use *poder* in phrases such as *¿Ves aquel pájaro?* Can you see that bird?; *desde aquí se ve el castillo* you can see the castle from here
□ often used to mean 'watch', especially with TV, films etc: *estaba viendo la tele cuando me llamaste* I was watching TV when you phoned me
□ as in Eng, 'to understand' *¡Ya veo lo que quieres decir!* Now I see what you mean!
□ 'to do with', in the following sense: *esto no tiene nada que ver con aquello* this has got nothing to do with that; *tiene algo que ver con el clima* it's got something to do with the climate
□ several common idioms: *vamos a ver …* let's see …; or a with little more urgency: *¡a ver!* let's see! *a ver lo que piensan!* let's see what they think!; *¡a ver si lo puedes hacer!* let's see if you can do it; *¡(ya) veremos!* we'll see!; *véase el párrafo 2* see paragraph 2; *a mi (modo de) ver* in my opinion
□ **visto** *past part* seen: used in a

number of expressions, eg *por lo visto* apparently; *visto que* seeing that; *visto que no puede hacerlo …* seeing that you can't do it …

□ **vista** *nf* the noun from *ver*: it has various connotations and occurs in many expressions, of which the following are a selection …
□ sight, vision: *vista doble* double vision; *a primera vista* at first sight; *estar a la vista de* to be (with)in sight of; *hacer la vista gorda a* to turn a blind eye to; *¡hasta la vista!* see you later! *echar una vista a* to take a look at; *perder de vista* to lose from sight; *volver la vista* to look back, look away
□ view: *con vistas al mar* with a sea view; *una vista del puente* a view of the bridge; cf also *panorama*
□ appearance: *tiene la vista muy pobre* it has a very poor appearance; cf also *aspecto*
□ **vistazo** *nm* look, glance: *echar/dar un vistazo a* to (take a) glance at

verano *nm* summer: *en (el) verano* in summer
□ **veranear** *vi* to holiday, go on a (summer) holiday: *siempre veraneamos en la costa Blanca* we always go to the Costa Blanca for our summer holidays
□ **veraneo** *nm* summer holiday (not exactly same as cf *vacaciones*; even less so cf *fiesta, feria, festivo*)
□ **veraneante** *nmf* (summer) holidaymaker

verdad *nf* truth
□ but also frequently used idiomatically: *de verdad* real, proper; *una paella de verdad* a real paella; *es verdad* it's true; *¿verdad?* really?
□ also used when you convert a statement into a question: 'isn't it?' 'don't you' etc in phrases such as *Tú me crees, ¿verdad?* You believe me, don't you?

□ **verdadero** *adj* true, real: *un verdadero amigo* a real friend; often also implies reliability or trustworthiness

□ **verdaderamente** *adv* truly, really; *verdaderamente no puedo* really I can't

verde *adj* green (in colour and ecological sense)

□ also 'randy', 'dirty', 'blue': *un viejo verde* 'a dirty old man'; *un chiste verde* a dirty/'blue' joke

□ **verdura** *nf* greenness, verdure, greenery

□ used in *pl* as *verduras* greens, green vegetables (cf *legumbre*, *hortaliza*)

vergüenza *nf* shame: *tener vergüenza* to be ashamed; *¡Es una vergüenza!* It's a disgrace! (NOT *desgracia* misfortune)

□ also 'shyness', 'timidity': *la pequeña tiene vergüenza* the little girl is shy

□ **vergonzoso** *adj* shy, timid (person)

□ also 'shameful', 'disgraceful'

□ **avergonzarse** *vr* -güe-; -ce-, -cé to be/feel ashamed (of oneself) (listed also under *A*)

verificar *vt* -que-, -qué to check, inspect, verify

□ **verificarse** *vr* to take place, happen (cf *tener lugar*, *celebrarse* in this sense)

verter *vt* -ie-, -i- to pour (out), spill

□ but for pouring out drinks, use *echar*

□ also: to dump, tip

□ **vertedero** *nm* tip, dump (for rubbish)

vertical *adj* vertical

□ **verticalmente** *adv* vertically, 'down' (crossword clues)

vestir *vt* -i- to dress, clothe

□ *estar/ir vestido de* to be dressed in/as

□ can be used transitively with the meaning of the more usual *llevar* to wear: *vestía sombrero rojo* she was wearing a red hat

□ **vestirse** *vr* to dress, in the sense of 'to wear clothes': *siempre se viste de rojo* she always dresses in red

□ also 'to get dressed': *¡Vístete ahora mismo!* Get dressed right now!

□ **vestido** *nm* (woman's) dress

□ also 'costume': *museo del vestido* museum of costume

vez *nf pl veces* time (in the sense of occasion/instance)

□ used in many useful phrases: *¿cuántas veces?* how many times?, how often?; *una vez* once; *tres veces* three times; *muchas veces* many times, often; *a veces* at times, sometimes; *algunas veces* sometimes; *alguna vez* some time, ever: *¿Has estado alguna vez en Portugal?* Have you (ever) been to Portugal at all?; *cada vez* each/every time; *esta vez* this time; *a la vez* at the same time; *de vez en cuando* from time to time; *otra vez* again; *rara vez* seldom, rarely; *tal vez* perhaps, maybe; *en vez de* instead of; *por primera/segunda vez* for the first/second time; *a su vez* in one's turn; *dos veces tres* two times three

□ NOT same as cf *época, hora, tiempo*, all meaning 'time' in different senses!

vía *nf* road, route

□ rather more limited in use than cf *carretera*; used in such phrases as *vía de circunvalación* ring road; *vía pública* thoroughfare; *por vía aérea* by air (same as *por avión*); *autovía* dual carriageway, not 'motorway': use *autopista*

□ in railway context 'track', 'line', 'gauge': *vía ancha/estrecha* broad/narrow gauge; *vía 3* platform 3

□ in the common prepositional phrase *en vías de* in the process of: *los países en vías de desarrollo* the developing countries

□ *prep* via, by way of

víctima *nf*   victim
- NB *fem* regardless of sex of victim!

vida *nf*   life
- NB *en mi vida* can have a negative meaning: 'never in my life', and behaves like *nunca* 'never', requiring *no* before verb if it occurs after it: *en mi vida he visto tal cosa* or *no he visto tal cosa en mi vida*   I've never seen such a thing in my life
- other useful phrases: *¡qué perra vida!* it's a dog's life!; *quitarle la vida a alguien*   to take sb's life
- also 'living', 'livelihood': *ganarse la vida*   to earn one's living

vídeo *nm*   video (recorder or tape): *grabar en vídeo*   to videotape, record

vidrio *nm*   glass (ie the material); cf also *cristal* used in this sense
- you don't drink from it; use *vaso*, *copa*
- use *gafas* for 'spectacles'

viejo *adj*   old
- in most senses, but cf *anciano*, *antiguo*, for some overlap in their rather more specific meanings
- don't use comparative *más viejo* talking of people, unless they are actually <u>old</u> – use *mayor*: *tu hermano es mayor que el mío, ¿no?*   your brother is older than mine, isn't he?
- also NB position changes meaning: *una vieja amiga*   an old friend (ie you've known a long time), but *una amiga vieja*   an old (elderly) friend

viento *nm*   wind
- NB *hace* or *hay (mucho) viento*   it's (very) windy

viernes *nm inv*   Friday
- *Viernes Santo*   Good Friday

vínculo *nm*   link, bond: *hay un vínculo medioambiental*   there's an environmental link
- **vincular** *vt*   to link, bind: *estar*

vinculado con   to be connected/ linked with: *está vinculado al problema del medio ambiente*   it's linked to/connected with the problem of the environment

violento *adj*   violent, in most contexts
- NB also has meaning of 'embarrassing/embarrassed', 'awkward': *es una situación un poco violenta*   it's a rather embarrassing/awkward situation; *me encontraba algo violento/a*   I felt rather embarrassed/awkward
- **violar** *vt*   to violate (in general sense); also 'to rape'
- **violación** *nf pl violaciones*   violation; rape

violeta *nf*   violet (flower)
- when used as *adj*   violet (colour), it is invariable: *cortinas violeta*   violet curtains

virgen *nf pl vírgenes*   virgin
- can also be used as adj: 'virgin', 'blank': *tierra virgen*   virgin soil; *una cinta virgen*   a blank tape

virtud *nf*   virtue
- **en virtud de** *prep*   by virtue of, by reason of

visita *nf*   visit: *estar de visita a/en*   to be on a visit to/in; *hacer una visita a*   to pay a visit to
- can also mean 'visitor': *'no se admiten visitas'*   'no visitors allowed'
- **visitante** *nmf*   visitor (the all-purpose word)

víspera *nf*   eve, day before: *en vísperas de*   on the eve of

vivir *vi*   to live
- means both 'be alive', and 'dwell'
- **vivo** *adj*   living, alive: *está todavía vivo*   he's still alive
- also 'lively', 'vivid'
- **vivienda** *nf*   housing, accommodation: *el problema de la*

vivienda the housing problem

□ also 'dwelling' (a neutral word that doesn't specify the type of accommodation): *se venden viviendas* dwellings for sale

vocablo *nm* word, term, expression: *una lista de vocablos españoles para …* a list of Spanish expressions/terms for …; more comprehensive than *palabra* 'word'

volar *vi* -ue- to fly

□ also used to express haste: *¡voy volando!* I must dash/fly!

□ *volar a + inf* to dash to, hasten to

□ also, totally different meaning – *vt* to blow up (with explosive): *los terroristas volaron el puente* the terrorists blew up the bridge

□ **vuelo** *nm* flight (most senses, eg action of flying, aeroplane flight)

□ but for 'fly/flight' in sense of 'flee/ing' use *huir/huida*

volcar *vt* -ue-; -que-, -qué: *vuelco, vuelcas; vuelque, vuelques; volqué, volcaste* to overturn, tip over, upset (in that sense)

□ **volcarse** *vr* to overturn, capsize, tip over: *el barco se volcó* the boat capsized

□ **vuelco** *nm* (action of) overturning, tipping over

volumen *nm pl volúmenes* volume

□ senses as in Eng of bulk/capacity, sound and book

voluntad *nf* will, desire

□ *buena/mala voluntad* good/bad will; *por voluntad propia* of one's own free will; *voluntad libre* free will; *tener la voluntad de + inf* to have the will to

□ **voluntario/a** *adj* voluntary; *nmf* volunteer

□ **voluntariamente** voluntarily

volver *vti* -ue-; *past part: vuelto* a frequently used verb, with a range of meanings, all involving turning or returning

□ to turn (sth) round or over: *volver la*

carne varias veces turn the meat over several times; *volver la cabeza* to turn one's head; *volver la espalda a alguien* to turn one's back on sb; *volver la página* 'turn over (the page)'; can be used for 'to give back', but better to use *devolver*

□ to return, come/go back

□ to turn (change direction): *vuelva a la izquierda* turn left

□ *volver a + inf* to do something again: *volvió a toser* he coughed again

□ **volverse** *vr* to turn round: *me volví para ver mejor* I turned round to see better

□ *volverse + adj* to become, turn (in that sense): *el tiempo se volvió amenazador* the weather turned threatening; *la pobre se volvió loca* the poor girl went mad

□ **voltear** *vti* often preferred in Sp Am to *volver*, with most of the above meanings; not used as such in Spain

□ cf also the less used *tornar*

□ **vuelta** *nf* the noun from *volver*, with a general idea of turning; used in a large number of idiomatic expressions:

□ turn, revolution: *dar la vuelta al mundo* to go around the world; *dar vueltas* to revolve; *dar una vuelta* to turn right round

□ bend, curve: *a una vuelta de de la carretera* at a bend in the road

□ circuit, round: *la Vuelta a España* the Tour of Spain (cycle race)

□ return: *a vuelta de correo* by return of post; *un billete de ida y vuelta* return ticket; *estar de vuelta* to be back (from somewhere)

□ change (money): *quédese con la vuelta* keep the change; not same as cf *cambio* (exchange) or *moneda* (small change)

□ walk, stroll: *dar una vuelta* to take a stroll

□ both verb and noun merit further research in a dictionary!

vosotros/as *pron* you (familiar plural form of subject and disjunctive pronoun)
- □ takes *2nd person pl* of verb
- □ note *f* form *vosotras*
- □ used in Spain, but little in Sp Am (use *ustedes* instead)
- □ **vuestro** *poss adj* your and *pron* yours
- □ ie belonging to *vosotros/as:* don't use it with other forms of 'you'!

votar *vi* to vote (*por* for)

- □ also: to vow
- □ **voto** *nm* vote; vow

voz *nf pl* **voces** voice: *en voz alta/baja* in a loud/low voice; *de voz en grito* at the top of one's voice;
- □ also 'shout': *dar voces* to shout, yell

vuelco see **volcar**

vuelo see **volar**

vuelta see **volver**

W *(uve doble)* is not really regarded as a letter of the Spanish alphabet, although it does of course figure on keyboards. It is principally used nowadays in foreign names, mainly of British/American or German origin: Washington, Glasgow, Weimar.
- ◆ In most other words from these sources *w* has been converted to *v:* *váter* loo (from 'water closet', although *W.C.* is still used as a notice); also *vatio* watt.
- ◆ However, some more recent imports retain the *w* and their English 'w' sound: *walkman, windsurf, web;* for the last one, it may well be that Spanish speakers will eventually settle to using their own word *red*, rather than convert to an almost unpronounceable *veb*!

X *(equis)* occurs quite frequently, though not often at the beginning of a word.
- ◆ It is pronounced like *-s-* before a consonant: *excursión, excelente*; and like *-cs-* between vowels: *éxito, examen.*
- ◆ The handful of words beginning with *x*, when it is pronounced *s*, include: *xenofobia, xerocopia, xilófono* – all pretty obvious!
- ◆ *x* is also used in Galician *(gallego)* and Catalan and Valencian where *j* is used in Castilian (ie Spanish); it is pronounced *-sh-*: *xunta (gallego)* for *junta, Xavia* for Jávea (Valencian).
- ◆ In Mexico (or Méjico!), it also tends to have the same pronunciation as the Castilian *-j-*: *Oaxaca* (pron *Oajaca*).

Y

> **Y** (*i griega*) can be used as a consonant in some parts of Spain and Spanish America. It is pronounced with rather more spring in the jaw muscles than in English, making it sound almost like an English j: *ya, vaya, suyo*.
> - Note that in between vowels, it always begins a syllable: *va-ya, su-yo, ma-yo, le-ye-ron*.
> - It takes the place of *-i-* on the end of a word: *hay, rey, hoy, muy*.

y *conj* and
- □ becomes *e* before a word beginning with *-i-* or *hi-* for the sake of the sound: *padres e hijos, Fernando e Isabel*

ya a little word frequently used with both literal and idiomatic meanings …
- □ *adv* already (referring to past): *ya hemos visitado la catedral* we've already visited the cathedral
- □ now, right away (referring to present or immediate future): *ya viene el camarero* the waiter's coming now, here comes the waiter
- □ *ya no* no longer, not any more: *ya no vamos a verles* we no longer go and see them
- □ used as *interj*: *¡ya!* often said when you agree with something: 'indeed!' or simply 'yes'
- □ sometimes with no translatable meaning, especially to emphasise short verbs: *¡ya lo sé!* I know!; *¡basta ya!* that's enough!; *¡ya voy!* I'm coming!; *¡preparados! ¡listos! ¡ya!* ready, steady, go!
- □ *conj* now … now … *ya me quiere, ya no me quiere* now he loves me, now he doesn't
- □ **ya que** *conj* since, as, in sense of: 'seeing that …': *ya que no me quiere* since he doesn't love me

yacer *vi* -*zc*- to lie (mainly used of the dead): *aquí yace …* here lies …
- □ **yacimiento** *nm* deposit (eg mineral): *yacimientos de carbón* coal deposits

yo *subj pron* I
- □ generally used with verb for emphasis: *yo voy, tú te quedas* <u>I'm</u> going, <u>you're</u> staying
- □ NB *soy yo* it's me

Z

> **Z** (*zeda* or *zeta*) is pronounced 'th' (as in 'thin') in most of Spain, and as 's' in the south of Spain and Latin America.
> - There is a strict spelling rule that *c* must be used for the 'th' sound whenever possible, ie in the combinations *ce* and *ci*. Therefore, *z* will occur only in the combinations *za, zo, zu* and at the end of a syllable (**za**pato, **zo**na, **zu**mbar, ga**z**pacho, arr**oz**), except in non-Spanish words (*Nueva Zelanda* New Zealand, *zigzag*).
> - NB words ending in *-z* change this to *-ces* in the plural: *vez/veces, feliz/felices*.

zafarse *vr* to escape, run away
- □ *zafarse de algo* to dodge, get round something (eg an obstacle)

zambullirse *vr ger*: *zambulléndose*; *pret*: *se zambulló, se zambulleron* to dive (*en* into)

zona *nf* zone
- ☐ used more widely than its Eng equivalent in the sense of 'area', 'district', 'park': *zona peatonal* pedestrian precinct/area; *zona industrial* industrial zone/park/area

zumbar *vi* to buzz, hum (insects, motors etc)

- ☐ **zumbido** *nm* buzz(ing), hum(ming)

zumo *nm* juice: *zumo de fruta* fruit juice
- ☐ alternative to *jugo* in Spain, but stick to *jugo* in Sp Am

zurcir *vt* -zo, -za-: *zurzo, zurces,* etc; *zurza, zurzas* to darn, mend (clothes)